BASIC REFERENCE SOURCES

A Self-Study Manual

Preliminary Edition

by

MARGARET TAYLOR

The Scarecrow Press, Inc.
Metuchen, N.J.   1971

BASIC REFERENCE SOURCES
A Self-Study Manual

Preliminary Edition

by

MARGARET TAYLOR

The Scarecrow Press, Inc.
Metuchen, N.J.   1971

Copyright 1971 by Margaret Taylor

ISBN 0-8108-0469-7

Library of Congress Catalog Card Number 70-175233

CONTENTS

34578

LIST OF SOURCES

Section 1a: National bibliographic records, U.S., current

       Publishers' Trade List Annual (AA347)
       Books in Print (AA348)
       Subject Guide to Books in Print (AA349)
       Paperbound Books in Print (AA346)
       El-Hi Textbooks in Print (see AA352)
       Children's Books in Print
       Law Books in Print (CJ12)
       Large Type Books in Print

Section 1b: National bibliographic records, U.S., current

       Publishers' Weekly - "The Weekly Record" (AA350)
       American Book Publishing Record (AA344)
       BPR Cumulative (1AA54, 2AA59)
       Forthcoming Books (1AA55, 2AA60)
       Subject Guide to Forthcoming Books

Section 1c: National bibliographic records, U.S., current

       Cumulative Book Index (AA345, AA343)

Section 2a: National bibliographic records, U.S., retrospective

       United States Catalog (AA342)
       American Catalog of Books (AA341)
       Kelly: American Catalog of Books (AA339)
       Roorbach: Bibliotheca Americana (AA338)

Section 2b: National bibliographic records, U.S., retrospective

       Sabin: Dictionary of Books Relating to America (AA334)
       Evans: American Bibliography (AA333, 1AA52, 1AA53)
       Shaw & Shoemaker: American Bibliography (AA336)
       Shoemaker: Checklist of American Imprints (AA337)

Section 3: Search strategy and review

Section 4: National library catalog and union list

       Library of Congress /National Union Catalog author lists (AA63, AA64, AA65)
       NUC 1952-56 Imprints (see AA65)
       NUC Pre-1956 Imprints (Mansell) (2AA12)
       LC /NUC 1942-62 author list, Master Cumulation (Gale)
       NUC Register of Additional Locations (1AA14)
       LC Subject Catalog (AA66)
       LC Catalog--Motion Pictures and Filmstrips (BG68)
       LC Catalog--Music and Phonorecords (BH38)
       NUC of Manuscript Collections (DB33a)
       National Register of Microform Masters (1AA17a)
       Newspapers on Microfilm (AG12, 2AG6)
       Catalog of Copyright Entries (AA353, BD223, BD67, BH37, BH37a)

Section 5: Bibliographic sources for serials--current lists

       Ulrich's International Periodicals Directory (AF18, IAF2)
       Irregular Serials and Annuals (2AF3)
       Standard Periodical Directory (AF17)
       Ayer Directory of Newspapers (AF13)

Section 6: Bibliographic sources for serials--union lists

      Union List of Serials (3rd ed.) (AF98)
      New Serials Titles (AF99)
      NST Classed Subject Arrangement (AF100)
      Subject Index to NST (2AF4)
      Gregory: American Newspapers...a Union List (AF5)
      Brigham: History and Bibliography of American Newspapers (AG8)

Section 7: Indexes to serials--indexing services

      Readers' Guide to Periodical Literature (AF122)
      Abridged Readers' Guide
      Social Science and Humanities Index (AF124)
      Public Affairs Information Service Bulletin (CA22)
      Kujoth: Subject Guide to Periodical Indexes
      Poole's Index to Periodical Literature (AF119)
      -- Date and Volume Key (AF120)
      Nineteenth Century Readers' Guide
      Wellesley Index to Victorian Periodicals
      New York Times Index (AG32, 2AG9)

Section 8: Bibliographic sources for government publications

      Monthly Catalog of U.S. Government Publications (AH18, 2AH4)
      GPO Price Lists (AH20)
      Selected U.S. GPO Publications
      Document Catalog (AH17)
      Poore: Descriptive Catalog (AH13)
      Ames: Comprehensive Index (AH14)
      Checklist of U.S. Public Documents (AH16)
      Andriot: Guide to U.S. Government Serials and Periodicals (AH11, 1AH1)
      Jackson: Subject Guide to Major U.S. Government Publications (2AH1)
      Leidy: A Popular Guide to Government Publications (2AH2)
      Monthly Checklist of State Publications (AH34)

Section 9: Sources for miscellaneous types of publications

      Vertical File Index (AA355)
      Dissertation Abstracts International (AI11, 1AI2)
      American Doctoral Dissertations (AI9, AI10)
      Masters Abstracts (AI13)
      Black: Guide to Lists of Masters Theses (1AI1)

Section 10: Bibliographic records for other countries--Great Britain, France, Germany

      British Books in Print (AA512, 1AA61)
      Paperbacks in Print (AA513)
      Bookseller (AA510, AA511)
      Whitaker's Cumulative Book List (AA508, AA509)
      The Publisher (see AA506)
      English Catalogue (AA505, 2AA69)
      British National Bibliography (AA507)
      Pollard and Redgrave: Short-Title Catalogue (AA498)
      Wing: Short-Title Catalogue (AA504)
      British Museum: General Catalogue of Printed Books (AA67, AA68, 2AA13)
      Biblio (AA472)
      Bibliographie de la France (AA473)
      Librairie Française, Catalogue Général des Ouvrages en Vente (AA474, 2AA66)
      -- Les Livres de l'Année (AA47a)
      Catalogue Général de la Librairie Française (Lorenz) (AA470)
      Vicaire: Manuel de l'Amateur de Livres du XIXe Siècle (AA471)
      Quérard: La Littérature Française, 1827-49 (AA469)
      Quérard: La France Littéraire...XVIIIe et XIXe Siècles (AA468)
      Bibliothèque Nationale. Catalogue Général des Livres Imprimés. Auteurs (AA72, AA460, 1AA15, 1AA16,
        2AA15, 2AA16)
      Deutsche Nationalbibliographie (AA483)
      Jahresverzeichnis des Deutschen Schrifttums (AA485)
      Deutsche Buecherverzeichnis (AA486)

Deutsche Bibliographie (AA487, 1AA60)
--; Halbjahresverzeichnis (AA488)
--; Fuenfjahresverzeichnis (AA489)
Boersenblatt fuer der Deutschen Buchandel, Frankfurt
Boersenblatt fuer der Deutschen Buchandel, Leipzig
Heinsius: Allgemeines Buecher-Lexicon (AA478)
Kayser: Vollstaendiges Buecher-Lexicon (AA479)
Hinrichs: Fuenfjahrskatalog (AA480)

Section 11: Review of Part I

Section 12: Dictionaries

Webster's Third New International Dictionary (AE8)
Webster's New International Dictionary (2nd ed.) (AE7)
Funk and Wagnalls New Standard Dictionary (AE6)
Random House Dictionary (1AE2)
Century Dictionary and Cyclopedia (AE4)
Oxford English Dictionary (AE20, AE21)
Dictionary of American English (AE80)
American College Dictionary (AE9)
Funk and Wagnalls Standard College Dictionary (AE10)
Random House Dictionary, college edition (2AE1)
Webster's 7th New Collegiate Dictionary (AE12)
Webster's New World Dictionary (AE11)
New Century Dictionary (AE5)
Shorter Oxford English Dictionary (AE22)
American Heritage Dictionary

Section 13: Supplementary language sources

Fowler: Dictionary of Modern English Usage (AE44)
Evans: Dictionary of Contemporary American Usage (AE43)
Follett: Modern American Usage: a Guide (1AE9)
Webster's New Dictionary of Synonyms (2AE12, AE79)
Roget's International Thesaurus (AE77)
Lewis: New Roget's Thesaurus of English in Dictionary Form
Wentworth and Flexner: Dictionary of American Slang (2AE9, AE72)
Berrey and Van den Bark: American Thesaurus of Slang (AE65)
Partridge: Dictionary of Slang and Unconventional English (2AE7, AE67)
Mathews: Dictionary of Americanisms (AE81)
De Sola: Abbreviations Dictionary (2AE2, AE27)
Acronyms and Initialisms Dictionary (Gale) (1AE53, AE79)
NBC Handbook of Pronunciation (AE56)
Wood's Unabridged Rhyming Dictionary (AE62)

Section 14a: Encyclopedias

Encyclopedia Americana (AD1)
Encyclopaedia Britannica (AD2)
Collier's Encyclopedia (AD4)
Columbia Encyclopedia (AD5, 1AD1a)
Lincoln Library (AD6)
Compton's Pictured Encyclopedia (AD14)
World Book Encyclopedia (AD16)
Encyclopedia International (AD15)
Grolier Universal Encyclopedia
American Peoples Encyclopedia
Britannica Junior
Subscription Books Bulletin Reviews (AA309a)
General Encyclopedias in Print (see 2AD4)

Section 14b: Foreign encyclopedias

Chambers's Encyclopedia (2AD1, AD3)
La Grande Encyclopedie (1886-1902) (AD27)
Larousse. Grand Dictionnaire universel du XIXe Siècle Français (AD28)
Grand Larousse Encyclopédique en Dix Volumes (AD31, 2AD8)
Encyclopaedia Universalis (2AD7)
Brockhaus Enzyklopaedie (1AD8, 2AD9)

Brockhaus' Konversations-Lexikon; Der Grosse Brockhaus (AD34)
Meyer Neues Lexikon (AD38)
Meyers Konversations-Lexikon (see AD338)
Enciclopedia Italiana di Scienze, Lettere ed Arti (AD48)
Enciclopedia Universal Illustrada Europeo-Americana (AD68)

Section 15: Yearbooks and Almanacs

Americana Annual (AD8)
Britannica Book of the Year (AD9)
Collier's Year Book (AD11)
World Book Year Book (see AD16)
Annual Register; World Events (DA50)
Facts on File (DA51)
Keesing's Contemporary Archives (DA52)
World Almanac (CG55)
Information Please Almanac (CG47)
New York Times Encyclopedic Almanac
Whitaker's Almanac (CG109)
Statesman's Year-Book (CG29)

Section 16: Yearbook supplements: statistics

Statistical Abstract of the United States (CG49)
Historical Statistics of the United States (CG51, 1CG6)
Statistical Yearbook of the United Nations (CG32)
Statistics Sources (CH108)

Section 17: Handbooks and manuals

Kane: Famous First Facts
Guinness Book of World Records
Benet: The Reader's Encyclopedia (BD18)
Brewer's Dictionary of Phrase and Fable (BD48)
Bartlett: Familiar Quotations (2BD16, BD75)
Stevenson: Home Book of Quotations (BD38)
Evans: Dictionary of Quotations (2BD18)
Douglas: American Book of Days (CF22)
Hazeltine: Anniversaries and Holidays (CF25)
Steinberg: Historical Tables (DA47, (1DA8)
Langer: Encyclopedia of World History (DA42, 2DA5)
Everyman's Dictionary of Dates (DA30)
Emily Post's Etiquette (CF36, 1CF6)
Menke: Encyclopedia of Sports (CB167)
Roberts' Rules of Order (CI171)
How-to-do-it Books: A Selected Guide (CB156)

Section 18: Directories

Encyclopedia of Associations (2AC1, AC28)
Foundations Directory (2AC2)
Research Centers Directory (2AC3, 1AC5, 1AC6)
Yearbook of International Organizations (CJ143)
Klein: Guide to American Directories (CH98)

Section 19: Biographical sources: universal

Webster's Biographical Dictionary (AJ25)
Chambers's Biographical Dictionary (AJ14)
Lippincott's Biographical Dictionary (AJ23)
New Century Cyclopedia of Names (AJ19)
International Who's Who (AJ29)
Current Biography (AJ28)
Biography Index (AJ2)

Section 20: Biographical sources: national and subject

Who's Who in America (AJ45)
Who Was Who in America (AJ40)
Who's Who (AJ155)

PREFACE

The material in this self-study manual is the result of a three-year project at the University of Hawaii. It was initiated under the guidance of Dean Robert D. Stevens, and began with the idea that basic bibliographic expertise might be taught by leading the students to the sources instead of by presentation and discussion of the sources in class. Mrs. Margaret Taylor was available to explore this idea, having recently resigned as a full-time faculty member, and Dean Stevens succeeded in obtaining funds to support her initial research. She developed a learning sequence for two units of our beginning reference course, LS 601: Bibliography and Reference Sources. In each, the student was led step-by-step to examine basic reference sources, building as he did so concepts of general bibliographic structure and search strategy. The early results were promising, and Mrs. Taylor went on to develop a programmed format for all of the source-centered content of the course. The School has been involved from the beginning in general guidance of the project and in testing the effectiveness of its approach.

The first units were tested in the Spring 1968 semester, using a test (T) group and a control (C) group. The students in these groups were not specially selected. Analysis of their backgrounds revealed that the median grade point average for academic work prior to library school was 2.94 among members of the T-group and 3.13 in the C-group. Records of academic performance in the School revealed an overall mean of 3.5 for students in both groups; the distributions of averages above and below this mean were virtually identical in both groups. Examinations on the content of the first units yielded a median grade of 88 in the T-group and a median grade of 80 in the C-group. Students using the programmed sequence did better than those taught conventionally when tested on the same material.

The two programmed units were used in the course for five classes a year over the next 2-1/2 years. Faculty were not asked to use them but chose to do so voluntarily. Student response was favorable in the overwhelming majority of cases.

Under a grant from the Grolier Foundation, the sequence for the entire course was completed in the 1970-71 academic year. It was tested throughout the Spring semester, using two concurrent sections of the course. In their midterm examination, students in the test (T) group had a median of 2 wrong answers, compared to a median of 4.5 wrong answers in the control (C) group. In the final examination, the T-group students had a median of 0 wrong answers, compared to a median of 2 wrong in the C-group. T-group students averaged less than half as many errors as the C-group students. Again, no special selection of participants was involved, and the two groups were not appreciably different in their other academic achievement; prior to library school,

T-group members had a median grade point average of 3.01, C-group members had a median of 3.00. Records of performance in library school revealed an overall mean of 3.6 for students in both groups, and again distributions of the averages above and below this mean were virtually the same in each group. Time requirements for the self-study program were recorded by participants. While time varied over a considerable range, the average amount spent fell within the normal load of two hours preparation time for each class hour. Use of the self-study manual resulted in substantially less classroom time to cover the same material. The test of the entire sequence confirmed the findings of the earlier experiments.

These tests were limited in many ways. The number of students who participated in the testing was small. Grade ranges were not extreme. There were variables in the test situations that could not be fully accounted for. The objective nature of the examinations was restricting. Even by the most conservative interpretation of the evidence, however, it seems clear that students perform at least as well under this system as they do when conventionally taught. This basic indication, coupled with the marked and consistent student enthusiasm for the self-study program, appears to us to justify a wider audience. Publication of this preliminary edition hopefully will encourage further testing.

At best, the self-study approach can have substantial advantages. It offers a viable alternative to the stupefying task of memorizing lists of titles and to the attendant tedium of show-and-tell in the classroom. Students are led into working contact with the sources themselves, just as they will be on the job. The self-instructional plan allows for individual pace, requires each student to respond to exposure to the material, and assures constant reinforcement. It can be used without mechanical aids, as in the present manual, or put in machinable form. The program reduces the amount of class time spent in reviewing sources, class time that can be used to more fully cover other important aspects of reference work; i.e., the communications skills involved in service to the public. There are obvious possibilities for continuing education, extension and refresher courses for working professionals.

The School is a better place for having been involved in the development of this program. This is a preliminary edition; it does need much more extensive testing, and by its very nature it will require continuous revision. Yet we feel that its potential is sound and that library educators and students alike will welcome its publication at this time.

Ira W. Harris
Acting Dean
Graduate School of Library Studies
June, 1971   University of Hawaii

INTRODUCTION

With this self-study manual, you will begin a careful examination of a specified list of reference titles. The manual consists of a long series of questions relating to your examination, use, and comparison of these specified reference sources. The question pages allow you enough room to jot down your answers as you proceed through the problems. The answers to these questions are given to you on separate pages at the end of each section, so that you may check your own answers against them to make sure that you are finding the correct information and using the sources in the correct way. You should check your answers quite frequently. In the beginning, you will find it best to check your answer for each question as you proceed. The questions are designed so that the correct answer to a question frequently depends upon an understanding of the answer to preceding questions.

Since you have been given the answers, you will be tempted to go immediately from the question to the answer, without trying to work out the answer for yourself. You could learn a certain amount from doing only this. The point of this whole type of exercise, however, is not to give you another textbook to read, but to give you a method through which you can most effectively learn how to examine and use these sources. The questions are set up to give you a great deal of information about the sources themselves. They are also set up as a device through which you can train yourself in the technique of examination and evaluation of reference sources, and through which you can get some actual experience in search strategy, in using the sources in the most effective and most efficient way. Both of these are techniques which you will need to use in your job situation. So it is to your own advantage in every way to try to work out the answers to the questions.

It will be necessary for you to refer to and use the actual reference sources in order to work out the answers to the questions; therefore you must plan to do the self-study manual in the library or wherever you have access to these sources. Winchell's Guide to Reference Books (8th edition) and the ALA Glossary are also used extensively throughout this manual as guides and as resource tools, and it would be easier if you have your own copies (or can borrow copies) of these two titles to keep with you as you work the questions.

One of the purposes of the self-study manual is to allow you to cover this material at your own pace. It has been set up to accommodate, as far as possible, a variety of learning and background differences among students. Previous experience in libraries or with the material, plus differences in reading speed, ability to integrate details, and psychic energy all contribute to the time variation among students. Therefore, you may want to make some adjustments in your use of the sequence as you proceed through the material, to fit it into your own specific needs.

Some of the sequence may seem unnecessarily simplified or repetitive to you. You may find that you can skip over some of the questions quickly because the answers will seem quite obvious to you. You may even find that you can work out some of the questions "in your head" rather than referring back to the sources, if you are clear about the sources. Even though your progress through the sequence may seem rather slow at the beginning, until you become familiar with the method and the material, it is strongly recommended that you do not attempt any skipping or modification until you are well into the sequence and feel that you understand its purpose and its relation to the sources. Some suggestions have been made in the sequence itself about "skipping" and reviewing. Otherwise it is up to you to judge to what extent you can modify it for your own purposes. Keep in mind the basic importance of actual use and handling of the sources.

Also keep in mind the probability that, the slower you are in working your way through the sequence, the more you may be in need of this detailed, repetitive, reinforced type of guidance, so try not to get discouraged about the amount of time consumed. If you feel that you are working too slowly and that it is taking too much of your time, then CONSULT WITH THE INSTRUCTOR.

It is not necessary to work through the entire sequence at one time, of course. The questions have been divided into smaller units, with an average estimated time of two to three hours each. You should plan, as far as possible, to work through an entire unit at one time.

If you come across problems, questions, or items which still seem confusing to you, even after you have referred to the answer sheets, do not hesitate to go to your instructor for help or clarification.

Note to Instructors and Students

The self-study manual is designed to be self-explanatory and self-contained when used in conjunction with the sources to be examined and with such aids as Winchell's Guide to Reference Books and the ALA Glossary. Therefore it is possible for the manual to be used without any additional textbook assignments or classroom sessions. However, the primary use of the manual in its present form is as a teaching resource or tool to cover certain aspects of a basic reference course, to be used with other resources such as readings, lectures, discussions, seminars, written assignments, etc.

It is helpful but not absolutely necessary if the student has, prior to beginning the manual, some general introduction to library reference services and information sources, such as is found in Chapters 1

and 2 of Basic Information Sources by William A.
Katz (Introduction to Reference Work, vol. 1; New
York, McGraw-Hill, 1969) and in more detail in
Katz's companion volume, Reference Services (Introduction to Reference Work, vol. 2; New York, Mc-
Graw-Hill, 1969). Also helpful would be some brief
background reading on the general subject of bibliography (for example: Basic Information Sources,
chap. 3, p. 35-44). Further supplementary readings
related to the specific sections of the self-study manual can similarly be found throughout a basic reference
text such as Basic Information Sources.

The manual as it is now set up is designed to
be used only in sequence; each section is dependent
upon information established in preceding sections.
Thus the student should start at the beginning and work
through each section in its proper order. Part I
should precede Part II. In general, he should not expect to work Section 2, then skip to Section 7, then
go back to Section 3, etc. Some flexibility to fit with
course requirements can be obtained by omitting sections or parts of sections (for example, Section 8 on
government publications; Section 10 on foreign bibliographic records; Section 14b on foreign encyclopedias,
etc.), but the student and instructor should keep in
mind that there may be references to the omitted
material in other following sections, particularly in
the review questions and review sections.

The answers in the self-study manual are
keyed to the latest editions of the sources available
in early 1971. Editions used are noted within the
question-answer sequence itself. Other editions can
be used for examination, but the student should realize that his answers will vary from those given in
the manual and that therefore some of the specific
reinforcement value of the manual will be lost. It
is best if the student has access to the editions referred to in the manual, at least in the early sections when he needs more specific guidance.

Margaret Taylor
Associate Professor
Graduate School of Library Studies
University of Hawaii

June, 1971

PART I

BASIC BIBLIOGRAPHIC SOURCES

Section 1a

National Bibliographic Records (U.S.)--current

Questions #1-66

With this first set of problems, you will begin your examination of the major sources which make up the current and retrospective bibliographic record of publications for the United States. While doing the questions and examining the sources, you should keep in mind the extent of the overall bibliographic coverage of U.S. publications, and the aims and objectives of bibliographic control itself.

1. First of all, how would you define "a bibliography" or "a bibliographical source"?

2. From this definition, and from what you may know or may have read about bibliographies, try to think of as many reasons as you can why you--either as a librarian or as a user of a library, as a user of bibliographical sources--would turn to these sources for information. What would some of these information needs be?

Before you begin examining the sources in this unit, you may find it helpful to read the brief survey of current publishing practices which is included at the end of this section (Appendix A). Then, keeping in mind that survey, and keeping in mind the potential information needs from your answer to #2, you should go on to examine carefully your first group of sources. Starting with the current sources, the first group consists of:

> Publishers' Trade List Annual (PTLA) (AA347)
> Books in Print (BIP) (AA348)
> Subject Guide to Books in Print (AA349)
> Paperbound Books in Print (AA346)
> El-Hi Textbooks in Print (see AA352)
> Children's Books in Print
> Law Books in Print (CJ12)
> Large Type Books in Print

You should first locate the titles, then if possible sit down with or near them so that you can look at them together. The letter and number symbols following each title are item references to Winchell's Guide to Reference Books (8th edition).

3. Take Publishers' Trade List Annual (PTLA) first, and note the basic physical characteristics about the set itself. For example, how many volumes does it contain?

4. It was already mentioned in the brief survey of publishing that each individual publisher is likely to issue, probably annually, a catalog or list of the firm's publications which are still "in print." What does "in print" mean?

5. These catalogs are themselves available directly from the publisher. PTLA is in fact, a collection of such catalogs. How often does PTLA come out (how often is it published)? (This is a very easy one and you can get it simply from the title of the set.)

6. Who is the publisher of PTLA itself?

7. How recent is the set you are looking at (what is its date of publication)?

8. So far, then, you've established the basic bibliographic information about PTLA: its full title, its publisher, the fact that it comes out annually, the number of volumes, and which edition you are looking at.

   The next step is the "scope." You have already established that PTLA is a collection of publishers' catalogs, but this doesn't tell you all you need to know.
   What catalogs does it include?
   Is it a comprehensive coverage?
   Does it include catalogs for all publishers in the United States?
   Does it include catalogs for publishers other than in the United States?
   This is not an easy problem to answer at this point, so you should begin by thinking: where might you look to find such information?

9. Do any of the three possibilities listed for the answer to #8 in fact give you an answer?

10. Put off this aspect of the "scope" of PTLA until later, in hope it will clear up, and go on to the "arrangement." Again, you have already established that PTLA is a collection of publishers' catalogs. How are these catalogs arranged? (In the set as a whole.)

11. Is this single alphabetical arrangement by publisher the only listing in the set?

12. Does PTLA contain a list of publishers whose catalogs are included?

13. Does this list or index tell you more than simply the names of the publishers?

14. Can you find the catalog of the East-West Center Press?
    Where is it located in PTLA?

15. What about the Scrimshaw Press in San Francisco?

16. The University of California Press has published a book by Donald Ritchie called The Films of Akira Kurosawa. Is this still in print and if so, what is its price?

17. Is Crime in a Changing Society by Howard Jones still available from Penguin Books?

18. You have now established that PTLA itself is arranged alphabetically by the name of the publisher, with a special supplementary section in the front. How are the items arranged within the catalogs themselves?

19. Do any of the catalogs list books by subject?

20. F. E. Peacock Publishers have published a book on nongraded schools by Sidney Rollins. Can you find out if it is still in print?

21. Thus far, then, you have been able to determine the arrangement (although not yet the scope) for PTLA. Can you make a brief, concise, succinct statement of the arrangement of PTLA?

22. Using PTLA only, can you find out whether or not a book is in print if you know only its author and title? For example, if you knew only that the book Crime in a Changing Society was written by Howard Jones, could you have found out its in-print status and price as you did in #17?

23. What do you need to know about a book or publication in order to use PTLA?

24. Therefore, what would you need to have in PTLA in order to answer #22?

25. What is BIP exactly? Look at the title page for its full title.

26. Who is the publisher of BIP, and how often is it published, what edition do you have, and how many volumes is it?

27. Has PTLA always had BIP as an index? You will probably have to go to Winchell for this one.

28. You still have not established the "scope" of PTLA (and therefore of BIP). In #9, you found that PTLA did not have a preface or an introduction. Does BIP have a preface?

29. Does this preface give you any answer to your problem in #8; that is, what publishers are included in PTLA/BIP?

30. This establishes, as closely as you are going to get it, the "scope" of BIP and therefore of PTLA. Next is the arrangement. What is the "arrangement" of BIP?

31. Look up Crime in a Changing Society by Howard Jones in both sections (author and title) of BIP. Is it listed in both sections? Is the same information given in both sections, or does one section refer you to the other section for fuller information?

32. BIP is, according to the subtitle, an author-title-series index. What is a series? Since you probably can't answer this one directly, think first: where would you go to find out?

33. The Golden Press is the publisher of a number of dictionaries especially designed for young people, but you do not really know the correct titles. Nor, for most of them, are you sure of the author. How then would you find out what these dictionaries are and how much they cost, so that you could purchase them, or select from them?

34. Is <u>Shaw and the Charlatan Genius</u> by John O'Donovan still in print? What is the publisher and price?

35. Since you found it listed in BIP, would you then have to check as well in PTLA?

36. Why, then, is it ever necessary to have or to use PTLA if you have BIP?

37. Is Samuel Eliot Morrison's <u>Vistas of History</u> (published in 1964) still in print? What is the publisher and price? BE CAREFUL.

38. Where are two places that you can find the address of the Bedminster Press?

39. What is the in-print status, price, and publisher of <u>Goya and His Sitters</u>, by Elizabeth du Gue Trapier?

40. On the previous question, the author was listed under Du rather than any other part of the name. If this had confused you and you had wondered what to search under--du, Gue, or Trapier--what could you have done?

41. What is the full name and address of the publisher of <u>Goya and His Sitters</u>?

42. The Denoyer-Geppert Co. is a publisher of maps and other geographical aids. Are their maps included in BIP? How do you know?

43. Can you, however, find the address for Denoyer-Geppert Co.?

44. BIP gives you author and title (and sometimes series' title) access to PTLA. What is a third major access you might need to have for bibliographical searching? In other words, what is a third kind of information you might have about any particular book or publication for which you are searching?

45. Do you have this third type of access through BIP, or PTLA itself?

46. Could you, then, find out what books are still in print in the U.S. on, for example, "data processing" or "air pollution"?

47. What is the basic bibliographical information you need to know about the Subject Guide to Books in Print?

48. Has BIP always had a "subject guide"? Where would you look to find this? (See #27)

49. The "scope" of the Subject Guide to BIP would, presumably, be the same as that of BIP and PTLA. Are there, however, any omissions?

50. What is the arrangement of the Subject Guide to BIP?

51. What U.S. books <u>are</u> in print on the subject of data processing?

52. The assigning of subject headings is a major part of library cataloging procedures, and libraries generally use a standard list of subject headings so that there will be some uniformity and consistency. The two major lists in use are the <u>Sears List of Subject Headings,</u> and the <u>Library of Congress List of Subject Headings.</u> Does the Subject Guide to BIP make use of either of these lists?

53. Would this be of help to librarians?

54. Will the books in Subject BIP be listed under only one subject heading?

55. What is the publisher and price of <u>Bits of Old China,</u> by W.C. Hunter?

56. If you wanted to find a listing of all the editions currently in print of Mark Twain's <u>Tom Sawyer,</u> would you expect to find such a list in Subject BIP?

57. Where and how would you find such a list?

58. Look in the correct source for a listing of all the editions currently in print of Mark Twain's <u>Tom Sawyer.</u> How many places would you have to look to be sure to cover <u>all</u> of the editions?

59. Since these are all editions of the same book by the same author, why is it necessary to look in so many places? Why aren't they all listed in the same place? (Refer back to last part of answer for #40.)

60. What is a pseudonym?

61. There are some listings in Subject BIP under the heading of Clemens, Samuel Langhorne. What are these, then, if Subject BIP does not include fiction entries?

62. In #57, the problem was to find a list of all editions currently in print of <u>Tom Sawyer.</u> Where would you look to find a list of all the editions which have ever been published of <u>Tom Sawyer?</u>

63. Where would you look to find out if such an author bibliography existed? You should be able to come up with at least four possible sources.

64. Would you be able to locate such a bibliography in BIP?

65. There are several other titles in this first group of sources. Three of these--Paperbound Books in Print, El-Hi Textbooks in Print, and Law Books in Print--are discussed briefly in the preface to BIP. What, if anything, is the difference between BIP and Paperbound Books in Print?

66. In #60, you wanted a list of currently available, in-print editions of <u>Tom Sawyer</u>. Where are <u>two</u> places you might look for this information?

The other sources in this first group--Paperbound Books in Print, El-Hi Textbooks in Print, Children's Books in Print, Law Books in Print, and Large Type Books in Print--are included here as examples of sources similar to and supplementary to those basic sources you have been looking at. As you can see from looking at the titles, they are subject (or form, in the case of Paperbound BIP) oriented. You should at least be aware of the existence of such supplementary sources, but it is not necessary to examine them in any detail at this stage. If you have extra time, you might find it interesting and good practice to compare them briefly with the BIP/PTLA/Subject BIP group for similarities of arrangement and access.

So far you have examined carefully three major bibliographical sources: Publishers Trade List Annual, Books in Print, and Subject Guide to Books in Print. These three sources are, in fact, very closely inter-related. You have <u>examined</u> each for the basic bibliographic information, the scope, the arrangement, and special features such as address lists. You have <u>compared</u> these three sources. You have also had several opportunities to <u>use</u> these sources, to search for information in these sources; often it is the search for information itself which gives you added clues about the scope and arrangement of the source. Keep these sources in mind as you proceed through the following questions, because you will have reason to refer back to them again. Now that you understand these three sources fairly well, you can use them for purposes of comparison when you examine other similar sources.

So far, if much of this is new to you, you may have had considerable difficulty in coming up with the proper answers to these questions. This in itself is not too surprising. If you have understood the answers when you turned to them in this manual, and if you have understood fairly well where you got off the track in trying to locate the answers yourself, then you can expect to continue working your way through the questions and profiting from your experience. But if you still feel very confused and uncertain at this point, then it is time to consult with your instructor to see what the trouble is.

Appendix A

Brief Survey of U.S. Publishing

Before you can make much sense out of the bibliographic records which you will examine in this section, it would be helpful for you to have some very elementary background information about the publication and distribution of books.

Books are produced by business firms called publishers. There are literally thousands of publishers in the United States. Each publisher is responsible for the publication of individual titles, ranging in number from two or three to several hundred. (The word "title" is used here as distinct from "copy"; i.e., the title, Valley of the Dolls, by Jacqueline Susann was published in over 10,000 copies). In general, except for classic works which are no longer protected by copyright, publishers have exclusive right to those titles which they have published; in other words, Valley of the Dolls in its hardcover edition is published only by Bernard Geis, not also by Doubleday or McGraw Hill.

For each new title which he publishes, a publisher will have printed the number of copies which he expects or hopes to sell. This is usually called a "printing"; it may also be called an "edition." If the publisher's stock of printed copies is sold out, he may or may not--depending perhaps on the demand--decide to have another printing run off. Presumably these second, third, etc., "printings" will be done without changing the content or the text or the format of the publication. If the publication is changed in any real way, it should therefore constitute another "edition," rather than "printing." Usually, publishers will indicate these changes by such terms as "second edition," "new edition," "revised edition," etc. The term "edition" has a number of other uses as well. A "reprint" may mean simply a "second printing" following directly on the first printing; or it may mean that the title has been re-set and reprinted, usually at a much later date than the original printing. Unfortunately, publishers do not use these terms of "printing," "edition," "new edition," "reprint," etc., as consistently or as carefully as we would like; it is sometimes a major bibliographical problem to figure out what changes, if any, have been made.

As long as a publisher still has copies in stock of a title, or as long as he continues to have new printings, or reprintings, made available as needed, then the title or the book is considered to be "in print." When the title is no longer available from the publisher's stock, and he does not intend to have another printing made, the title is considered to be "out of print," or "o.p."

The books, when in print, are available directly from the publisher who publishes them. (Some publishers may have other, usually larger, publishing firms act as agents for them.) They are also sold, or distributed, through book stores or book dealers, who stock copies of titles from a large variety of publishers. The book dealers must, of course, get their copies directly from the publishers.

The "book trade" is made up of the publishing industry, which produces the books, and the book dealers or book stores, who distribute and sell the books. Books sold through book stores to the general public (such as novels, poetry, cookbooks, travel books, etc.) are generally referred to as "trade" books. "Non-trade" publications, therefore, are those items not usually carried in the stock of most book stores; for example, textbooks, materials published by the government on any level, encyclopedias, etc. The distinction between "trade" and "non-trade" or "in the trade" and "out of the trade" is not always clear, and some publications have moved from one category to another. (For example, books published by university presses have in the past been considered as "non-trade," but now they are commonly carried "in the trade.") It is a useful distinction to begin to think about, however, since it is often a criterion for inclusion or exclusion of materials in many bibliographies.

The "book trade" is certainly just as dependent as librarians--perhaps even more so--on complete, up-to-date, and accurate information--or bibliographic control--of books and other publications. Many of our bibliographic records, therefore, will be compiled primarily by and for the book trade itself. This does not, of course, necessarily make them any the less use to librarians.

All new books, or new titles, are not published on the same day, or at the same time of year. New titles are published every day of the year, although there are a few seasonal surges, such as before Christmas. Advance information about new titles is given in Publishers Weekly, a periodical published by and for the book trade (and therefore referred to as a "trade publication," which is a somewhat different use of this term than the trade/non-trade distinction mentioned previously). Announcement of the actual publication of the title (meaning that it is "out" and therefore now available) is, in effect, its listing in the "Weekly Record" section in the back of each issue of PW; you will be examining this PW Weekly Record as one of the bibliographical sources.

In addition to announcements, advertisements, and listing in such book trade journals as PW, publishers also mail out advertisements and announcements, and often issue at various intervals throughout the year lists of new and/or forthcoming books. Publishers also issue from time to time, usually annually, lists or catalogs of their complete stock, older titles which are still in print/in stock/available, as well as new titles. It is essentially these annual stock catalogs or lists which make up the volumes of the Publishers' Trade List Annual, which you will also examine.   The only way in which you can definitely determine whether or not a particular title is still in print (available) is by writing to the publisher to inquire, or by looking it up in the publisher's stock catalog.

This rough survey of the "book trade" has been quite elementary and simplified, in order to give you some kind of working background for your examination of the bibliographical sources.   There are many more complex aspects of the publishing and distribution of books, some of which may become clearer to you as you proceed through this course.

Section 1a

National Bibliographic Records (U.S.)--current

Answers #1-66

1. A: If you do not feel you can give an answer to this from your own knowledge or experience, then you should begin by trying to look it up, either in any standard English language dictionary, or in a more specialized dictionary like the ALA Glossary, or in the text you are using for this course or in any readings you have been assigned on bibliography. Actually, the definitions of the term bibliography vary somewhat from source to source, and it may be necessary to read several different writers on the subject, and examine and work with many bibliographies over a period of time before the definition becomes really clear to you. However, for purposes of starting this manual, we can begin by defining a bibliography simply as a list of publications, which has some unifying element (such as: by a specific author, on a specific subject, published in a specific country...) and is organized in some systematic manner (such as: alphabetically by name of author, by subject, by date of publication...).

2. A: For example: to find out what books have been published and are available; for book selection for the library collection, or for recommendation to readers; to find out the prices of such materials, and their sources of purchase; to verify and identify publications; to compile bibliographies of authors or subjects; to locate materials for inter-library loan; etc.

3. A: 6 (in the 1970 set).

4. A: Still available from the publisher (refer to Appendix A).

5. A: Annually (once a year). Title: Publishers Trade List Annual.

6. A: R.R. Bowker Company in New York (and London). This appears on the title page.

7. A: 1970. Again, this appears on the title page, as part of the title itself: Publishers Trade List Annual, 1970. It also appears as part of the copyright statement (Copyright © 1970) on the verso of the title page.

8. A: There are a number of possibilities:
(a) the title page (does it tell you?)
(b) the Preface (is there one?)
(c) the annotation in Winchell (does this in fact tell you?)

9. A: The title page--does it tell you? No.
The Preface--is there one? No.

The annotation in Winchell--does this tell you? No.

10. A: Alphabetically by the name of the publisher. This should be quite obvious to you simply by glancing through the volumes themselves, but it is also pointed out in the annotation in Winchell. This is one of the reasons why it is very important to realize that the set consists of more than one volume; vol. 1 for example contains only A-B; vol. 2 contains Blo-F, etc. (See answer to #2.)

11. A: No, actually there are two alphabetical lists: one called "Index to Publishers" in the yellow section in the front of vol. 1 (in the 1970 edition), followed in the yellow section by a collection of shorter lists (Supplement), more or less but not entirely alphabetical, followed by the major alphabetical section running through all four volumes.

12. A: Yes, the "Index to Publishers" in the (yellow section in the 1970 edition) front of vol. 1 (See #11.)

13. A: Yes, it tells you where you will find the catalog: i.e., in the regular alphabetical order, or in the Supplement and on what page of the Supplement.

14. A: Yes. It is in the regular order (the symbol *** meaning in the regular alphabetical order), in vol. 2 between the catalogs of Dutton and Eardmans.

15. A: Yes. This one is in the yellow supplement section. Since the Supplement is not in strict alphabetical order, you have to look in the index which appears at the beginning of vol. 1, which tells you that the Scrimshaw Press appears in the Supplement on p. 669.

16. A: Yes, it is still in print, and the price is $11.00. You know it is in print because you can find it listed in the publisher's catalog. You have to find the University of California Press' catalog (in regular order, alphabetized under U-); then in the catalog itself, look under the alphabetical list of authors for Richie.

17. A: Yes, it is and the price is 95¢. The list of Penguin Books appears in regular order, alphabetized under P. However, this publisher's list is alphabetical by title only, so you had to find it under "Crime" rather than "Jones."

18. A: They vary from publisher to publisher. University of California Press had an author listing (and also title index); Penguin Books listed by title only.

19. A: You'll have to glance through the set at several of the catalogs to determine this. Actually, most of these do not, but some do: Arco Press is a good example of subject listing which includes annotations as well.

20. A: Yes, it is and the price is $5.75. The title is Developing Nongraded Schools and it was published in 1968. The Peacock catalog (located in the Supplement, p. 320-1) lists by title only, and you did not have the title, only the author, but the catalog itself is only two pages long, and you can easily go through it to search out a similar title by that author.

21. A: Catalogs arranged alphabetically by name of publisher. Shorter lists in Supplement, front of vol. 1. Location shown by index preceding Supplement. Arrangement within catalogs varies from publisher to publisher.

22. A: No, you couldn't.

23. A: The name of its publisher.

24. A: An author or title index, or both. Which brings you to Books in Print (BIP).

25. A: "An author-title-series index to the Publishers' Trade List Annual."

26. A: The publisher is the Bowker Company (same as PTLA), it is published annually (same as PTLA), and the 1970 edition has two volumes: vol. 1 is "authors" and vol. 2 is "titles." This information is all on the title pages of the two volumes. (A third set which may be shelved nearby is the Subject Guide to Books in Print, not part of BIP itself and to be considered later.) Both BIP and PTLA usually "come out" or appear or are published in the late fall of the year, and are presumed then to contain listings of books in print from the various publishers through the late summer, or about July, of that year. Thus, the 1970 edition of BIP will be available in about October of 1970, and will be presumed to contain a listing of books in print as of about July 1970. And therefore, from January 1971 through October or November of 1971, you would be using the 1970 edition of BIP.

27. A: No. PTLA began annual publication in 1873, and BIP did not begin publication until 1948. The Winchell annotation tells you clearly that from 1873 until 1948, there were no indexes, except briefly in 1902-04.

28. A: Yes, called "How to Use Books in Print," following the title page. It is very informative and you should read the entire preface carefully.

29. A: The actual scope of PTLA/BIP is never really clearly stated, but it is generally considered to include catalogs from all major American publishers and--in more recent years--from a large proportion of minor or smaller publishers as well. As more and more publishers are added to the roster, or persuaded to make their catalogs available to the Bowker Company for this publication, the size--and the scope--of PTLA/BIP increases considerably. It is almost easier to say what is not in BIP/PTLA than what is in it. See the section headed "Types of Publications not fully represented in BIP" (in the preface) for a statement on this and on specific omissions.

30. A: Alphabetically by author (and/or editor) and title (and series' title). These have been separated into two alphabetical lists, and into two volumes, with authors (and editors) in vol. 1, titles (and series' titles) in vol. 2--rather than mixing authors and titles together into one alphabetical list. This information can be seen from the title pages themselves, or in the preface, first paragraph. Note from the preface and from observation that vol. 2 also contains an alphabetical list of U.S. publishers with addresses.

31. A: Yes, both author and title sections list it, but the author volume gives more information. See BIP Preface regarding this ("Information included in author and title entries.")

32. A: See the ALA Glossary, definition #1 under "Series." An example of a publisher's series with which you might be familiar are those published by Time-Life Books, such as Foods of the World, Nature Library, World Library. These are unnumbered series. These series are not listed in BIP as such, although the titles of the individual books are. In order to find a list of the titles in these series, you would have to know that the publisher was Time-Life Books and turn to that publisher's catalog in PTLA for a listing.

33. A: Here you could best go directly to the publisher's catalog in PTLA and see what dictionaries are listed. You would probably have to go through all the titles, unless the dictionaries happened to be listed separately, but the Golden Press catalog is a less imposing list to go through than, for example, the entire title section of BIP.

34. A: Yes, it is listed in BIP (Authors, under O'Donovan, or Titles, under Shaw...). The price is $4.50; the publisher is Dufour, and the date of publication--given only in the Authors volume--is 1966.

35. A: Theoretically, no. Since BIP is an index to PTLA, the listing of a title in BIP automatically tells you that, since it came from the publisher's catalog, the title is in

print--as the title of the source itself tells you, Books in Print. BIP, of course, is subject to errors, as are all bibliographical sources, and if you wanted to be doubly sure, you could also check the publisher's catalog as well, but this is probably not always necessary.

36. A: As you could see from your answers to #32 and #33, sometimes it is more direct to go to the publisher's catalog itself when you are not sure of authors or titles. And the publisher's catalog itself in PTLA may give you more complete information than is found in BIP.

37. A: BE CAREFUL. Yes, it is still in print ($4.95; Knopf). In this case, the name you were given was misspelled. This is a far more common hazard than you might think, and you should always be on guard for it. If you were aware that Morison is one of our foremost historians and that therefore his book would not be likely to have gone out of print so soon, you might have suspected either a misspelling or a mistake in BIP. In either case, double checking under the title entry would have answered your problem. Or possibly you might have glanced at Morison as an alternate spelling in BIP-authors at the same time you looked under Morrison. Eventually (after you've been misled by enough errors), such automatic consideration of alternate possibilities will begin to be second nature to you. Of course, if you had looked in the title volume first, you would have found it, but don't forget that you could similarly have been given an incorrect title.

38. A: In the publisher's catalog itself in PTLA, and in the list of publishers at the end of volume 2 of BIP (remember your answer to #30 about the arrangement of BIP).

39. A: BIP-Authors, under Du Gue Trapier, lists the book as in print, from "Hispanic," at $10.00. It would also be correct to look in BIP Titles, under Goya.

40. A: You could have looked under all three possibilities till you either found the correct one or eliminated all three; you could also have looked it up under title, since you had the title. In this case, BIP-authors does give you cross-references from Gue and from Trapier to Du Gue Trapier. See BIP preface on listing of cross-references and variant forms of authors' names ("Special Note on How to Find an Author's Complete Listing.").

41. A: Hispanic Society of America, Broadway between 155th and 156th Streets, New York, N.Y., 10032. BIP gives only "Hispanic," and you have to refer to the "Key to Publishers' Abbreviations" to find the full name and the address.

42. A: No. You can tell this by
    (a)   looking in the publisher's name index to PTLA (vol. 1); Denoyer-Geppert is not listed;
    (b)   the statement in the preface to BIP, noted in the answer to #29, that the editors of BIP do not attempt to include maps--among other things-- even for those publishers whose catalogs are included in PTLA.

43. A: Yes, in the full list of U.S. publishers in the end of vol. 2 of BIP.

44. A: Two pieces of information you might have are the author and/or the title. Other pieces of information are the date of publication and the publisher, but probably they will not be as important to you as the possibility that you would be searching for a book or publication because of its subject matter. (For example, you might want to find a book on the subject of air pollution.) So you can then say that the three major accesses you need for bibliographical information, or for bibliographic control, would be: author, title, subject.

45. A: BIP does not have a subject index. In #19, you noted that some of the publishers' catalogs in PTLA included subject listings, but not all.

46. A: Not from BIP or PTLA as such, unless you wanted to go through all of the titles to pick out those dealing with data processing. But by now it should have begun to dawn on you that the third item in your list of sources to examine--the Subject Guide to Books in Print--is just the sort of thing you want for this problem.

47. A: Publisher: Bowker
    How often published: annually, as with BIP
    How many volumes: the 1970 edition has two volumes

48. A: As with #27, you would most easily check in Winchell, and find that the Subject Guide has existed only since 1957, although BIP has existed since 1948. At this stage, such information may seem superfluous to you; you may not see the point of knowing when, for example, the Subject Guide began, since you are unlikely to use it for any but the current year. However, it is a very revealing aspect of the overall picture of bibliographical control in this country that such sources do not spring fullblown into existence, but rather develop in stages over the years, as a need for specific tools or for another access to such tools is demonstrated. This is particularly evident with the current bibliographical sources; their structure--their scope and arrangement-- may change from year to year, even from month to month or from week to week; it is part of your job to deal with these sour-

ces, to realize that such changes are being made and to try to keep up with them.

49. A: The introduction or preface, "How to Use Subject Guide to Books in Print," following the title page, tells you about specific omissions, both for omissions from the BIP listings (i.e., fiction, poetry and drama, Bibles, etc.), and for the same statement of omissions you found in BIP itself.

50. A: As you might expect, it is alphabetically by subject, and the introduction (which you should read) gives you a good deal of information on the various types of subject entries or "subject headings" which are used, and how they are alphabetized.

51. A: "Data processing" is not used as a subject entry or "subject heading" in Subject BIP, but at least it is listed and refers you to other words which are used: "Electronic data processing," plus "information storage and retrieval systems," and "Punched card systems." You would probably want to check under all three subject headings, then. One of the problems with subject headings is that they tend to change from year to year as new terminology and new emphases come into being. You should always keep in mind as many different possibilities as you can, and hope that your source will give you sufficient references to the headings or entries which are actually used.

52. A: Yes, it follows the Library of Congress List of Subject Headings. See the preface.

53. A: Yes, because it uses a list which is likely to be familiar, and they can expect some consistency of headings, perhaps, with those used in their own card catalog.

54. A: No, since Library of Congress subject cataloging may assign more than one subject heading, the Subject BIP will list titles under all assigned subject headings. This also is in the preface.

55. A: Paragon Reprint, $5.50. Where do you go to find this? You could perhaps have found it under "China-Description and Travel" in Subject Guide to BIP, but why bother? You had the author and the title, and no reason to think either was incorrect, so BIP is much more direct. Also the title does not clearly indicate whether the subject is China-- the country or China as in porcelain.

56. A: No, since Subject BIP specifically excludes fiction listings (see the preface).

57. A: You want to find a list of in-print titles; therefore you go to BIP. You could look under author or title; probably you should get into the habit of looking under the author when you have that information.

58. A: In the author volume under Twain, also under

Clemens, Samuel Langhorne which gives you a cross-reference back to Twain. In the title volume under Tom Sawyer, and also under Adventures of Tom Sawyer (for which you have a cross-reference under Tom Sawyer).

59. A: BIP lists authors and titles as given in the publishers' catalogs or listing in PTLA, with some attempts to bring variants together by cross-references (see answer to #40). The publishers' listings may vary in use of the author's full name, or use of a pseudonym, or in complete title.

60. A: See the ALA Glossary or a dictionary. (Mark Twain is Samuel Langhorne Clemens' pseudonym.)

61. A: Biographical and critical works about Clemens (Twain), which are included, and which would be listed under the author as the subject.

62. A: Probably an "author bibliography" (for Clemens/Twain) would give you the best answer here, if one exists. If such a bibliography is not too recent, you might then have to supplement it by searching through more current bibliographical sources such as those you are examining in this unit.

63. A: (1) your library's card catalog (which will tell you of the existence of such a bibliography only if your library has a copy; the fact that you do not find one listed in the library's card catalog does not eliminate the existence of such a bibliography).
        (2) a bibliography of bibliographies, such as Bibliographic Index or Besterman's Bibliography of Bibliographies.
        (3) Winchell--using the index and looking under both Twain and Clemens.
        (4) You might expect to find one in the Subject BIP under Clemens as a subject, as you found biographical and critical works in #61.

64. A: Not unless you knew the author and title. But as indicated in the answer to #63, you could find it through Subject BIP, if the bibliography is still in print.

65. A: You can get this directly from the preface to BIP, which tells you that BIP includes most paperbound editions but Paperbound Books in Print is more complete and is revised more often. Therefore Paperbound BIP would include more recent information than you would find in BIP.

66. A: BIP and Paperbound Books in Print.

Section 1b

National Bibliographic Records (U.S.)--current

Questions #67-125

67.   Assume that you were to find information on the publisher and price of a novel published last month. You know what the author and title are.   Would you expect to be able to find this information in BIP?

68.   Obviously, then, you must have some more current source of bibliographical information than BIP for such recently published books.   Does the preface to BIP tell you whether or not you can expect such information from BIP, and if not where else you can find it?

The various sources mentioned in the preface to BIP take you into the second group of titles to be examined, which are:

> Publishers' Weekly - "The Weekly Record" (PW) (AA350)
> American Book Publishing Record (BPR) (AA344)
> BPR Cumulative (1AA54 & 2AA59)
> Forthcoming Books (1AA55 & 2AA60)
> Subject Guide to Forthcoming Books

Again, it would be best to try to examine the titles in this group together.   Since both PW and BPR are periodicals, try to get together several recent issues rather than simply one issue or just the most recent issue.

69.   Publishers' Weekly (PW) is a journal (a periodical) published by and for the "book trade."   What is the book trade?

70.   It should be quite obvious that PW comes out weekly; this is part of the bibliographical information which you should note.   Just for practice, see if you can find the date, volume, and issue numbering on any recent issue, and see if you can find the statement (the masthead) which tells you how frequently PW is published, how much it costs, who publishes it, etc.   Who does publish PW and what else do they publish?

71.   You may want to become more familiar with PW as a whole later.   Now you are concerned with the "Weekly Record" part of PW, which is included at the very back of each issue.   The implication, although it is not so stated, is that those weekly listings record new books as they are actually published-- that is, that books listed in the "Weekly Record" of June 22, 1970, were published on or about that week. You can also safely assume that the titles as listed in PW "Weekly Record" have in fact actually been published, not just announced for publication.   What is the "scope" of the "Weekly Record" in PW?

72.   What does "conscientious" mean in this context?

73.   Are there any specific exclusions noted in the scope of the "Weekly Record"?   That is, what are the limits which the Bowker Company has set for this listing?

74.   Would you expect the list to include such things as maps, films, records, globes, etc.?

75.   An important part of the "scope" for bibliographies is the amount of information given for each entry, or for each citation, within the bibliography itself. What does the introductory paragraph tell you to expect in each individual citation in the PW "Weekly Record"?

76.   Look at the attached sample page from PW "Weekly Record," at the citation for <u>Science in Elementary Education</u> by Peter Gega. The elements of the citation are identified as follows:
author (Gega, Peter C.)
title (Science in elementary education)
edition statement (2d ed.)
publisher (Wiley)
place of publication (New York)
date of publication (1970)
paging (xii, 631p)
size (26cm.)
contents information (illus, pt. col.; Bibl. = illustrations, part colored; bibliography)
International Standard Book Number (ISBN 0-471-29507-8)
Dewey Decimal classification number (372.3'5 in upper right)
Library of Congress classification number (LB1532.G4 1970)
Library of Congress card order number (74-101977)
price ($10.95)
catalog tracings for subject headings and added entries (1. Science--study and teaching (Elementary); I. Title)

Compare this with the citations in BIP, for example. Was all of this information given to you in BIP?

77.   Look at the entry on the attached sample sheet for <u>Churches in Rock</u> by Georg Gerster. Who is the publisher? What is the price? Was the book ever <u>published elsewhere</u>?

78.   What is the arrangement of the PW "Weekly Record"?

79.   Look through some recent issues. Besides author names, do you see any "corporate author" entries (such as organizations or associations, etc.)? Do you see any title entries?

80.   Do you see any subject entries?

81.   Do you see any cross-references from title to author? Choose any item entered under author and check to see if there is also an entry under title.

82.   Therefore we can say that the arrangement of the PW "Weekly Record" is alphabetical by main entry (whether author--personal or corporate, or title) <u>only</u>, with no cross-references. Is this similar to BIP?

83.   Could you locate in the PW "Weekly Record" a book if you knew only its title? Such as a novel called <u>The Nice and the Good</u>?

84.   You must therefore know, or be able to make an educated guess, at the main entry of the item in order to locate it. In #80, you noted that there were no subject entries as such in the "Weekly Record." However, do you have <u>any</u> subject access at all to the "Weekly Record"?

85.   In #67, you had the problem of finding information about a novel published last month, which presumably

‡FURET, Francois, 1927-   744.04
French Revolution [by] Francois Furet &
Denis Richet. Tr. by Stephen Hardman. [1st
Amer. ed. New York] Macmillan [1970]
416p. illus., ports. 25cm. Tr. of La Revolution. Bibl. [DC148.F8713 1970b] 70-81243
9.95
1. France — History — Revolution. I. Richet, Denis, 1927- joint author. II. Title.

FURTH, Hans G.   371.3
Piaget for teachers [by] Hans G. Furth.
Englewood Cliffs, N.J., Prentice [1970] xii,
163p. illus. 22cm. ISBN 0-13-674937-2 (pbk.)
Bibl. [LB775.P49F8] 72-106001 6.95; pap.,
2.95
1. Piaget, Jean, 1896- 2. Child study. I. Title.
Cloth ed. carries ISBN 0-674945-3.

FUTURE of empirical theology, (The),   230
by Fred Berthold [others] Ed. by Bernard E.
Meland. Chicago, Univ. of Chicago Pr. [1969]
x, 387p. 24cm. ISBN 0-226-51955-4 (Essays
in divinity, v. 7) "Several . . . of the essays
. . . were presented at the Alumni Conf. of
the Theological Field of Divinity Sch., Nov.
7-9, 1966." Bibl. footnotes. [BT83.53.F8] 78-
83980 11.00
1. Empirical theology — Addresses, essays,
lectures. I. Berthold, Fred, 1922- II. Meland,
Bernard Eugene, 1899- ed. (Series)

GALLANT, Ruth   372.4'13
Handbook in corrective reading: basic tasks.
Columbus, Ohio, Merrill [1970] 156p. 23cm.
ISBN 0-675-09379-1 (Merrill reading ser.)
Bibl. refs. [LB1050.5.G3] 77-103421 pap.,
2.25
1. Reading—Remedial teaching. I. Title.

GARDINER, Alfred George, 1865- 824'.9'12
1946
Windfalls [by] Alfred George Gardiner (Alpha
of the Plough, pseud.) With illus. by Clive
Gardiner. Freeport, N.Y., Bks. for Libs.
[1970] xvi, 270p. illus. 23cm. (Essay index
reprint ser.) ISBN 0-8369-1467-8 Reprint of
the 1920 ed. [PR6013.A6W5 1970] 70-105014
9.50
1. Title.

GEGA, Peter C.   372.3'5
Science in elementary education [by] Peter C.
Gega. 2d ed. New York, Wiley [1970] xii,
631p. illus. (pt. col.) 26cm. ISBN 0-471-
29507-8 Bibl. [LB1532.G4 1970] 74-101977
10.95
1. Science — Study and teaching (Elementary)
I. Title.

GEISSMAN, Theodore Albert, 1908- 581.1'3
*Organic chemistry of secondary plant metab-
olism* [by] T. A. Geissman [&] D. H. G.
Crout. San Francisco, Calif., Freeman, Coo-
per [1969] ix, 592p. illus. 25cm. Bibls. [QK8
87.G4] 71-81384 14.50
1. Botanical chemistry. 2. Plants — Metab-
olism. I. Crout, D. H. G., joint author. II.
Title.
Publisher's address: 1736 Stockton St., San
Francisco, Calif. 94133.

GENEVA Institute of International   341.12
Relations
The problems of peace; lectures delivered at
the Geneva Institute of International Relations
at the Palais des Nations, August 1926, together with appendices containing summary of
discussions. First ser. Freeport, N.Y., Bks. for
Libs. [1970] xii, 365p. 23cm. (Essay index reprint ser.) ISBN 0-8369-1468-6 Reprint of the
1927 ed. [JX1937.G4 1970] 73-105015 12.50
1. League of Nations. 2. International Labor
Organization. 3. Arbitration, International. 4.
World politics - 1919-1932. I. Title.

GEORGE, James Zachariah,   326'.0973
1826-1897
*The political history of slavery in the United

States.* Foreword and with a sketch of the author's life, by William Hayne Leavell. And
with a pref. somewhat in the nature of a personal tribute, by John Bassett Moore. New
York, Neale Pub. Co., 1915. Detroit, Mich.,
Negro Hist. Pr. [1970?] xxiv, 342p. port.,
plates. 23cm. [E415.7.G34 1970] 72-90132
13.00
1. Slavery in the United States — History. 2.
U.S. — Politics and government. 3. Recon-
struction. I. Title.

GEORGE, Norvil Lester,   658'.91'64799
1902-
Effective school maintenance [by] N. L.
George. West Nyack, N.Y., Parker [1969] xv,
224p. illus. 29cm. ISBN 0-13-245449-1 Bibl.
[LB3235.G4] 75-76884 17.95
1. School buildings — Maintenance and repair.
I. Title.

‡GERASIMOVICH, Liudmila   894'.2
Konstantinovna
*History of modern Mongolian literature,
1921-1964,* by Ludmilla K. Gerasimovich. Tr.
from Russian by members & friends of the
Mongolia Soc. Bloomington, Ind., Mongolia
Society, 1970. 22cm. ISBN 0-910980-16-0
(pubns. of the Mongolia Soc. Occasional
papers, no. 6) Tr. of (romanized: Literatura
Mongol'skoi Narodnoi Respubliki) Bibl.
[DS798.M575 no. 6] 68-19042 pap., 8.00
1. Mongolian literature — History and criticism. I. Title. (Series: Mongolia Society. Occasional papers, no. 6)
Publisher's address: P.O. Box 606, Bloomington, Indiana 47401.

‡GERSTER, Georg, 1928-   726'.5'0963
Churches in rock; early Christian art in Ethiopia [by] Georg Gerster, with contributions by David R. Buxton [& others] Pref.
by the Emperor Hayla Sellase I. Tr. by Richard Hosking. [New York] Phaidon [dist.:
Praeger, c.1970] 148p. illus. (pt. col.), map,
plans. 33cm. ISBN 0-7148-1381-8 Tr. of Kir-
chen im Fels. Bibl.: p. 144-146. [N7988.G4613]
69-19806 29.50
1. Cave churches - Ethiopia. 2. Art, Coptic.
I. Title.

GIBSON, J. Sullivan   631.4
Soils: their nature, classes, distribution, uses,
and care, by J. Sullivan Gibson & James W.
Batten. University, Univ. of Alabama Pr.
[1970] xvii, 296p. illus. 21cm. ISBN
0-8173-2875-0 Bibl. [S591.G52] 68-14555 6.00
1. Soil science. I. Batten, James W., 1919-
joint author. II. Title.

GIBSON, Walter Brown, 1897-   FIC-M
Grove of doom, by Walter Gibson (alias
Maxwell Grant) [New York] Grosset
[1969, c.1966] 154p. 18cm. ISBN 0-448-
05320-0 (Tempo bks., 5320) At head of title:
The weird adventures of the Shadow. The 1st
vol. in the author's trilogy, the 2d of which is
Voodoo death; & the 3d, Murder by moon-
light. [PZ3.G3594Gr4] [PS3513I2823] 813'.5
'2 74-86705 pap., .60
1. Title. II. Title: The weird adventures of the
Shadow.

GILFILLAN, S. Colum, 1889-   301.2'4
The sociology of invention; an essay in the social causes, ways, and effects of technic invention, especially as demonstrated historicly
[sic] in the author's Inventing the ship
[by] S. C. Gilfillan. Cambridge, M.I.T. Pr.
[1970, c.1935] xiii, 185p. 21cm. ISBN
0-262-07009-X Subtitle varies slightly. Bibls.
[T212.G5 1970] 75-97497 7.50; pap., 2.45
1. Inventions. 2. Ships. I. Title.
Pbk. ed. has ISBN 0-262-57020-3.

GILKEY, Langdon Brown, 1919-   215
Religion and the scientific future; reflections
on myth, science, and theology, by Langdon
Gilkey. [1st ed.] New York, Harper

[1970] x, 193p. 22cm. (Deems lects., 1967)
Bibl. refs. [BL240.2.G54 1970] 72-109070
5.95
1. Religion and science — 1946- — Addresses, essays, lectures. I. Title. (Series)

GILPATRICK, Eleanor   658.37'3621097471
G.
*The occupational structure of New York City
municipal hospitals* [by] Eleanor G. Gilpa-
trick, Paul K. Corliss. Foreword by Sar A.
Levitan. New York, Praeger [1970] xxi,
190p. illus. 25cm. (Praeger special studies in
U.S. econ. & social development) Bibl.
[RA972.5.G55] 76-105407 12.50
1. New York (City) — Hospitals — Staff. I.
Corliss, Paul K., joint author. II. Title.

GINSBERG, Louis, 1896-   811'.5'2
Morning in spring; and other poems. New
York, Morrow, 1970. 125p. 22cm. [PS3513.
I75M6] 79-107067 5.00
1. Title.

*GIRDLER, Reynolds   741.23
Crayon techniques [by] Reynolds Girdler,
Jr. New York, Pitman [1969] 32p. illus.
(pt. col.) 19½x28cm. pap., price unreported
1. Crayon drawing — Juvenile literature. I.
Title.

*GLASS, Justine   133.3
They foresaw the future; the story of fulfilled
prophecy [New York] Berkely [1969]
256p. 18cm. ISBN 0-425-01833-4 (Medallion
bk., Z1833) pap., 1.25
1. Prophecy. 2. Predictions. I. Title.

†GLASSER, Paul H., comp.   301.42'08
Families in crisis, ed. by Paul H. Glasser,
Lois N. Glasser. New York, Harper [1970]
vi, 405p. 21cm. (Readers in social problems)
Bibl. refs. [HQ728.G45] 79-103916 pap.,
5.95
1. Family — Addresses, essays, lectures. 2.
Social problems — Addresses, essays, lec-
tures. I. Glasser, Lois N., joint comp. II.
Title.
L.C. card lists contents.

GOETHE, Johann Wolfgang von,   535.6'01
1749-1832
Theory of colours. Tr. from German, with
notes, by Charles Lock Eastlake. Introd. by
Deane B. Judd. Cambridge, Mass., M.I.T.
Pr. [1970] lxii, 423p. illus: (pt. col.) 21cm.
Tr. of Farbenlehre. Reprint of the 1840 ed.
[QC495.G5 1970] 74-84656 10.00; pap.,
2.95
1. Color. I. Title.

GOLDWIN, Robert A., 1922- ed.   327'.08
Readings in world politics, ed. by Robert A.
Goldwin. 2d. rev. by Tony Pearce. New
York, Oxford Univ. Pr. [1970] 644p. 21cm.
Bibl. refs. [JX1391.G6 1970] 70-83001
pap., 3.95
1. International relations — Collections. I.
Pearce, Tony, 1928- II. Title.

GONZALES, Ambrose Elliott,   398'.0973
1857-1926
With Aesop along the black border. New
York, Negro Univs. Pr. [1969, c.1924] xiv,
298p. 23cm. ISBN 0-8371-2732-7 Dialectal
paraphrases from Aesop's fables. "The fables
contained in this vol. were . . . pub. in The
State between August 1923 & Feb. 1924."
[GR103.G65 1969] 73-97424 11.00
1. Folk-lore, Negro. 2. Folk-lore — South
Carolina - Sea Islands. I. Aesopus. II. Title.

GOOCH, C.H.   621.32'9
Gallium arsenide lasers; ed. by C.H. Gooch.
London, New York, Wiley-Interscience
[c.1969] 333p. illus. 24cm. ISBN 0-471-
31320-3 Bibl. refs. [TK871.3.G65] 78-93559
14.50
1. Lasers. 2. Gallium arsenide. I. Title.

would not be in BIP. Now, where and how would you go about finding it?

86.   Review: If the citation you located did not give you the address of the publisher, where would you look to find the address of the publisher?

87.   The "Weekly Record" is published weekly, therefore 52 times a year. Suppose you had to find, in PW, the listing for a title which you knew had to be published last year but did not know what part of last year. Would you then have to go through every weekly issue of PW, to a possible total of 52 issues?

88.   Look at a recent issue of American Book Publishing Record (BPR), and read the introductory note on the inside front cover. What connection does BPR have with PW?

89.   Therefore, what is the scope of BPR?

90.   And as a further aspect of the scope, what (how much) information will be included in the individual entries or citations in BPR?

91.   What is the arrangement of BPR? Is it the same as PW Weekly Record?

92.   BPR is arranged by subject. Is it therefore alphabetically by subject?

93.   How would you find books on travel in a recent issue of BPR?

94.   How would you find books on advertising?

95.   BPR, then, is a classified subject arrangement. In order to use this type of arrangement most successfully, what type of index (other than author/title) might you need?

96.   What title have you examined previously which was arranged by subject?

97.   Is the subject arrangement of BPR similar to the Subject Guide to BIP?

98.   In BPR, books on the subject of "pottery" are listed in the 730's, within the broad subject division of "The Arts," the 700's. Are they therefore listed in proximity to all of the books on crafts, regardless of whether these books are on the subject of pottery, weaving, woodcraft, leather work, etc.?

99.   Is a similar arrangement followed in Subject Guide to BIP?

100.   If you are looking in BPR for a book for which you have the author (Clive Hart) and the title (<u>Kites; an Historical Survey</u>), could you find it without determining the subject area?

101.   The <u>scope</u> of BPR then is the same as PW "Weekly Record," but the arrangement is classified (by Dewey Decimal Classification) with author /title /subject indexes.   What are two basic differences between PW "Weekly Record" and BPR?

102.   Does PW "Weekly Record" have a subject approach?   Does BPR have a subject approach?   Therefore, can you look in PW "Weekly Record" and find all books published on travel as easily as in BPR?

103.   In #87, you found that in order to locate the listing for a title published last year, you would have to go through each weekly issue of PW "Weekly Record" to a possible total of 52 issues.   Now that you know about BPR, what advantage would you have?

104.   What then are two advantages of BPR over PW "Weekly Record"?

105.   What is one advantage of PW "Weekly Record" over BPR?

106.   When did BPR begin publication and what does this tell you about access to PW "Weekly Record" information prior to that time?

107.   Review: what information does the BPR /PW citation give you which you do not get from BIP?   (#75)

108.   You have seen that the <u>weekly</u> issues of PW "Weekly Record" cumulate or combine citations into a <u>monthly</u> listing in BPR.   Do the monthly issues further cumulate or combine?

109.   How often does the BPR Cumulative come out?

110.   How long has the BPR Cumulative been coming out?

111.   What is the <u>scope</u> of BPR Cumulative?

112.   What is the <u>arrangement</u> of BPR Cumulative?

113.   If, then, the BPR Cumulative has exactly the same scope and arrangement as BPR, what is its specific use?

114.   Review: of all the sources you have had so far, where would you look to find the publisher of <u>Beautiful Losers</u> by Leonard Cohen, published in 1966?

115.   Who is the publisher?   What is the price?

116.   You can get that information from either BIP or BPR Cumulative 1966.   What does BIP tell you that BPR Cumulative does not?

117.   Where would you look to find out how many new editions of Shakespeare's plays appeared (in the U.S.) in 1969?

118.   Where would you look to find a list of all the different versions of the Bible which are in print?

119.   Would the listing in BIP give you enough information to distinguish sufficiently between the various versions or editions?   (If you are not sure how to answer, check it in BIP to see.)

120.   Where would you go to find further information?   (Two sources which you have had so far in this section.)

121.   Suppose you wanted to make a choice between editions, for purchase, or for recommendation to a patron. Do you think either of the sources from #120 would give you really sufficient information for that choice? (Again, if you are not sure how to answer, choose one of the Bibles cited as in print in BIP and search it out in both sources.)

122.   So what other possible type of bibliographical source might you find helpful in this case?

123.   Suppose that you want a current book on a very specific aspect of advertising. You could, as we have already noted, look in BPR in the appropriate classification number, and find out what books have been published on advertising during the past year, and go back to BPR Cumulative for previous years if you wished. You could look over the titles of all of these books and see if any of them covered the specific aspect of the subject you are concerned with. Perhaps none of them do; you might then wonder if it is possible that any new books on the subject will be coming out soon. How would you find this out? (Remember the preface to Books in Print.)

124.   These next two publications--Forthcoming Books and Subject Guide to Forthcoming Books--can be examined quite quickly because they can easily be compared to other sources you have already looked at in detail. They are in fact very similar to two of the sources you have previously examined. Look over the two titles--considering basically their arrangement and the amount of information given; which of the earlier sources are they similar to? The titles alone might give you a clue.

125.   In #67, you had the problem of finding information about a novel published last month, about which you know the author and title. At that point, you would have had to look through each weekly issue of PW for such information. In #85, you found that you could solve that problem more directly by going through monthly issues of BPR. Now, do you have any further choices?

Section 1b

National Bibliographic Records (U.S.)--current

Answers #67-125

67. A: No, you wouldn't. Remember that BIP is published in the late fall of the year (see the answer to #26), and that therefore it will not necessarily include listing for titles published after that date. (For example, the 1970 edition of BIP is published in October 1970; the 1971 edition is published in October 1971. Books published in November and December 1970, and in 1971 until October, will not necessarily appear in the 1970 BIP which you would be using until October 1971.)

68. A: Yes, it does.

69. A: Refer back to the Appendix A.

70. A: The date, volume and issue numbering appear on the front cover, upper right corner. The masthead statement appears on the inside front cover, bottom of page. The publisher is the Bowker Company, and they also publish BIP/PTLA/Subject Guide to BIP/Paperbound Books in Print, etc.

71. A: Read the paragraph at the head of each week's list: "A conscientious listing of current American book publication."

72. A: That's hard to tell--basically it means that they will try to be all-inclusive (within the limits they have set) but do not count on it--because actually the Bowker Co. is dependent upon the individual publishers to contribute information, as it is with PTLA/BIP.

73. A: Yes, there are specific exclusions. This is set forth in the introductory paragraph to each week's listing: "Not included in these listings are ..."

74. A: No. "Book publication" is specifically stated. Also, these items have been excluded from listing in BIP (see #29). Who publishes PW? Who publishes BIP?

75. A: Library of Congress cataloging, published price, address of publisher if required. (The citation in the Weekly Record is intended to be a complete library catalog entry, and the cataloging itself is done by the Library of Congress in cooperation with the Bowker Co.)

76. A: No. Basically, BIP gave only author, title, publisher, price (and by implication, the in-print status), and sometimes the date of publication. (Sometimes fuller information is given in the PTLA listing.)

77. A: Publisher is Phaidon (distributed by Praeger). Price is $29.50. The book is a translation of a German title, Kirchem in Fels. The translator is Richard Hosking. The citation does not actually tell you that the book has been published elsewhere, in German or English.

78. A: Basically, the entries are listed alphabetically.

79. A: Yes to both. (On the sample page attached for #76, the Future of Empirical Theology is an example of a title entry; Geneva Institute of International Relations is an example of a corporate author entry.)

80. A: No.

81. A: No on both counts.

82. A: No, BIP had entries under author and title (and sometimes series), with some cross-references.

83. A: No, not unless it happened to be entered under title, which is certainly unlikely for a novel.

84. A: In a way, but awkwardly. The Dewey Decimal number in the upper right corner of each citation is a clue to the subject, and you could, for example, locate all the medical books in a week's listing by running down the right side of the columns and looking at every item with a 610 number. (This is not quite the same thing as a "subject entry," noted in #80. A "subject entry" would mean that the subject itself would be used as the key element in the citation--for example, the subject word "Medicine" would be used as the entry word for the citation, and the citation would be filed alphabetically under "medicine." In general, a subject access would have to be through a subject entry, but you can see from this example of the PW "Weekly Record" that it is possible to have other types of subject access.)

85. A: You would have to search through the weekly issues of PW "Weekly Record," probably starting from the most recent you had on hand and working back, looking under the author's name (main entry), until you found the citation.

86. A: BIP, Vol. 2, list of publishers; possibly in PTLA if the publisher's catalog is included.

87. A: Yes, you would, if you were using the PW

"Weekly Record" only. However, your task is made much easier by the existence of the next bibliographical source on your list of titles to examine: the American Book Publishing Record.

88. A: It is, of course, also published by the Bowker Co., but more than that, BPR is a "monthly cumulation from the Weekly Record listing of PW..."; that is, the weekly entries from PW are cumulated (added together, or combined) once a month to form the BPR.

89. A: Same as PW "Weekly Record" from which it is taken (except that it comes out only monthly instead of every week).

90. A: Same as PW "Weekly Record" again, since the citations are taken directly from the PW "Weekly Record." (See your answer to #88.)

91. A: No, it is not the same as the PW "Weekly Record." BPR is arranged by subject. Check the introductory paragraph at the beginning of an issue, on the first page-- "The basic arrangement is ...."

92. A: No, it follows the scheme of the Dewey Decimal Classification itself, and is therefore arranged by classification number. It is necessary to know where your subject falls in the classification scheme in order to locate it in the monthly listing. Once you have established that medicine is "610" you can go to the "610" section, numerically, and see all in one place all the books on medicine.

93. A: Look under 910 for travel (as indicated in the introductory paragraph), or look up travel as a subject in the alphabetical index in the back of the issue, and find the page number for the travel classification.

94. A: The introductory paragraph does not tell you this specifically, but you might guess they would fall into the general area of "business." It is more direct and less liable to error, however, to look up advertising in the subject index in the back and be referred to the specific Dewey Decimal classification number.

95. A: A specific subject index, which tells you where the subjects will be found in the classification scheme--such as you used for travel in #93 and advertising in #94. In BPR, the subjects are indexed with the titles in the back of each issue.

96. A: Subject Guide to Books in Print.

97. A: No, not really. Subject Guide to BIP is arranged alphabetically by Library of Congress subject headings. BPA is arranged numerically by Dewey Decimal classification, with broader subject divisions than in Subject Guide to BIP.

98. A: Yes.

99. A: No. In Subject BIP, books on pottery are listed alphabetically under "pottery," between "Potters' Marks" and "Potting (Electronics)". Books on weaving are listed under "weaving," alphabetically between weaverbirds and Webb, Beatrice.

100. A: Yes. Each monthly issue of BPR has an author index and a title index.

101. A: The frequency of appearance, and the arrangement.

102. A: Not really (see #84). Yes. No.

103. A: You could go through each monthly cumulation, in BPR, to a possible number of 12 issues--searching by author, as you have noted in #100.

104. A: (1) Easy subject access; (2) one list (monthly) compared to four or five lists (weekly) in PW Weekly Record.

105. A: More frequent, up-to-date information. (Since PW "Weekly Record" comes out once a week, compared with BPR's monthly, you will get the information on new books faster or sooner.)

106. A: 1960. Winchell again. So that prior to 1960, there was no monthly cumulation of the PW "Weekly Record" entries, and searching would have to be done through the entire 52 issues. Furthermore, prior to 1960, there was no reasonable--or quick-- subject access to the entries in PW "Weekly Record" (refer back to #84).

107. A: Cataloging information, basically: LC classification number, Dewey classification number, LC card order number, added entry and subject tracings, etc. (See #75).

108. A: Into the BPR Cumulative, the next title on your list to examine. Again, you might be a jump ahead of the titles, seeing a need and wondering if there is a bibliographical tool or source which fills that need.

109. A: Annually (title page)

110. A: As before you would look in Winchell for this one. BPR Cumulative is first listed in the Winchell first supplement (1AA54), indicating that it began--as an annual cumulation from BPR weekly issues--in 1965. (This annotation and the annotation for BPR weekly in the basic Winchell (AA344) indicates that there was an annual index to BPR, from 1962; this is an index only, referring you back to the issues of BPR weekly, not a cumulation of the individual entries into one further volume.) However, a glance at the BPR Cumulative on the shelves will show you that volumes exist for 1960-64 as well as 1965 on. Examination of these will show you that the 1960-64 volumes are a five-year

cumulation published in 4 volumes, and the title page of volume 1 will show you that the set was published in 1968. In fact, the Bowker Company, after beginning publication of the annual cumulations in 1965, then went back to cumulate earlier BPRs (from its beginning in 1960 through 1964) into a single cumulation. A similar five-year cumulation for 1965-69 is planned for publication in late 1970 or 1971. The five-year 1960-64 cumulation is listed and annotated in Winchell second supplement (2AA59).

111. A: Record of American book production for the year 1966, etc. Basically, the same as BPR (monthly issues) and PW "Weekly Record," of course.

112. A: Same as BPR, see #91 and following.

113. A: Mainly that it is much easier to look in one alphabetical or subject list (annual cumulative) rather than in 12 separate monthly lists. This is the basic principle behind "cumulation" and it is one which is very useful to the construction of reference sources, particularly bibliographies.

114. A: BIP (by author or title), or BPR Cumulative 1966 (by author in the index); (or BPR monthly issues for 1966, or PW "Weekly Record" issues for 1966).

115. A: Viking (NY), $5.75, and Compass paperback, $1.75, according to BIP.

116. A: The in-print status.

117. A: BPR Cumulative is best--all in one spot, and gives 1969 publications only. BIP will tell you all editions in print, including other than 1969 so it is more confusing.

118. A: You want to know in-print status. Therefore, BIP.

119. A: No.

120. A: One possibility is to refer to the publisher's catalog in PTLA itself, in the hope that it would give you further information. A second possibility is to search out each edition in its listing in BPR Cumulative / BPR monthly /PW "Weekly Record" to see if that citation would give you further information.

121. A: Probably not unless you know a lot about Bibles.

122. A: A selective, annotated bibliography (if it happens to include Bibles). The Readers' Advisor (Winchell #AA269), for example, is a particularly helpful source. Look it up and see what it tells you about Bibles; this should help you to see the usefulness of such "selection aids" or selective bibliographies or readers' advisory type sources.

Another similar source, which might also have occurred to you as an answer to #120, is a bibliography of Bibles. Here, as you did with Mark Twain, you could go to Winchell or to the bibliographies of bibliographies for some suggestions.

123. A: Two other Bowker publications, Forthcoming Books and its companion Subject Guide to Forthcoming Books, would probably give you this information. These are discussed briefly in the preface to Books in Print. They are also the next titles to examine in this section.

124. A: Forthcoming Books is arranged by author and title, and only the basic bibliographical information--including price--is given for those items listed. Subject Guide to Forthcoming Books is arranged by more or less specific subjects listed alphabetically--in other words, just like the Subject Guide to Books in Print. Forthcoming Books is similar in arrangement (although in one volume rather than two) to BIP and Subject Guide to BIP. Reading the short preface in any of the recent issues of Forthcoming Books will tell you that it is in fact, to be used in conjunction with the annual edition of BIP--and therefore serves to update or supplement BIP. Similarly Subject Guide to Forthcoming Books serves to update or supplement Subject Guide to BIP. Since you already know what types of publications are listed or excluded from BIP (and Subject BIP), you know approximately what types of publications you will expect to find listed in or excluded from Forthcoming Books. The same assumption can be made about the amount and kind of bibliographical information included in the citations.

125. A: You could go to Forthcoming Books, which not only updates BIP but serves as an announcement of forthcoming books--therefore your title should be listed if it has come out since the last publication of BIP, and it should also be listed even if the novel is in fact not yet published.

Section 1c

National Bibliographic Records (U.S.)--current

Questions #126-184

All of the titles you have examined so far (except for Law Books in Print) are publications of the Bowker Co., so by now you should be aware that the Bowker Company is one of the major publishers of current bibliographical information. The Bowker Company is a commercial publishing firm, but one which is very closely associated with the "book trade" and is well known for publishing materials, such as Publishers' Weekly itself, which are of use to the book trade and to librarians. Remember that sources of national bibliographic records are not necessarily always from the library profession; this is especially true in the United States.

There is another major commercial firm involved in the publishing of current bibliographical sources, particularly useful to librarians, and in your future examination of bibliographical and reference sources, you will learn about many of their publications. The next title to examine, of current sources in the U.S. national bibliographic records, is a publication of the Wilson Company:

Cumulative Book Index (CBI)   (AA345 & AA343)

126.   Your first problem is to determine the scope and the arrangement of CBI. Judging from your past experience, where might you look for this?

127.   Probably then the most effective way to approach CBI is to use the annotation in Winchell, which is quite full although not entirely currently accurate, plus the preface in a recent two-year cumulated volume of CBI, plus an examination of the source itself in comparison to the information you get from Winchell and from the CBI preface. Who publishes CBI, when did it begin publication, and how often does it come out?

128.   Locate the volumes of the Cumulative Book Index on the shelves, and look at the title page of one of the recent issues or volumes (in the paper-covered recent issues, the cover itself constitutes the title page). What is the full title of CBI, including the sub-title?

129.   This full title tells you a great deal about this source, and you begin with the first word. What does "cumulative" mean, and where have you had it before?

130.   What is the major effect, or advantage, of cumulation?

131.   Remembering that CBI goes as far back as 1928, look at all of the bound volumes and paper-covered current issues on the shelf, and see if you can figure out the cumulative pattern. This pattern will be fairly easy to determine for the bound volumes, less easy to determine for the current paper-covered issues. For the current issues, check carefully on the title page (or cover) for a statement that the issue you have "supersedes" or replaces earlier issues, as this will indicate a cumulation. (And remember that your classmates, and the reference librarians, may also be using current issues from the shelves so that some may be missing when you look at them.) What does the cumulation pattern appear to be?

132.   Does CBI appear to cumulate more often than BPR?

133. So far we have concerned ourselves with sources of bibliographical information on current publications-- this year, this month, this week. We also need at times to have information on older or past publications; in other words, retrospective information. What might some of these retrospective bibliographical information needs be?

134. Of course, any current information becomes, eventually, retrospective; any current bibliographical record will then become, eventually, a retrospective record. There is no clear-cut point at which current becomes retrospective. Usually, one would consider the present year, perhaps also the past year, as "current", and anything prior to that as "retrospective." But for the needs of some people, last week's information could be considered retrospective.

Suppose you wanted to find the publisher and the correct publication date for Medieval Days and Ways, by Gertrude Hartman, published by MacMillan, which you know to have been published in the United States in the 1930's. Of the sources which you have had so far in this unit, which ones could you use? CBI? PW Weekly Record? BPR Cumulative? BPR (monthly)? BIP? PTLA? (Assume that you are searching specifically for the 1930 edition so that you are considering retrospective sources--that is, do not assume the title is still in print or has been reprinted. If it happens to be still in print, or if it happens to have been reprinted and the reprint is still in print, then of course it would be listed in the current BIP. What about using older editions of BIP or PTLA?)

135. Of the three yes answers for the preceding question, which would be the easiest to use and why?

136. If in fact you did not have access to CBI, and had only PTLA and PW Weekly Record, what other possibility would you have for answering #134?

137. PTLA and the PW listings are certainly a source of retrospective information, but they are extremely inefficient to use. Why is this? What is lacking in these sources which would make them easier to use?

138. CBI, then, is a source of current information (how often is it published?), but it is also the first source you have had which gives you any reasonable retrospective access to information. How long has it been published?

139. So far you have concentrated mainly on the "cumulative" aspect of CBI, and as you have seen, this is one of its most effective features. This is part of the arrangement of the set. But there is much more to determine about the scope and arrangement. Go back to the full title (#128), and consider the sub-title itself. What does this tell you about the scope of this source?

140. Is this any different from the scope of the Bowker publications examined earlier? (BIP/PTLA/PW/BPR, etc.)

141. Does CBI then list all books from all countries?

142. Does CBI list only books in English, regardless of where published?

143. What types of publications are included in the scope of CBI? (The full title gives you a clue; a more complete answer is in the preface.)

144.   Does CBI include periodicals?

145.   The "scope" of CBI, then, is a record of book publication, basically, with some specified exceptions, in
        the United States, and in English anywhere in the world. How does this differ from the record in the
        PW Weekly Record (and therefore in BPR)?

146.   Is the scope of CBI broader, narrower, or the same as PW Weekly Record?

147.   What information is given you in the individual entries in CBI? Is this more, less, or the same as that
        given you in PW Weekly Record entries?

148.   Is this more, less or the same as that given you in BPR?

149.   Using CBI, what is the publisher and price for Johnny Under Ground by Patricia Moyes, published in 1966?

150.   In the entry for Moyes, how were you to have known that "16s '65 Collins" was the information for the
        British publication?

151.   Could you have found the answer to #149 by looking in CBI under the title?

152.   What is the arrangement of CBI? (You must already have had to figure this out in order to locate Moyes:
        Johnny Under Ground in #149, and you probably did not have any real trouble. You see how far you have
        progressed?)

153.   In #147, you indicated the information found in the individual entries. In these entries is there any indi-
        cation of the subject of the book (as you have with the LC or Dewey classification numbers, and the sub-
        ject heading tracings, in the PW Weekly Record listings)? Is there anything else in CBI which appears
        to indicate subject?

154.   Review: What are the three main kinds of access which we need for bibliographical information? (Refer
        back to #44).

155.   Does CBI have all of these three accesses, and how are they arranged?

156.   Is this the same as the arrangement of PW Weekly Record?

157.   Did BIP have all of these three accesses?

158.   Is the arrangement of CBI the same as BIP, then?

159.   Does BPR have all three of these accesses, and is the arrangement similar to CBI?

160.   This arrangement of author/title/subject in one alphabetical list is often called a "dictionary" arrange-
       ment (see "Dictionary Catalog" in the ALA Glossary), and is very typical of Wilson Company publica-
       tions.   Keep it in mind as you will come across it again.

       Do the CBI title and subject entries give you all of the bibliographical information found under the author
       entry, or do they serve more as cross-reference to a basic entry?   Look up two or three examples and
       compare them.

161.   Can you find a list of detectives, in England, published late in 1967?

162.   What kind of "access" did you need, and use, to answer the preceding question?   Author?   Title?
       Subject?

163.   Is the CBI subject access a classified one?

164.   What other subject access source uses subject headings?

165.   In #51, you looked up "data processing" in the Subject Guide to BIP.   Refer back to your answer for
       that problem, and then see how CBI treats it.   Is it similar?

166.   How does this compare to the treatment in BPR?

167.   How is fiction listed in BPR and BPR Cumulative?

168.   How is fiction listed in Subject Guide to Books in Print?

169.   How is fiction listed in CBI?

170.   Where could you go to find, most easily, some titles (and authors) of recently published science fiction?

171.   Since CBI attempts to record all English language publications, would you then expect it to be a fairly
       good and complete record for Great Britain as well as the U.S.?   For any other countries?

172.   In the front of recent issues of CBI is a special list called "Checklist of English Language Publications
       issued in countries other than Great Britain, Canada, and the U.S."   Do the publications listed appear on-
       ly in this checklist or are they included also in the regular listing?   (How would you find out?)

173.   What then is the point of the Checklist? You may have to use your imagination on this one.

174.   In examining these sources so far, you have stressed only "scope" and "arrangement" from the general criteria for evaluation of reference sources. Another criteria often mentioned is that of "Special Features," and here the checklist in CBI may be considered as an example of a special feature. Does CBI have any other things which might be considered as special features? Can you recall any other special features from previous sources you have examined?

175.   Find in CBI the entry for They Talk and Walk by Norbert Brown, published in 1966 by the Magna Carta Press. How many pages does it contain?

176.   And the moral is: just because a book is published in 1966, can you necessarily expect to find it in the 1966 volume of CBI?

177.   You have the information that Growing Up in Religion by Evelyn Derry was published in London in 1963. Who is the publisher?

The next few questions, from #178-184, are set up as a short review, covering all the sources you have looked at so far in this section. It is not necessary to go back to the sources themselves and look up all the answers, but you may find it helpful to do so, particularly for those aspects which still may not be clear to you.

178.   You want to find the titles of some books on anthropology published in 1955 or 1956. Where would you look?

179.   You need the price of the Dell edition (paperback) of H. Rider Haggard's King Solomon's Mines. What are three possible sources in which you could find this?

180.   Could you find the answer to the previous question in CBI?

181.   A book entitled Travel While you Work by Joan L. Owens was published in England in 1963. Where would you find the publisher and price?

182.   Where would you look to find if there is a "variorum" edition of Yeats' poems available for purchase?

183.   Could you have found the answer to the previous question--a "variorum" edition of Yeats' poems--by checking in BIP under title? What problems would you run into?

184.   You want to find the titles of books on art published recently, this year and last year. What are at least three different sources you could turn to for this information? Which one would be the easiest to use, and why? (If you can't immediately come up with the answer to this last question, then try actually looking up such books in all three sources and see what you find out.)

Section 1c

National Bibliographic Records (U.S.)--current

Answers #126-184

126. A: Probably you should look for a preface
         or introduction. In fact, the current issues
         of CBI do not contain any very effective pre-
         faces or introductions, and you have to go
         back as far as the two-year bound cumula-
         tions (1963/64; 1965/66) for such a state-
         ment.

127. A: The publisher is the Wilson Company. It
         began publication in 1928 and it comes out
         currently more or less monthly. (Winchell
         says "monthly;" the July 1970 issue of CBI
         says "monthly except August".)

128. A: Cumulative Book Index; a World List of Books
         in the English language.

129. A: Cumulative is a combining or an adding to-
         gether (check a dictionary or the ALA
         Glossary for a fuller explanation), and
         you have already seen it at work with the
         PW Weekly Record/BPR/BPR Cumulative
         sequence.

130. A: Basically, it reduces the number of places
         in which you have to search. You have
         seen it, for example, cumulate weekly is-
         sues into monthly issues, and then into
         annual volumes, reducing the possible
         search places from 52 to 1.

131. A: The cumulation pattern for the early vol-
         umes is every five years: 1928-32, 1933-
         37, 1938-42. Then a six-year cumulation
         (1943-48), followed by two four-year cumu-
         lations (1949-52; 1953-56). From 1957 on,
         the pattern has been two-year cumulations:
         1957-58, 1959-60, 1961-62, 1963-64 (the
         1963-64 cumulation was so large that it
         was necessary to bind it in two volumes,
         but it is still only one cumulation for that
         period, as the volumes are divided alpha-
         betically), 1965-66 (also in the two vol-
         umes), etc. and cumulated quarterly (for
         example, January and February with March)
         and then semi-annually. (The bound semi-
         annual volumes are likely to be delayed in
         publication, so it is possible that you would
         see, for example, the September and
         October papercovered monthly issues on
         the shelves well before the January-July
         bound semi-annual cumulation is received.)

132. A: Yes, BPR cumulates annually (from monthly
         issues), then every five years. CBI
         cumulates at the first three months, then
         semi-annually, as well as annually, then
         every two years. Frequent cumulation is
         one of the basic principles behind the Wilson
         Company publications.

133. A: Identification of older published materials--

determination of correct author, correct
title, etc.; further information on older pub-
lications--such as the edition, the series (if
any) in which published, the publisher, etc.,
the date of publication; selecting and ordering older publications to fill in a library's
collections (last week's publications on a particular subject is not always the best, just
because it is the newest; there are "classics"
in subject areas as well as in literature);
identifying and locating older publications for
research purposes; compiling bibliographies.

134. A: CBI: yes, it goes back to 1928
         BIP: no, it began in 1948
         PTLA: yes, it began in 1960
         BPR Cumulative: no, it began in 1960
         BPR (monthly): no, it began in 1960
         PW Weekly Record: yes, it began in 1872
            (and even the early volumes carried some
            sort of a list)

135. A: CBI, because you would have to search
         through considerably less places--three of
         the five year cumulations. In PTLA, you
         would have to go through each yearly vol-
         ume to a possible total of 10. (And you
         can only do that because you have the pub-
         lisher's name). In PW Weekly Record, you
         would have to go through each weekly issue
         (52) for each year (10), a possible total of
         520 places--and in fact, you would probably
         not bother unless you were desperate.

136. A: A subject bibliography might tell you.

137. A: Cumulation (remember #135).

138. A: CBI is currently published on a monthly
         basis, more or less. It has been published
         since 1898--as a supplement to the U.S.
         catalog until 1928; thereafter, the volume
         came out as CBI.

139. A: "A World list of books in the English
         Language." It tells you that it includes
         books published in the English language,
         published anywhere in the world. The pre-
         face (see #126 and #127) also tells you this:
         "it aims to be a complete bibliography of
         works in English..."

140. A: Yes, it is. Those covered only American
         (or U.S.) publications, none from other
         countries unless distributed by a U.S. firm.
         CBI covers all countries.

141. A: No, only those in English.

142. A: You might well think that it does, but in
         fact, it also records all U.S. publications,
         including those in languages other than

English. (As an example, see the 1965-66 cumulation under Miller, S.H. and Jacobs, C.: Michel et la pieuvre.)

143. A: Cumulative Book Index; a World List of Books.... Books primarily, excluding government documents, maps, music, paperbound editions, pamphlets, and other items as listed in the preface.

144. A: Basically, no. Nowhere is this specifically stated, but the fact that it is called a "Book Index" or list indicates this to some extent, and the fact that you won't find any periodicals as such listed in its pages should cinch it. (You will find "annuals" listed in CBI, and these may sometimes be considered as periodicals.)

145. A: The type of publications covered is basically similar; CBI also includes English publications from other countries.

146. A: Broader

147. A: Author, title, paging, price (usually), publisher, date of publication, LC order card#. It doesn't give you the cataloging information (Dewey classification #, LC classification #, subject headings and added entry tracings) which you got from PW Weekly Record. Nor does it give you as full a statement of the size and the binding, usually. The information in CBI is therefore somewhat less than in PW.

148. A: Your answer should be the same as in the preceding question, since the BPR entries are exactly those from the PW Weekly Record.

149. A: In the 1965-66 cumulation, volume 2, under Moyes. Following the title, it gives you the paging (253p.), the price ($3.95), the year of publication ('66), the publisher (Holt); and then the British price (16s=16 shillings), the date of the British publication ('65), and the British publisher (Collins), followed by the LC card order #(66-10121).
   If you could not find this at all, go ahead temporarily to #151.

150. A: You were not. But you could have looked up "s" in the list of abbreviations in the front ("Explanations") and found out it meant "shillings," which might have helped, and you could have looked up "Collins" in the publishers list in the back of the volume and found from the address that it was a British publisher named Collins. It helps when using CBI to remember that it includes publications from other countries.

151. A: Yes, CBI has items listed under both author and title, in one alphabet.

152. A: Basically, it is alphabetically, with all entries in one single alphabet. Read the

introduction ("Suggestions for finding information") in the front of one of the bound cumulative volumes if you had trouble with this one. (If you skipped to this from #149, go back again now and do #149-151.)

153. A: No, subject indication in the entry itself unless you can tell or guess from the title. However, there are some entries which have a subject or "subject heading" above the entry. Check in a recent issue to find an example of this, then double check the entry under the author to see if it is entered under author and subject.

154. A: Author, title, subject.

155. A: Yes, it has author/title/subject entries, and all are in a single alphabet, as stated in #152.

156. A: No, CBI includes author, and title, and subject entries, in one alphabet. PW Weekly Record lists, in one alphabet, only the author or main entry. No titles (unless used as a main entry). No subjects.

157. A: Yes; author, title, and subject (in Subject Guide to BIP)

158. A: No; CBI has all three--a/t/s--in one alphabet. BIP has them in three separate alphabets. (Actually in separate volumes.)

159. A: Yes, BPR has author, title, and subject access. The basic arrangement is by subject (classified rather than alphabetical), and authors and titles are in separate alphabetical indexes, so again they are separate.

160. A: Usually the fullest information is found under the author entry, or the main entry. The title entries and the subject entries give enough information to refer to the main entry for more information.

161. A: In the October 1967 issue or whatever cumulation may now include it. Under Detectives--Directories. (Regency publicity service. Enquiry agents, private detectives ...1967, library edition at 35 shillings, and diary edition at 42 shllings...)

162. A: Subject

163. A: No. BPR is an example of a classified subject listing. CBI uses "subject headings."

164. A: Subject Guide to Books in Print

165. A: In the July 1970 issue of CBI, for example, there is no subject heading for "data processing" and no cross-references. This does not prove that CBI does not use that heading at all, simply that there were no titles on that subject listed in that issue. You would have to go through several issues of CBI to determine whether or not the heading is used, unlike the Subject Guide to

Books in Print where it is all listed in one volume. Subject BIP referred you to other headings, such as "Electronic Data Processing," "Information Storage and Retrieval," and "Punched Card Systems." The "July 1970 CBI issue <u>has</u> some titles listed under "Electronic data processing," and under "Information Storage and Retrieval Systems." In the January-July 1969 cumulation, there is a reference: "Data processing Electronics see Electronic data processing." A real advantage in using Subject BIP is the cross-references (or sees and see-alsos) which help you to cover all possibilities.

166. A: BPR is a classified arrangement and therefore you have to find out where in the classification the various "subjects" will be listed, so you need to check the alphabetical list of what are, in effect, subject headings, in the back of the issue or front of the annual cumulation. In BPR Cumulative 1966, "data processing" is listed in the index, and refers you to 651.8 of the classification; these books then are listed under the general area of "Business." The BPR Subject Index does not refer you to any other possible headings, but from your earlier experience with Subject BIP, you might think of looking under "Information Storage and Retrieval." This also is listed in the BPR subject index, referring you to 029.7 of the classification scheme. These titles are listed in quite a different place than "Data Processing," in with library science rather than business. Check BPR on "Electronic Data Processing."

    With both CBI and BPR, since you do not always have cross-references for subject headings, you are really on your own --more so than with Subject BIP--in locating all possible headings which might cover your subject.

167. A: In a separate section at the end of the classification scheme.

168. A: It is not listed at all; remember #56.

169. A: By author and title in the regular alphabetical listing. Also, according to the Winchell annotation, under subject where appropriate.

170. A: Most easily and directly, to CBI, checking under the heading "science fiction" (see the answer to #169). Check the January-July 1969 CBI for examples. You could also look in the separate fiction list in BPR (or in the PW Weekly Record), checking the entire list for the designation of FIC-S in the upper right corner of the citation; this is an awkward way of searching in the same way that you found it awkward to search PW Weekly Record by subject classification number (#84).

171. A: Yes, you would, and it is, although the

information from other countries may be somewhat slower in being listed than that from the U.S. It is also useful as a basic source for Australia, New Zealand, and Canada--other English-speaking countries.

172. A: The easiest way to find out is simply to choose an item listed in the checklist and look it up in the regular list to see if it also appears there, and you should find that it does.

173. A: The Checklist appears as a kind of an added attraction, or <u>special feature</u>, bringing together in one convenient place most of the non-U.S. publications. It could be useful as a book selection feature for libraries, for example.

174. A: The list of publishers with addresses, included in most of the bound volumes of CBI, is a good example of a special feature, and the same feature is included in BIP, v. 2. (Lists of abbreviations should not properly be considered as "special features" since an explanation for abbreviations used should be a mandatory feature of any reference source if it is to be most useful.)

175. A: It contains 242 pages. The entry for this item is not in the 1965-66 CBI. It is in the 1967-68 cumulation. There is a moral in this.

176. A: No, obviously not. You should expect that it will appear in the year of publication, or if it is published at the end of the year, it may of course appear in an early issue or cumulation of the following year. But if you do not find it as expected, you should then expect to keep searching forward (to the present date) on the assumption that it may have been listed late. (You might also think in terms of searching backward, in earlier years, in case your given date is incorrect.)

177. A: The only source you have so far covering British publications is CBI, and 1963 would be covered in the cumulative volumes for 1963-64. This title is not listed in that cumulative volume. You could then, as you did with #175 and 176, work your way forward to the present date, but you would still not find it. In fact, in this case the date was wrong--the publication date should have been 1962, not 1963, and you will find the publication listed in CBI 1961-62. The publisher is the Christian Community Press. When you check in what appears to be a correct source and you don't find the item you are looking for with reasonable searching, you should ALWAYS suspect your information as well as the source itself. And in bibliographical searching, it would not hurt to check a few years back from the date you have, as well as forward.

178. A: CBI is the only place you <u>can</u> look. Subject

BIP and BPR have subject access, it is true,
but they did not exist in 1955 or 1956.
This is another reason (in addition to that
in #48) for knowing when the bibliographical
sources began publication.

179. A: BIP, PTLA (under Dell), Paperbound Books
in Print.

180. A: Yes, you could, but since you do not know
the date of publication you would have to
work back through each issue and year
until you located it. It is more direct to
go to the other sources.

181. A: This is an English or British publication
(in English, but also in the sense of published in England). The only source you
have so far which gives you information
on English or British publications is CBI.

182. A: "Available for purchase" presumably would
mean "in-print," so you would want BIP,
the author volume, under Yeats. One of
the confusing elements in this problem
might have been the use of the word
"variorum," if you were not already familiar with it. But by now you should
realize that you can clear up most such
problems by checking in either a dictionary or in the ALA Glossary.

183. A: In the first place, you do not know what
the title is--presumably it would be something like "Poems," "Poetry of ...,"
"Collected Poems," "Complete Poems,"
etc.--and you do know the author's name
(Yeats), so it would make more sense to
check under author directly. You might
be able to find it also in the title volume.

184. A: You have to look in those sources which
have subject access, so you could use:
Subject Guide to BIP (considering that
books published last year and this year
would probably still be in print); CBI;
BPR (Cumulative and Monthly Issues).
BPR would probably be the easiest to use
because of its classified arrangement--
"art" is a very broad subject heading, and
it would probably be broken up into
several more narrowly defined headings
in the CBI and Subject BIP, which would
mean you would have to look in all of
those places; whereas in BPR all the art
books would be together in the 700
classification.

Section 2a

National Bibliographic Records (U.S.)--retrospective

Questions #185-227

185.   You have examined the major current sources of bibliographical information for the U.S., and you can move on to those sources which are primarily retrospective. What is meant by "retrospective"?

Keeping in mind that current sources become retrospective, or that sources which are now retrospective, may have been current at the time of their publication, you should now go on to examine the next group of titles:

United States Catalog (U.S.Cat.) (AA342)
American Catalogue of Books (AA341)
Kelly: American Catalog of Books (AA339)
Roorbach: Bibliotheca Americana (AA338)

186.   All four of these sources were current, at the time of their publication, as CBI is now current. Now, however, they serve us as retrospective sources. The United States Catalog is in fact the forerunner of what current publication?

187.   Who was the publisher of the United States Catalog? Who publishes CBI?

188.   When actually was the US Catalog published?   Go to Winchell for this.

189.   Look at the full title, including sub-title, of the US Catalog for 1928.   What was it similar to, of the current sources you have already examined?

190.   Where would you look to determine the scope of the US Catalog (4th edition, 1928)?

191.   Of the two possibilities in the preceding answer, which would be the best?

192.   In this case, the preface itself (to the 4th edition, 1928, of the US Catalog) is a very interesting statement of the history of such bibliographical records during the 19th and early twentieth century, and you may want to read it entirely as well as looking through it for information on the scope. What is the scope of the US Catalog?

193.   Is the scope of the US Catalog then the same as the current CBI?

194.   What information is given in the citations in the US Catalog?

195.   What is the arrangement of the US Catalog?

196.   What is the correct title of a Spanish American cookbook by Pauline Kleemann, published in the late 1920's?

197.   The US Catalog, after the 4th edition, was supplemented, or kept up to date, by CBI. You have then an unbroken record of US book production from about 1899 through the present date. What years are covered by the American Catalogue of Books? How did you find this?

198.   Who is the publisher of the American Catalogue, and what is the publication date?

199.   Can you think of any reason why it would have been necessary, or desirable, for a reprint to be made of the American Catalogue?

200.   Who is the publisher of a book by Lumholtz, titled <u>Among Cannibals: an Account of Four Years' Travels in Australia and Queensland</u>, published in 1889?

201.   How many volumes are there in the complete set of the American Catalogue, and how are these volumes arranged? You can get this answer very directly simply by looking at the spines of the volumes as they sit in their correct order on the shelf. (Assuming, of course, that they are sitting in their correct order...)

202.   What are the three basic accesses which we need for bibliographical sources, and does the American Catalogue have all of these?

203.   Does it have all three accesses for the entire scope of the set?

204.   Are these three accesses listed in a "dictionary" type arrangement?

205.   In the volumes for the American Catalogue, is each year of the scope (1876-1910) covered by a separate volume or separate list? That is, is the material listed for 1906 in a volume or list by itself, or cumulated (as in CBI) with other years?

If you did not fully understand the answer to #201, then questions #202-205 are the types of questions which you must ask yourself in order to understand completely the arrangement of such bibliographies. If you had difficulties earlier (#200) in locating the publisher of Lumholtz' <u>Among Cannibals</u> (1889), try it again now and see if you find it easier. (And if you are still having trouble, perhaps it's time to see your instructor.)

There is a great deal of introductory material in the various volumes of the American Catalogue; if you have time to read them these prefaces will give you an interesting picture of the historical development of U.S. bibliographical control. However, you probably will not have the time, at this point, to read them carefully. If you were to do so, you would find that the listings in the American Catalogue, from 1876 on, were compiled from the weekly record listings called "Annual Catalogues," which were then cumulated --with some additions--into the larger cumulations as indicated in question #205.

206. Who is the publisher (that is, the original publisher; not the reprint publisher) of the American Catalogue series? (See #198).

207. When you examined the Bowker Company publications, as part of the current sources, you found that PW and PTLA, although they began publication in the late 1800's (1872 and 1873 respectively), did not serve as effective retrospective records because they did not really cumulate in any reasonable pattern. Now you find that the records from the early issues of PW did in fact cumulate, in a sense, to form the retrospective record of the American Catalogue, which you are now examining. The Bowker Company (or its predecessor, Mr. Leypoldt) is then responsible for an annual record of book production from 1876-1910, and again from the 1960's to the present. What company moved in to pick up this record during the years 1910 to approximately the 1960's?

208. Preceding the American Catalogue in coverage are Roorbach's Bibliotheca Americana and Kelly's American Catalogue of Books. These are separate publications but are so similar that they are often considered or cited together as Roorbach and Kelly.

What is the scope of Roorbach? That is, what years are covered by this record? What types of publications are included? Are these publications limited in any way by language or by country of publication?

209. What years are covered by Roorbach, bibliographically? When was Roorbach published, originally?

210. Note then that the years covered and the years published are not necessarily similar. With Roorbach, the first cumulative volume was not published until 1852, but its coverage goes back to 1820. What are the years covered by Kelly, bibliographically?

211. When was Kelly published, originally? Is this the same as the "years covered"?

212. Otherwise, is the scope of Kelly similar to that of Roorbach?

213. What information is given in the entries for Roorbach and Kelly? How does this compare with more current sources, such as CBI, BPR, etc.?

214. What is the publisher and original price of Durrie's A Genealogical History of the Holt Family, published in 1864?

215. What is the first name of the author of Scampavias from Gibel Tarek to Stamboul published in 1857?

216. Who is the author of France and England in North America, a Series of Historical Narratives published in 1865?

217. If you were able to find answers to the last three questions, #214-216, you have probably then already figured out the arrangement of Roorbach and Kelly. It is, in fact, quite similar to that of the American Catalogue, with one exception. What is the difference? Are Roorbach and Kelly lacking any of the basic accesses?

218.   However, is it possible to find in Roorbach and Kelly, the bibliographical information (author, title, imprint) of a book on Arctic expeditions, published in the U.S. in the latter half of the 19th century?

219.   Therefore, you do have a kind of subject access, through the title. It is limited, however. Could you have found the answer to #218 if you had looked under "expeditions, Arctic?" Why or why not?

220.   What then is the basic limitation to using titles as a subject index?

221.   What is the arrangement of Roorbach and Kelly? Use your experience with the last several questions as the basis for this.

222.   What is the cautionary comment made about Roorbach and Kelly in Winchell?

223.   In #218, you found under the title entries, two books by Sargent on Arctic expeditions, one titled Arctic Adventures by Sea and Land published by Phillip in 1857, and one titled Arctic Explorations and Discoveries during the Nineteenth Century, also published in 1857 by Mason Brothers. Look in the same source (Roorbach, 1855-1858) under the author (Sargent, Epes). Is the information you find there similar to the title entries?

        The next four questions are REVIEW.

224.   Where would you go to find out who is the author of a biography of William C. Macready, published in 1894?

225.   James Reeves is the editor of a recently published book of Emily Dickinson's poetry. Where would you go to find the publisher and price?

226.   Where would you find the publisher and price for the book Teacher by Sylvia Ashton Warner?

227.   So far, what are the years for which you have a bibliographical coverage? What are the sources which cover these years?

Section 2a

National Bibliographic Records (U.S.)--retrospective

Answers #185-227

185. A: Older, past, or earlier publications. Not necessarily beginning or ending at any specific date, simply those which are "not current." Probably earlier than the past year or two.

186. A: CBI.

187. A: Wilson Company.

188. A: The last edition was the 4th, in 1928. Three earlier editions were in 1899, 1902, 1912, with some supplementary publications in between. The US Catalog then was published from 1899 through 1928.

189. A: The sub-title on the title page is given as "Books in Print, January 1, 1928," so it was at the time of its publication, therefore, similar to the current BIP.

190. A: You would go to Winchell, which gives a very full statement of the scope of the US Catalog in the annotation for CBI; or you would go to the preface of the source itself.

191. A: The preface is usually the more complete statement and in a sense the more accurate, but the annotation in Winchell is usually more concise, and easier and quicker to read.

192. A: Basically, American publications--primarily books, excluding most documents, music, pamphlets--plus Canadian publications and importations of American firms. This information is from the preface; the statement in the preface (first page, fourth and fifth paragraphs) on the inclusion of state and then of federal documents is one which will be very interesting to keep in mind when you examine sources for government publications later.

193. A: Somewhat, but not quite. The scope of the US Catalog is not as broad as CBI because it does not include publications (in English) from other countries. It is worth noting that the US Catalog did attempt to include some government documents, but later volumes of CBI specifically exclude such publications.

194. A: Basically, the same information--and in the same form--as in CBI; in fact, the US Catalog sometimes includes some additional information.

195. A: Like CBI

196. A: You have the subject and the author; the author is probably easier, at least more direct, to search under. You need to check in the US Catalog covering 1928, and it is not there; so you need to go on to the next in the series, CBI five-year cumulation for 1928-32, where you find, under Kleemann: Ramona's Spanish Mexican Cookery, the first, complete and authentic Spanish Mexican Cookbook in English... published in Los Angeles in 1928.

197. A: 1876-1910 (a slight overlapping with the US Catalog). You could, of course, turn to Winchell for this answer, or you could get it from the spines of the volumes on the shelves.

198. A: These bibliographical records were published currently with the years they cover, and the years covered are 1876-1910 as in #197. The set you are examining may be the original set, or a later reprint. The reprint was made by the Peter Smith publishing firm in New York and the publication date given on the title pages is 1914; the actual dates of the original publication are given on the verso of the title pages, 1876-1910. The original publisher is the R.R. Bowker Co.

199. A: As a basic bibliographical record, it would be much in demand by American libraries, especially new libraries just building up their collections, and the demand would probably far exceed the supply of the original publication.

200. A: Scribner's Sons. First you had to refer to the volumes covering the year 1889. These are the volumes for 1884-1890. Then you had to look in the volume covering authors (you could have also looked under the title, but remember that it is usually more direct to look under the author when you have that information), and find Lumholtz. The name of the publisher is given in Italic type at the right of the entry. If you had difficulty finding this answer, go on to the next questions for a discussion of the basic arrangement of the set, and then return to look up this problem again. By now, you should find that you can figure out the basic arrangement of these bibliographies on your own, more or less automatically, as soon as you begin to look for some specific item.

201. A: 13 volumes altogether (in the 1941 reprint). The date groupings (as indicated on the spines of the volumes) are: 1876, 1876-1884, 1884-

1890, 1890-1895, 1895-1900, 1900-05, 1905-07, 1908-10. From 1876-1900, each date grouping (such as 1884-1890) has two volumes, one covering authors and titles (in one alphabet), one covering subjects. From 1900-1910, author and title and subject are all in the same volume. If you feel sure that you fully understand this answer, and that you fully understand the arrangement of the American Catalogue, you could probably then skip over the next few questions, #202-205. If you do not understand this answer, then questions #202-205 should help to make it clear to you.

202. A: Author, title, subject; yes, the American Catalogue has all three.

203. A: Yes. From 1876-1900, the subject access is listed separately--in separate volumes in fact, from the author title accesses. From 1900-1910, the author/title subject accesses are listed in the same volume.

204. A: From 1876-1900, they are not, as the subject access is listed separately. From 1900-1910, they are, as all three accesses are listed in one alphabet. CBI is representative of a "dictionary" arrangement.

205. A: The years are grouped together approximately every 5 or 10 years. Earlier volumes are grouped together every 10 years; as the set proceeds, the cumulations come more often.

206. A: Frederick Leypoldt and "The Publishers Weekly" (forerunners of the R.R. Bowker Co.) (See the verso of the title-page of the reprint volumes.)

207. A: The Wilson Company with the U.S. Catalog and then CBI.

208. A: The years covered are 1820-1860 (and January of 1861). The type of publications included is not too clear, but is basically books, with some documents, some pamphlets, even some periodicals (listed separately). The publications included are limited, presumably, to those published in America. Sources for this information: the preface of Roorbach, and Winchell.

209. A: The years covered--as indicated in the scope--are 1820-1860 (and January of 1861); the volumes of Roorbach as you now see them were originally published from 1852-1861. (As with the American Catalogue, there is also a Peter Smith reprint, 1939, and you have to go to the verso of the title page for the original publication and copyright information.)

210. A: 1861-1870 (and January of 1871).

211. A: Kelly was originally published from 1866-1871 (and again, in a 1938 Peter Smith

reprint). Again, the publication dates are not the same as the years covered. The first cumulative volume of Kelly was published in 1866, but the years covered go back to 1861.

212. A: Yes, except for the years covered, the scope of Kelly and Roorbach are similar-- regarding types of publications included, and the limitations by language or country. See the answer to #208.

213. A: The information is very brief--author, title, publisher, size, price. In Kelly, the date of publication is given. In Roorbach, the date is not always given. The information is usually not nearly as complete as in current sources.

214. A: J. Munsell (of Albany), at $3.00. In Kelly, the volume covering 1861-66, p. 59, under Durrie, D.S.

215. A: Roorbach, the volumes for 1855-58, covers this date. The title entry (under Scampvias) lists "Lieut. Wise" as the author, and a reference to the author entry (under Wise) does not give you any further information, so you can't answer this question from Roorbach.

216. A: F. Parkman. In Kelly 1861-66, p. 71, under France...(title). Again, the author entry does not give you any further information.

217. A: Roorbach and Kelly have no subject access. The American Catalogue does.

218. A: Yes, it is, but only when the title of the book is the same as or very similar to the "subject heading" you are using. For example, in Roorbach, volume for 1855-1858, under the title entry Arctic Explorations and Discoveries during the Nineteenth Century... by Epes Sargent, and one above this, also by Sargent titled Arctic Adventures...

219. A: No, you could not have found it, because the entry was under the first (real) word of the title: Arctic.

220. A: The subject for which you are searching must be the same as the first word of the title, or you will not find it listed. You may find a few books on your subject, if the title is helpful, but you will not find all of them.

221. A: The volumes themselves are arranged chronologically, by cumulations of years, as with the American Catalogue and with CBI. Within each volume, covering specified years, the arrangement is by author and title in one alphabet, with no subject access, and no other indexes. A few items, such as some periodicals, law books, etc. are listed separately in appendices. In Roorbach and Kelly, each cumulation is

published in only one volume. In the
early years of the American Catalogue, the
cumulations were published in two volumes--
one for authors and titles, one for subject.
The cumulation pattern for Roorbach and
Kelly is rather erratic, as it is with the
American Catalogue, but it is clearly indicated on the spine of the volumes themselves, so there is no reason to remember
it.

222. A: In the annotation: "Both Roorbach and Kelly
          are unsatisfactory..."

223. A: No. As a matter of fact, there is only one
          title listed under the author's name, the
          1857 Phillips publication, and that one is
          titled Arctic Expeditions... rather than
          Arctic Adventures. How do you know which
          is right, and in fact if either or any of
          them are right? This is just one example
          of the "unsatisfactory" aspect of Roorbach
          and Kelly.

224. A: To begin with, since the date you have is
          1894, you need to go to the American Cata-
          logue, which is the source covering that
          year. Then, because you do not have
          either the author or the title, you need a
          subject approach, which you do have for
          the American Catalogue, and for that
          year, it is in a separate volume. The
          subject in this case is the name of the
          biographee--Macready, W.C.

225. A: Your main key here is that you are after
          information on a "recently published" book.
          (Don't be misled here by the fact that
          Emily Dickinson lived during the time
          covered by Roorbach and Kelly; new edi-
          tions of well-known writers are always
          being published currently--and in fact,
          none of Miss Dickinson's poems were pub-
          lished during her lifetime.) Since it is a
          recent book and you want to know the pub-
          lisher and price, BIP would be your most
          direct source. You do not have the title,
          so you would look in the author volume
          under the author (which is Dickinson not
          Reeves).

226. A: You have no date, and not even an indica-
          tion of the date ("recently") as you did with
          the preceding question. (You may be aware
          however, that this is a recent publication,
          which will help you considerably.) In any
          case, the fact that you are looking for the
          price indicates that enquirer suspects that
          the book is still in-print. BIP is always
          a good place to start a search, and is your
          first source of information on current or
          recent books.

227. A: 1820-61 Roorbach
          1861-71 Kelly
          1876-1910 American Catalogue
          1899-1928 US Catalog
          1928 "to date" (meaning, "to the current
              time") CBI

1872-date PW Weekly Record
1873-date PTLA
1960-date BPR
1948-date BIP

Section 2b

National Bibliographic Records (U.S.)--retrospective

Questions #228-314

All of the sources examined so far are listings compiled more or less at the time of publication of those titles which they list or include--therefore, current or contemporary sources which have now become retrospective.

The next group of sources to examine for this unit are retrospective sources which were compiled retrospectively. They are:

      Sabin: Dictionary of Books Relating to America (AA334)
      Evans: American Bibliography (AA333, 1AA52, 1AA53)
      Shaw & Shoemaker: American Bibliography (AA336)
      Shoemaker: Checklist of American Imprints (AA337)

228.   Taking Sabin's Dictionary of Books first, and looking at it on the shelf, as usual, the first thing you should be aware of is its general physical aspect--and in this case probably the first thing which should occur to you is that Sabin is a set of many volumes, rather than a work in a single volume. By now, you should be quite used to seeing the bibliographical sources as multi-volumed sets. Like many similar undertakings, the set of Sabin was not published all at once, but in fact was published "in parts" over a very long period of time. What is the publication date of Sabin?

229.   In examining Sabin for use, what are the two major criteria which you should determine? (You've been over these again and again with previous sources.)

230.   In the past you have been examining for scope first, then arrangement. With Sabin, for a change, take the arrangement first, as it is far easier to determine. Sabin, as you found in #228, is a multi-volumed set. You have seen other bibliographical sources which contained several volumes, such as CBI, or the American Catalogue. Are the volumes of Sabin arranged, within the set itself, in the same way as those of CBI or American Catalogue? What is the relationship between the volumes of Sabin? Is this the same as the relationship between the volumes of the American Catalogue, or CBI?

231.   Who is the publisher of Electron: a telegraphic epic for the times by W.C. Richards, which was published in 1858?

232.   Could you have found the publisher of Electron (in #231) if you had not known that the author was W.C. Richards? (If you are unsure of how to answer this, look up Electron in Sabin and see what you find, or don't find.)

233.   If Electron; a telegraphic epic for the times had been published in 1956, and you had not known the author, could you have found the information?

234.   Sabin lists--according to the Winchell annotation--"some title entries for anonymous works," meaning that when the work or publication cited has been published anonymously, it will be listed in Sabin under its title. What does "anonymous" or "anonymously" mean?

235. How does an "anonymous" work differ from a "pseudonymous" (see #60) work?

236. Can you determine, so far, any general rule for the ways in which bibliographies treat anonymous and/or pseudonymous works?

237. The main arrangement of Sabin is then alphabetical. It is basically an author list, with anonymous works entered by title, and some entries under place-name. Is there anything in the full title of the Sabin bibliography which would have indicated this arrangement?

238. You have had the use of "dictionary" arrangement before, with CBI and other Wilson Company publications, meaning author/title/subject in one alphabet. Is this therefore the use of the term as it appears in the title to Sabin? Does Sabin have author/title/subject access?

239. Taking scope next, there will be four specific items which you will want to determine--that is, there will be four specific questions which you should ask regarding this particular source. What are these four questions?
    (If you have trouble, go back to #205 on Roorbach, #212 on Kelly, and #213 on both of them.)

240. For Sabin, the scope is not nearly as clear cut as it might be. It is, in fact, quite difficult to determine. Take your four questions, then, one at a time, beginning with: the years or dates covered by Sabin. First, think where, from past experience, would you go to find this?

241. What is the full title of Sabin? And what does this tell you about the years covered by this source?

242. What then is the beginning date covered by Sabin?

243. What is the closing or ending date covered by Sabin?

244. This seems to be very straight-forward. It is, in fact, very misleading. Does the annotation in Winchell give a clear statement regarding the years covered?

245. The title page of the source, and the Winchell annotation having failed you here, your only other recourse is to go to the preface or introductory material in the source itself. The only preface in vol. 1 of Sabin is an introduction entitled "Prospectus," published in 1868 in the first part issued. Remember that the actual publication of the Sabin bibliography took place from 1868 through 1936--a period of 72 years. Sabin himself died long before it was completed, and the work was continued and completed by other bibliographers; under these circumstances, one might expect that the scope of inclusion might have changed somewhat. It is necessary to look further into the set for further statements of scope and procedure.

These consist of a "Statement" in vol. 20 (1928), and a Preface, Introduction, Final Statement, and "Bibliographia Americana, 1866 and 1936" in vol. 29 (1936).

These statements, telling as they do the story of one of the most monumental and magnificent achievements of American bibliography, give you a very good picture of the frustrations and problems of the compilation of such a bibliography. You should at least read p. ix-xi of the "introduction" of vol. 29: "The scope of Sabin," for a clearer statement of the changing scope of the bibliography until the time of its completion.

Having read this statement, then, now what do you think is the closing or ending date of the Sabin entries?

246.   Probably the closest you can come to a statement of the years covered by Sabin is: 1492 to 1800/1870. Admittedly, this is somewhat vague. It is simplest to think of Sabin as covering, more or less, the 19th century; in other words, when in doubt check Sabin.

      If you are trying to locate information on a title published in the U.S., in the 18th century, and you do not find it in Sabin, is this then an indication that the title did not exist?

247.   The next aspect of the scope is simpler: What types of publications are included?

248.   Are the publications listed in Sabin limited in any way by language or country of publication? Go back to the full title on this one for a clue.

249.   Would you expect to find in Sabin a book by Edouard Auger, titled <u>Voyage en California,</u> published in Paris in the 1850's?

250.   What is the correct date, the publisher, and the number of pages of the item mentioned in #249?

251.   In the entry for Auger, a notation "H 2376" is given at the right side of the page. What does this stand for? How would you expect to find out?

252.   Still referring to the scope of this bibliography, what kind of information is given to you in the individual citations?

253.   Why might it be important or useful to include, in bibliographies, such location symbols as you had with the Auger item (#249)?

254.   Writings describing the voyages of Amerigo Vespucci were printed in Europe in 1503 and 1504. Where might you expect to find listings of such early books?

255.   Would you expect to find in Sabin any information about a book titled <u>References for Literary Writers</u> by H. Matson published in 1892?

256.   Where would you be able to find such information?

257.   Could you find through Sabin the names of some books on Witchcraft, published in the early 1800's?

258.   You may remember, however, from #218 (arctic expeditions) that sometimes title entries can give you a kind of subject access. Is this helpful for #257, books on witchcraft, in Sabin?

259.   Would you expect to be able to find in Sabin any books relating to the state of New Jersey, for example: surveyors' lists, public documents, statistics, laws, etc. even if you did not have the author or exact title?

260.   Would you then expect to be able to find in Sabin any books on or about the Hawaiian Islands?   Can you?

261.   Why do you think this is?

262.   Don't give up so easily.   What's another name by which the Hawaiian Islands have been called, particularly in the 19th century?

263.   You have the information that a book by Wharton titled A Treatise on Theism was published in 1859 (in the U.S.).   You need to verify and complete this bibliographical information.   Would you expect to find this in Sabin?

264.   Where then can you look to verify and complete the bibliographical information?   What can you find?

265.   In the answer to #246, it was stated that one of the reasons you might not locate a title in a given bibliography would be that either the information you had was incorrect, or the information in the bibliography was incorrect.   You have already seen (notably with Roorbach and Kelly, as in #223) that some of the bibliographies do list incorrect, inconsistent, and/or confusing information.   Aside from careful checking and proofreading, how could the compiler of a bibliography guard against such errors?   (See the last page of Sabin's Prospectus in volume 1 of the Sabin Bibliography.)

266.   What was the price of "Hughey Dougherty's Staggering-Home-to-Bed Songster?" when it was published in New York in 1870?

267.   Sabin's bibliography is generally considered as the achievement of one man, although it was in fact completed, eventually, with the help of an organization.   It is a retrospective bibliography; and unlike such lists as CBI, American Catalogue, Roorbach and Kelly, it was compiled retrospectively--after the publication of the books, rather than at the time of the publication of the books--by searching library collections, book dealer lists, catalogs, other bibliographies, etc.
       Another such retrospective bibliographic compilation is that of Charles Evans: The American Bibliography.   How many volumes comprise the entire set of Evans?

268.   If you turn to the title page of volume 1 of Evans, you should be able to get a very clear statement of the scope and the arrangement of this bibliography.   What is the scope?

269.   And the arrangement of Evans?

270.   Like Sabin, the Evans bibliography was compiled and published retrospectively.   When was it published?

271.   The scope of Evans is indicated on the title page of vol. 1 as from 1639 through 1820.   Did Evans in fact complete the bibliography to that date (1820)?   Did anyone?

272. The scope of Evans, then, is actually 1639 through 1800. Why do you think Mr. Evans set 1820 as his original closing date?

273. Would you expect to find in Evans, Voyage en California by Auger, from #249?

274. Would you expect to find the early printings of the Voyages of Amerigo Vespucci (#254) in Evans?

275. Is the scope of Evans the same as that of Sabin?

276. Does Evans, like Sabin, include location symbols for libraries holding copies of the items listed?

277. In general, do you think that the information given in the entries in Evans is similar to that in Sabin?

278. Is the arrangement of Evans similar to that of Sabin?

279. The arrangement of Evans is chronological, and vol. 1 covers 1639-1729. Is this similar to the chronological arrangement of Roorbach, in which vol. 1 covered 1820-52?

280. Locate in Evans a sermon by Enoch Huntington, called Political Wisdom, or Honesty the Best Policy, printed in 1786. When it was actually delivered, how many pages does it consist of, and what library has (or had in 1903) a copy of it?

281. How do you find out what AAS stands for in the preceding entry?

282. Evans is arranged chronologically. Do you have author or title access?

283. Do you have subject access?

284. Did you have subject access in Sabin?

285. The years covered by the Sabin Bibliography overlap Evans, but the arrangement of the two bibliographies is basically quite different. Can you think of any reasons why Evans chose to arrange his bibliography chronologically? Can you think of any advantages of this over an alphabetical arrangement?

286. Thomas Foxcroft (1679-1769) wrote Character of Anna, the Prophetess, consider'd and Apply'd which was published in Boston in the early 18th century. Locate this in Evans. What is the actual date on which it was published?

287. The date in the citation for Foxcroft (see the preceding question, #286) is given as MDCCXXIII,

in Roman numerals.   How do you translate this into Arabic numerals, and what is the date then in Arabic numerals?

288.   Would you expect to find the Foxcroft item (#286) in Sabin?

289.   The Foxcroft item is in Sabin, but is not easy to find.   Where is it?   Give it a try.

290.   What was the first publication printed in America?

291.   Which do you think is the easiest to use--the chronological arrangement in Evans, or the alphabetical arrangement in Sabin?

292.   What are the two basic differences between Sabin and Evans?

293.   Did Evans, like Sabin, try to examine copies of the books he described?   Remember #265.

294.   When he began publication of his bibliography in 1903, Evans intended to take it from the beginning of printing in the United States up to 1820, to the beginning of Roorbach, Kelly, etc., to form an unbroken chronological record of publication in the United States.   In fact, the Evans bibliography was completed only through 1800, leaving a gap of some 19 years before the beginning of Roorbach.   Has anything been done to fill in this gap?   (Don't consider Sabin here.)   Look ahead.   Be alert.

295.   What are the publication dates of the Shaw/Shoemaker bibliography?   (Dates of publication, not dates of coverage.)

296.   This, then, is a very recent addition to our retrospective bibliographical coverage.   The preface in vol. 1 of this set is, like those mentioned earlier, well worth reading for its picture of the processes of bibliographic compilation--in this case providing a comparison of twentieth century procedures with those used by earlier bibliographers such as Sabin and Evans.
        What is the scope of the Shaw/Shoemaker American Bibliography?

297.   What about the information given in the citations themselves?   Is this also similar to Evans?

298.   A short publication entitled "A Few observations on the government of R.I." (Rhode Island) was published in 1807.   The author was Benjamin Cowell.   Find a citation or entry which will give you the number of pages in this publication.   Where would you look?

299.   The entry you find in the preceding question shows the author's name in square brackets ([ ]).   What does this mean?

300.   Could you have found the information on these 1807 observations on the government of R.I. if you did not already possess the information that the author was, in fact, Mr. Benjamin Cowell?

301.   What is the arrangement of Shaw/Shoemaker?

302.   Is there a cumulated author and/or title access, as in Evans?

303.   Is there a subject access?

304.   The sub-title of the Shaw/Shoemaker American Bibliography is "A Preliminary Checklist," and the pre-
        face begins "This bibliography has been gathered entirely from secondary sources." What is meant by
        these statements?

305.   Were the Sabin and Evans bibliographies compiled from secondary sources?

306.   What are "ghosts," bibliographically-speaking, as referred to in the Shaw/Shoemaker preface (p. ix)?

307.   All of the major bibliographies you have examined so far have been an attempt at a comprehensive re-
        cording of American publications. In bibliography, comprehensiveness is an aim; completeness is rarely
        an achievement. Some bibliographies have achieved more than others. Evans is considered as a very
        comprehensive record, but even Evans is not complete. Have there been any attempts to supplement
        Evans, to fill in gaps, and make additions and corrections to the record? (Think: assuming that such a
        thing has been done and that it then exists as a published record, where would you best look to find out
        about it?)

308.   The preface to the Shaw/Shoemaker American Bibliography has indicated that any list--even a preliminary
        checklist compiled entirely from secondary sources--of publications of the period for 1801-1819 is better
        than no record at all. A similar statement has been made about the Roorbach and Kelly lists. Is any
        attempt being made, or has any attempt been made, along the lines of any of the previous sources you
        have examined, to complete, supplement, fill in, etc., the Roorbach and Kelly records?

309.   What is the purpose of Shoemaker's Checklist of American Imprints?

310.   What then would you expect the scope of Shoemaker's Checklist to be?

311.   You would expect the scope to be the same as Shaw/Shoemaker, but in fact, is it entirely the same? For
        instance, does the Shaw/Shoemaker list include periodicals? Does the Shoemaker checklist include peri-
        odicals?

312.   This bibliography is still "in progress" or "in process of compilation and publication." How would you
        find out about publication dates of future volumes, and how would you find out when--and if--it is com-
        pleted?

313.   What is the arrangement of Shoemaker's Checklist?

314.   Are there any variations in procedures of methods used, and in information given, between the Shaw/ Shoemaker and the Shoemaker Checklist?

Section 2b

National Bibliographic Records (U.S.)--retrospective

Answers #228-314

228. A: 1868-1936. You want the publication date,
         not the coverage (although you will find that
         the two are not entirely unrelated). As with
         Roorbach and Kelly, you will need to check
         the publication date on the title page of the
         first volume, for the beginning date, and
         then refer to the publication date on the
         title page of the last part of the last vol-
         ume for the closing date (1936).

229. A: Scope and arrangement.

230. A: The entire set of Sabin is arranged alpha-
         betically. The entire set of CBI or the
         American Catalogue is arranged chrono-
         logically, that is by year or by date. Vol-
         ume 1 of Sabin contains "A-Bedford." Vol-
         ume 1 of the American Catalogue contains
         the year 1876; volume 1-2 of the American
         Catalogue contains the years 1876-1884.
         Within these volumes of the American Cata-
         logue, the arrangement is alphabetical. For
         CBI and the American Catalogue (as with
         Roorbach and Kelly), the arrangement is
         first chronological then alphabetical. The
         arrangement of Sabin is only alphabetical.

231. A: The publisher is D. Appleton and Company--
         found in Sabin by looking in vol. 17, cover-
         ing "Remarks to Ross," under the author
         Richards.

232. A: No. Sabin contains, basically, no title
         entries--primarily author entries, with
         title entries when the author is anonymous,
         and some entries under name of place.
         (See the Winchell annotation.)

233. A: Yes, for that publication date you would
         have had CBI to check in, and you could
         have checked under title, because CBI
         gives title entries as well as author entries.

234. A: Use the dictionary or the ALA Glossary.

235. A: There is considerable similarity, and it
         might be necessary for you to get into li-
         brary cataloging rules in some depth in
         order to clarify the exact difference. Bib-
         liographically speaking, in both cases the
         author is presumably unknown, and both are
         therefore published anonymously. Many
         pseudonyms are very well known, however--
         such as Mark Twain. Although a book pub-
         lished with Mark Twain given as the author
         is published "under a pseudonym," it can
         hardly be said to be published anonymously.

236. A: Probably not. The rules vary from bibliography
         to bibliography, which is one of the reasons

why it is so important to READ A PREFACE.
Frequently, the prefaces or introductions will
tell you what the specific bibliography in question does. Winchell annotations may also tell
you. In the case of a book published under a
pseudonym, in which a pseudonym (Mark Twain)
is used in place of the author's correct name
(Samuel Clemens) it is not always understood or
known that the name used is a pseudonym. You
may find the work entered under the pseudonymous name, or under the correct name if the
correct name is known; and if the work is fully
cross-referenced, you would find a reference
from the pseudonym to the correct name, or
vice-versa. If a book is published with no
author's name in it at all, or completely anonymously, then it would probably be entered under
the title, or in some bibliographies, under the
general heading of "Anonymous." If a book is
published anonymously, but the correct author
is known (or surmised) by the bibliographer,
then the book may be entered under the correct
name, or it may be entered under the title but
indicating the correct name in an annotation or
note. Adequate cross-references are enormous-
ly important in this whole problem. Bibliographies do not always have such adequate cross-
references. Therefore, in using them it behooves you to be aware of all possibilities.

237. A: It is called a "dictionary of books"--which
         would certainly imply (although not assure)
         an alphabetical arrangement.

238. A: No, not really. Sabin does not have com-
         plete title access nor, really, any subject
         access at all. Sabin only has, basically,
         author access, but that is alphabetical, and
         the use of the word "dictionary" here un-
         doubtedly implies only the basically alpha-
         betical arrangement.

239. A: 1. What are the years or dates covered?
         2. What types of publications are included?
         3. Are the publications included limited in
            any way by language or country of publi-
            cation?
         4. What bibliographical information is given
            in the entries or citations about the indi-
            vidual publications cited?

240. A: The places you could look for this answer are:
            the title page of the source;
            the preface or introduction to the source;
            Winchell

241. A: A Dictionary of Books Relating to America,
         from its Discovery to the Present Time (as
         shown on the title-page and in Winchell). It
         tells you that the years covered are: "From its
         discovery to the present time."

242. A: "From its discovery." The discovery of
          what? America. Which was discovered
          in what year? 1492. Therefore, the be-
          ginning date for Sabin's coverage is:
          1492, the discovery of America.

243. A: "To the present time." What is "the
          present time?" Presumably, the time at
          which the bibliography was being com-
          piled or published, and the date of original
          publication of Sabin was (see #228) 1868-
          1936. The closing or ending date covered
          by Sabin would presumably be, then, about
          1868 for those items in volume one, and
          proceed to later and later years as the
          compilation of the bibliography itself pro-
          ceeded on toward the publication of the last
          volume in 1936.

244. A: No. As regards "years covered" by Sabin,
          the annotation in Winchell simply avoids
          the issue. This is a very good example
          of the fact that you cannot always rely on
          some published source such as Winchell,
          and you must learn to determine these fac-
          tors on your own, for yourself.

245. A: In general, the closing dates of the early
          volumes (vol. 1-20) will be approximately
          the 1860's; from vol. 21 on, the ending
          date is progressively moved back to the
          1800's, growing more and more restric-
          tive as it became more imperative to
          finish the task. The closing dates of
          Sabin could be considered then as 1800-
          1870, more or less.

246. A: Not at all. It merely means that it is
          not listed in Sabin, either because it was
          unknown to the compilers, or because it
          fell outside of the increasingly restric-
          tive scope. It may also mean that it is
          listed in Sabin but you did not find it
          there--either because you looked incor-
          rectly, or not thoroughly enough, or be-
          cause your information was faulty, or
          because the compilers' information was
          faulty, or because it was entered in the
          bibliography in some fashion unsuspected
          by yourself.

247. A: The Winchell annotation tells you "books,
          pamphlets, and periodicals," and by glanc-
          ing through several of the volumes and look-
          ing at the types of materials listed, you can
          see that the scope of Sabin is very broad,
          in this aspect. All types of publications
          appear to be included.

248. A: The full title tells you "...Books Relating
          to America...," which implies at least a
          broader scope than simply U.S. publica-
          tions or English language publications, and
          again you can confirm this by glancing
          through the volumes themselves and look-
          ing at the entries, and by referring to the
          Winchell annotation ("printed in the
          Western Hemisphere, and works about the
          region printed elsewhere").

249. A: Yes, because the date falls within the scope
          of Sabin (it would be in the early volumes,
          under A-), and it relates to America, even
          though published in Paris.

250. A: The date is 1854, the publisher is Hachette
          et Cie, the number of pages is 238.

251. A: Look in the introductory pages of vol. 1 for
          a list of abbreviations, or in the preface
          for an explanation. The preface ("Pro-
          spectus") does not give any information
          here. There is a page entitled "Explana-
          tory" which indicates what the "initials
          which precede the numbers at the end of
          the description" stand for. H stands for
          Harvard College Library and is therefore a
          "location symbol," indicating that (at least
          in Mr. Sabin's day) the Harvard College Li-
          brary possessed a copy of the book or pub-
          lication cited. The number following the H
          is not explained, but a glance up and down
          the page on which it appears should show
          you that each item listed is followed by
          such a number, and that the numbers follow
          one another consecutively through the listing;
          therefore the number can be surmised to be
          an "item number"--or an inventory number,
          within the bibliography itself. If further
          reference should be made to the Auger title,
          it can be referred to as item #2376, with-
          out repeating the entire citation, and the lo-
          cation of the citation can quickly be found.

252. A: The usual basic bibliographical information
          of author, title, publisher, date, paging, etc.,
          and often the names, or abbreviations or
          symbols for the names of libraries having
          copies. Furthermore, you often get lists of
          contents, bibliographical notes, references
          to reviews, descriptions, etc.--the Winchell
          annotation tells you this, and you could see
          it for yourself by glancing through the entries.

253. A: In this way the person who uses the bibli-
          ography, and who finds a title of interest
          cited there, then has at least one source he
          can go to, to look at or use the title. An
          important aspect of bibliographical control
          is the location of copies (both provision of
          copies to be used, and indication of the lo-
          cation of such copies). This is very useful
          for interlibrary loan (although the location
          indications as given in Sabin may be just a
          bit outdated by now). This whole question
          will be of great importance later in examina-
          tion of "union catalogs" and "union lists."

254. A: First of all, it helps if you realize that
          Vespucci was one of the first discoverers of
          America, and these writings would therefore
          be included in Sabin as "relating to Amer-
          ica." They are listed, under Vespucci. The
          bibliographical descriptions of these books,
          in Sabin, are good examples of analytic bib-
          liography. Note the very careful, very full,
          very complete physical description of the
          volumes, the leaves, the way the text is set
          on the page, etc. This also is an example

of the unexpected treasures of information to be found in Sabin.

255. A: No, since it was published in 1892--this date falls outside the scope covered by Sabin.

256. A: In the American Catalogue (1890-95, authors, p. 284. The publisher was McClurg).

257. A: Basically, no, since Sabin does not have a subject approach.

258. A: Not much. Sabin lists no titles beginning with "witchcraft," and only two--both apparently novels of some sort--beginning with "witch." Remember, however, that Roorbach and Kelly had both author and title access for all entries; Sabin has only author access (except for some anonymous titles). No doubt there would be other books in Sabin whose titles begin with the word "witchcraft" but they would be listed under their authors only, so you could not locate them by title.

259. A: Yes. In #232, you found that the entries, although basically by author only, did include some place names, and you will in fact find quite a bit in Sabin under the general entry of New Jersey.

260. A: Yes, you would expect to, since that is a place name. But you do not find anything under Hawaii or Hawaiian Islands.

261. A: You might surmise that in the 1860's, the Hawaiian Islands were not considered a part of America, or of the Western Hemisphere. There is a better reason, though.

262. A: Try the Sandwich Islands and see what you find. This is an example of the way in which some change in usage--place names, subject headings, etc.--can throw you off the track in your search if you do not keep this factor of change constantly in mind. One of the best clues to the effective use of older reference books, whether bibliographies or any other type of reference source, is to try as much as possible to think in terms of the time the source itself was published. One of the things librarians can be most grateful for in modern reference book publishing is the concept of extensive cross-references.

263. A: No, not really. The early volumes of Sabin did go through 1860 or later, more or less, but "W" would be very far along in the compilation of the set, after the scope had been restricted to the early part of the 1800's. Just to make sure, you can check in Sabin to see, but this publication is not there.

264. A: You can look in the source covering that period, Roorbach for 1858-60 (p. 155), under Wharton. You find that the author's

initial is F., but you cannot find his first name. You can verify the title, and find that the rest of the title is "and on modern skeptical theories." You can find that the publisher was Lippincott. But, as is frequently the case in Roorbach, no date is given, so you cannot verify that.

265. A: It would certainly help to reduce such errors if the compiler or compilers worked directly from the books--that is, if they actually saw, and examined, the books which they were listing and describing. Often it is necessary for compilers to "content" themselves with secondary sources, such as library catalogs, bookdealer catalogs, and other lists. As Mr. Sabin points out, if he were to strive to examine in detail every item listed, he would never complete his task (nor would anyone else).

266. A: Here again you are on doubtful ground as regards the date of publication--this title might or might not be in Sabin. But in any case, you have been asked to find the original price, and Sabin does not list prices, so you must go to a source which does, and the source which covers that date and which also lists prices is Kelly, 1866-71, p. 197. This item is listed simply as if it were a title entry (which it is) under the first word of the title, Hughey. If you considered Hughey Dougherty as the author, and looked under Dougherty, you would not find an entry. The price of the item, by the way, was ten cents.

267. A: There are 14 volumes.

268. A: Years covered "From the genesis of printing in 1639 down to and including the year 1820." Types of publications included: "Books, pamphlets, and periodical publications." Limitations of publications: "Printed in the United States of America." Information given in citations: "Bibliographical and bibliographical notes." Some of these answers will need to be further clarified.

269. A: "Chronological dictionary"--that is, chronological, by year (as with American Catalogue, Roorbach and Kelly, etc.), and within the year, alphabetically by author.

270. A: The original publication dates (verso of title page of the 1941 reprint) were 1903-34, for vols. 1-12, 1955 for vol. 13, 1959 for vol. 14.

271. A: By checking Winchell and/or the last volumes of the bibliography itself, you will see that Evans completed the bibliography through the letter M of 1799 (in vol. 12). The bibliography was completed later (1955) through 1800, in vol. 13.

272. A: This would bring his compilation up to the beginning of Roorbach, which--having been published in 1852-61--was therefore already in existence when Evans began the publication of his retrospective compilation in 1903.

(Presumably, of course, Evans began compilation of the information long before he began actual publication of it. The preface to vol. 13 tells you that he began recording information as early as 1880. Roorbach was in existence even then.)

273. A: No, for two reasons: first of all because it was published in 1854, and Evans goes only to 1800; secondly, because it was published in Paris, and Evans does not include non-American publications.

274. A: No, for two reasons: first of all because they were published in 1503, 1504, before printing in the United States, and because they were published in Europe.

275. A: The dates overlap but Sabin begins earlier (1492) and ends, more or less, later at least in the early part of the alphabet. The types of publications included are similar. Evans is limited to items printed in America, Sabin includes those items relating to America regardless of where published.

276. A: Yes, to the right of the entries; in capital letters.

277. A: The information given in Evans is quite full, and similar to that in Sabin, but Sabin often gives a tremendous amount of additional information.

278. A: No. Sabin is strictly alphabetical. Evans is chronological.

279. A: In Evans, each year is listed separately, and vol. 1 includes separate lists for 1639, 1640, 1641, 1642, etc. In Roorbach all entries for 1820-52 were cumulated together into the volume covering those years.

280. A: It was delivered on the 20th of April, 1786, in Middletown (presumably Connecticut); consists of 20 pages, and the AAS (American Antiquarian Society) has a copy. Found in vol. 7, under 1786, then alphabetically under the author's name.

281. A: On p. xi of the Preface to vol. 1, the statement is made that such abbreviations would be sufficiently well-known not to need further identification. However, a list of identification is given in vol. 13.

282. A: Yes. Each volume has an author index (although no title index). Volume 14 has a cumulated author/title index.

283. A: Each volume has a "Classified Subject Index" which is some help, but is not as usable as, for example, the subject access in more modern bibliographies. There is no cumulation of these subject indices.

284. A: No.

285. A: In the preface in vol. 1 of Evans, on p. xi,

are stated some of the advantages to the chronological arrangement, at least from Evans' point of view.

286. A: In order to locate this in Evans, you have to go first to volume 14 and look under either the author or the title (if under the author, then to the correct title listed under Foxcroft), which gives you the "item number," which tells you where, in the main bibliography, you will find the entry. A location guide for the item numbers is given in the lower corner of each set of facing pages, in vol. 14. In Evans, the item numbers for each title are given on the left side of the page, rather than following the entry as in Sabin. The item number for Foxcroft is #2431, and the date on which the book was published was MDCCXXIII.

287. A: The ALA Glossary does not seem to be much help here, but any common dictionary should tell you about the formation of roman numerals if you do not know it already. For example, Webster's New World Dictionary of the American Language (c1964) gives a short explanation in the definition for "roman numerals," and a fuller explanation under "Special Signs and Symbols" in the back. The date, for Foxcroft, is 1723. (M= 1000+ D= 500+ CC= 200+ XX= 20+ 111= 3).

288. A: Since it is the early part of the 18th century (you had that information to begin with) you would reasonably expect to find it there.

289. A: You have to go through all of the Foxcrofts listed, since their first names are not indicated clearly in the author entries, and they do not seem to be alphabetized according to the first name. You also have to look at all of the small print (this is important in Sabin), and you will find the Character of Anna listed, along with many other titles, in the note to the last Foxcroft entry. This is typical of Sabin. Remember the annotation in Winchell: "...does not count the added editions and titles mentioned in the various notes."

290. A: This is where Evans' arrangement can be very helpful. Presumably the first item listed in his bibliography is the first publication in America: The "Oath of a Free-Man," printed in 1638.

291. A: It depends primarily on the information you have to work with. Ordinarily, in identifying a specific item, you would have the author's name, and it is certainly easier to go directly to that name in one alphabetical list and find your information, than to check through year after year of names, or to refer from names in an index back to the fuller information under the year.

292. A: One is the arrangement; the second is the coverage or scope--Sabin is broader.

293. A: Like Sabin, he tried to, but could not always. This is noted in his own preface to vol. 1,

the middle of p. xi. But an even more revealing statement on this problem is in Mr.
Shipton's preface to vol. 13, p. vii and the
top of p. viii.

294. A: The next title on your list--Shaw and Shoemaker's American Bibliography--was compiled and published precisely to fill that
gap. (Sabin is so erratic on its inclusion in
publications from 1800-1820 in the later
part of the alphabet, that it cannot be said
to form a real record for this period;
furthermore Sabin does not show a chronological record because of its arrangement.)

295. A: 1958-1966.
(1801-1819 pub. 1958-1963);
Addenda /list of sources /Library Symbols;
    1965;
Title Index: 1965;
Corrections /author Index: 1966.)

296. A: It covers 1801-1819, and like Evans, is intended as a listing of "American publications"
--including those published or printed in the
United States, and including a rather broad
range of type of publications. It is necessary to go to the preface of the work, to see
specifically its variations from Evans'
methods (see p. ix of the preface.)

297. A: See p. vii of the Preface; information given
is that available, and is "uneven in quality."
Library location symbols are given when location is known.

298. A: The year 1807 is covered by the Shaw-Shoe-
maker American Bibliography, the citation is
found in the volume for 1807, under Cowell,
and the number of pages is 18.

299. A: According to the ALA Glossary entry under
"bracket," square brackets indicate that the
enclosed information has "been supplied."
Therefore, in this case, it means that the
author's name does not appear in the publication itself. The item was therefore published anonymously. (see #234 on "anonymous.")

300. A: Yes, since you have a title index which
would (and does) refer you to the entry
under Cowell, by means of an item number
as in Sabin and Evans.

301. A: Like Evans, chronological, each year
separately (in this publication, each year
is in a separate volume, so it is easy to see
at a glance that there has been no cumulation).
Within the year, alphabetical by author or
main entry.

302. A: Yes, in the final volumes. See answer to #295.
(The Winchell annotation indicates this author
and title cumulation as "in progress").

303. A: No.

304. A: It is necessary to go to the preface to find
out. (Winchell only repeats the information.)
The preface tells you, in essence, that any
kind of a checklist at all was better than
none, and that this one is admittedly incomplete and uneven--hence "preliminary" (pre-

sumably, to be used as the basis for a more
comprehensive and reliable bibliography--
perfecting citations, laying ghosts, and fill-
ing gaps--see p. ix). The use of secondary
sources means that the compilers worked
from lists, catalogs, other bibliographies--
and not from the books themselves.

305. A: Refer to #265 and 293. Both used secondary
sources; both attempted as much as possible,
however, to examine and check the publications.

306. A: See the ALA Glossary.

307. A: If such supplements, additions, further
records exist in published form, one of the
places where you would expect to find them
listed is, of course, in Winchell--along
with the rest of the bibliographical sources.
And in fact Winchell does list three such
supplementary publications (AA333b).
AA333c, AA333d), plus an index of printers,
publishers, and booksellers as listed in
Evans (AA333b).

308. A: Again you might go to Winchell for this one,
and the answer happens also to be the next
title on your list: Shoemaker's Checklist of
American Imprints.

309. A: "Planned as a continuation of Shaw /Shoe-
maker to give more complete listings than
those in Roorbach." (Winchell) Similar
information is given in the Preface to vol.
1 (1820).

310. A: Since it is a continuation of Shaw /Shoemaker,
you would expect the scope to be approximately the same as that record, beginning
however with the year 1820.

311. A: This is a good example of why it is important to read the prefaces and not take too
much for granted. The Preface to vol. 1
(1820) of the Shoemaker Checklist tells you
that periodicals are not to be included in the
scope of this bibliography, although they were
included in the Shaw /Shoemaker list.

312. A: Since this is a current publication (although
a retrospective bibliography), each new volume as it appears would presumably be listed in the PW Weekly Record. The completion of the bibliography would be noted in
future editions (or supplements to) Winchell,
or in similar listings of reference and bibliographical sources.

313. A: Basically, the same as the Shaw /Shoemaker
bibliography.

314. A: This is the kind of information you would
expect to find in the Preface. The Preface
to vol. 1 (1820) does not indicate any significant variations in method, but going on
to the Preface in vol. 2 (1821), p. iii, you
will find that: the compiler is now attempting to check the publications listed somewhat
more carefully than in previous lists, with
resulting more accurate and fuller descriptions for the titles listed. Cross references
for pseudonyms, and for anonymous titles,
are given.

Section 3

National Bibliographical Records (U.S.)--search strategy and review

Questions #315-349

You have now examined the major bibliographical records, current and retrospective, for American or U.S. publications. The next several questions will refer you, randomly, to all those sources you have so far examined. Before going on to these questions, it would probably be useful to make a rough chart of the coverage (or scope) and access (or arrangement) of these bibliographical sources, so that you can tell quickly which ones would be the best sources to use in answering the questions. Making the chart and answering the search questions in this set will serve you as a review of the material.

To begin with, you should indicate which sources cover which specific years. (Refer to your answer to #227)

315. After having listed the sources and the years they covered, do you notice any obvious gaps so far (such as the gap between Evans and Roorbach, which has been filled in by Shaw/Shoemaker)?

316. What do you have which you can use as a bibliographical source for this period? Will it or they be satisfactory?

317. Consider the three major accesses we need to bibliographical sources--author, title, subject--and fill these in on your chart. Are any of the sources so far lacking author access?

318. What about title access?

319. What about subject access?

320. Subject access is often considered our weakest area of bibliographical control. Do you think our present subject coverage is an improvement over earlier subject coverage? In other words, do we appear to be making progress?

321. If you wanted to compile a list of books published in the United States on witchcraft, what sources could you refer to?

322. In searching for bibliographical information, what kinds of information--what elements or pieces of information--could you either have or need?

323. One of the most important elements to determine, at least approximately, in searching for bibliographical information, is the date, or the general time period. Why is this? (If this is not immediately clear, then think about the overall, basic organization and structure of the bibliographical sources.)

To answer the following questions, then, you will need to make a choice from the various bibliographical sources of information which you now have available. You could of course search aimlessly through all of the sources until you found an answer, somewhere. But a more effective approach, which you should be learning, is to search _systematically_ through the sources available, choosing first those sources and that procedure most likely to give you the information you need. You have already been doing this, to some extent. But now your choice of sources begins to widen, so your thinking must be more careful.

In order to choose your source--in other words, in order to set up your strategy--you must first examine your problem or question, to decide what kind of information you _need_, and what kind of information you already _have_. Here you are confined to bibliographical sources and bibliographical information.

324. Suppose then that you need to find out who is the author of a book called _Inquest_, about the assassination of President Kennedy and the Warren Commission report. How would you go about it?

325. What would you have done if the book in the previous question had not been in print or had been very recently published? (And therefore not in the source noted in the answer.)

326. Why would you choose to go to BIP as your first search stop in #324, instead of directly to CBI or BPR?

For the following _review_ questions, as you have done with previous review questions, you can either search out the specific answers in the sources, or simplify the process and save some time by just deciding where (and why) you would be most likely to find the answer. Searching in the sources is excellent practice and helps you to get the feel of using them and to remember them in more detail. Searching may also clarify your understanding of the sources. You will need to judge for yourself how much review and practice and clarification you may need at this point.

327. Who is the publisher of Henry Frost's _The Communion of Saints_, published in 1821? What library or libraries have copies? (Does this mean that these are the only libraries having copies?)

328. You have a note about a book by Humphrey Desmond, called _Does God Love Irish_, which you believe to have been published in the early 1900's. Can you find a citation for it, with the correct date?

329. What is the publisher and date of _Miscelanea Americana, Escritos Publicados en la prensa Americana_ by Luis Ricardo Fors, published in Paris in the 1800's?

330. Josephine Blackstock's _Songs for Sixpence, a Story about John Newberry_ was published by Follett in 1955. Is this still in print, and what is the price?

331. What is the date of publication of a book by S.P. Godwin, titled _Heart Breathings, or, The Soul's Desire Expressed_?

332. Is Ray Bradbury's science fiction novel _Fahrenheit 451_ available in paperback?

333. Julia Child is a popular figure on TV these days, as the "star" of a program called "The French Chef" on the ETV channel. She is the author of some cookbooks currently in print, but you might well expect (and, if you are a fan, you might hope) that she would have another cookbook in the offing. How would you find out if Mrs. Child does have another cookbook scheduled for publication in the near future?

334. You have in your library a broadside which contains seven four-line verses called "Fellow Craft Hymn,

for the use of Holland Lodge, composed by Brother Low." In one corner someone has penciled "NY, 1790." You need to find Brother Low's first name or complete name; you need to verify the date, if possible. Where would you look, and what is Brother Low's first name?

One of the most interesting things about search strategy is that it soon becomes so automatic and instinctive that you tend to forget about it. The way to approach any problem--but especially a seemingly difficult one--is not by moving aimlessly, or frantically, from one source to another, but by taking the time to analyze the problem and figure out a systematic approach. You may be surprised at how soon you will do this sort of thing instantaneously, sometimes even subconsciously, perhaps without being aware that you are doing it. But you need to get into the habit of working this way, before it will become both instinctive and instantaneous. Remember too that a problem which appears simple and straightforward may turn out to be difficult and complex, and you may need to rethink and revise your strategy in midstream. Keep an open mind and keep your imagination working.

335.   Has Robert Graves written and had published a book of poetry for children? Try to search this one out for yourself, and if you can, move ahead to #348 for the answer. If you do not come to the correct answer, or you cannot come to any approach at all, then work through the following questions, #336 through #348.

336.   First of all, this problem is unlike the others you have been working on, in that you are following up a surmise, not necessarily a fact. You need to find out if such a book has been published. Obviously, if you find the information that it has, then you have answered your question. If you cannot find such information, then you are faced with deciding: (a) that such a book was never published, or (b) that such a book may have been published but you cannot find the information, either because your search was not thorough enough or because your sources were inadequate or incorrect. Deciding how far to go before you stop searching is, therefore, part of your problem--or it may become part of your problem as you proceed. The more experience you have, the better you can make such a decision. However, lacking such experience, you can at least plan your approach carefully so that you will not overlook the obvious.
       To begin with, what information do you have, and what further information can you make an educated guess about?

337.   What current source(s) do you have with subject or author (or both) approach?

338.   Which of these would you turn to first and why?

339.   Do you find an answer to your problem in Subject Guide to Books in Print, then?

340.   So what are your possible conclusions from this? Can you conclude then that Robert Graves has not written and had published a book of poetry for children?

341.   Assuming that you searched correctly in the source (you did find what clearly seems to be the proper subject heading) and that you have not been careless and overlooked the information, you may then consider that your source may have been inaccurate. You must keep this possibility in mind at all times. But even so, you must then search elsewhere. Put this possibility of inaccuracy aside for the moment, and consider your conclusion that the book is therefore not in print in the United States. What possible ideas for further search does this leave you?

342.   From these possibilities, what sources should you then search in?

343.   Following the sources indicated in the answer to #342--BPR/PW Weekly and/or CBI, working back from the current issue--what if anything do you find?

344.   Does this answer the question posed in #335?

345.   Can you think of something else which you might also want to know, or which your inquirer might want to know, about this book--now that you have determined its existence and identified it?

346.   Is it still in print? Did you already answer this question? Is it worth checking again, now that you know the full bibliographical information?

347.   Your problem, in #335, was to find out if a book of poetry for children had been written by Robert Graves, and published. If you had gone directly to BIP, instead of to Subject Guide to Books in Print, or through the CBI/BPR/PW sequence, would you have been able to answer your question?

348.   Where would you go then in the hopes of getting further information about the entry (Penny Fiddle, gr. 4-6) in BIP?

It would appear that the information (or actually, the lack of information) in Subject BIP was in error. In #340, one of your conclusions was that your first source (Subject BIP) might be inaccurate, but even if this was so, you would still need to determine other sources to search in. These other sources could well have been those you used in #342 (CBI and/or BPR/PW, working back from the current issue). If you had used them, you would have eventually found the correct information, as you did in the answer to #343. Or if you had immediately double-checked the accuracy of Subject BIP by going to BIP under author, you would have found, as you did in #347, only the title and the grade level clue, and you would have had to go on to PTLA for further information.

You could have found the information through at least three sources: a listing in CBI, a listing in BPR Cumulative, and a listing in BIP used in conjunction with further information from PTLA. What would seem to be your most reasonable source, Subject BIP, did not give you the correct information, apparently due to an error in the source.

Another possible source which has not been considered so far would be an author bibliography (for Graves), but it would have had to have been a very recently compiled one in order to include the particular book you are after. If you had looked in an author bibliography for Graves, compiled in 1955, you would still have had to search in recent and current sources to cover the period from 1955 to date.

As you can see, there are a number of possible ways to approach this problem, and all of them have some validity; the main point is that you must remember to cover all possibilities. Again, as you can see, there are a number of sources in which you might find the answer, although you should expect some variance in the type and amount of information given to you from source to source.

349.   For example, is there any information given in the CBI citation for Graves' The Penny Fiddle which you did not find in the BIP/PTLA citations?

Section 3

National Bibliographic Records (U.S.)--search strategy and review

Answers #315-349

315. A: There is a gap between Kelly and the American Catalogue--1871-1875.

316. A: PW Weekly Record, which begins in 1872; and
PTLA which begins in 1873. Neither will be
very satisfactory to use, as both would be extremely tedious to search in, but they do exist and are--if you are desperate enough--bet-
ter than nothing. Be alert later on for
further possibilities to cover this period.

317. A: Only PTLA prior to 1948 (BIP), which is
of course what makes it basically so unsatis-
factory as an answer to #316.

318. A: Again, PTLA does not have any prior to
1948. Sabin does have title access except
for anonymous works, and the Shoemaker
Checklist does not presently have title access
but presumably will in due time. Otherwise
all the sources do have title access, more
or less completely.

319. A: Sabin has none, Evans is spotty, Shaw/
Shoemaker and Shoemaker have none. Roorbach and Kelly have none. American Catalogue, U.S. Catalog, and CBI have subject
access. PW/BPR now have subject access
and PTLA/BIP/Subject BIP now have subject
access.

320. A: Yes

321. A: Those with subject access. (See #319).

322. A: Author, title, subject, date of publication,
publisher--primarily. You could be searching for any of these or a combination of any
of these. You could already have any of
these or a combination of any of these;
more likely you would have a combination
of elements rather than a single element,
however. (You should also keep in mind
that the information you have, of any of
these elements, could be either approximate
or inaccurate.)

323. A: As a group, the bibliographical sources you
have examined tend to be organized chronologically (by date). For example, in the
broadest possible grouping: current and
retrospective. (Individually, bibliographical
sources tend to be organized either by author
or by subject.) In order to determine where
to begin your search, you should know or at
least make an educated guess at the date, at
the general time period, at whether or not
it is likely to be current or retrospective.
This is why it is important for you to think

about these sources both as individual,
specific sources, and also as a group, in
relation to each other.

324. A: First you would figure out the elements
which you have, and the elements which you
need, and you would consider the date or
general time period of major importance.
You need to find out the author. You have
the title (Inquest), and the subject (assassination of President Kennedy). You do not
have the date or any indication of the general
time period, but you can certainly figure it
out from the subject. The subject is recent
(since 1963), so you would begin with recent
or current sources. Recency combined with
popular subject matter would lead you to
think that the book would now be in print
(BIP), or very recently published (PW
Weekly Record, BPR, CBI). BIP does have
a title access, so you might as well begin
there. (You could also get this information
from your library's card catalog, of course,
by checking for a title added entry, but this
sort of thing works only if your library has
the book in question.)

325. A: You still have the title and subject, so you
could have searched either forward or back
in BPR (monthly and Cumulative) or CBI,
both of which have title and subject access.

326. A: BIP is a one-stop source, and if you find it
there, you will have solved your problem by
checking in only one place. If you had gone
directly to CBI or BIP, since you had only
the vaguest idea of the date, you would
probably have had to look through several
issues or volumes of either one before you
located the title, and therefore your answer.
Also by locating it in BIP, you have at the
same time established its in-print status.

327. A: You have most of your basic bibliographical
information--author, title, date. The date
(1821) is covered by Roorbach and by the
Shoemaker Checklist. Since you need an
indication of what libraries might have
copies, you can find this information only in
Shoemaker. (This title is not in Roorbach
anyway). The publisher is James Hughes.
Libraries having copies are CSmH (Huntington Library in California) and Wis-Ar
(probably the Wisconsin state archives?).
(The symbols used in the Shoemaker Checklist to identify libraries holding copies are,
according to the Preface of vol. 1, those
used in the National Union Catalog; you will
find out in the next group of sources what

this refers to, so do not bother with looking it up now.) The location symbols given in the Shoemaker Checklist (as with Sabin, Evans, and the Shaw/Shoemaker) do not list all libraries having copies, only those libraries known to have copies, or those which have reported copies. It is therefore quite possible that libraries other than the two listed would have copies of The Communion of Saints.

328. A: You might as well begin with the American Catalogue in 1900 and work forward (to the current date). The book was published in 1918, and its correct title is Why God Loves the Irish. You can assume this is the book you are looking for, since there is nothing else similar to it, published at that time. You will find it listed in the United States Catalog, 1928 volume. Or you could have started with the U.S. Catalog 1928 as it contains all books still in print at that date and therefore might include publications from the early 1900's.

329. A: This was published in Paris and the only source you have so far likely to include such publications is Sabin; the publication is about or "relating to" America, and the date would be covered by Sabin, and you have the author's name. (Even if you do not read Spanish, you should be able to get the general drift of this title.) Sabin does have the book listed; the publisher is E. Denne Schmitz, and the date of publication is 1872. The author's name is listed under Fors; remember that if you are uncertain about what part of the name to search under, you should probably search under all parts.

330. A: Since it is in BIP (price $3.48), you can assume that it is in print.

331. A: Here you have author and title, but no date, not even approximately, so you can begin either with very current sources (PW, BPR, CBI, BIP) and work back, or with the very old sources (Sabin, Evans, etc.) and work forward. If you have no clue to the date of the book, it is probably six of one and half a dozen of the other which end you start at. However, the title of this book has a peculiarly non-current air, so proceeding on this "feeling," you might decide to start with the early sources, beginning with Sabin, Evans, Shaw/Shoemaker, etc., working through until you find your publication listed. You should also get in the habit of noting down where you have searched, and what you searched under, and what results you did or did not find, so that if you have to backtrack, you do not have to repeat all your steps. In this case you will find the book was published in 1867, the publisher is Lippincott.

332. A: "Available," again, meaning "in print," meaning BIP (or Paperbound Books in Print) is your first source. It is listed in BIP, in a paperback edition (Ballantine publishers), so it is available in paperback (and the price is 75¢).

333. A: You might find it out from reading Publishers Weekly, but a more direct source would be Forthcoming Books (checking under Child), or Subject Guide to Forthcoming Books (checking under cookbooks).

334. A: You have the title, the author approximately, and the date approximately. The date is covered by Sabin and Evans. You can check Sabin under Low, as author, but it is not listed. In Evans, you can go directly to the volume for 1790 and check alphabetically under Low for that year, and you will find a citation for your broadside, which tells you that Brother Low's first name is Samuel. The fact that the imprint information, in Evans, appears in square brackets, is an indication that this information did not appear on the publication itself but in fact was "supplied" by the bibliographer. On your copy, remember, it was only written in pencil, presumably at a later time. (If you didn't know what a broadside is, why didn't you look it up in the ALA Glossary?)

335. A: See #348.

336. A: You have the author (Graves) and the subject (poetry for children). In the problem as stated, you do not have an indication of date or time period, but you can certainly make an educated guess (you have already done this in #324--Inquest, and #331--Heart Breathings). In this case you can get information about the author. You may already know that Robert Graves is a modern (and living) author, you may be able to find this out from the person making the inquiry, or you will eventually have biographical sources in which to look it up. You can therefore figure that your time period is more likely to be current than retrospective (but do not rule retrospective out entirely).

337. A: Subject Guide to Books in Print (subject approach); BIP (author approach); BPR and BPR Cumulative (subject and author approach); PW Weekly Record (author approach).

338. A: Probably Subject Guide to Books in Print, because it is a one-stop source (as in #326).

339. A: First of all, you have to find the subject heading(s) under which to look. There is no subject heading for "poetry for children." You might then think of "children's poetry." (The subject heading "poetry" does give you a see-also reference to "children's poetry" if you did not happen to think of this alternative possibility yourself.) However, there is no book by Robert Graves listed under this

subject heading.

340. A: You cannot conclude that the book does not exist or has never existed. You can conclude that the book is not in print in the United States (your knowledge that Graves is British--gained from the same sources as indicated in the answer to #336--leads you to this conclusion). You can also conclude that (a) you did not search correctly in the source, or (b) your source is inaccurate.

341. A: The book was once published in the U.S. and is no longer in print. The book has been published in the U.S. but so recently that it does not appear in Subject BIP. The book is in print in Great Britain, the book was once published in Great Britain but is no longer in print, or the book has been published very recently in Great Britain.

342. A: (a) No longer in print--retrospective sources (BPR/PW Weekly Record and CBI, working from current date back).
(b) Too recent to appear in Subject BIP-- very current sources (BPR/PW Weekly Record and CBI, working from current issue back).
(c) Published and/or in print in Great Britain: the only source you have so far for British publications is CBI, again working from current issue back.
You should note that your answer is effectively the same for all three possibilities.

343. A: CBI cumulative volume for 1961/62 lists, under Graves: The Penny Fiddle; Poems for Children (published in 1961 by Double-day at $2.50, and in 1960 by Cassell--in London--at 12/6). BPR Cumulative for 1960-64, under Dewey 821, also lists the 1961 Doubleday publication.

344. A: Yes, it does. You have found that such a book (of poetry for children by Robert Graves) has been published.

345. A: You, or the inquirer, might want to know if you can still "get" or buy the book--in other words, is it still in print?

346. A: Since in #339 you did not find it in the Subject Guide to Books in Print, you might assume that it is not in print. However, it probably is worth checking again, now that you have the title, and you can now check either under author or title in BIP, or in the publisher's catalog (Doubleday) in PTLA. In BIP, under Graves, you find that The Penny Fiddle is listed as in print.

347. A: The listing in BIP tells you only the title. It does not give a sub-title nor does it tell you it is specifically a book of poetry for children. (You already know from your searching in CBI that The Penny Fiddle is a book of poetry for children, but you cannot tell this from the entry in BIP). The BIP entry does tell you that the book is for grades 4 through 6, which still does not tell you that it is poetry, but does tell you that it is for children, so it is a clue worth following up.

348. A: To the publisher's catalog in PTLA, Doubleday, which does tell you that the full title is Penny Fiddle: Poems for Children.

349. A: CBI citation gives you the number of pages (62), the British publisher and price (Collins, 12/6), and the LC card order number, none of which are given in BIP/PTLA. PTLA gives you the size (6-1/8 x 9-1/4) and the grade level ("up to 12"), neither of which are given in CBI.

Section 4

National Library Catalog and Union List

Questions #350-400

One of the purposes of this self-study manual is to instruct you in the method or technique of examining reference sources; so far you have been given a great deal of specific guidance in what to look for and where to look for it.   Now, you should find that you are growing more and more independent of such specific guidance.   You should have a fairly clear idea of the type of information which you must look for in each of these bibliographic sources, and where you are likely to find it.   When you are examining a new or unfamiliar source, you should look for similarities and make comparisons with what you already know.

The next set of sources from the bibliographical records of the United States are:

> Library of Congress /National Union Catalog author lists (AA63, AA64, AA65)
> NUC 1952-1956 Imprints (see AA65)
> NUC Pre-1956 Imprints (Mansell) (2AA12)
> LC /NUC 1942-62 author list, Master Cumulation (Gale)
> NUC Register of Additional Locations (1AA14)
>
> LC Subject Catalog (AA66)
>
> LC Catalog--Motion Pictures and Filmstrips (BG68)
> LC Catalog--Music and Phonorecords (BH 38)
> NUC of Manuscript Collections (DB33a)
> National Register of Microform Masters (1AA17a)
> Newspapers on Microfilm (AG12 & 2AG6)
>
> Catalog of Copyright Entries (AA353, BD223, BD67, BH37-BH37a)

350.   Before you begin with the first source, review in your own mind how you are to proceed.   If necessary, go back to the questions on the other sources you have already examined.   What do you need to find out or determine about this source, in your examination of it?

Often you will find that there is considerable overlapping of this information.   For example, you can frequently tell a great deal about the scope and arrangement of a source from its title, or from its publication dates.   Sometimes it in necessary to determine the publication dates of a source before you can make a clear statement of its scope.   Sometimes you will need to determine the basic arrangement of the source before its publication dates, or therefore its scope, will be clear to you.

This is very true of the LC /NUC catalogs.   Because of this complexity, it would probably be easiest for you to begin by turning to the Winchell entry and annotation (AA63 /64 /65), which is quite extensive, and read that as background, before you turn to the source itself.

Note that this particular source is listed in Winchell first under "Universal Bibliography," and then under the sub-heading of "Library Catalogs."   Read the few paragraphs of text under this heading.   Then note that the LC /NUC catalogs are further listed specifically as library catalogs of "national libraries."

It would be helpful if you had as background some understanding of what a national library is, and of what the Library of Congress itself is.   If you are not already familiar with either of these, then you might try to look them up.   Definitions in the ALA Glossary are not satisfactory for either.   Try a general encyclopedia for the Library of Congress (probably within the article on "libraries"), plus reading the few comments on national library catalogs in Winchell (8th ed., p. 7), plus the brief definition for "national library" in the ALA Glossary.

The Library of Congress in Washington, D.C. functions as a national library for the United States.   One of its functions has been to make available to other libraries printed catalog cards for most of its own holdings (the items in its collections), and sometimes items from the collections of other libraries in the country.   These printed catalog cards are the same as those which you can see in the card catalogs of most large college and university libraries.   The LC "printed catalog," which you are examining, is a reproduction in book form, or in bound volumes, of these printed catalog cards.

351.   According to the annotation in Winchell, are the LC catalogs then a catalog of Library of Congress holdings?

After having read the full information in Winchell, turn to the source itself.   Keep in mind that the LC/NUC catalogs consist of several series, or several sets of volumes, and you should be sure that you have located the entire set.   The Library of Congress/National Union Catalog printed catalogs have been published at fairly regular intervals over a number of years, and are still being published currently, and at various times have been cumulated into larger sets.   Glance through some of the volumes and you will see that the entries are in the familiar form of a catalog card entry.

By using the Winchell annotation and by examining the physical volumes themselves, you should first try to determine the publication pattern of the LC/NUC catalogs--what the various series consist of, what they represent, how many volumes they contain, what the cumulation pattern is, etc.   While you are doing this, you can get from the titles a general idea of the scope of the work.   You may prefer to do this by yourself, or you may prefer to do it with the aid of the following sequence of questions.

352.   Locate the first, or the basic, series of the LC set.   What are the publication dates (not necessarily the dates of coverage) of this set, and how many volumes are there?   What is the title?

353.   The publication dates for the basic series are 1942-1946.   Does this then include printed catalog cards issued from 1942-1946?

354.   The next series is the first supplement to the basic set.   How many volumes does it consist of?   In what year(s) were they published?   What are the issuing dates of the cards which they contain?   Does this mean that you would find in the First Supplement only titles published from 1942-1947?

355.   Does the 1942-1947 supplement then supersede the basic set?   Would titles in the basic set appear also in the 1942-1947 supplement?   If you were searching for a book published in 1937, where would you look (so far)?

356.   What is the next series?   How many volumes does it have?   Is there anything special about the last volume?

357.   What is the next series?   Is there any difference between the title of the fourth series and the title of the earlier series?

358.   What does this title change represent?   See the Winchell annotation for help on this one.

359.   Do you think then that the scope of the printed catalogs has increased, decreased, or remained the same since its change to the National Union Catalog?

360.   One of the changes in the LC/NUC catalogs at this point was the inclusion of location symbols in the entries.   Of the bibliographies you have already examined, in the previous questions, which ones included library location symbols?

361.   How do you find out what the library location symbols stand for?   What does HU stand for?

362.   Review: What is the importance of such location symbols?

363.   What is the union catalog?

364.   What is the purpose or usefulness of union catalogs or union lists?   Try to think about this one, but if you cannot come up with any possibilities turn to the answer.

365.   With the fourth series, 1953-57, the title, the scope and function of the catalogs changed, from just LC printed cards to that of a union catalog listing.   The fourth series was published throughout 1953-57 and then cumulated into the set you are looking at now.   The title and function change came in 1956, and the national union catalog listings were included for only 1956+ imprints.   Would you expect to find in the 1953-57 cumulation an entry with NUC location symbols for a book published in 1954?

366.   Is there any way in which NUC information is available for imprints during the earlier part of the 1953-57 cumulation?   See Winchell annotation or think about other titles on your list to examine.

367.   Look at the last series you have examined, and at those which follow.   So far, has any cumulation pattern appeared?   Look at the current issues.   What cumulation pattern is there for currently appearing issues?

368.   Can you make a brief indication or chart of the pattern for the entire source from the basic set to date?   Show coverage for imprint date of publications included.

369.   This is a large number of places in which to search.   Is there anything being done to cut down this searching?

370.   In the various parts of this source which you have examined so far, where would you look to find information on a book published in 1887?

371.   Would you expect to find library locations indicated for it?

372.   Is anything being done to supply library locations for early imprints, such as the 1887 title?

373.   When the NUC Pre-1956 Imprints is completed, will it and the current NUC be thought of as a "national bibliography"?

374.   You have determined the publication and cumulation pattern of the various older series of the LC/NUC catalogs, and the current issues as well.   What is the basic arrangement of the material within the source?   Is it alphabetical or classified?   You can quickly tell this by glancing through a few of the volumes.

375.   The Winchell annotation states that the LC/NUC catalogs are arranged by "author and main entry." What does this mean? Do you remember any earlier source which was also arranged in this way?

376.   If you know the title of a book, but do <u>not</u> know the author, would you be able to locate it in the LC/NUC catalogs?

377.   If you specifically wanted to locate the entry in the LC/NUC catalogs for a book of which you knew only the title--for example, <u>The Nice and the Good</u>--and you do not know the author, how could you go about it?

378.   Are there any cross-references in the LC/NUC catalogs?

379.   Locate in the LC/NUC catalog the entry for <u>We Bark at Midnight</u> by Van Lane Ferguson, published in Rutland, Vermont in 1958. In what year and volume did you find it? Who is the publisher? How many pages are there in the book?

380.   Look at the entry for the Ferguson book from the preceding question. What does the "58-7495," in the lower right corner of the entry, mean? Where would you look to find out?

381.   Is there anything in the entry for the Ferguson book (from #379) which might give you a clue to what the book is about?

382.   Is there any subject access at all for the LC/NUC catalogs? You may need to go to Winchell for this.

383.   Locate in the LC/NUC catalog the entry for <u>Unfolding Character: The Impact of Gordonstoun</u> by Adam Arnold Brown, published in London in 1962. This may be difficult to find. Use your imagination. In what year and volume did you find it?

384.   In the entry for <u>Unfolding Character</u> from the preceding question, can you find the library location symbols for libraries reporting this title to the NUC? What are the names of two of these libraries, besides the Library of Congress?

385.   In the entry for <u>Unfolding Character</u> (see #383), several libraries are listed--or their symbols are listed--as having copies of this title. Does this indicate that these are the only libraries in the U.S. holding this title?

386.   Libraries cooperating in the national union catalog project may report that they have a copy of a specific book after the entry for that book has appeared in the published NUC. Suppose you are trying to get a specific book on interlibrary loan and the NUC lists only two libraries who hold copies and neither can fill your request. Do you have any way of finding out additional libraries holding copies and reporting them later?

387.   In earlier questions, you tried to locate and verify information for a book by Wharton entitled <u>A Treatise on Theism,</u> published in the U.S. in 1859. This was not in Sabin, and the other source for the period,

Roorbach, listed the title but did not actually give a date so you could not verify that information. Can you now verify it from the LC/NUC catalogs?

388.   You have already considered the <u>scope</u> of the LC/NUC catalogs, to some extent, when you considered its title change and expansion to the National Union Catalog in 1956 (#358). The scope of material listed or included in the LC/NUC catalogs is more or less that of the collections of the Library of Congress and of the collections of the libraries reporting to the NUC. Obviously, this is an extremely <u>broad</u> scope.

Most of the sources you have examined previously have been much more limited, to materials published in the United States, materials published in English, materials relating to America. Does the material listed in the LC/NUC catalogs have any such limitations?

389.   Why are the LC/NUC catalogs listed, in Winchell, under "universal" bibliographies?

390.   Why, then, would we be considering the LC/NUC catalogs as part of the bibliographical records of the United States?

391.   Remember that ideal bibliographical control should cover more than just books. Many of the earlier bibliographical sources you examined were quite limited in the <u>types</u> of publications included. For example, they might exclude periodicals, pamphlets, government publications, dissertations, serials, maps, audio-visual materials, etc. Do the LC/NUC catalogs seem to have any of these types of exclusions? (Read the Winchell annotation, glance through the catalogs themselves, and read the preface to one of the recent issues.)

392.   For example, are serials and periodicals included in the NUC?

393.   What kind of bibliographical information do you find in the entries themselves, in the LC/NUC catalogs? Is the information extensive? Do you think it is authoritative? Why or why not would it be considered authoritative?

394.   Is there any kind of information which has not generally been given in the LC/NUC entries and which might be very important to librarians?

395.   Then where do you look for the price, if it is not given and you need to know it?

There are a number of other publications which supplement and complement the materials included in the basic LC/NUC catalogs. These are listed with Winchell numbers at the beginning of this section. Some of them have been referred to in the previous questions, and some will be taken up in more detail in later sections of this manual. You may have time now to look up some of these further sources and examine them briefly; if not, it would be helpful to read the Winchell annotations for these additional sources and see how they fit into the scope of the basic LC/NUC author catalog.

In summary, then, the scope of the LC/NUC catalogs, which you have examined, plus the various supplementary publications you have also considered, is very broad, and the information given in the entries is--in general--very complete and quite accurate. So you can see that this source serves as one of our most useful, most complete, most accurate sources of bibliographical information, not only for publications of the U.S. but for publications from all countries as well. It serves us as part of our own national bibliographic records, and as part of a "universal" bibliographic record.

396. Can you see any weaknesses or loopholes in the use of the LC/NUC catalogs as a complete national bibliographical record? For example, do you remember that any of the prefaces or Winchell annotations said that all publications (for example, all books) published in the United States would automatically be listed in the LC/NUC catalogs? Is any provision made to require all publications to be deposited in the Library of Congress or any other official source?

397. What is copyright and copyright registration?

398. Is there any record of publications which have been sent to the U.S. Copyright Office for registration? Is this record then a complete listing of all U.S. publications?

399. Can you tell from the annotation in Winchell how the Catalog of Copyright Entries compares, in a general way, with the LC/NUC catalogs? Consider type of materials covered.

400. It would appear that the scope of the CCE is perhaps in a way much broader than the LC/NUC catalogs since it includes all types of written matter sent in to be copyrighted--for example, games, children's coloring books, etc. Can you see any ways in which the CCE is more limited for bibliographical use than the LC/NUC catalogs? It may not be possible to answer this question without actually examining the source itself, by looking at the entries and the information included in them, and the dates of the material as it is included and published, or made available.

Section 4

National Library Catalog and Union List

Answers #350-400

350. A: In general you will want to determine: the basic bibliographical information about the source itself; the arrangement of the source, its access; the scope of the source (including the amount of information given in the individual citations or entries); any special features you may note about the source. (This is the information outlined in Winchell's 8th edition, p. xiv-xv.)

351. A: No, not really--it is a catalog only of the items "for which Library of Congress printed cards were available" (see note under "scope" in Winchell, p. 8) and in some cases from collections other than those in the LC. The LC printed catalogs do not record all of the LC holdings, and include as well holdings from other libraries.

352. A: The first or basic series of the LC catalog was published from 1942-46, and consists of 167 volumes, or volumes 1-167. The volume numbering and the publication dates appear on the spines of the volumes as well as on the title pages. At that time it was called "A Catalog of Books Represented by Library of Congress printed cards..." (This is item AA63 in Winchell.)

353. A: No, according to the title of the source (title page and Winchell annotation), it includes printed cards issued up to July 1942. In other words, dates of coverage for publications would be from the earliest printed books to July 1942.

354. A: The first supplement (also Winchell AA63) to the basic set consists of 42 volumes (volumes 1-42), published in 1948. They contain cards issued from 1942 through 1947. 1942-47 is the date of issue of the cards, not the imprint dates of the publications covered. As in the basic set, coverage for imprint dates of the publications would be from earliest printed books through, now, 1947.

355. A: No, it does not supersede the basic set; it supplements it--adds to it--to be used in addition to the basic set. In theory, titles in the basic set would not appear also in the 1942-47 supplement. If you were trying to find an entry for a book published in 1937, you would look first in the basic set (imprints to 1942) and if you did not find it there, then look also in the 1st supplement (imprints to 1947).

356. A: The third series is a five-year cumulation,

containing printed cards issued from 1948-1952. The original catalogs were published from 1948-1952 and the cumulation was published in 1953. (Winchell item AA64). It has 24 volumes. Vol. 24 contains only listings for "films."

357. A: The fourth series (Winchell AA65) is another five-year cumulation, covering cards issued from 1953-1957. The cumulation was published in 1958, in 28 volumes, of which vol. 27 covers "music and phonorecords" and vol. 28 "motion pictures and filmstrips." With the fourth series, 1953-57, the title changed to the "National Union Catalog." Earlier titles were some variation of "Library of Congress."

358. A: The change of title from LC to NUC represents an important change in the scope and function of the printed catalog. See the Winchell annotation, p. 8, under the scope of "1953-1957." The printed catalog now includes titles reported to the LC by other libraries, and indicates location of these titles as well.

359. A: Basically, the scope has broadened, or increased, since the catalogs now contain many titles from other libraries.

360. A: Sabin, Evans, Shaw/Shoemaker, Shoemaker Checklist.

361. A: Look them up in the front of each cumulative set. HU stands for the University of Hawaii Library.

362. A: See the answer to #253.

363. A: See the definition given in the ALA Glossary.

364. A: Some of the things you might have suggested would be: location of materials (for inter-library loan, for example); cooperative buying, cataloging, etc., between libraries, on a local/regional/national basis; a further bibliographical source for information.

365. A: No, because NUC information was included for 1956+ imprints only. You might expect to find an entry--but for an LC printed card, not for the national union catalog information.

366. A: Yes, in the NUC 1952-56 imprints. In 1961 the LC decided to print NUC cards for those 1952-56 imprints which were not

included in the 1953-57 cumulation. The National Union Catalog 1952-56 imprints (a 30 volume set) then serves as a supplement to the 1953-57 cumulation.

367. A: Since the publication of the first supplement, the cumulation pattern has been every five years or quinquennial. The currently appearing issues come out monthly, cumulating quarterly, then annually (and eventually the annual cumulations you see will cumulate into another five-year or quinquennial cumulation.)

368. A:
1. LC cards only   1942 (imprints to 1942)
2. "   "   "   1942-47   "   to 1947)
3. "   "   "   1948-52   "   to 1952)
4. LC/NUC   1953-57   "   to 1957)
   (plus 4a. NUC 1952-56 imprints)
5. LC/NUC   1958-62   "   to 1962)
6. LC/NUC   1963-67   "   to 1967)
7. LC/NUC   1968, 1969, etc. including
                 monthly and quarterly issues

369. A: Publication of the Library of Congress/National Union Catalog Author Lists, 1942-62; a Master Cumulation (published by Gale Research, not LC) which aims to cumulate into one alphabet items 1-4 in the answer (#369) above.

370. A: For a book published in 1887, you would have to go back to the LC basic set, and if you did not find it there, work forward, searching through the various series as indicated in the answer to #369. Since libraries currently purchase many books with older imprint dates, you could reasonably expect it to appear at any point, depending on when the LC received and cataloged it and made an LC card available.

371. A: You would not expect to find library locations--i.e., NUC information--since that is included in the LC/NUC only for 1952+ imprints (including the 1952-56 imprints catalog published to supplement the 1953-57 cumulation).

372. A: Yes, the National Union Catalog Pre-1956 Imprints, which will make available bibliographical information on all titles with imprint dates prior to 1956 held by cooperating libraries and reported to the national union catalog in the Library of Congress. It is expected to be completed in 1979 in 610 volumes.

373. A: No, more truly as a universal bibliography. It will cover, as does the current NUC, publications from all countries, all languages. The addition of the vast pre-1956 imprints section will extend it to cover all periods. The national union catalog which actually exists on cards in the LC is "national" in the sense of being part of our "national" library, and is contributed to by some 600 libraries in North America.

374. A: The basic arrangement is alphabetical.

375. A: Think back to the PW Weekly Record, arranged by "main entry only." This means that you will find only one entry for each item, primarily author entries but in some cases title entries. There will not be any entry under both author and title (as with CBI and BIP).

376. A: No.

377. A: Look it up in some other source which does give you title access (for example, CBI) to find out the author, and then look it up in LC/NUC under the author.

378. A: Yes, there are some. The Winchell annotation tells you this, and you should be able to see it from glancing through several pages of entries in the source itself.

379. A: The entry is located in the 1958-62 series, vol. 14 (p. 372) under Ferguson. The publisher is Tuttle and the paging is given (87 pages) in the "body" of the card, just as it appears on a regular catalog card which you might find in a university library card catalog.

380. A: Probably you would not know what this number stands for and would have to look it up. You should expect that reference sources will give you some adequate instructions about abbreviations, numbers, symbols, etc., which are used in the source, and usually these explanations will be located in the prefatory or introductory material in the front of the volume. In this case you will need to go back to vol. 1 of the 1958-62 set, and on p. x there is a description and explanation of the various parts of the entries. The number in the lower right corner is the order number for the LC card (of which the entry itself is a reproduction), so that libraries wishing to order copies of the card may do so by using that specific number.

381. A: In this particular entry, the LC classification number or call number is given in the lower left corner (PZ4 F352 We), and if you knew the classification scheme, or where to look it up, you would be able to tell that PZ is the class number for Fiction in English.

382. A: There is no subject access in the volume you have been examining. There is, however, another series called Library of Congress Catalog, Books: Subjects (Winchell AA66), which begins in 1950, and which does give an alphabetical subject access to all publications, mainly with imprint dates of 1950+. It does not include all NUC contributions, only those items for which LC printed cards are available; however, some library location symbols are given, and the NUC itself can be checked for other possibilities.

383. A: The entry is in the 1963-67 set, vol. 3, under Arnold-Brown, not under Brown. There is no cross-reference from Brown to Arnold-Brown, so this is a case where you have to use your imagination and try all the possibilities of entry that occur to you. You do not have the option in the LC/NUC catalogs, as you do with for example CBI, of finding the entry also under the title or of finding a cross-reference from the title to the correct author entry. Also, although the book was published in 1962, the entry does not appear until the 1963 volume, meaning that the card from the LC/NUC was not issued in time for its appearance in the 1962 volume. As with most of the other bibliographical sources, the appearance of the listing will not necessarily coincide exactly with the publication of the book.

384. A: The library location symbols are located in the lower left, beneath the LC classification number or call number: "MH DLC OC," etc. MH stands for Harvard University Library, DLC stands for the Library of Congress, OC stands for the Public Library of Cincinnati, etc. You can look up these symbols in the front of volume 1 of the series.

385. A: No, only that these libraries have reported it to the NUC. Not all libraries report to the NUC. Many libraries may have this title but not have reported it to the NUC. Other libraries may report it but at a later date so that they would not be included in this particular list.

386. A: Yes, in the NUC Register of Additional Locations (Winchell 1AA14), published in the last eight volumes of the 1963-67 cumulation, then continued on a semi-annual and annual basis. This is a listing of LC card numbers (given in the original NUC entry) only, plus additional location symbols.

387. A: Yes, this book is listed, in the basic (to 1942) set, under Wharton. It shows the same information you found in Roorbach, plus the author's full name, plus the number of pages, plus the date of publication (1859).

388. A: No, certainly no more so than the collections of any college or university library, for example. The LC/NUC will include foreign publications, foreign language publications, as well as U.S. or English language publications.

389. A: Because they do not attempt to limit themselves to listings of the publications of one language or one country, but rather include publications in all languages from all countries. (See #373.)

390. A: The LC functions as a national library for the U.S. One of the functions of a national library is to collect and preserve the literature (in a broad sense) of that country. The LC does attempt to fulfill this function. Also, as a basic research library, its collections of U.S. publications will be extensive. Most of these publications--current and retrospective--will be represented by LC printed cards or reports to the NUC; and will therefore appear in the LC/NUC catalogs.

391. A: In general, the LC/NUC catalogs include a much broader range of types of materials or publications than any of the preceding sources. According to the Introduction ("Scope") in a recent issue, they include: books, pamphlets, maps, atlases, periodicals and other serials, government documents, and some theses and dissertations.

They also include music and recordings, and motion pictures and filmstrips. In the past these were included in the LC/NUC catalogs (although in separate volumes in the cumulations); since 1953 they have been published in separate series--LC Catalog: Music and Phonorecords; LC Catalog: Motion Pictures and Filmstrips--with their own cumulations and their own current issues.

So the range of coverage is extremely broad. It is not always clear whether all of these materials are included as LC printed cards or as NUC listings; you must read the introduction carefully to make these distinctions. But at this point all you need to realize is that some entries for all of these various types of materials will appear in the LC/NUC catalogs.

392. A: Yes (see the introduction of a recent issue under "Scope"), but only if LC printed cards are available, and generally library locations are not given. Serials/periodicals reported by other libraries, with library locations, are given in another LC publication, New Serials Titles.

393. A: The entries represent, in general, library cataloging, and would therefore include all the kinds of information that you would expect to find in a library catalog card--including notes, subject heading tracings, added entry tracings and call numbers. This information is usually much more extensive than that which you find in most bibliographical sources, and--because it does represent cataloging from the publication itself--it can generally be considered as quite authoritative and accurate.

394. A: Yes, the price. However, many of the entries in the recent issues do include the price.

395. A: BIP, PTLA, PW, BPR, CBI, etc.

396. A: There was no indication that all publications would automatically appear in the LC/NUC catalogs nor that any provisions had been made to require all publications to be deposited there. Coverage would still be extensive, however, since the NUC includes

entries from the LC itself plus 600
other libraries. In addition, LC is the
depository for all books sent in to the
U.S. Copyright Office for copyright registration.

397. A: See the ALA Glossary or a general diction-
          ary. Essentially, copyright is the exclusive
          right--granted in some legal or official way--
          to reproduce a work. Copyright registration
          is the official registration of this right, ac-
          complished in the United States by sending
          copies of the work in to the U.S. Copyright
          Office.

398. A: Yes, the Catalog of Copyright Entries, pub-
          lished continuously by the Copyright office
          in the Library of Congress. (Winchell
          AA353, etc. as noted at the beginning of
          this section.) No, it lists only those pub-
          lications sent in for copyright registration.

399. A: Materials covered include books, pamphlets,
          serials, contributions to periodicals, peri-
          odicals, dramas, lectures, musical compo-
          sitions, maps and atlases, works of art,
          scientific and technical drawings, photo-
          graphic works, prints, pictorial illustrations,
          motion pictures and filmstrips, prints and
          labels. (See general Preface to volumes
          of the CCE, and Winchell annotation.) "The
          works listed include not only the current
          output of the publishing industry of the U.S.
          and many works in English and in foreign
          languages published abroad, but also the
          products of many specialized publishing enter-
          prises..business reports and yearbooks, trade
          catalogs and directories, manuals, instruction
          books, business and legal services, research
          studies in many fields...printed matter at-
          tached to or accompanying games, filmstrips,
          and other articles." (Introduction to Part I,
          Books and Pamphlets).

400. A: Entries in the CCE, although reasonably
          full, do not include as much information as
          the LC/NUC entries (see #393). Entries
          are listed in the CCE according to the date
          they were copyrighted (which is usually al-
          though not necessarily the date of publication):
          however, the gap between the copyright
          date and the publication of the CCE is con-
          siderably more than in the LC/NUC. For
          example, publication of the CCE covering
          copyright registrations made in 1967 was
          published in 1970, a gap of 3-4 years.

Section 5

Bibliographic Sources for Serials--Current Lists

Questions #401-464

The sources which you have examined thus far comprise the major bibliographical records of publication in the United States, both current and retrospective. Some of them overlap, particularly the current ones, but differences in scope and information given are still sufficient to make it necessary to consider using all of them together to provide an adequate record.

However, national bibliographical control must include coverage of all types of publications: books, serials, periodicals, newspapers, pamphlets, dissertations, maps, music scores, etc. (And as our needs move more in the direction of the multi-media concept, bibliographical control must also be extended to include other types of informational and educational materials such as films, filmstrips, recordings, transparencies, etc.) One of the primary deficiencies of the sources you have looked at so far is that they tend to limit their coverage mainly to book publication. The sources you will be examining in this and following sections will deal with publications other than books: serials (periodicals, newspapers, annuals, etc.), government publications, dissertations, pamphlets, etc.--those publications which have generally been excluded from the previous sources. The bibliographical sources in the following sections are not always considered as part of our national bibliography but in fact they must be in order to give us proper coverage.

This section, then, begins with sources for bibliographic information about serials, and the first group to examine are specifically sources of current information--bibliographies, lists, directories of the periodicals themselves:

        Ulrich's International Periodicals Directory (AF18, 1AF2)
        Irregular Serials and Annuals (2AF3)
        Standard Periodical Directory (AF17)
        Ayer Directory of Newspapers...(AF13)

401.   What is a serial?

402.   "Serials," then, is a broad term which covers several types of publications, similar mainly in their successive (serially) or continuous form of publication. One type of publication broadly defined as a "serial" is a periodical. What is a periodical?

403.   In laymen's terms, periodicals include magazines and/or journals, whether of general interest or specific subject interest, whether of popular, mass-circulation appeal or professional, technical, scholarly appeal. (There is a tendency, not clearly defined, to label general interest, popular content, mass-circulation, commercial publications as magazines, and the special subject interest, professional, technical, scholarly publications as journals.) Thinking in terms of magazines and journals, which you have some familiarity with, and of the definitions in #402, can you give two significant points about periodicals, one dealing with the format, and one dealing with the content?

404.   Why are periodicals important items in library collections?

405.   Of the various bibliographical sources which you have examined so far, which ones are themselves periodicals? In other words, which ones are published periodically? PTLA? BIP? Subject BIP? PW? BPR? BPR Cumulative? CBI? U.S. Catalog? American Catalog? Kelly? Roorbach? Sabin? Evans? Shaw/Shoemaker? Shoemaker Checklist?

406. Of the various bibliographical sources which you have examined so far, which of them attempted to include periodicals (or serials) in their listings? Did the Bowker publications (BIP/PTLA/Subject BIP; BPR, etc.)? Did CBI? What about the retrospective records--Sabin, Evans, Roorbach, Kelly, American Catalog, Shaw/Shoemaker, Shoemaker Checklist?

407. Would you say that periodical or serial publications had been adequately covered in the retrospective and current records you have seen so far?

The next set of sources you will examine deal specifically and only with records of serial (and/or periodical) publication, and even more specifically they deal with the periodicals themselves, as opposed to the separate articles contained in the periodicals. A separate set of sources will cover the separate articles. It is important to keep in mind this distinction.

408. Review: What is the basic bibliographical information which you should ascertain about each source as you examine it?

409. What then is the basic bibliographical information about the first title, Ulrich's International Periodicals Directory?

410. Looking at the title and subtitle only, what can you tell immediately about the scope of this source? What, if any, are its limitations, in terms of: comprehensiveness, type of publication included, time period covered, country of publication?

411. Again, looking only at the title and subtitle, can you tell immediately anything about the arrangement of this source? If the title page doesn't give you a clue, what else can you do immediately to determine the arrangement?

412. The basic arrangement then is by subject, with periodical titles listed under the subject they deal with, using subject headings, or subject classifications. The breakdown is a broad separation of science and technology (in volume 1) from humanities and social sciences (in volume 2). Within the volumes themselves, the more specific subjects are listed alphabetically. Can you find in Ulrich's a list of periodicals (that is, the titles of the periodicals) dealing with the subject of folklore?

413. Can you find the title of a periodical dealing specifically with the folklore of gypsies?

414. How often is this periodical, which deals specifically with the folklore of Gypsies (see answer to #413), published? (In other words, what is its frequency of publication; how often does it "come out" or "appear?")

415. Why would it be important for a library to know the frequency of publication?

416. What introductory material is included in Ulrich's?

417. What bibliographical information is included in each citation?

418. How would you find the title of a periodical on knitting? (If you have trouble with this, go on directly to #419 and #420).

419. Review: If you have a bibliographical source with a basic subject arrangement, what additional access do you need and where would you expect to find it?

420. Does Ulrich's have these other accesses?

421. Can you find the titles of some periodicals on UFO's (unidentified flying objects)? If you can't decide whether UFO's would be considered "Science and Technology" or "Social Sciences and Humanities," would you have to look in the index to both volumes?

422. What about periodicals which do not seem to be limited to one subject--e.g. Time, Life, Reader's Digest?

423. If you need to find ordering information (such as price, address of publisher, frequency of publication, etc.) for the UNESCO Bulletin for Libraries, would you expect to find it in Ulrich's and how would you go about it?

424. What is meant by "back volumes" or a "retrospective file" of a periodical? If you wanted to get not only a current subscription to UNESCO Bulletin for Libraries but also a complete file of all that had been published to date (so far), can you tell from the Ulrich's citation how much has been published?

425. If you were searching in Ulrich's for a specific title, such as the UNESCO Bulletin for Libraries, or for titles on UFO's, and you did not find listings in Ulrich's could you assume then that such titles did not exist? Why, or why not? (As always, of course, you should keep in mind that you might be searching, or using the source, incorrectly, or that your information might be faulty, but for this question, assume you did search correctly and your information is right.)

426. On what basis are periodicals selected to be included in Ulrich's? Does this seem to be a narrow or broad basis for selection/inclusion?

427. If you were looking for a specific title which would appear to meet the requirement for inclusion in Ulrich's and it was not there, what else might you suspect? In regard to periodicals, what is meant by the term "current" in the subtitle to Ulrich's?

428. Ulrich's is a list of current, or currently appearing, periodicals, giving ordering/acquisitions information (price, publisher, etc.). Is it similar in any way to any other source you have looked at? (Who publishes Ulrich's?)

429. BIP appears annually and is kept up to date through Forthcoming Books. Does Ulrich's appear annually? How frequently does it appear? How is it kept up to date? Where would you look to find all of this information?

430.   Would you expect the supplements to have the same scope and arrangement as the main volumes?

431.   Review: What is a periodical? How are periodicals defined for inclusion in Ulrich's? How often does a periodical have to be issued in order to be included in Ulrich's?

432.   Would you expect PTLA or BIP to be listed in Ulrich's?

433.   Where would you find them listed?

434.   Who is the publisher of this source and what does this tell you?

435.   Note that the title of this source refers to "serials" rather than periodicals. What are serials and how do they differ from periodicals?

436.   What is the full title of Irregular Serials? What does this title tell you about the scope and arrangement of this source? Is it similar to Ulrich's? What is the main difference between Ulrich's and Irregular Serials?

437.   Would you expect a title to be included in both Ulrich's and Irregular Serials?

438.   Even though the scope differs, would you expect to use Irregular Serials in the same way as Ulrich's and find generally the same type of information in it?

439.   Look up the Educators Grade Guide to Free Teaching Aids in Irregular Serials. How often is it published and what does it cost? Is the publisher's name and address given?

440.   What can you find out about the Publications of the Indiana Historical Society?

441.   What can you find out about the publication schedule of Irregular Serials? When is a new edition expected? How will it be updated? Will it be handled in a similar manner to Ulrich's?

442.   Review: Where would you look to find out if, by any chance, a new edition or a supplement to Irregular Serials is expected in the next few months?

443.   A source similar to Ulrich's is The Standard Periodical Directory, which can be looked at briefly by comparing it to Ulrich's. What does its title page tell you about its scope, and how does this compare to Ulrich's?

444.   Does the introductory matter (Preface) to the Standard Directory give you any further comparisons to Ulrich's regarding scope?

445.   How does the arrangement of the Standard directory compare with Ulrich's?

446.   Look up unidentified flying objects in the Standard Directory. How does its location compare with Ulrich's? How do the listings themselves compare to what you found in Ulrich's?

447.   In general, how does Standard compare to Ulrich's?

448.   Does Ulrich's include newspapers?

449.   Where would you find information on newspapers?

450.   What is the full title of the Ayer Directory?

451.   Is the publisher of this next source one that you are familiar with?

452.   How frequently is the Ayer Directory published? Can you tell this from the title page or the introduction (Guide to the Use of the Directory)?

453.   Does the Ayer Directory limit itself to newspapers, or does it overlap Ulrich's in any way? In regard to type of publication included, is its scope broader or narrower than Ulrich's?

454.   What about place of publication? Does Ayer cover more or less territory than Ulrich's?

455.   What is the basic arrangement of Ayer's? Is this similar to any arrangement you have looked at previously?

456.   Is it possible to locate in Ayer the information about a publication if you do not know exactly where it is published?

457.   Is there any subject access to Ayer's? For example, if you wanted to look up publications on UFO's, as you did in Ulrich's and Standard, could you do it?

458.   Can you find, in Ayer's, a list of newspapers and periodicals published in the Chinese language in the United States?

459.   Is there a daily newspaper in Oxford, Nebraska? How big is Oxford, Nebraska, anyway?

460.   What is the ordering information for the St. Louis (Mo.) Post Dispatch? If you did not know that the Post Dispatch was published in St. Louis, Missouri, could you find it in Ayer's?

461.   How would you find out how many daily newspapers are published in Tennessee?

462.   Besides bibliographical information on publications listed, what other useful information can you get from Ayer's? Why do you think all of this is included in the source?

463.   When you examined Ulrich's, you also looked briefly at a similar source, the Standard Periodical Directory. Are there any other sources similar in scope and use to Ayer's? Where would you look to find out?

464.   So far the sources for serial publications which you have examined have been concerned primarily with providing bibliographical information on current (i.e., currently-appearing) serials /periodicals /news-papers. Such information is useful for selection and ordering (acquisitions) of materials, and is also useful for bibliographical identification. Is there anything in the sources which you have just examined which might give you retrospective bibliographical information on serials?

Section 5

Bibliographic Sources for Serials--Current Lists

Answers #401-464

401. A: See ALA Glossary, 1st definition ("A publication issued in successive parts, usually
at regular intervals, and as a rule, intended
to be continued indefinitely. Serials include
periodicals, annuals (reports, yearbooks,
etc.) and memoirs, proceedings, and trans-
actions of societies.") The exact definition
of a serial is a difficult problem. The American Library Association's Library Statistics:
A Handbook of Concepts, Definitions, and
Terminology (published in 1966) gives essentially the same definition as the ALA
Glossary but amends it to include newspapers, and perhaps monographic and publishers' series. (Monographic and publishers' series have been referred to in this
manual in question #32.) The significant
points to keep in mind at this stage about
serials are "issued in parts," "intended to
be continued indefinitely"; that is, the idea
of continuous publication.

402. A: ALA Glossary again: "A publication with a
distinctive title intended to appear in successive (usually unbound) numbers or parts
at stated or regular intervals and, as a
rule, for an indefinite time. Each part
generally contains articles by several contributors." The ALA Glossary then goes
on to exclude newspapers, and memoirs,
proceedings, journals, etc., of societies
(all of which would seem to fall within the
definition of a periodical) from this for
purposes of library cataloging rules. The
ALA's Library Statistics: A Handbook
defines a periodical as "A serial publication
which constitutes one issue in a continuous
series under the same title, usually published at regular intervals over an indefinite
period, individual issues in the series being
numbered consecutively or each issue being
dated" and neither includes nor excludes
newspapers, and the memoirs, etc., of
societies. Periodicals, then, are serials,
but all serials are not periodicals. All of
which goes to show that the exact definitions of the word "serials" and "periodicals"
are confusing at best, and it behooves you to
keep this confusion in mind when dealing with
bibliographical sources which purport to include
or exclude serials, periodicals, newspapers,
etc. When in doubt, double check.

403. A: Format: from the definitions given in #402:
the fact that the issues appear or are issued
at intervals, such as weekly, semi-weekly,
monthly, quarterly, etc.
Content: each issue usually contains several
different articles by different authors or
contributors, sometimes on unrelated subjects,

sometimes related by the subject of the
periodical or theme of the issue itself.

404. A: There are many reasons, among them:
they are sources of current, up-to-date information (for popular subjects, current
events, research, etc.); similarly, retrospective periodicals or "back files" are
historical sources for contemporary comment and detail not found in book-length or
monographic treatises; they are the largest
single type of publication of the total publishing output; many people who will not read
books, will read periodicals; etc.

405. A: PW is clearly a periodical: published at
periodic intervals, and with articles by several contributors; the Weekly Record of
book publication which you examined specifically is only part of the journal, a regular feature contained in it. BPR and CBI
are also periodicals--although like the rest
of the titles on the list, they are only bibliographic records and do not contain articles, so they are not journals or magazines
in the sense that PW is, but they do appear
in successive parts at stated or regular
intervals and are expected to continue indefinitely.

PTLA/BIP/Subject BIP and the BPR Cumu-
latives are annual publications, and would be
considered as periodicals by some libraries
and as annuals by other libraries, but
probably as serials by all libraries.

The U.S. Catalog, American Catalog, Kelly
and Roorbach would probably have been considered as periodical publications at the time
they were published, as at that time they
were probably expected to continue indefinitely, but they have since ceased publication,
and are not appearing currently, and would
most generally now be referred to as "sets."

Sabin, although published in parts periodically
over an extensive period, did have a foresee-
able end, and would probably not have been
correctly thought of as a periodical; in any
case, it also has ceased publication; similarly with Evans and Shaw/Shoemaker.

The Shoemaker Checklist is presently being
published, but although volumes are appearing at periodic intervals, the intervals are
not really regular or clearly stated, and
presumably it does have a forseeable end.
It also would probably be defined as a set
or a series, currently coming out.

406. A: The Bowker publications and CBI do not
         say that they specifically exclude serials,
         but by their nature they are limited to book
         publication; "books" does sometimes in-
         clude certain serials--for example, year-
         books and annuals--but pretty generally ex-
         cludes periodicals.

         The retrospective records vary a great deal
         in what they include. Surprisingly, many
         periodical and serial publications are in-
         cluded in these bibliographies; when in
         doubt, check.

407. A: No.

408. A: Full title (and subtitle if significant); author,
         editor, compiler, etc., if significant; imprint
         (publisher, place of publication, date of
         publication); number of volumes; specific
         edition you are looking at.

409. A: Full title: Ulrich's International Periodical
             Directory
         Subtitle: A Classified guide to a selected
             list of current periodicals, foreign and
             domestic
         Editor: Marietta Chicorel (this is probably
             of limited significance to you at this
             point; in earlier editions the editor was
             Carolyn Ulrich, hence the title.)
         Published by: Bowker Company in New York
         Edition: 12th
         Number of volumes: 2 in the 12th edition
         Date of publication: vol. 1 in 1967; vol. 2
             in 1968.
         (All of this information is given on the title
         pages of both volumes except the fact that
         there are 2 volumes, but since the title
         page does indicate "Volume 1," this should
         be a clue that there is at least more than
         one volume.)

410. A: Title and subtitle: Ulrich's International
         Periodicals Directory; a Classified Guide
         to a Selected List of Current Periodicals,
         United States and Foreign.
         Type of publication included: periodicals
         Time period covered: current
         Country of publication: International:
             United States, foreign
         Comprehensiveness: selected

411. A: Subtitle: A Classified guide... "Classified"
         may ring a bell from the examination of
         American Book Publishers Record (BPR)
         and the BPR Cumulative (see #92-99 and
         #163). "Classified" is also defined in the
         ALA Glossary (as part of "classified
         index"; "grouped under broad subjects").
         The subtitles for volumes 1 and 2, dividing
         the source by very broad subject breakdown
         into science and technology in one volume
         and humanities and social sciences in the
         second volume, might also give you a clue.
         Beyond this, the easiest and quickest method
         is to flip through the pages of the source it-
         self: subject headings at the top of the
         pages (i.e., agriculture, chemistry, engineer-

ing, etc.) should alert you to a subject
arrangement. You could also check the
introductory matter of the Winchell annotation, but in this case the arrangement is very
simple and should be obvious to you from the
source itself.

(Note: the use of the word "classified" may
seem to connote the use of some specific
subject classification scheme, such as the
Dewey Decimal Classification scheme which
was used in BPR. Here, in Ulrich's, there
is no reference to a specific scheme other
than the very broad separation of vols. 1
and 2; within this breakdown the subjects
are listed alphabetically, as for example
they were in Subject Guide to BIP. However, there is some grouping of minor subjects under a major heading--see "Hobbies,"
for example.)

412. A: Yes, in the volume for humanities and social
         sciences (vol. 2), under the heading "folk-
         lore" (under "F"), p. 754-6.

413. A: Yes, Journal of the Gypsy Lore Society.
         After finding the list dealing with folklore
         in the previous question, you look through
         that list till you find a title which seems to
         fit the requirements.

414. A: Semi-annually (s-a.). If you didn't know
         what "s-a." means, you should look for and
         expect to find a list of explanations for the
         abbreviations used in the sources--this is in
         the introductory material.

415. A: Particularly from an acquisitions point of
         view, to know how often to expect receipt of
         the issues so that they can be properly
         checked in. (In some libraries the reference
         department is responsible for handling of cur-
         rent issues of periodicals.) This is also im-
         portant from a reference point of view be-
         cause the frequency of publication will give
         you some clue to the currency of the ma-
         terial in the periodical (i.e., annual or
         even quarterly publication will not be as "up
         to date" as weekly, daily, or even monthly).

416. A: In volume 1: Contents, Key to Subjects,
         preface, introduction (how to use),
         acknowledgments, abbreviations (including
         those for indexing services, money symbols),
         foreign exchange conversion tables. The same
         in volume 2 plus a periodicals price index
         and a key to citation elements.

417. A: See the Key to Citation Elements in the
         introductory material of vol. 2 (see #416).
         Look at this carefully to see how extensive
         the information given can be.

418. A: Method A:
         (1) Look in the main body of vol. 2 under "K"
             for knitting and find nothing, so
         (2) refer back to the front matter to key to
             subjects and go through it to see what
             else knitting might be under and guess

"Hobbies--Needlework" (or maybe "Home Economics"?) and look under that classification for a title on knitting; or (and this is probably better), look in the index in the back of vol. 2 for knitting, which refers you to the broader heading of Hobbies--Needlework in the main body of the source.
Method B:
   Assume knitting would be too specific a subject classification to be found alphabetically in this source, and look directly in the index as in (2) above.
If you had trouble with this, then go on to #419 and #420.

419. A: Author and title; found usually in indexes. Possibly a more specific subject access than is found in the basic arrangement; this too is usually found in an index form.

420. A: No author access, since for this type of bibliographical record (listing of the periodical itself, not the specific articles within the periodical) an author access would not be significant.

   Title access and specific subject access is a single index in the back of each volume; the index in volume 2 is a combined index for both volumes, making it necessary to look only in one place.

   Now go back to #418 on knitting if you need further clarification by an example.

421. A: Look in the combined index to both volumes, in the back of volume 2, which tells you to see Aeronautics--Missiles and Space, /and leaves it to you to realize that Aeronautics would be in vol. 1. Missiles and Space is a sub-division under Aeronautics, and there are several UFO titles listed.

422. A: Look under the section "General periodicals" which is then subdivided by country of publication. You more or less have to figure this out for yourself since the introduction does not note it.

423. A: You would expect to find the information there since this information is included in Ulrich's citations (see #417), and you have a title index so you can look it up directly. (Without a title index, you could look under the subject heading of "libraries" and then through the list for this title, as you did for gypsy folklore in #413). If you are not sure whether the title would be in vol. 1 or 2, you would look in the "Combined" index in vol. 2, (under UNESCO at the beginning of the U's, not under Unesco). The index refers you to a specific page (the title is listed under "Library Periodicals"). The subscription price is $3.50 per year. How do you know this? By referring to the "Key to Citation Elements" which tells you that the price given is annual (per year) unless otherwise noted...), it can be ordered from the UNESCO Publication Center

in New York (address given), and it appears / comes out /is published bi-monthly (bi-m). (It also tells you that the periodical contains bibliographies and book reviews, and that it is indexed in Library Literature, Library Science Abstracts, and PAIS.)

424. A: Back volumes (or basic issues) are generally those volumes of a periodical rather than the current volume (or issues). A retrospective file would be a set of back volumes, or past /retrospective volumes of the periodical. (See #404).

   The Ulrich's citation gives you the beginning date--for the UNESCO Bulletin, it is 1947. That means that the periodical has been published since 1947. It does not tell you specifically how many volumes there would be (you can guess at one per year, but this is not always true), and it does not tell you that the periodical was published continuously during that time.

425. A: You could not assume that the titles did not exist. Is Ulrich's comprehensive? Does it claim to include all periodical titles? See subtitle: a selected list...

   Therefore if a periodical title is not listed in Ulrich's, it may be only because it was not included, not because it does not exist.

426. A: See introduction, "III. | Scope of Inclusion" (which defines a periodical--compare with your answer to #402) and notes policies in regard to U.S. government publications, as well as some specific inclusions and exclusions) and "IV. Selection Policies." This is called a selected list but it is actually quite broad in what it attempts to include; the main criteria for exclusion is the frequency of publication (i.e., within 5 days a week to twice a year).

427. A: A selected guide to Current Periodicals... Periodicals, although by definition intended to be "continued indefinitely," do have a way of stopping publication--or "ceasing" publication--for lack of financial support, lack of interest, lack of staff, change of interests, etc. The Saturday Evening Post is a well-known example of this. Every year there are hundreds of new periodicals which start publication and similarly hundreds which cease publication; some do not even last out their first year. Periodicals also "merge" with other already existing periodicals--again for financial or staffing reasons, or they change their titles (Saturday Review of Literature to Saturday Review, for example), or they suspend their publications temporarily (many European periodicals did this during the war periods), or they cease publication for a time and then start up again, sometimes continuing the volume numbering before they "ceased," sometimes starting new volume numbering or a new series of numbers, etc. All of which makes bibliographical searching and identifica-

cation of periodicals quite complex, and which makes library acquisitions /ordering / processing /handling /cataloging /use of periodicals equally complex. Note the list of "Cessations" in the back of Ulrich's, which also includes mergers, suspensions, changes of title, etc.

Here, currently means "currently appearing."

428. A: Ulrich's is a kind of Books in Print for periodicals, or perhaps more accurately BIP and Subject BIP together. Both are published by Bowker.

429. A: The title page of the 12th edition only shows the edition and the year, but the fact that the latest edition is 1967-68 at least shows that it is not an annual publication. You would hope to find this information about frequency of appearance and up-dating in the introductory matter (or in the Winchell annotation). The Preface to Vol. 1 doesn't tell you, but the Introduction to Vol. 2 (II. Timetable of publication) tells you that each volume is to be published in alternate years--which has not in fact been carried out--updated by annual supplements.

430. A: Yes, and a glance through the introductory matter and through the latest available supplement itself would show this to be true.

431. A: See #402, and #426.

432. A: No, they are published annually (once a year).

433. A: In the next title on your list: Irregular Serials and Annuals. You would probably also find them listed in PW Weekly Record and BPR, and in CBI, since annuals /yearbooks and other similar publications are often considered to fall into the category of "books," as well as "serials." When in doubt, check. (See #406).

434. A: The publisher is Bowker Company and this might tell you that the source would have some relation to Ulrich's Directory--the physical format is very similar also.

435. A: See #401. But a better idea of what constitutes a serial and how this differs from a periodical can be gotten from reading the Preface to Irregular Serials.

436. A: Irregular Serials and Annuals: an International directory.
Subtitle--A classified guide to current foreign and domestic serials, excepting periodicals issued more frequently than once a year.
Scope: Current, international (foreign and domestic)--same as Ulrich's; "Serials, excepting periodicals issued more frequently than once a year." ---Ulrich's scope: periodicals issued "more often than once a year."
Arrangement: Classified (subject arrangement, with--presumably--a title index)-- same as Ulrich's.

The main difference is in definition of the type of publication included, and even more specifically in the frequency of publication.

437. A: No, the defining factor is mutually exclusive. Basically, Irregular Serials includes those serials which have been excluded from Ulrich's on the basis of (1) the irregularity of their publication, and (2) the frequency of their publication--annual, once a year and less often.

438. A: Yes, since it was published as a complementary or companion volume to Ulrich's, and is arranged in basically the same manner.

439. A: The title in the index refers you to the page number; it is listed under "Education." It comes out annually and costs $20 for each annual volume. The publisher's name and address are given.

440. A: This title is listed in Irregular Serials under "History," then alphabetically under "I" for Indiana. Or the title is listed under "Indiana..." in the index which refers you to the page number. The series began publication in 1897, is published irregularly, the last part published was vol. 24, #3 in 1966, and the price per part varies. Publisher's name and address are also given.

441. A: The Preface (last paragraph) of the 1st, 1967, edition tells you that new editions are planned, probably biennially (every other year) with annual supplements. It would appear that, so far, this publishing schedule has not worked out.

442. A: Forthcoming Books.

443. A: Title and subtitle: The Standard Periodical Directory. The most complete guide to U.S. and Canadian periodicals..information on more than 50,000 periodicals.

Standard is limited to the U.S. & Canada; Ulrich's is international--all countries. Standard claims to be "most" complete, with 50,000 titles (as compared to 35,000 titles in Ulrich's)

444. A: The Preface to Standard indicates a broader definition of periodicals: "A regular frequency of at least once every two years," meaning it will overlap Ulrich's and will include some (annuals and bi-annuals, for example) but not all (only those with "regular" frequency) of the Irregular Serials.

445. A: The arrangement of both is by subject with title index. Standard's subject arrangement is alphabetical, with all subjects in one alphabet, not separated into science /technology vs. humanities /social sciences as in Ulrich's. Standard has a kind of a classification number for each subject heading, which looks like the Dewey Classification but isn't, and is apparently Standard's own numbering scheme.

446. A: In the Standard directory, UFO is in the index with reference to its own classification (181.1) rather than as part of a larger subject heading as in Ulrich's. The listings include most of those in Ulrich's but not the one published in France.

447. A: The arrangements are similar, the same basic information is given; the scope of Standard is broader than Ulrich's in some ways--i.e., inclusion of titles--but narrower in others-- i.e., exclusion of foreign titles.

448. A: No, the introduction (under III. Scope of Inclusion. 3. a.) specifically excludes newspapers published more often than five days a week, which would therefore cover most daily newspapers. Presumably newspapers with a less than daily publication--i.e., once or twice a week--would be included.

449. A: In the Ayer Directory, the next title on your list.

450. A: Full title: Ayer Directory; Newspapers, magazines and trade publications; a guide to publications printed and published in the United States and its Territories, the Dominion of Canada, Bermuda, the Republics of Panama and the Philippines; descriptions of the states, provinces, cities and towns in which they are published; classified lists; 70 maps.

451. A: The publisher is Ayer Press in Philadelphia, and is not one of the publishers you are familiar with through this manual so far, so this doesn't give you any handy clues to the source as you had with all the Bowker publications.

452. A: Neither the title page nor the introductory matter tells you, and you have to go to the Winchell annotation to find out that it comes out annually, and in fact has been coming out annually since 1880. You can guess from the date on the title page (i.e., 1970 Ayer Directory); if it were a biennial publication the date would probably be given as 1970-71; if it were less frequent than every other year, it would probably indicate an "edition" rather than a date (as in Ulrich's).

453. A: Since it includes newspapers, magazines, and trade publications (see subtitle) it will include things which are also in Ulrich's and some-- primarily newspapers--which are not. Its scope for type of publication included is therefore broader.

454. A: Ulrich's is international in scope; Ayer is basically U.S. and Canada (like the Standard directory). Therefore its scope for place of publication is narrower than Ulrich's.

455. A: The basic arrangement is geographical-- titles are listed under the name of the state and then city in which they are published; the states are listed alphabetically and the cities are listed alphabetically, within the state. You have not previously examined through this manual any source with this type of arrangement.

456. A: Yes, there is an alphabetical index of titles (except for newspapers).

457. A: There are some subject lists (called "Classified lists") in Ayer's--see the Table of Contents. You can look up certain things by subject. You could not, however, look up UFO's, or folklore, or knitting.

458. A: Yes--see the classified list, "Foreign Language Publications."

459. A: There is no daily newspaper in Oxford, Nebraska. Look under Nebraska, then Oxford, then for a publication which comes out daily. There is one newspaper in Oxford (as of 1970), published only on Thursdays. The subscription price (presumably annually) is $3.50. The population of Oxford is 1,090 (as of 1970).

460. A: Look first under Missouri, then St. Louis, then Post Dispatch. It is published evenings except Sunday and Sunday mornings. The local subscription price is $22.50 per year (presumably then plus postage if it were to be mailed out of town), and the address of the publisher is given. Since it is a newspaper, it would not be included in the title index, and presumably then could be located only through the geographical location.

461. A: You could get this information by counting all the daily newspapers listed under Tennessee, but a more direct way is to look at the list of "Tennessee newspaper and periodical statistics" following the general information on Tennessee at the beginning of that section.

462. A: Ayer's includes "descriptions of the states, provinces, cities and towns in which they (i.e., the publications) are published" (see subtitle) including a fantastic amount of statistics and information on population, income, employment, manufacturing, agriculture, marketing, etc. (See Table of Contents.) Also maps, and airline and railway information. All of this information--besides being a bonus to librarians--is of value to potential advertisers, developers, marketing surveys, etc.

463. A: As in the past, the first place to look for this type of information would be in Winchell's Guide to Reference Books. Similar sources to Ayer's would be found in the same section in which Ayer's is listed and annotated. Two publications giving extensive coverage of newspapers as well as related general statistical information are Editor and Publisher International Yearbook (AF14) and Working Press of the Nation (AF19).

464. A: You have been looking at these sources--
          Ulrich's, Irregular Serials, Standard,
          Ayer's--as if they existed only in the most
          current editions; in fact, both Ulrich's and
          Ayer's have been published for some time--
          Ulrich's more or less regularly every two
          or three years since 1932; Ayer's annually
          since 1880. In their earlier editions, they
          are rich sources for information on peri-
          odicals and newspapers no longer published,
          and many libraries do keep back files of
          Ulrich's and Ayer's.

Section 6

Bibliographic Sources for Serials--Union Lists

Questions #465-511

465.   Besides basic bibliographical identification both current and retrospective, ordering information for ac-
quisition, and subject control, what other type of information do we need for full bibliographic control?
(Think back to the kinds of information provided in other sources you have examined, particularly in the
LC/NUC series and to some extent in the retrospective sources for books.)

466.   Location of copies tends to be even more important for serials than for books.   Why would this be?

The next set of sources to examine provides both location of copies and bibliographic information; retrospective and current:

            Union List of Serials (3rd ed.) (AF98)
            New Serials Titles (AF99)
            NST Classed Subject Arrangement (AF100)
            Subject Index to NST (2AF4)
            Gregory: American Newspapers...A Union List (AF5)
            Brigham: History and Bibliography of American Newspapers (AG8)

467.   With this set it is easiest to begin with a retrospective source.   The first title on the list is the Union
List of Serials.   What is a union list?

468.   What is the basic bibliographical information about this first source, Union List of Serials (ULS)?

469.   What introductory material is contained in the first volume of this source?

470.   What does the title tell you about the scope of this source?   Are there any limiting factors indicated in
the title?

471.   Does the phrase "in libraries of the United States and Canada" in the title mean that the ULS would include only those serials published in the U.S. and Canada?

472.   Would you say then that the scope of the ULS is international?

473.   Are all serial publications included in ULS?   Are there any exceptions or exclusions?

474.   How does the scope compare with Ulrich's?   Think in terms of definitions and policies for types of publications to be included.   (Refer back to #426 on Ulrich's if necessary.)

475.   Look through the volumes at several of the entries. What information is given in the entries? Is full bibliographical information given? How does this compare to what was given in Ulrich's?

476.   Look up in ULS the title <u>Biochemical Bulletin</u>. What information can you find out about it?

477.   What is the arrangement of ULS?

478.   Is there any subject access to the ULS?

479.   Look up in ULS the title <u>American Ski Annual</u>. When did this series begin publication? What is the frequency of publication? Is it still being published?

480.   How can you find out if it is still being published?

481.   When was the Union List of Serials published? (See #468) Is there a limitation by date on the publications included? Will there be another edition? How will it be kept up to date?

482.   Locate New Serials Titles on the shelves. Look carefully at its physical format, keeping in mind that the purpose of NST is to serve as a current supplement to ULS. Basically, the source is similar in format to other current sources you have examined previously. What does it remind you of?

483.   What is the basic bibliographical information about New Serials Titles? (Look in one of the recent issues).

484.   Can you tell, in a general way, what the cumulation pattern is for NST?

485.   Did the LC/NUC catalogs ever include library holdings/locations for serials/periodicals? What is the relation of New Serials Titles to the National Union Catalog?

486.   What is the scope of NST? What type of publications are included? What are the limitations, if any, for inclusion? What type of bibliographical information is given for each entry?

487.   Is there any indication of subject given in the individual entries in NST itself?

488.   A periodical called <u>Karate-Do</u> is put out by the All American Karate Federation, and it began publication recently. Where is it published, when did it begin publication, and from what library could you borrow the first issues? Does this mean that that library is the only library holding copies of this periodical?

489.   What then is the arrangement of NST?

490.   Is there any subject access to the ULS? Is there any subject access to NST?

491.   What are at least two sources in which you could find some titles of currently-appearing periodicals on the subject of linguistics?

492.   Specifically, what is the NST Classed Subject Arrangement? What is its relation to the NST? What is its usefulness?

493.   Does the NST Classed Subject Arrangement cumulate, as the NST itself does? Suppose you wanted to find titles of periodicals on the subject of linguistics which had begun publication in the past 15 or 20 years. Could you do this through the NST Classed Subject Arrangement? Could you do it through anything else?

494.   What is the scope of the Subject Index to New Serial Titles 1950-65? What is its basic arrangement?

495.   Would you expect the Subject Index to NST to continue beyond the 1965 date?

496.   What would be the primary usefulness of ULS and NST from a reference point of view?

497.   Does the Union List of Serials include newspapers? Does New Serials Titles include newspapers?

498.   Where would you go then for bibliographical information and for library locations on newspapers (primarily American, since you are basically concerned with U.S. bibliographic records)?

499.   Locate both Gregory's American Newspapers and Brigham's History and Bibliography and examine both together. How does the scope differ between the two publications?

500.   Compare the arrangement of Gregory and Brigham. Are they similar? Are they similar in arrangement to ULS and NST?

501.   Can you locate items in Gregory or Brigham if you know only the titles?

502.   Would you expect to find listed in Brigham newspapers which might have been published in Hawaii in 1800, or in California in the 1780's?

503.   Who was the printer of a daily newspaper called "Porcupine's Gazette," published in Pennsylvania and New York City at the end of the 16th century?

504.   Gregory and Brigham provide a union list for newspapers only through 1936. Where would you look to see if any more current such bibliographical sources exist? What can you find that might serve the purpose?

505.   For purposes of reviewing the bibliographical source for serials--current lists, bibliographies, directories; and union lists--you have examined so far, go over the sources in this section and the preceding section and make a rough chart of the coverage/scope (dates, type of publications, kinds of information) and access/arrangement for these sources, as you did at the beginning of Section 3 for the major bibliographical sources. Use this chart, then, as a basis for answering the following review questions.

505.   "Heraldica; revue d'histoire nobiliaire et de documentation" was published in Paris beginning in 1911. Where would you go to find out when it ceased publication and how many volumes make up a complete set?

506.   Where would you look to find price and publisher for the magazine titled Environment?

507.   You need to find some specific information about the various editors of "The Boston News-Letter" which was published until the time of the American Revolution. You are also concerned about possible changes in title, and you would like to examine some of the actual issues, but your library does not have any holdings of it. Where would you look to find all of this information?

508.   Where would you look to find the beginning date of the periodical "Education and Psychology," published in Delhi, India? (You don't know if it is being published currently.)

509.   If you wanted to find some periodicals on the subject of business administration, where would you look?

510.   Where would you look to find information about the daily newspaper in Sacramento, California?

511.   Suppose you wanted to look at, borrow, or in some way get copies of some issues of a newspaper published in Sacramento, California, in the early 1900's?

Section 6

Bibliographic Sources for Serials--Union Lists

Answers #465-511

465. A: Location of copies (see #253).

466. A: Back volumes of serials are often harder to
get than out of print books, and are in many
ways more costly to acquire, process, and
handle.
For libraries serving research needs, peri-
odicals--especially back volumes--are a source
of basic research information, frequently more
important than books.

467. A: See #363 or see the ALA Glossary. An excellent short discussion of union lists and
their uses, particularly for periodicals, is
given in Winchell, p. 141 (8th ed.), preceding
the information on specific union lists for U.S.
periodicals.

468. A: Full title: Union list of Serials in libraries
of the United States and Canada.
Publisher: Wilson Co. in New York
Edition: 3rd
Publication date: 1965
Number of volumes: 5

469. A: The title page is preceded by (1) list of cooperating libraries and their symbols and
(2) explanations. Following the title pages
comes (3) Preface, (4) Introduction, and
(5) Sample Entries.

470. A: "Union list" tells you that it will include
information on library holdings. One limiting
factor indicated in the title is that the type
of publication is limited to serials. The
only other limiting factor in the title is "in
libraries of the United States and Canada."

471. A: No, it means it includes serials in the collections of/held by/contained in "libraries
of the United States and Canada." It would
not list serials unless they were held by
one of the cooperating libraries. (Furthermore, it does not list serials unless they
are reported to ULS by one of the cooperating libraries.) Presumably many libraries
in the U.S. and Canada would contain serials
published in countries all over the world.

472. A: In regard to the publications listed in it,
yes, it is international in scope. In regard
to the libraries whose holdings are indicated,
no, it is limited to U.S. and Canada.

473. A: See Introduction, a very specific list of
"Classes of Serials Generally Excluded."

474. A: Both are international in scope. Ulrich's
includes only periodicals with publication frequency of less than one year; ULS, even with

its list of exclusions, still includes a wider
range of serial publications than Ulrich's.
Ulrich's includes only current periodicals;
ULS includes both current (as of its publication in 1965) and retrospective or ceased
serials.

475. A: Title is always given, place of publication
is usually given, publisher or issuing organization is sometimes given. Beginning
date of publication is usually given, and
ending date if publication has ceased.
Changes of title are usually indicated, as
well as whether the periodical merged,
suspended, ceased, etc. Location symbols
are given for cooperating libraries who report holdings of the title. Current ordering
information (price, address of publisher,
frequency of publication) is not given. In
fact, there is no sure way of telling from
ULS whether or not a publication is still
being published. (See "Sample Entries" in
the introductory material.)

476. A: In volume 1, under B. Published by the
Biochemical Association of Columbia University. Published in New York. The
series has ceased publication in 1916("//"
indicates ceased publication, see "Sample
Entries"). The entire set consists of volume 1-5 (parts or issues continuously numbered no. 1-21), published Sept. 1911-May
1916. Part or issue no. 16 was never published. (You can guess from the number of
issues indicated and the approximate way
they might be spread over the 5-6 years of
publication, that it was probably issued
quarterly.) Copies are held by Stanford
College Libraries, Stanford in California
(CST), etc.

477. A: You already had to figure this out to locate
the answer to #476, and in fact you may
have done it without being aware of it. The
arrangement is alphabetical by title. As in
Ulrich's (see #420) there is no need for
author entries.

478. A: No, except what you might accidentally get
through title (see #218-20).

479. A: American Ski Annual began publication in
1928. You can guess from the title that
the frequency of publication is annually. The
ULS entry does not show that it has ceased
publication.

480. A: You can check in Ulrich's for current information. Since this title is presumably
an annual, however, you should check first

or also in Irregular Serials. You could try also in Ayer's under the place (Vermont, Brattleboro). Since the organization responsible for publication (United States Eastern Amateur Ski Association; presumably later called the National Ski Association?) is given in ULS, you could write to that organization for information. (Eventually you will examine sources which will give you addresses, etc., for organizations.)

481. A: Third edition, 1965 (title page of source). Covers publications begun up to December 1949, i.e., before 1950 (introduction and Winchell annotation). This will be the last edition and it will be kept up to date by New Serials Titles (introduction and Winchell annotation), the next title on your list.

482. A: It should most specifically remind you of the LC/NUC series. It might also remind you of CBI. NST has several bound cumulated volumes, plus current (this year, perhaps still last year) issues.

483. A: Full title: New Serials Titles; A Union List of Serials Commencing Publication after December 31, 1949.... Supplement to the Union List of Serials, Third Edition. Published by: The Library of Congress, Washington, D.C. (Third Edition on the title page may look as if it refers to NST, but actually it is a continuation of the reference on the previous line: ULS, 3rd edition.) Date of publication: 1950 and (to date).

484. A: 1950-60 (10 year cumulation) in two volumes, followed by 1961-65 (5-year cumulation) in two volumes (published by Bowker), followed by 1966-68 (3-year cumulation) The current pattern, as indicated in the Preface to recent issues, is 8 monthly issues, plus quarterly cumulations, plus an annual cumulated volume, following that of NUC.

485. A: See the Preface in a recent NST issue. LC had previously issued Serial Titles Newly Received, a list of periodical titles received by the LC, serving as a serial supplement to the LC Catalog of Printed Cards. In 1953, this list was superseded by New Serials Titles, which included serial listings for LC and for cooperating libraries, as a supplement to ULS. The NUC catalogs (see #391) do not include entries and library holdings for serials, only catalog cards for those titles cataloged by the Library of Congress. Thus NST serves also as a supplement to NUC for serials.

486. A: Information given would be the same as ULS (see #472, 473, 475). Because NST is an ongoing publication, you can expect some changes from time to time--usually increases in the coverage or scope. The "Introduction" in recent issues of NST will give you the current coverage. A primary limiting factor is that publications included must have begun publication after 1949. Unlike ULS, NST sometimes but not always includes ordering information (frequency, address of publisher, price) for U.S. publications, especially for more recent issues.

487. A: Yes, see Dewey Decimal classification numbers above and to the right of the entries (see Introduction, "Subject Classification").

488. A: Look in NST--beginning either with 1950 and working to date or with the most recent issue and working back. In the 1966-68 cumulation, the title is shown, published in Los Angeles, beginning in 1967, and the University of Illinois (IU) has copies from no. 1. The University of Illinois library is not the only library to hold copies--it is the only library, at that point, to report holdings. (As with NUC, see #385.) Later reports of holdings may appear in later issues, and if you started with the most recent issue and worked back, you might have found these before you came to the first listing.

489. A: Alphabetically by title, same as ULS. A special section in some issues shows "Changes in Title," with various kinds of changes noted as in a similar list in Ulrich's (see #427).

490. A: No subject access to ULS (see #478). Yes, through the New Serials Titles Classed Subject Arrangement.

491. A: In Ulrich's (also in the Standard Directory). In recent (i.e., this year, possibly last year) issues of NST Classed Subject Arrangement.

492. A: The Classed Subject Arrangement is simply another printout of the entries from NST, arranged according to the Dewey Decimal classification numbers above and to the right of the entries (see #487), thus forming a classified (or classed) subject arrangement of the list, allowing users to see quickly what periodicals are being published on certain subjects rather than searching through an entire NST issue looking at class numbers in each entry.

493. A: NST Classed Subject Arrangement itself appears only monthly with no cumulation. If you wanted to go through 12 issues per year, and if your library had kept all the back issues, you could find that list of linguistic periodicals in the Classed Subject Arrangement, but only back to 1955 when the Classed Subject Arrangement began.

    You could also find it in the Subject Index to New Serial Titles 1950-65, the next title on the list.

    (You could also find some in Ulrich's by checking beginning dates of all linguistic periodicals listed there, but this would be very tedious.)

494. A: The scope of the Subject Index to NST is the same as NST itself, to which it is an index. The arrangement is classed, by Dewey Decimal Classification (as is the Classed Subject Arrangement to the NST). The Subject Index, however, is purely an index, listing Dewey class numbers followed by item numbers referring you back to the NST publication itself. For example, to find linguistics, look in "Table of Contents Second Summary Division," p. vii, finding "Comparative linguistics" listed as 410 (under Language 400.) Look in the main body of the volume under 410, Comparative linguistics. Each 410 listed is followed by an item number referring you back to the NST for titles and bibliographical information.

495. A: The introduction states that the publishers will consider compiling additional subject indexes as further cumulations of NST appear.

496. A: For inter-library loan (locating libraries with copies of back volumes of specific titles) and for general bibliographical identification.

497. A: Since newspapers are generally defined as serials, you would expect so, but in fact newspapers have been entirely excluded from NST (see Introduction) and generally from ULS (see Winchell annotation of ULS Introduction).

498. A: To the next two titles on your list, Gregory's American Newspapers, 1821-1936; a Union List...and Brigham's History and Bibliography of American Newspapers, 1690-1820.

499. A: Basically by date. Brigham covers 1690-1820 and Gregory covers 1821-1936. Both cover newspapers. Both give basic bibliographical information; Brigham gives considerably more historical and bibliographical information. Both give library locations.

500. A: Both Gregory and Brigham are arranged geographically--by state alphabetically, by cities alphabetically within states, by title of the newspaper alphabetically within the city of publication. This is similar to Ayer's. Both ULS and NST were arranged alphabetically by title.

501. A: In Brigham, yes, since there is a title index. In Gregory, no. There is no title index.

502. A: No. Brigham goes to 1820, but includes only American newspapers of that time period--i.e., newspapers which were published in what was then the United States. Neither California nor Hawaii were states in 1820.

503. A: The time period is covered by Brigham. Brigham is arranged by place of publication. with title and printer index. You don't know the printer yet so you can't use that. You know the place but only generally (Pennsylvania and New York) so it is easier to use

the title index. There are several listings with that title or a similar one; take any and look under the place indicated; (Pennsylvania is in volume 2, as is the index), so looking there first, you find under Philadelphia, a listing for the "Porcupine's Gazette" and the information that the printer was William Cobbett.

504. A: Go to Winchell. (Section AG on Newspapers, look under "Bibliographies and Union Lists.") In fact, there are no more current bibliographies or union lists; the closest approximation to such a source is Newspapers on Microfilm published by the Library of Congress (AG12), which is a union list of microfilms of newspapers to be found in libraries in the U.S. and Canada, and in its latest edition (6th) brings the information up to 1966. The extensive use of microfilm to preserve old newspapers, and the growing use of microfilm in inter-library loan has made this union list of microfilms a more currently useful source.

505. A: Union List of Serials. This is international in scope, therefore would include French (Paris) publications. So would NST but that covers serials beginning only after 1949. Since it has presumably ceased publication, it would not be in Ulrich's.

506. A: Ulrich's (or Standard). You want ordering information; this is given in Ulrich's. It is also given in NST (see #486) but not consistently. The primary purpose of Ulrich's is to give such current ordering information; the primary purpose of NST is to list new titles and give library locations. (And you are assuming, of course, that the magazine is currently published.)

507. A: In Brigham. "News-Letter" implies perhaps a newspaper, and Brigham includes newspapers and covers the time period. You want library locations, and Brigham gives this information. You also want information about editors and title changes, and this means you would need the kind of extensive discussion given in Brigham.

508. A: Since you do not know the beginning date, you would probably start with ULS and work through NST from 1950 to the current issue until you found it. You could also check Ulrich's, since beginning dates are given there, but it would be listed there only if it is currently published.

509. A: You need subject access, and you have therefore only Ulrich's (or Standard) and NST. Ulrich's is the easiest and most direct to use, and you would certainly find a large number of periodicals on that subject listed there.

510. A: Newspaper and current--Ayer's. (Ulrich's, Standard, and Irregular Serials do not

cover newspapers.)

511. A: Since you want to locate copies, you want
          a union list.   ULS/NST do not generally
          include newspapers.   Gregory does, and
          covers this time period.   Newspapers on
          Microfilm (see answer #504) would also be
          a possibility, to get or locate microfilm
          copy.

Section 7

Indexes to Serials--Indexing Services

Questions #512-611

So far the bibliographical sources you have examined for serials /periodicals /newspapers have been lists or directories for only the titles of the serials. One of the distinguishing features about most serials (periodicals and newspapers) is that they consist of a number of different articles, by different authors, which are basically separate entities brought together in one publication (see #403). In order to have complete bibliographic control, we need also to have some sort of analytic access to these individual articles or items published within a larger publication.

This brings us to the next set of sources to examine--indexes to serials:

> Readers' Guide to Periodical Literature (AF122)
> Abridged Readers' Guide
> Social Science and Humanities Index (AF124)
> Public Affairs Information Service Bulletin (PAIS) (CA22)
>
> Kujoth: Subject Guide to Periodical Indexes
> Poole's Index to Periodical Literature (AF119)
> --Date and volume Key (AF120)
> Nineteenth Century Readers' Guide
> Wellesley Index to Victorial Periodicals
>
> New York Times Index (AG32 and 2AG9)

512. How do you define the word "index?"

We can say that basically we have two types of "indexes" to deal with:

those which appear within a publication--i.e., an index in the back of a book, or in a set of books such as an encyclopedia, or in an issue or volume of a periodical. These indexes are an integral part of the publication itself and index, or refer to, material only within that specific publication of which they are a part. In a sense, you have been dealing with this type of index all along in the various bibliographical sources--for example, an author /title index to a source which is arranged by subject (BPR, Ulrich's) or chronologically (Evans), or geographically (Brigham).

those which appear separately from the publication or publications which they index, and which themselves form a specific publication. Generally these indexes are in periodical form, appearing at regular intervals. Those which appear currently and regularly are usually referred to as "indexing services" (or "indexing and abstracting services" if they abstract the material as well as index it).

513. Begin by looking at a source with which you may already have some familiarity, the Readers' Guide to Periodical Literature. This is an example of a current indexing service. As such you can expect that, like many of the bibliographical sources you have already examined, it is published on an on-going periodical basis, at regular intervals, and presumably has been coming out for some time; therefore you should be prepared to think in terms of a large number of volumes and parts with possible cumulation patterns, as you have had in so many of the bibliographical sources you have already examined (CB1, LC /NUC, NST, etc.)
     Look first at one of the most recent issues. What is the full title of the source?

514. What does this tell you about its scope? What limitations are there to its coverage? Is it limited to a certain type of publication? Is it international or more limited by country of publication? Is it comprehensive or selective?

515.   Readers' Guide is an index to a "selected" list of U.S. periodicals.   What is the basis for selection?
       Where would you expect to find a full statement of the basis for selection?

516.   Specifically, by title, what periodicals are indexed in Readers' Guide?   Approximately how many?

517.   Is the periodical Physics Today indexed in the Readers' Guide?   What does this tell you about Physics
       Today?

518.   Does the Readers' Guide index any periodicals published by the government (federal, state, local, inter-
       national)?

519.   Who publishes Readers' Guide and does this fact tell you anything?

520.   Can you think of two primary distinguishing features of CBI, in regard to its arrangement?

521.   How frequently is the Readers' Guide published, currently?   Can you tell quickly what the general cumu-
       lation pattern is?

522.   When did the Readers' Guide begin publication?   (Because you are dealing with a long and rather complex
       set, you might find it easiest to go first to the Winchell entry and annotation, and then check this against
       the set you are examining.)

523.   In the dictionary arrangement of CBI, all authors, titles, and subjects were included in one alphabetical
       listing.   Is this exactly the same in the Readers' Guide?   Does Readers' Guide have all three of these
       accesses?

524.   Are there any title entries at all in Readers' Guide?

525.   If, however, you were searching in the index for a specific article, and you did remember only the title
       and not the author, could you still find it?

526.   Are there cross-references in the Readers' Guide?

527.   Are there any indexes within the Readers' Guide?   Do you need any?   Why or why not?

528.   Using the March 1969-February 1970 annual cumulation, find a citation for an article on the teaching of
       ecology.   Where would you find the article itself--that is, in what specific periodical issues would you
       find the article?

529.   Why is it important to know the volume number for the periodical, if you have the exact date of the issue?

530.   Would you expect to find the article cited in #528 also in the Readers' Guide under the author?

531.   If you wanted to subscribe to Science News, where would you look for the ordering information? (Price, frequency of publication, name and address of publisher.)

532.   William F. Buckley wrote an article about Gore Vidal which appeared in Esquire Magazine recently. Can you find the title of it, and specific information about the issue in which it appeared? What about an article which Mr. Vidal wrote about Mr. Buckley?

533.   If you wanted to compile a short list (or bibliography) of the magazine articles written by Mr. Buckley, how would you go about it?

534.   How far back, retrospectively, would you need to search? Would searching through Readers' Guide give you a list of all the magazine articles Mr. Buckley had written?

535.   Can you find citations to articles which would give you some information on the problems of poor people living in the city, and specifically what was happening to them because their housing was being torn down and replaced?

536.   You could have found at least a dozen articles cited in Readers' Guide under the various headings given in the answer to #535. How would you know which of these would specifically deal with your topic, or which would be of most use to you?

537.   Suppose you wanted to find out also how this problem of displacement of the urban poor had been dealt with, if at all, in the 1920's and 1930's. Could you find information on this through Readers' Guide? Would you expect the subject headings to be the same?

538.   The full title to the Readers' Guide (see #513) is the Readers' Guide to Periodical Literature (Unabridged); an index to... This would lead you to suspect an abridged edition. Is there an Abridged Readers' Guide and what is its nature and use? Where would you look to find out?

539.   The Readers' Guide is relatively limited in the number of periodicals it indexes (160) but it is still one of the best known and most used of the periodical indexing services because of the general and popular nature of its scope. Another indexing service similarly general in nature is the Social Sciences and Humanities Index. Locate some recent issues of this source. What is its full title, and who is the publisher?

540.   Knowing that the Social Sciences and Humanities Index is a Wilson publication you can assume that it will have certain similarities to other Wilson publications (CBI, Readers' Guide) which you have already examined. The easiest and quickest way to familiarize yourself with the Social Sciences and Humanities Index is to compare it with the Readers' Guide. Presumably both indexing services would not have the same scope, as they are published by the same company. What is the scope of SSHI and how does it differ from the Readers' Guide?

541.   The Social Sciences and Humanities Index does not have as broad a scope or coverage as the Readers' Guide, in one sense, since it is limited to social science and humanities subjects, while RG covers

science also. Is there any difference in the scope or depth of coverage of social sciences and humanities between SSHI and RG?

542. How can you tell specifically what periodicals are indexed in SSHI? Who selects the periodicals to be indexed?

543. How is the Social Sciences and Humanities Index arranged?

544. What kind of subject headings are used? Is this the same as those used in Readers' Guide? In CBI? Can you remember any other source you have examined so far which used the same kind of subject headings?

545. What is the advantage of this use of the LC subject headings?

546. How frequently is the SSHI published and how frequently does it cumulate? How does this compare to Readers' Guide?

547. When did SSHI begin publication? Has it always been called the Social Sciences and Humanities Index?

548. Was there any difference in the scope or coverage of the International Index and the Social Sciences and Humanities Index? Probably the easiest way to answer this is to read the annotation for SSHI in Winchell.

549. If you were searching for material on the study of the stylistics of early Middle English prose, where would you look? Can you in fact find any such articles? Assume for purposes of limiting your search that such an article was published in late 1968.

550. Would you expect to find articles on urban renewal and ecology indexed in the Social Sciences and Humanities index?

551. The Social Sciences and Humanities Index does not include science and technology in depth (although RG does in a popular, non-technical way). Does the Wilson Company publish an indexing service which would complement SSHI in covering the sciences in a more specialized way? Where would you look to find this out?

552. The Wilson Company publishes several other indexing services which are even more specifically subject-oriented. These also can be located in Winchell, or by looking in the pamphlet "Cataloging and Indexing Services" put out by the Wilson Company, or in the Wilson Company publications catalog (in PTLA). Some examples are Education Index, Library Literature covering librarianship and related subjects, and Art Index. Some of these indexing services have a broader scope than just periodicals (as in RG and SSHI) and also index or list books, pamphlets, parts of books, etc., thus becoming true current subject bibliographies. How would you find out if such an indexing service covered material other than periodical articles?

553.   An example of an indexing service which does list books, pamphlets, etc., as well as articles in periodicals, is the Public Affairs Information Service Bulletin (PAIS). PAIS is limited to the social sciences, but is still very broad in its coverage. What is its full title, and what does this tell you about its scope?

554.   What is the arrangement of PAIS?

555.   Look through one of the recent larger cumulations at the subject headings. What ones do you note that would seem relevant to some of the current problems?

556.   Some of these headings were also in the Readers' Guide and in the Social Sciences and Humanities Index. What would you expect to find through PAIS that you would not find in the other indexes?

557.   Who publishes the PAIS Bulletin? What is the P.A.I.S. itself?

558.   The Wilson Indexing services are sold to libraries on the "service basis" method of charge. What is this method of charge?

559.   The Wilson Company is by no means the only publisher of indexing services, however. Many other indexing (or indexing and abstracting) services are available for specialized fields, and can be located through Winchell under the appropriate subject. None of the indexing services you have examined so far is an indexing/abstracting service. What is meant by an abstracting service? What is an abstract?

560.   Another source besides Winchell for locating indexing/abstracting services on a subject field is one of the titles on your list to examine: Subject Guide to Periodical Indexes and Review Indexes, by Jean Kujoth. Unlike most of the sources you have examined so far, this one is simply a book, in one volume, and a small one at that. If you wanted to locate an indexing service which would index periodicals or cite articles dealing with architecture, how would you find it through Kujoth? What can you find out about the index through Kujoth?

561.   How can you tell in which one of the several indexing services a periodical will be indexed? If you wanted some articles on the international aspect of librarianship, and you knew that such articles were published in the UNESCO Bulletin for Libraries, and you wanted to know which indexing services would cover this periodical, how would you find out?

562.   Like CBI, the Readers' Guide and the Social Sciences and Humanities Index are current sources which, in their earlier volumes, also serve as retrospective sources. How far back can you search in them retrospectively?

563.   You have coverage by the Wilson Company indexing services back to 1900. What do you have as retrospective sources for the 19th century or earlier?

564.   Look at Poole's Index first. Poole's Index is, now, entirely a retrospective index; it is no longer published. What is the basic bibliographic information about Poole's? What is its full title, how many volumes does it have, when was it published?

565 /   What are the dates of its <u>coverage</u> (as opposed to its publication)?   What are the dates of coverage for
566.   each volume in the set?

567.   What is the <u>scope</u> of Poole's Index? (You would normally expect to get this information from the
         preface or introductory material; the Preface to vol. 1 of Poole's is worth reading but is quite time-consum-
         ing. As with some of the retrospective bibliographies for books (Sabin, etc.), the prefaces in the various
         volumes of Poole's Index are in themselves a series of comments on the historical development of this
         form, on the need for periodical indexes, and on the early concepts of and problems of such indexing. How-
         ever, as a time-saving device at this point, you might most easily go directly to the Winchell annotation
         to find the scope of Poole's Index.)

568.   Is there a list in Poole's Index of the periodicals covered (as there was in Readers' Guide)? What intro-
         ductory material is given in Poole's?

569.   Does the arrangement of Poole's Index differ from that of the Readers' Guide? (Consider: does it have all
         the accesses you have with RG?)

570.   What kind of subject access does Poole's Index have? Does it appear to be the same as the Readers'
         Guide? Does it appear to use subject headings as does Readers' Guide?

571.   Refer back to #218-220 (re Roorbach and Kelly) on the use of titles as subject access. Poole's Index is
         <u>not</u> a title index, but a subject index. Have the titles been modified in any way to create a subject index?
         (Look, for example, at the entries under "indians" on pages 316-17 of the fifth supplement, 1902-1906.)

572.   How would you go about using Poole's to find articles written about the Indians in the nineteenth century?
         Would you have to look under other headings? Would you expect to find articles about, specifically, the
         Hopi Indians and the Navajo Indians all in the same place, or under other headings?

573.   Look specifically under Hopi Indians on p. 296 of the fifth supplement of Poole's Index, at the articles en-
         titled (presumably) "Sky-god personations in worship of Hopi Indians" (or possibly "Worship of Hopi Indians
         in Sky-god Personations" or even "Worship of Sky-god Personations in Hopi Indians"). Who is the author
         and where would you find the article? What is the <u>date</u> of the article?

574.   The information in the front of the fifth supplement to Poole's Index indicated that the Journal of American
         Folk-lore was published in Boston from 1902-1906 in five volumes, which seems unclear if 1902 is vol. 15.
         If you wanted to get more information about the Journal of American Folk-lore, when it actually did begin
         publication, etc., where would you look?

575.   If you wanted to find out if the Journal of American Folk-lore is still being published, currently, where
         would you look?

576.   Is there any other way to determine the volume dates in Poole's than checking through the "Chronological
         Conspectus?"

577.   If you wanted to make a list of the periodical articles written by Andrew Lang during the nineteenth cen-
         tury (as in #533 for William F. Buckley), could you do so through Poole's Index? What about Lord
         Macaulay?

578.   Are there any entries at all in Poole's Index for Lord Macauley?   What are they?

579.   If you were doing research on Robert Burns, the Scottish poet (1759-1796), would you find Poole's Index helpful?

580.   Look at the next retrospective source on your list, Nineteenth Century Readers' Guide.   What period does this source cover?   Who published it and when was it published?

581.   The Nineteenth Century Readers' Guide then covers some of the same period as Poole's Index, and was in fact published much after Poole's Index was in existence.   Why was this?   What was the point of the duplication?   How does the Nineteenth Century Readers' Guide differ from Poole?   (Read the Preface.)

582.   Look up the Fewkes article (from #573) in the Nineteenth Century Readers' Guide.   Look it up by subject, not author.   How does it contrast to Poole's Index?

583.   The Nineteenth Century Readers' Guide is a retrospective source which was published more or less currently (1944).   (According to the Preface, it was intended to continue it back through the entire nineteenth century, but this has not yet come to pass.)   It was published specifically to correct defects of an older source covering the same time period.   What other bibliographical sources does this remind you of?

584.   Are Poole's Index and the Nineteenth Century Readers' Guide the only periodical indexes we have for retrospective general subject coverage?

585.   Poole's Index, the Nineteenth Century Readers' Guide, and the Social Science and Humanities Index all cover English-language periodicals, thus including British periodicals as opposed to being limited to U.S. periodicals.   It is very typical of the periodical indexes and current indexing services to cover both the U.S. and Great Britain; this can be seen from the group heading in Winchell (Periodicals--Indexes-- United States and Great Britain), p. 145-47, for these sources.   The sources you have looked at so far have been published in the United States.   Would you assume that similar periodical indexes published in Great Britain would also cover American or U.S. periodicals?   Where would you look for such British indexes?   Are there any other retrospective sources with general (i.e., very broad subject) coverage of periodical articles?

586.   The Wellesley Index to Victorian Periodicals (1824-1900) is a retrospective source which is currently being compiled and published.   It will cover mainly British periodicals of that cultural period with a broad subject base.   The first volume was published in 1967.   This is not listed in the section of Winchell as noted in #584 and #585.   Where would you look to find more information on the source?   Where would you look to find if a second volume is due momentarily?

587.   Have the indexes and indexing services you have looked at so far covered newspapers?

588.   What are newspapers?   How do they differ from what has been generally referred to as "periodicals?"

589.   Think about a possible indexing service for newspapers, in comparison to the ones you have seen for periodicals.   Would you expect them to differ in any way?   Consider all of the basic, possible accesses you

could have to bibliographical sources. Do you need all of these for newspapers? What kind of access would you need for newspapers?

590. There are no indexing services for newspapers comparable to those for periodicals. In fact, there are very few newspaper indexes of any kind. Our primary newspaper index is that specifically to one of the best known, major U.S. newspapers, the New York Times. Look at the New York Times Index. Is it published continuously as the other indexes are? How often? Is it cumulated? How often?

591. Is there any introductory or prefatory material in the NY Times Index which tells you how to use it, what the abbreviations stand for, etc.?

592. Look through some recent issues of the New York Times Index. How does it differ from the other indexing services you have seen?

593. In the answer to the previous question, it was suggested that you look up in the 1969 volume to see how much information is given on the Apollo moon landing. How did you find it--that is, under what heading(s) was it listed?

594. Could you find out through the New York Times Index alone (that is, without going to a further source to which it leads you) who won the Nobel Peace Prize for the current year? And what he won it for?

595. In searching for the winner of the Nobel Peace Prize for the current year, you would presumably have to look under the appropriate subject heading in each of this year's issues (to a possible total of 24) until you found the specific item you were searching for. Is there any way you can think of to shorten this search?

596. Suppose you want some further information about the awarding of the prize to Dr. Bourlog, but your library does not subscribe to the New York Times so that you can look up the article referred to in the Index. What else can you do?

597. Can you tell if the New York Times Index uses standardized subject headings, such as those used in the Wilson indexes? Can you think of any limitations to the use of standardized subject headings in a newspaper index?

598. The NY Times Index has subject access only. Are there any names in the subject headings--i.e., names of persons, places, organizations, etc.? What about cross-references?

599. Can you find--through the New York Times Index only--the date on which the New York State abortion law went into effect? Can you find further information about what happened when the law went into effect?

600. How would you find access to contemporary accounts of the stock market crash preceding the "Great Depression" in 1929/30? Would you expect this to be in the NY Times Index? Would you expect to find it indexed under "Depression," or "Great Depression?"

601. What about contemporary accounts of the Civil War? Would you expect to find them indexed under "Civil War?"

602.   What other newspaper indexes are there in addition to the NY Times Index?

The following series of eight questions are <u>review</u> questions covering all of the bibliographic sources for serials. Before trying to answer them, you might make a chart of the sources covered in this unit-- indexes--to add to what you already have for directories and union lists (see #505).

603 /   You plan to subscribe to <u>Science and Children</u> for your school library. Where will you find out how many
604.   issues you should expect to receive each year?

605.   Where would you look to find recent critical articles on the novels of Iris Murdoch (contemporary English novelist)?

606.   A book titled <u>Travel While You Work</u>, by Joan Owens was published in England in 1963. Where can you find the name <u>of the publisher and price</u>? Where can you find out if it is still in print?

607.   You want to borrow on interlibrary loan some recent issues of the San Francisco Free Press, the Berkeley Barb, and the San Francisco Oracle. How would you find out which libraries have copies?

608.   Where would you look to find information on the oil spill off the coast of California in 1969?

609.   Where would you look to find out where <u>Time Magazine</u> is indexed?

610.   If you wanted "news" type information (details, dates, comments, figures, etc.) on the oil spill off the coast of California in 1969, and you were in a library which did not have the NY Times Index, where else could you look?

611.   Where would you look to find some recent publications on the formal theory of differentiation in organization?

Section 7

Indexes to Serials--Indexing Services

Answers #512-611

512. A: See the ALA Glossary or any dictionary. Basically, an index is a list of items (names, subjects, etc.) in a work or works, with reference (usually page numbers) to that work or works.

513. A: Readers' guide to periodical literature (un-abridged); an index to selected U.S. general and non-technical periodicals of reference value in libraries.

514. A: Limited to periodicals (more specifically, items within periodicals); limited to those published in the U.S.; "selected."

515. A: According to the title, "general and non-technical," "of reference value in librar-ies." A fuller statement should be found in the prefatory or front matter, and the "Policy Statement" in the front of the annual bound volumes does give an explanation of the general basis and philosophy of selec-tion.

516. A: A list is given in the front pages or front matter of the RG itself. All issues contain a list of "Abbreviations of periodicals in-dexed" and some issues contain also a fuller list of "periodicals indexed." Ap-proximately 150-160 periodicals.

517. A: Yes, it is indexed in RG. Look in the list of periodicals indexed in an annual cumula-tion. The fact that it is indexed in RG tells you that the periodical is considered to be of general interest, more or less on a popular level; that is, it is not a highly technical or highly specialized journal in the field of physics.

518. A: Yes. You can tell this by looking through the list of periodicals indexed, included in the front matter of recent issues. You will find, for example, American Education published by the United States Government Printing Office, Conservationist published by New York State, UN Monthly Chronicle published by the United Nations.

519. A: The publisher is the Wilson Company, which also publishes CBI, so you might therefore expect some similarities to that source.

520. A: The idea of cumulation (see #129-132) and the dictionary (author/title/subject in one alphabet) arrangement.

521. A: RG is published semi-monthly (twice a month). These issues cumulate quarterly

(in green covers), and then annually into a bound volume. (Until recently it also cumulated every two years, and earlier in a three, four, or five-year pattern.) You can find this information from looking at the titlepage covers of recent issues (dates are given in the upper right corner of the cover) and at the dates of coverage given on the spines of bound volumes; or by look-ing at the masthead (see #70) on the bottom of the first page of recent issues; or by checking the Winchell annotation.

522. A: Its coverage begins with 1900 (publication of the first cumulated volume was in 1905). There is also a Nineteenth Century Readers' Guide for 1800-1900+, which will be taken up later.

523. A: No, actually Readers' Guide is only an author/subject list--but it is still in a general dictionary arrangement, since all entries are in the same alphabet.

524. A: Yes, in a way--titles are listed for fiction (i.e., novels and short stories) and drama with a see reference to the author, under which full information will be found. (See "Suggestions for the use of the RG..." in the front of a recent issue.) In general, however, there is no real title access to Readers' Guide--probably because in search-ing for material from periodicals, one is far more apt to be searching by subject, or if searching for a specific item, to know the author than the title.

525. A: Yes, you could find it by looking under the subject--since presumably if you remembered the title, you would also remember the sub-ject.

526. A: Yes, from various forms of personal names and various forms of subject headings to the form of name or headings used in RG. Also titles of fiction and drama as noted in #524. (See "Suggestions..." in the front of a recent issue.) However, all of these cross-references do not appear in every is-sue, only in the issues in which they are significant, as in CBI (see #165).

527. A: There are no indexes; you don't need any; you already have the accesses you need (author/subject) in the main arrangement.

528. A: Searching by subject, you would look first under "ecology," then under that for the sub-heading "teaching." The citation is: Ecology in the classroom: uniting the

specialists.
   J. Potter. il Sci N 97:44-5 Ja 5'70
The periodical in which this article would
be found is Science News (look up Sci N
in the periodical abbreviations in the front)
on pages 44-5 at the January 5, 1970 issue,
which happens to be in volume 97. (See the
explanation for the sample entry in "Suggestions..." in the front.)

529. A: Because "back issues" of periodicals in li-
         braries are usually bound and marked by
         the volume.

530. A: Yes, you would.

531. A: In Ulrich's International Periodical Directory,
         or in Readers' Guide itself (see List of Peri-
         odicals indexed in front).

532. A: The title of Mr. Buckley's article is "On Exper-
         iencing Gore Vidal" and it appeared in the
         August 1969 issue of Esquire, page 108-113
         and following (volume 72). This is indexed
         in the 69/70 annual cumulation of Readers'
         Guide. You could have found it by looking
         under Buckley as the author or Vidal as the
         subject. Mr. Vidal's article is "A Distaste-
         ful Encounter with William F. Buckley, Jr.,"
         in the September 1969 issue of Esquire, and
         similarly it would be found under either
         Buckley as subject or Vidal as author, so
         that whichever way you looked you should
         have found both articles together.

533. A: Search through issues and cumulations of
         Readers' Guide, under Buckley as author,
         noting down what you find, cited, or indexed,
         there.

534. A: How far back retrospectively you would need
         to search would depend on the purpose of
         your list. If you just wanted recent articles,
         then you could decide your own cut-off date
         of 1960 or 1965, etc. If you wanted a
         comprehensive, complete listing, then you
         would have to go as far back as Mr. Buckley
         was presumably capable of writing articles,
         which would in any case not be any earlier
         than the date of his birth. However, if you
         wanted a comprehensive list--a list of all
         the magazine articles Mr. Buckley had
         written--then you would find in Readers'
         Guide only the articles in those magazines
         indexed by Readers' Guide. You would need
         then to cover other sources as well.

535. A: The problem here is what subject headings
         to look under, and there are several pos-
         sibilities. "City" or "urban" would be a
         good start. Remember that RG will give
         some cross-references but not in every issue.

         The 69/70 bound cumulation cites articles
         under "city and town life" (with a cross-
         reference from "urban life"), under "urban
         renewal," under "housing" (with a cross-
         reference from "urban housing"). Another
         possibility is "poor" which cites more articles

plus referring you to see also entries under
the headings "poverty," "public welfare,"
"slums," etc. Some of the citations will
probably be duplicated under some of the
headings.

536. A: You could jot all of the citations down and
         search them all out in the library's collec-
         tions (assuming the library had all the peri-
         odicals cited), and judge each for itself by
         looking at it. You could also make an edu-
         cated guess at their usefulness from the
         titles of the articles and to some extent from
         the periodicals in which they appear.

537. A: You could search back in RG as far as 1900,
         since RG does go back that far. Subject
         headings always have a tendency to change
         as our language changes and as the sig-
         nificance of subjects themselves change.
         In the January 1929-June 1932 bound cumu-
         lation of RG, there are many citations under
         "housing," nothing under "urban renewal,"
         for example.

538. A: One of the most direct places to look is in
         Winchell--item AF123, directly following the
         annotation for the Readers' Guide itself. The
         Abridged Readers' Guide is simply what it
         implies--an abridged edition covering only
         about one-third of the periodicals indexed
         in the unabridged edition, issued only once
         a month, cumulating only once annually, for
         libraries which cannot afford the larger
         service.

539. A: Social Sciences and Humanities Index (no
         sub-title), published by the Wilson Company.

540. A: Both are limited to periodicals (i.e.,
         articles within). SSHI limited to social
         sciences and humanities (RG includes also
         science and technology). SSHI includes
         English-language periodicals, both U.S. and
         British (RG includes U.S. publications only).
         SSHI covers approximately 200 periodicals
         (RG covers 160).

541. A: SSHI indexes periodicals which deal with those
         subject areas in more depth; more scholarly,
         more specialized, as compared to the popu-
         lar level of the periodicals indexed in RG.

542. A: As in RG, the periodicals indexed are listed
         in the front (List of Periodicals Indexed),
         giving also the ordering information. And
         also as in RG, a committee of users selects
         the periodicals to be indexed (see Policy
         Statement).

543. A: Like the Readers' Guide: author and subject
         in one alphabet, some cross-references.
         (See Policy Statement in front of a recent
         issue).

544. A: The subject headings used follow those used
         by the Library of Congress (see Policy State-
         ment in front of a recent issue). Neither
         Readers' Guide nor CBI stated specifically

that they used LC headings, but one would assume they would be similar. The Subject Guide to Books in Print also used LC subject headings (see #52). And of course, the LC Subject Catalog itself (see #382) would use LC subject headings.

545. A: See answer to #53. It is a familiar and standardized list, and there will be some consistency of headings with those used in library card catalogs and in other bibliographical sources.

546. A: SSHI is published quarterly (every three months) as compared to semi-monthly (twice a month) for the Readers' Guide. See masthead statement on Policy Statement page of front matter in a recent issue. SSHI cumulates annually (as does RG).

547. A: SSHI was formerly titled the International Index and began publication in 1916; the title was changed to Social Sciences and Humanities Index in 1965.

548. A: Coverage has varied over the years as titles have been added and dropped. Earlier years of the International Index included some foreign (i.e., non-English) periodicals, and also some scientific periodicals.

549. A: Because this seems more of a scholarly nature than a popular nature, SSHI would probably be better than RG. Late 1968 would take you to the April 1968/March 1969 cumulation. The problem is finding the correct subject heading. Looking under "Middle English," you are directed to see "English language." Looking under "English language," then the subhead "Middle English," then the sub-subhead "style," you find listed an article titled "Early Middle English prose: three essays in stylistics," by C. Clark, published in Essays Crit (Essays in Criticism), October 1968, vol. 18, pages 361-82.

550. A: You could find material on those subjects through both the SSHI and RG, but the articles found through SSHI would be, perhaps, of a more technical, more specialized nature than those you would find through RG.

551. A: You would need to look in Winchell for this, and you would have to turn to the section for sciences (E. Pure and Applied Sciences), then under General Works (EA, p. 526), then to the section for "Indexes and Abstract Journals" (p. 531), where you would find the Applied Science and Technology Index (EA63) published by the Wilson Company.

552. A: The simplest way is to look through one of the issues, if available, to see if entries are included for books, etc. Or read the prefatory statement or policy statement in the front of one of the recent issues. Or read the annotation in Winchell (but be sure it is currently applicable). Or read the

annotation for the service in "Cataloging and Indexing Services."

553. A: The full title (from the title page--or cover page--of recent issues of the source itself): Public Affairs Information Service Bulletin; a selective subject list of the latest books, pamphlets, government publications, reports of public and private agencies and periodical articles, relating to economic and social conditions, public administration and international relations, published in English throughout the world.

554. A: Subject access only, alphabetically by subject headings. Neither PAIS nor the Winchell annotation indicate whether a specific subject heading list (e.g., LC) is followed, but presumably it would be related at least to some standard form such as the LC list.

555. A: Abortion, city planning, civil rights, consumer credit, ecology, housing, poverty, school lunches, taxation, urbanization, Vietnamese conflict, women (May 2, 1970 cumulation).

556. A: PAIS would include books, pamphlets, and government publications (other than periodicals). For example, in the May 2, 1970 cumulation under Poverty--United States, there is listed a periodical article from Public Policy, a Rand Corporation report on an analysis of poverty, a U.S. Dept. of Agriculture publication (for 25¢) on rural Indians in poverty, and a U.S. Senate committee report on poverty and malnutrition in the United States.

557. A: The publisher is the Public Affairs Information Service, Inc., a non-profit association of libraries (see verso of title page, or cover page).

558. A: It means that the library pays according to the indexing it actually uses; for example, for the Readers' Guide, the library pays according to how many of the indexed periodicals it subscribes to. "Service basis" is defined briefly in the ALA Glossary. It is also explained in more detail in the "Cataloging and Indexing Services" pamphlet put out by the Wilson Company.

559. A: See the ALA Glossary on abstract and abstracting service, or a dictionary on abstract. An abstracting service is an indexing service similar to those you have looked at, which includes not only the basic bibliographic information (author, title, periodical, volume number, paging, date, etc.) for each entry, but also includes an abstract, or content summary, of the article (or book, or report, or whatever is being cited). An example of an indexing service which includes abstracts in its citations is Documentation Abstracts (or Library Science Abstracts).

560. A: First, look under the Academic-Subject Index (p. 9 of the 1969 edition) for "architecture" (p. 12). Several titles are listed, including some--such as Applied Science and Technology Index (see #551)--which are obviously of a much broader scope than architecture itself. In the list, Architectural Index seems a likely source. You then look up this title under the Title Descriptions (see p. 49), finding it alphabetically by title on p. 55. The citation there gives you publisher, beginning date, form, content, subjects included, and a type of information code (AIP), to decipher which you have to turn back to p. 7 where you find that AIP means that the service "indexes articles in periodicals" (i.e., as opposed to indexing parts of books, etc.). The same information can be found in the Summary of Titles section, again alphabetically by title, on p. 113, in chart form.

561. A: You could guess that it would be in Library Literature. You could look in the front of Library Literature in the list of periodicals indexed, and find out for sure. You could also find out from Ulrich's. The citations in Ulrich's indicate the indexes which cover that periodical (see #423), so if a periodical is listed in Ulrich's, you can find it there.

562. A: Readers Guide to 1900
SSHI to 1916

563. A: Nineteenth Century Readers' Guide, and Poole's Index: the next two titles on your list.

564. A: Full title: Poole's Index to Periodical Literature
Number of volumes: in most editions there will be 6 or 7 volumes (the basic index in two volumes, plus five supplements)
Dates of publication: in most editions, 1891 through 1908 (the basic index originally published in 1882, revised edition published 1891). There is also a 1938 reprint.
(from title pages of volumes or from Winchell.)

565 / A: 1802-1906.
566. Basic index, 1802-1881; 1st supp., 1882-86; 2nd sup., 1887-91; 3rd sup., 1892-96; 4th sup., 1897-1901; 5th sup., 1902-1906 (title page says "to Jan. 1, 1907"). (from title pages of volumes, or from spines of volumes, or from Winchell annotation).

567. A: The Winchell annotation tells you that Poole's Index covers 479 periodicals, American and English, (varying somewhat from volume to volume). The dates of coverage are given in #565. In addition, the Preface to vol. 1 of Poole's (1891 edition) tells you that, in the beginning, only those periodicals which were likely to be found in libraries and private collections were indexed, that medical, legal, botanical and other purely professional and scientific periodicals were omitted, that semi-professional periodicals were included if of general interest--that the main criteria was the wants of general scholars.

568. A: Volume 1 contains a Prefatory Note (to the 1891 edition), a Preface, a list of co-operating libraries (like Sabin, Poole's started out as the work of one man and eventually became the work of a committee), abbreviations/titles/imprints, (which is in effect a list of the periodicals indexed), and a "Chronological Conspectus of the Serials Indexed." Each succeeding supplement also contains a list of abbreviations and a Chronological Conspectus which indicates what specific periodicals are indexed in that supplement.

569. A: Poole's has only subject access (RG has both subject and author access).

570. A: Poole's Index does not use the subject headings in the same sense that RG does. By looking carefully at the way the entries are constructed, you can see that in fact the titles of the articles themselves are used as the entries.

571. A: The significant indexing word or "catchword" or "keyword" has been pulled out of the title for the subject entry or alphabetizing word. For example, in the first entry under "Indians," the title of the article is "The American Indians" (by C.F. Lummis, published in Land of the Sun...). The entry is indexed not under the first real word of the title (which would be American), but under the significant word, "Indians," and the title itself within the entry has been inverted (Indians, the American). In some cases where the title does not clearly contain the significant keyword, it has been entered under that keyword anyway, much as a regular subject heading (see "Indians. Cities of the Dead." at the top of the right column on p. 316; this would appear to be an example; it is not always easy to tell).

572. A: You would look in all the volumes under the heading "Indians." You would also find it helpful to think of other significant related keywords which might also have been used for entries. For example, articles specifically on the Hopi Indians are indexed separately, listed on p. 296 of the fifth supplement.

573. A: The author is J.W. Fewkes. The article is found in Journal of American Folk-lore (see abbreviations in front of the volume). "15:14" presumably means "vol. 15, page 14." Inclusive paging is not given, usually only the first page of the article. The

date is not given, but can be found--more or less--through the "Chronological Conspectus" also in the front of the volume. The abbreviation list tells you that the Journal of American Folk-Lore was published in Boston, 1902-06, in 5 volumes. It also tells you that the number for that title in the "Chronological Conspectus" is 341. You then look in the "Chronological Conspectus" under 341 (p. xiii) which tells you that 15 is 1902. Presumably then the article is in Journal of American Folk-Lore, vol. 15, p. 41+, 1902.

574. A: Union List of Serials. Which tells you that the Journal of American Folk-Lore began publication with vol. 1 in April 1888 (which would make vol. 15 in 1902) in Boston, N.Y., and Lancaster, Pa., by the American Folk-lore Society, and that it has been published through at least 48 volumes since library holdings are indicated through 48 volumes. (Since this information does not jibe with that which you found in Poole's, it would seem clear then that Poole's gives publishing information only for the dates or years covered by that specific volume.)

575. A: Ulrich's.

576. A: By using Poole's Index Date and Volume Key (by Bell and Bacon), see Winchell AF120. This is simply titles and dates in one alphabetical tabular form for the entire index. (The Date and Volume Key also contains, p. 5-8, a short and very interesting survey of the origin and development of Poole's Index, and particularly points out the rules for procedure used by the cooperating libraries.)

577. A: No for both. There are no author entries in Poole's.

578. A: Subject entries--the articles indexed under the entry "Macaulay, Lord" are articles about him, not written by him.

579. A: Yes, you could search Poole's under "Burns, Robert" as a subject entry and find critical, biographical, etc., writings about him.

580. A: 1890-1899 (with some indexing for 1900-1922). (See Preface to source.) It was published by the Wilson Company, in 1944 (2 volumes).

581. A: The Nineteenth Century Reader's Guide was undertaken specifically to offer a source which would correct some of the defects of Poole's Index, by using standard subject headings (see #53 & #545) and providing author access.

582. A: The subject heading is still specifically Hopi Indians, with a subhead of Religion and mythology. The entry itself gives the title correctly and the inclusive paging and the date.

583. A: The Shaw/Shoemaker American Bibliography and the Shoemaker Checklist, published relatively recently to re-cover the period of Roorbach and Kelly and to correct defects of those sources.

584. A: No. Winchell (same section as Readers' Guide, Poole's Index, etc.) notes other similar sources as Annual Magazine Subject Index, 1907-49 (AF129), Annual Literary Index, 1892-1904 and Annual Library Index, 1905-1910 (AF127 and 128), and the Catholic Periodical Index, 1930-date.

585. A: Yes, you could assume that British indexes would also cover U.S. publications. Reference sources (such as periodical indexes) published in Great Britain are included in Winchell as well as U.S.-published reference sources. Some of those indexes with retrospective general coverage are listed in the section of Winchell noted in the question (p. 145-47), such as: Subject Index to Periodicals (AF125), retrospective: 1915-1961; British Humanities Index (AF126), current: 1962-date.

586. A: Since the first volume was published in 1967, it would not be included in the basic volume of Winchell (published itself in 1967, with a general closing date of 1964/5). It does appear, however, in the first supplement, (item 1AF27). Forthcoming Books (you have the title) would be one place to look for information on volume 2. You might also look in the publisher's catalog in PTLA (finding the name of the publisher through Winchell or through BIP).

587. A: Generally not, considering the general definition of newspapers.

588. A: See ALA Glossary under "newspaper." A newspaper differs from a periodical partly in its physical format, but as regards content, it differs in that its primary purpose is to report, record, describe, discuss daily current news events.

589. A: Basic possible accesses would be: author, title, subject, and chronological (time, period, date of publication...). Do most newspaper articles have titles? (No, although they do have headlines which might possibly be considered as similar.) Do most newspaper articles have authors? (Some have author by-lines, but most do not.) You are left, then, with subject access and chronological access.

590. A: It is published semi-monthly (twice a month), with an annual cumulation. The annual cumulation is called a "Book of Record."

591. A: Not in the semi-monthly issues, but in the annual cumulations there is a page of "How to Use the New York Times Index" plus a foreword.

592. A: Under the subject heading, the date and location of the article or item is cited (for example: Ja 20, 1:8 = January 20, page 1, column 8), but in addition, <u>information</u>, content, facts from the article or <u>item are given</u>. In a way these entries are like "abstracts" of the news item--thus the New York Times Index can claim to provide not only a classified index to the news, but a summary, a condensed history of the news itself. Look, for example, in the 1969 cumulated volume to see how much specific information and detail (plus illustrations) can be found in the index alone, on the Apollo moon landing.

593. A: Looking under "moon" send you to see "Space--Moon" (which turns out to be, actually, "Space and upper atmosphere--moon"), under which there is considerable information plus references to "Astronautics." Looking under "Apollo" sends you to see "Astronautics--U.S. projects--Apollo," and this is the heading which gives the most extensive information plus several pages of illustrations, on Apollo flights 9, 10, 11 and 12.

594. A: Yes, since that information would be noted in the entry indexed under the subject. For example, in 1970, you would find indexed under Nobel (in the Oct. 13-31st. issue of the Index), the fact that Dr. N.E. Borloug won the 1970 Nobel Peace Prize for his contribution to spurring food products in developing countries.

595. A: You could shorten your search by looking in the last cumulated volume (in this case, 1969), where you would have to look in only one place under the approximate subject heading, to see from the date of the item approximately what time of year the Nobel Peace Prize was awarded in that year (October 21, 1969), under the assumption that it would be awarded approximately the same time this year. You could then look in the current issue for this time.

596. A: On the assumption that your local newspaper, or whatever newspaper(s) your library does have, would have carried a story on the awarding of the prize, and that it would have appeared approximately the same date of the New York Times story, then you could look it up in issues of your local newspaper for October 21, 1970, or thereabouts.

597. A: The index itself doesn't indicate whether or not standardized subject headings, such as LC, are used. One of the limitations to using such a list for a newspaper index is that the material to be indexed is basically current events, constantly changing, constantly new. The need is for frequent changes, for new words, for flexibility, for specificity. Actually, the Index uses its own set of subject headings (or "descriptors") called the New York Times Thesaurus of Descriptors (Winchell 2AB21).

598. A: Yes, there are name entries or headings, although generally with reference to the subject concerned. There are plenty of cross-references in general. See "How to Use the New York Times Index" for a detailed discussion of types of headings used, arrangement of headings (subdivisions, alphabetization, etc.), cross-references, etc.

599. A: It would help if you had a general idea of when the law went into effect--otherwise you would simply have to start from the most recent issue of the Index and work back in time till you found what you were searching for. If you knew that the law was passed in 1970, this at least narrows the search down to that year. The significant entry for this is found in the July 1-15, 1970 issue (or in the 1970 cumulated volume), under "abortion."

600. A: Since the NY Times Index goes back basically to the beginning of the newspaper itself in 1851, it therefore would cover events of 1929-1930, the stock market crash, the depression, etc. It would likely not be indexed under "depression," however, since that name for the period did not come in to such common use until later. You might need to look under several headings in the indexes for 1929/30. Look, for example, in the Oct-Dec 1929 Index (no annual cumulations then, only quarterly) under "Stocks and Bonds--Prices" for a long series of brief citations giving, in themselves, an interesting and revealing account of the crash. Look also at the volume for 1930 (an annual cumulation)--the arrangement of the entries and the subject headings should remind you of the Wilson indexes.

601. A: These would be covered since the Index goes back to 1851. The annotation in the basic volume of Winchell (AG32) shows the index going back to 1913, with earlier volumes from 1851-1905 on microfilm. This earlier period ("Prior Series") has since been published in book form (Winchell 1AG12 and 2AG9)--some of it in the original handwritten form, some newly prepared, etc. Since some of the indexing for the Civil War period has been more or less currently prepared, then you might expect the headings to reflect a more current view of those times, and entries would be found indexed generally under "Civil War." The Forewords to the volumes of these Prior Series Indexes, especially that to the Sept. 1851-Dec. 1862 volume, and to the July 1905-Dec. 1906 volume, are helpful reading background on the differences between earlier and current indexes, in depth of indexing and in subject headings used.

602. A: In Winchell, listed under "General Reference Works--Newspapers--Indexes--U.S.," you can find that there is also a current index to the <u>Christian Science Monitor</u> (AG33), and for the <u>New York Daily</u>

Tribune from 1875-1906 (AG34). In the same
location under "Great Britain," you can find
that there is an Index to the London Times,
which goes back to 1863 (AG37 and AG38).

603/604
A: Ulrich's. Since you plan to subscribe, it is
therefore presumably currently published.
Ulrich's gives frequency of publication in its
citations.

605. A: Social Sciences and Humanities Index. You
might also find some indexed in Readers'
Guide, but the use of the term "critical"
might lead you to the more scholarly SSHI.

606. A: Since it is a British (English) publication,
the only sources you have so far which will
cover it are CBI and LC/NUC. CBI is
more likely to give you the price, for a
1963 publication, than LC/NUC. The price
listed in CBI, of course, is the price of
the book at the time it was published, in
1963. As yet, you have no source to look in
to find out if British publications are still
in print. If it has been also published in
the U.S. (which is likely), then of course
you can look in BIP, which will give you
publisher, price, and in-print status.

607. A: Since you want location of copies, you want
a union list, and your choice then is ULS
and NST. Since the titles given are part of
the "underground press" you would assume
that they have probably begun publication
since 1949, and therefore check first in NST.
(If you weren't aware of the titles sufficiently
to make that educated guess, then you would
look first in ULS and proceed to NST, or
vice versa.) One problem might be whether
or not these publications qualify as newspapers and would therefore be excluded from
ULS/NST, or similarly whether as "underground" publications, they would be excluded from ULS/NST. In any case, all
three happen to be listed in NST.

608. A: Depending on what type of information you
wanted, you could look in the New York Times
Index for 1969 (under "Water--Pollution--
California Coast Incident"), which would give
you some specific facts and indicate the exact
dates of the incident so that you could then
search further through the newspapers themselves, or you could look in one of the indexing services, such as Readers' Guide, on the
assumption that by now some articles on the
subject would have appeared in periodicals.

609. A: Ulrich's. Time is currently published. Ulrich's gives information on indexing in its
citations.

610. A: If your library had the Readers' Guide, you
could look in it to find location of articles
in the various current events newsmagazines
(Time, Newsweek, Life, etc.

611. A: The subject matter is generally social sciences,
and it would seem as if a more specialized,

scholarly source would be in order. "Some
recent publications" could include books,
periodical articles, etc.--"recent" combined
with a very specific aspect of a topic might
lead you to an indexing service for periodical articles. The subject matter is
generally social sciences, and it would seem
as if a more specialized, scholarly source
would be in order: Social Sciences and Humanities Index.

Section 8

Bibliographic Sources for Government Publications

Questions #8/1-8/59

The bibliographical sources you have examined in the last few sections of this manual have covered serial publications--periodicals, newspapers, annuals, etc. Serial publications are not generally--or at least not consistently--included in the basic bibliographical records examined in the early sections of this manual. Another type of publication which is not generally or consistently included in these basic bibliographical records is "government publications." The bibliographical sources which cover government publications are the next set you will examine:

Monthly Catalog of U.S. Government Publications (AH18, 2AH4)

Price Lists, GPO (AH20)
Selected U.S. GPO Publications

Document Catalog (AH17)
Poore: Descriptive Catalog (AH13)
Ames: Comprehensive Index (AH14)
Checklist of U.S. Public Documents (AH16)

Andriot: Guide to U.S. Government Serials and Periodicals (AH11, 1AH1)

Jackson: Subject Guide to Major U.S. Government Publications (2AH1)
Leidy: A Popular Guide to Government Publications (2AH2)

Monthly Checklist of State Publications (AH34)

8-1   What are "government publications?"

Government publications are a good source of information on governmental organization and administration. They are also a basic source of statistical information. But furthermore--and this is not as clearly recognized by the layman--government publications are available in any field, of both popular and research interest: health, education, agriculture, business, home economics, cooking, child care, social welfare, economics, science and technology, etc.

The U.S. Government Printing Office (G.P.O.), located in Washington, D.C., is generally considered to be the largest publishing and printing plant in the world. Similar materials are also published on state and local (county, municipal or city, etc.) levels, although not to the same extent. Other countries also have extensive government publishing programs, such as the HMSO in Great Britain, the Queen's Printer in Canada, etc. Material is also published by international government organizations, such as the United Nations, UNESCO, League of Nations, etc.

Government publications are often considered and treated as a special form or type of publication. In fact, government publications may appear in the same form (books, periodicals, pamphlets, etc.) and in the same types (bibliographies, directories, yearbooks, etc.) as the materials available from any of the so-called "trade" publishers. Probably the principal reasons for treating government publications as a separate type or form lies in the fact that the bibliographical control over these materials is in itself quite separate. It does not usually appear in the "trade" bibliographies, but rather in bibliographies especially compiled and published by the government itself. Its "author/title/subject" access may be rather complex.

8-2   How many of the bibliographical sources which you have examined so far have included government publications? Current "trade" bibliographies--BIP, etc., PW/BPR, CBI? Retrospective sources: Sabin, Evans, Roorbach, Kelly, etc.? LC/NUC, etc.? Periodicals and newspaper directories: Ulrich's, Ayer's, etc.? Serial union lists: ULS, NST? Periodical indexing services: Readers' Guide, etc.?

8-3   Some of the bibliographical sources which you have examined are actually government publications them-selves.   Which ones?

8-4   The specific bibliographic sources covering government publications form a current and retrospective series.   Look first at the basic current source for bibliographical information on federal government pub-lications, the Monthly Catalog of U.S. Government Publications.   Who publishes it?   How often?

8-5   Is it comprehensive or selective?   Does it include publications from all levels of government?   Specifical-ly what publications are included?   Are any specifically excluded?   Does the source itself give you any clear statement of which is included?

8-6   How is it arranged?

8-7   Is there any relationship between access by "issuing agency" and the access by author/title/subject which you have become familiar with in previous sources?   Look in a recent issue at the publications listed under one of the issuing agencies, Office of Education, for example.

8-8   Searching for information by way of "issuing agency" sometimes requires an understanding of the structure of the government.   Is there any publication which explains this structure?

8-9   Is there any way you can get, through the Monthly Catalog itself, a very general, overall picture of the structure and organization of the issuing agencies?

8-10   If you wanted to find government publications on the general subject of urban problems, what issuing agencies could you search under?

8-11   If you have a broad subject classification on the basis of the issuing agency, do you have any specific sub-ject access?   For example, if you wanted to find publications specifically on the Head Start program, and you did not know which government agency was responsible for the program, how would you go about it? How would you find listings of publications on Vietnam?

8-12   In cases where a specific person is concerned with the publication, either as author or as subject, do you have any access to the publications through his name?

8-13   Is there a title access?   Is there need for a title access?

8-14   The Monthly Catalog is published monthly.   Does it cumulate in any way?   (Look at the source on shelves and see Winchell annotation.)

8-15   Presumably another decennial cumulative index (1961-70) is due.   Would you expect it soon?   When was the 1951-60 decennial cumulation published?

8-16   In the late fall of 1970, the U.S. Senate voted to return to the Taos Indians (of the Taos Pueblo, in New Mexico) the 48,000 acres of their sacred land surrounding Blue Lake in the Sangre de Cristo Mountains in New Mexico (after a struggle of some 65 years on the part of the Indians). Some hearings on the bill were held in the Senate during the summer of 1970. If you wanted to read what was said at the hearings, how would you go about it? Would you expect to find this material published by the U.S. government? Would you expect to find it listed in the Monthly Catalog? How would you locate it in the Monthly Catalog? (There are two ways in which you could do this.)

8-17   Can you actually find it listed in the Monthly Catalog? How many pages are there in the publication of this particular hearing? What is the number of the Senate bill which was finally passed into law in November 1970? Is a price given? How would you obtain the document if you wished to have a copy? Could you order the document through the Superintendent of Documents?

8-18   Is there any other way you might locate a copy of the hearings document? What does the black dot in the listing tell you?

8-19   What is a "depository library?"

8-20   In the entry or citation for the Taos Indian Blue Lake hearings, what is the significance of the letters and numbers to the right? (Y 4. In 8/13: T15/2/970.)

8-21   Hunger and malnutrition are two of the major problems faced in the world today. What inexpensive publications which might offer some help or solutions to this problem are available from the U.S. government? Think in terms of a broad range of subjects in using the indexes; hunger and malnutrition are, after all, the problems, not the solutions. Also look directly under appropriate issuing agencies.

8-22   Is there a "book in print" type of source for government publications? Does the Monthly Catalog list all government publications in print?

8-23   Is it expensive to subscribe to the Monthly Catalog? Where would you find out the cost of a year's subscription?

8-24   If a library or an individual did not wish to subscribe to the Monthly Catalog, is there any less expensive way of receiving information on current government publications?

8-25   The government published several bibliographies on American Indians during the 1950's. How would you find citations to these? One of these was a list of books for Indian schools. When was it published?

8-26   How far back can you search, retrospectively, in the Monthly Catalog?

8-27   What source(s) do you have which give you retrospective coverage prior to 1895?

8-28   What are the dates of coverage for these three sources (Poore, Ames, Document Catalog) plus the Monthly Catalog? Is there any overlapping?

8-29   The Document Catalog (full title: Catalog of the public documents of Congress and of all departments of the government of the United States for the period March 4, 1893-Dec. 31, 1940) overlaps the Monthly Catalog for all but two years of its existence. What is the difference in scope or coverage between the Monthly Catalog and the Document Catalog? Is there any difference in the access? (See Winchell.)

8-30   Where would you look to find listings of various publications of the U.S. government on the subject of children, published in the 1920's? Look specifically for a pamphlet titled "Campaign against malnutrition" published in 1923. Compare entries in the Document Catalog. Compare subject approach in both sources.

8-31   The Document Catalog was preceded by Ames (1881-1893) and Poore (1774-1881). These bibliographies (like Sabin and Evans, for example) were compiled somewhat retrospectively. Ames was compiled specifically to fill the gap between Poore and the beginning of the Document Catalog. Look at both sources together and comparatively. Are there any differences in scope or arrangement between Poore and Ames?

8-32   Poore is arranged chronologically. Is this the only access you have to the material? Are there any indexes to give you additional access to the basic arrangement?

8-33   How does this compare to the access in Ames? In the Document Catalog? In the Monthly Catalog?

8-34   Have you examined any other sources with a chronological arrangement like Poore's? Is there any advantage to the chronological arrangement? Would there be any special advantage to a chronological arrangement for government publications? Can you find a citation for the Declaration of Independence? Could you find this in Poore's without looking in the Index?

8-35   Another retrospective source listed in Winchell, with Poore and Ames, is Greely's Public Documents (AH12). Look only at the full title of Greely in Winchell and compare it to Poore and Ames. What time period is covered by Greely and what does it overlap? What is the difference in scope between Poore and Greely?

8-36   A report was made by the Geographical Survey in 1883 on volcanoes in Hawaii. Where would you find it?

8-37   Could you have used the index in Ames to find the report on volcanoes in Hawaii?

8-38   What is the "serial set" (or "Congressional edition")? How would you find the reports on the volcanoes in Hawaii in the "serial set"?

8-39   In what government publication would you find the original publication of John Adams' (not John Quincy Adams) Inaugural Address? What are the general contents of the address?

8-40   A presidential commission was established in 1967 to study and report on riots and disorders. The chairman of the commission was Otto Kerner and the resulting report is often referred to as "the Kerner report." Can you find a listing of its publication with price and ordering information?

8-41   The Kerner report was also published by a trade publisher in both hardbound and paperback editions. Where would you look to find publisher and price?

8-42   Where and how would you look to find what material--official reports, documents, etc.--about slavery which the government had published during the period preceding the American Civil War?

8-43   Where and how would you locate an official account or report of Custer's last stand? On this one, if possible, follow the citation all the way through the Serial set /Congressional Edition to find the actual account.

8-44   Many of the government publications are issued in serial or periodical form (see #401-402 for definitions). Did the bibliographical sources for serials include consistent and complete coverage for government serials /periodicals?

8-45   What sources do you have which list and give bibliographic information specifically about government-published serials or periodicals?

8-46   What is the scope and arrangement of Andriot's Guide to U.S. Government Serials?

8-47   Are these serial publications listed also in the basic bibliographical sources for government publications (Monthly Catalog, etc.)? Why are separate listings necessary? If you wanted to find a list of the periodical titles published by the U.S. government dealing with education, where would you look?

8-48   What is the annual subscription price and the frequency of publication of the Antarctic Journal of the United States (issued by the National Science Foundation)?

8-49   The bibliographical sources for government publications, which you have examined so far, give you to some extent both author (government and personal) and subject access. In dealing with government publications in general, which of these approaches would seem to be most useful, or most important?

        The subject access in the sources you have examined so far is ponderous to use, at best, and requires searching through numerous volumes and issues to give any kind of collective coverage. The next two titles on your list to examine--Jackson's Subject Guide to Major U.S. Government Publications and Leidy's A Popular Guide to Government Publications--are examples of basic and relatively up-to-date general subject approaches to U.S. government publications. Examine both titles together, comparatively.

8-50   What is the scope of the Jackson and Leidy lists? Perhaps this can best be answered by thinking in terms of their purposes or use. Is there any difference in the scope of the two lists?

8-51   Is there any difference in the arrangement or access between Jackson and Leidy?

8-52   What exactly is the American Ephemeris and Nautical Almanac? Look it up in both Jackson and Leidy, and compare ease of location and information given.

8-53   If you wanted a listing of short, inexpensive pamphlets published by the government on the subject of food preparation and nutrition, such as you found for #8-21, would you be more likely to find such a list in Jackson or Leidy?

8-54   Where is another place--other than either Leidy or Jackson--in which you could find such a list?

8-55   Where would you find a list of bibliographies and reference sources, with descriptive annotations, which would give information on reports, findings, programs, etc., of government financed and supported research work?

8-56   The Monthly Catalog covers only federal government publications. Where would you look to find publications of the states? Where would you look, for example, to find a list of current publications of the state of Kansas?

8-57   Who publishes the Monthly Checklist? Are there any limitations to the publications listed there?

8-58   What is the arrangement of the Monthly Checklist?

8-59   What type of publications are issued by state governments? (Look through a recent issue for examples.)

        For review, make a chart for the main bibliographical sources examined, showing dates of coverage (see answer to #8-28) and access (see answer to #8-33), plus indications for the serial sources and subject guides.

Section 8

Bibliographic Sources for Government Publications

Answers #8/1-8/59

8-1 A: See <u>ALA Glossary.</u> See also Winchell, 8th
edition, p. 155, at the beginning of the section on government publications. Basically,
government publications are those materials
published under the authority of or at the ex-
pense of the government. These include the
state papers, orders, proclamations, speeches,
treaties, laws, statutes, codes, bills, session records, proceedings, minutes, hearings,
etc., of the government itself: all of these
would seem to fall clearly into the category
of official papers or documents. The phrase
"government documents" (or "public documents") is often used interchangeably with
"government publications." "Documents"
seems to refer more to such official papers,
while the use of the phrase "government publications" gives more indication of the
astonishingly broad subject categories of
current government publications in the U.S.

8-2 A: Current trade bibliographies (BIP, PW/BPR,
CBI) quite specifically exclude government
publications, altho CBI (see #143) does
rather erratically include a few here and
there.
          The retrospective sources do include
some government publications but it is not
clear to what extent.
          LC/NUC includes government publica-
tions in so far as they are received, cataloged and reported by NUC libraries. (See
#391)
          The Catalog of Copyright Entries does
not include them (because in general
government publications are not copyrighted).
          Ulrich's and Irregular Serials do include
some government publications, <u>if</u> they fall
into the definition of "periodicals" or
"Irregular Serials" in the sources.
          ULS and NST include government publica-
tions <u>only</u> if they are periodicals or monographic series (therefore excluding government serials which are not periodicals).
          Some of the periodical indexing services
do, again if the government publication is
a <u>periodical</u>: see #518 on Readers' Guide,
for example.
          Other indexing services such as PAIS
which include books, pamphlets, etc., will
also include some government publications
if they fall within the subject categories
indexed. (See #553 and #556 on PAIS.)

8-3 A: All of the current sources published by the
Library of Congress: the National Union
Catalog, LC Subject Catalog, Catalog of
Copyright Entries, NST, etc. (See list pre-
ceding question #350.)   The older, cumu-

lative volumes of these sources have in many
cases been taken over and/or reprinted by
commercial publishers (Bowker for NST,
Mansell for LC/NUC, etc.)

8-4 A: Issued by the Superintendent of Documents,
U.S. Government Publications Office (GPO),
Washington, D.C. Monthly.

8-5 A: There is no statement in the Monthly Catalog itself about its scope, or its comprehensiveness. It is assumed, basically, to
be a comprehensive listing. Advertising for
the Monthly Catalog makes the claim that it
is a comprehensive listing of all publications issued by the departments and agencies
of the U.S. government, compiled by the
Library of the Division of Public Documents,
which according to law must receive one
copy of each publication authored by any
branch or bureau of the government including those for sale by the Superintendent of
Documents, those available at issuing offices,
and those for official use only. This implies
a complete listing, but as always, since the
listing is dependent upon the compilers' receiving a copy/copies of the publication,
such comprehensiveness/completeness cannot be totally relied upon.

8-6 A: Alphabetically by "issuing agency," with an
index.

8-7 A: The "author" for most government publications is considered to be the "issuing agency"
(Department of Agriculture, Bureau of the
Budget, Office of Education, etc.) Because
the issuing agency tends to issue publications in its general subject area--e.g.,
publications on education from the Office of
Education--the arrangement by issuing agency
also gives a kind of broad subject cate-
gorizing or classifying.

8-8 A: Look in Winchell, not under bibliographical
sources but under <u>subject</u>--i.e., United
States government organization, under the
very broad category of social sciences (C),
then political science (CI), then govern-
ment--United States--official registers:
item CI55, <u>United States Government
Organization Manual,</u> published annually.
Similar information can be found to some
extent in the "guides" to government publications listed in the AH section, such as
Schmeckebier's Government Publications and
their Use (AH9) or Boyd and Rips' United
States Government Publications (AH7).

8-9 A: Look at the "List of Government Authors" in the front, which lists the "issuing agencies" or "authors" for the government publications. This tells you, for example, that the Patent Office is part of the Commerce Department, that the National Park Service and the Geographic Names Board are part of the Department of the Interior, that the Science and Technology Office is under the Executive Office of the President, that the Peace Corps is under the State Department, etc.

8-10 A: Housing and Urban Development Department; Health, Education, and Welfare Department-- especially Community Environmental Management Bureau, Community Health Service, Social and Rehabilitation Service, etc.; Narcotics and Dangerous Drugs Bureau (Justice Department); Labor Department; etc.

8-11 A: There is specific subject access to some extent through the index. Material on the Head Start Program should be indexed there (see August 1970 issue); it would also be found directly under the Child Development Office of the Health, Education and Welfare Department. Vietnam should also be specifically listed in the index (see almost any recent issue), with reference to the item number(s) for the full citation.

8-12 A: Again, to some extent through the index. Names of person and places are included in the index. See the October 1970 issue under Parker, Patricia E. (maps, a MARC format) for an example of personal author listing.

8-13 A: Titles of government publications are frequently of a type not easily remembered (for example: "To extend Defense production act of 1950, as amended, hearings 91st Congress, 2d session, on H.R. 17880, June 16-July 6, 1970," item 12267 in September 1970 issue).

8-14 A: The index only cumulates annually. The index has been cumulated again on a 10-year basis (decennial) for 1941-1950, and 1951-1960.

8-15 A: Since the 1951-60 decennial cumulation was not published until 1968 (see date of publication in the imprint, title page), then you would not expect the 1961-70 cumulation for some time yet.

8-16 A: Headings, bills, documents, reports, etc., as part of the official business of the government, would be printed by the U.S. GPO and should be listed in the Monthly Catalog, although they would not necessarily be offered for sale by the GPO. See the note on hearings, etc., under "Congressional Bills..." in the "General Information" section of the Monthly Catalog issue. You can locate the listing for the hearings either through the index or directly under the agency, etc., issuing/publishing the document (i.e., the "government author").

8-17 A: The listing for the Senate hearings on amendments to this bill is found in the November 1970 issue of the Monthly Catalog. The index (Taos Indian Blue Lake area land conveyances, hearings) sends you to item 16064. The issuing agency or author is Congress--Senate--Interior and Insular Affairs Committee. There are 315 pages. The Senate bill was number 750 and the House of Representatives bill was number 471. No price is given, and there is no star to indicate that the item is for sale by the Superintendent of Documents. The dagger at the end of the listing indicates that distribution is made by the issuing agency (Congress, Senate, Interior and Insular Affairs Committee). If you wished to obtain a copy, you could not get it through the Superintendent of Documents. You would have to apply to the Interior and Insular Affairs Committee of the U.S. Senate, or perhaps write to your congressman as suggested in "General Information."

8-18 A: The black dot indicates that the publication has been or will be sent to depository libraries, and can therefore be examined in such a library. (Item 1040 following the black dot is a category number for document librarians requesting from the Superintendent of Documents.)

8-19 A: See ALA Glossary. See also page 103 of the September 1970 issue of the Monthly Catalog ("List of Depository Libraries as of September 1, 1970" with paragraph of explanation).

8-20 A: See "General Information." This is the classification number used in the Library of the Division of Public Documents. The same classification scheme is used in many Document Collections of other libraries. These classification numbers are also used as catalog or order numbers by the Superintendent of Documents, and should therefore be included as part of the ordering information.

8-21 A: For example: under Agriculture Department: "Food stamps to end hunger" (15¢) "Nutritive value of foods (30¢) (September 1970); "Food guide for older folks" (10¢), "How to buy dry beans, peas and lentils (25¢) (October 1970); "Food for family with young children (10¢), "Vegetables in family meals" (20¢) (August 1970). Also "Annotated bibliography on maternal nutrition" ($1.50) (item 11564, August 1970). Also hearings, etc., listed under the Senate Selection Committee on Nutrition and Human Needs. Subjects: nutrition, hunger, food, etc.

8-22 A: The Monthly Catalog lists, each month, only those items published during that period--as does CBI, BPR, etc. It does not attempt to list, each month, all publications available or in print as of that date. There is not a complete list of "in print" government publications. Specific subject lists (for example: Indians, home economics, education, national parks, consumer information, Library of Congress, census, maps, geology, plants, etc.) of "in print" or available publications can be obtained free from the GPO. These are the "Price Lists" (Winchell AH20) as noted in the "General Information" section of the Monthly Catalog. Look at an example of one or two if possible.

8-23 A: The Monthly Catalog including the annual index costs $7.00/year, which like most government publications is an excellent value. The subscription price is given in the masthead of the Monthly Catalog itself (see verso of title page). It could also be found in Ulrich's (Ulrich's will include some government publications if they are periodicals, which the Monthly Catalog is; see #8-2), in "Bibliography" section under United States Government Publications Monthly Catalog (price in 12th edition given as $4.50/year--now out of date).

8-24 A: Through the list of "Selected United States Government Publications" issued biweekly, and free upon application to the Superintendent of Documents. (See "General Information" in the front of a Monthly Catalog.) Look at a sample of this selected list if possible.

8-25 A: The Decennial Cumulative Index for 1951-60, under "Bibliographies on American Indians." The bibliography of books for Indian schools was published in 1953 (item number 11197 of that year). Other references are given under "Indian schools," including two more book lists (1955 nnd 1959).

8-26 A: See Winchell. To 1895 (the title varies somewhat over the years, and it has not always been as well indexed).

8-27 A: Ames, Poore, Document Catalog--the next sources on your list to examine.

8-28 A: Poore: 1774-1881
          Ames: 1881-1893
          Document Catalog: 1893-1940
          Monthly Catalog: 1895-date.
          The Document Catalog and Monthly Catalog overlap for most of the publication of the Document Catalog.

8-29 A: Basically, the Document Catalog is a more detailed, complete, permanent record for that period. According to the Winchell annotation, it gives "full catalog information" and includes a large amount of "analysis" or specific detail on publications. It is a full dictionary catalog, with author (personal and government), subject, and some title access.

The Monthly Catalog for that period was basically an ordering list, without as complete access or information about the publications. The Document Catalog was discontinued in 1947 (with coverage ending with 1940), and the Monthly Catalog was improved and expanded to take on some of the features of the Document Catalog and to become a single permanent record of publications.

8-30 A: The Document Catalog and Monthly Catalog both cover the period. Since you want broad coverage on the subject of "Children," the Document Catalog would be the best source, as all entries on this subject are brought together in that source; in the Monthly Catalog you would have to refer constantly from index references to the entries in monthly issues. The specific pamphlet titled "Campaign against Malnutrition" is in the Document Catalog, vol. 16, 1921-23, p. 380 under "Children"--National Child Health Council; in the Monthly Catalog July 1923-June 1924, p. 267, under Public Health Service. The Monthly Catalog gives price (5¢), which would have been important at the time of publication although it is not now.

8-31 A: In scope, both attempt to give comprehensive coverage of the government documents or publications of the periods covered. The main difference is in arrangement. Poore is arranged chronologically, Ames by subject. The arrangement of Ames by subject is not so clear from the Winchell annotation and can better be seen in the source itself--the middle column of entries on each page is the basic arrangement of the source, alphabetically by keyword (see #571 on keyword entries).

8-32 A: The index in Poore generally includes subjects (basically catchword or keyword subjects taken from the titles), some authors, names of people and places, etc. The index appears useful but on experience it is found to be incomplete (see Winchell annotation, AH13). However, insofar as it goes, the access in Poore is chronological, subject and author.

8-33 A: The access in Poore is chronological, subject (keyword and therefore possibly title to some extent), and author/name (personal).
          The main access in Ames is subject (keyword and therefore possibly title to some extent) with author/name (personal) index.
          Document Catalog has author (government and personal), some title, and subject access in one alphabetical (dictionary) arrangement.
          Monthly Catalog has main access by issuing agency (government author), with author/name (personal) and subject index.

Although the basic arrangements of all the sources differ, the accesses are generally the same; subject and author. The differences, and the difficulties, are in the extent of the indexing for specific subjects and names. This problem can best be appreciated in continued use of the sources.

8-34 A: Evans' American Bibliography was also arranged chronologically. See #290-291 on the uses of the chronological arrangement. With government publications, dates are the one fact you may know (as opposed to author and title) for a historical document. The citation for the Declaration of Independence is found in Poore, vol. 1, pg. 3. You could find it directly under the date, which you would presumably know: July 4, 1776. The citation in Poore shows the document to be published in Charters and Constitutions, vol. 1, pp. 3-6, and the original draft and document itself to be in the Department of State at Washington, D.C.

8-35 A: Greely covers 1789-1817, falling within the Poore period. Greely's full title is "Public Documents of the first 14 Congresses, 1789-1817. Papers relating to early Congressional Documents." Greely covers only publications and documents issued by Congress; Poore has a broader scope, including publications from departments and bureaus, etc., as well.

8-36 A: The date, 1883, would lead you to Ames for the citation, where you would look under Hawaii or under volcanoes as the keyword subject. Ames shows that the information on the volcanoes of Hawaii appears in the Report of the Director of the Geological Survey, and in the Report of the Secretary of the Interior for 1883. The column on the right indicates that these were published as a House Executive Document of the 48th Congress, 1st session-document no. 1, pt. 5, vol. 3, p. 75-219, with 29 plates and 3 figures.

8-37 A: Only if you knew the personal author (C.E. Dutton) of the report, since the index in Ames is personal author names only.

8-38 A: See ALA Glossary, but better yet see also Winchell, 8th edition, p. 156, comments on "The Serial set" under "Catalogs and Indexes." Winchell tells you that each bound volume of the set is given a serial number, and it is necessary to use the Checklist of U.S. Public Documents, 1789-1909 (AH16), the Document Catalog (AH17), and the Numerical lists and schedule of volumes (AH19) to find the serial volume number for specific documents.

The report on volcanoes in Hawaii was published as House Executive document no. 1 of the 48th Congress, 1st session. (See answer to #8-36). To find the serial number of the volume of the serial set in which this document will appear, you look in the Checklist (AH16, above) for 48th Congress, 1st session, which appears on p. 70, and then for House Executive Documents, in the middle of the page, then for no. 1, pt. 5,

vol. 3; the serial number given in the left column is 2192. Then, if your library has a complete set of the "Congressional edition," you would look in it for volume number 2192, in which (p. 75-219) you should find the report on volcanoes in Hawaii.

8-39 A: It helps to know generally that John Adams lived from 1735-1826 and was the second president of the United States from 1797-1801. This puts the original Inaugural Address within the Poore period. (Otherwise you would simply have to start from, presumably, the beginning with Poore and work forward in time till you found it.) If you knew specifically that Adams was president from 1797- (which is unlikely), you could go directly to that date in Poore, otherwise you would go to the index under "Adams, John" or "Inaugural addresses and messages--Adams, John" which would direct you to p. 36. On p. 36, second column, you find that Adams' Inaugural Address was first published in the Journal of the Senate, pp. vii-xvi, and the contents of the address are listed in the citation in Poore's, so it is not necessary to find the address itself to answer that part of the question.

8-40 A: You want price and ordering information for a recent publication so you would search in the Monthly Catalog from 1967 to date. Although you are looking for the "Kerner report," one of the problems in using the government publications' bibliographical sources is that the popular name for committees, commissions, reports, bills, etc., is not always used as in indexing word, and you must resort to a subject approach. The publication of the Kerner report is listed in the May 1968 Monthly Catalog; it cannot be found in the 1968 index under Kerner, but subjects such as "riots" and "civil rights" list the National Advisory Commission on Civil Disorders--report, item 6716. The report is available from the Superintendent of Documents for $2.00 (Pr 36.8: C49/R29).

8-41 A: Books in Print (assuming it to be still in print) under title (Report of the National Advisory Commission...) or Subject Guide to BIP under subject. BIP lists Dutton, $7.95, but no paperbound edition, so you could also check Paperbound BIP, but no paperbound edition is listed there either, so presumably it is by now out of print. The paperbound edition (Bantam, 1968, $1.25) is listed in BPR Cumulative 1968.

8-42 A: For slavery preceding the Civil War (1861-65), the material would be listed in Poore which covers that period. Your approach here would be subject so you would go to the index, which has about three columns of references on the subject "slavery."

8-43 A: You could begin by finding the date of Custer's last stand, which would narrow your search to that general period of time.

(American College Dictionary lists Custer, George Armstrong, 1839-76; assuming his last stand to be the date of his death, you could begin with 1876; or you could go on to an encyclopedia for further information--Columbia one-volume encyclopedia lists, under Custer, George Armstrong, that his final battle and death was in 1876 at Little Bighorn river in Montana.)

The date then falls within Poore, so you can search in the index under Custer, George Armstrong. There are two references, one of which (1084) is to a resolution to tender condolences to his family. The other (1081) leads you to p. 1081 where you have to search carefully through all the citations until you find: "Message on hostilities of the Sioux Indians. President U.S. Grant. Senate Ex. Docs, no. 81, 44th Cong., 1st sess. Transmittal of information in regard to the hostile demonstrations of the Sioux Indians and the disaster to the forces under Gen. Custer. July 13, 1876/6 p."

To locate the report in the serial set, you turn again to the Checklist (see #8-38), under 44th Congress, 1st session (p. 55) to find Senate Executive document no. 81 (S. ex. docs/1-94) which is in volume #1664 of the serial set. Then of course you have to find volume 1664 of the serial set and look through it for document no. 81 which should be the report on Custer's last stand.

8-44 A: No. Some government-published serials / periodicals are included in the serial bibliographies but the coverage is limited. Union List of Serials, for example, includes only those which are periodicals or monographic series, thereby excluding many government serials (see #8-2).

8-45 A: The February issues of the Monthly Catalog have a special section devoted to an alphabetical listing by title of current government periodicals.

There is a special Price List (see #8-22) devoted to periodicals and other publications sold on a subscription basis.

In addition, another source on your list-- Guide to U.S. Government Serials and Periodicals (Andriot)--lists and describes government serials.

8-46 A: Scope: "serials, periodicals, releases and other ephemeral materials, reports, looseleaf services, field agency publications and important reference works which are revised or updated from time to time" (Foreword to 1970 edition).
Arrangement: basic arrangement by issuing agency, more or less alphabetically with agency, subject, and title indexes.

8-47 A: Yes, serial publications are listed in, for example, the Monthly Catalog. These listings are for single issues or volumes only, as they appear, and they are listed only by

issuing agency (there is no title index to the Monthly Catalog). The February listings are by title, not by subject, and are for periodicals only.

Andriot gives more complete and useable bibliographical information for each source, with subject and title access.

A list of periodicals on education published by the U.S. government would probably most easily be found through the index in Andriot. The February issue of the Monthly Catalog could be used, by going through the entire list of titles and picking out those dealing with education.

8-48 A: See February 1970 Monthly Catalog, Appendix (Directory of U.S. Government Periodicals and Subscription Publications), item 2335, Antarctic Journal... $3.50/ year, issued bimonthly.

8-49 A: Subject access is most generally useful. Personal name or author is not always known. Subject access is similar to title access.

8-50 A: Neither is truly a "guide" in the sense that it guides one through the mass of bibliographical apparatus dealing with government publications, telling one how to locate and use government publications (although Jackson does include a short but useful chapter on "Guides, Catalogs, and Indexes"). Both are highly selective listings by broad subject categories, attempting to indicate-- through selection, categorization, and annotation--some of the wealth of inexpensive, authoritative information available to the general public through publications of the U.S. government.

Jackson (see "Foreword") has selected generally on the basis of titles "which appear to be of permanent importance from the earliest period to the present." Leidy has apparently selected more on the basis of popular and current appeal (see title and preface).

8-51 A: Both are arranged under subject categories alphabetically.

Leidy has a basic subject arrangement with a specific number (and name) index; Leidy also has a table of contents which shows at a glance the subjects covered.

Jackson has no index, no table of contents; the Foreword indicates that LC subject headings are used for the subject categories. A good indication of the general difference in type of publication included is to compare what Leidy lists under "American Indians" with what Jackson lists under "Indians."

8-52 A: It can be found quickly in Leidy by looking in the index under title. In Jackson, where there is no index, it is found under the general heading "Almanacs" (being in fact the only listing under this title). The information in Jackson is somewhat more detailed about the contents of the publication, and also indicates more clearly that it is an annual publication which has been coming out since 1855. The Leidy citation is only for the 1968 volume, since which other volumes have been published.

8-53 A: Leidy--more popular pamphlets. (Under Agriculture, Home Economics, Nutrition.)

8-54 A: In one of the subject-oriented U.S. GPO Price Lists (see #8-32), such as Home Economics or Consumer Information.

8-55 A: Jackson: Subject Guide to Major U.S. Government Publications (under "Research"). You would also find some listed in Winchell, but not so directly or so easily identifiable as government-oriented.

8-56 A: Monthly Checklist of State Publications. In addition, some states have their own published lists--see Winchell 1AH3, for Kansas, for example.

8-57 A: It is published by the Library of Congress. The limitation is that only those publications received by LC are listed, therefore its comprehensiveness is dependent upon the cooperation of various State agencies (see introduction to a recent issue).

8-58 A: By state, and then by issuing agency.

8-59 A: For example, reports and bulletins from agriculture experiment stations and extension services. Statistics and surveys. Publications of state universities and colleges.

Section 9

Sources for Miscellaneous Types of Publications

Questions #9/1-9/37

In addition to the major categories of serial publications and government publications, there are several other types or forms of published material for which our bibliographical control has been rather erratic and incomplete. These include pamphlets, dissertations, microfilms, manuscripts, reprints, maps, music scores, and if we want to extend our idea of bibliographic control or coverage beyond publications to recorded material, we can include also visual materials such as films, filmstrips, slides, transparencies, and audio materials such as recordings and tapes.

The next set of sources to examine attempts to fill in some of the gaps of bibliographic coverage for these materials:

> Vertical File Index (AA355)
>
> Dissertation Abstracts International AI11 & 1AI2
> American Doctoral Dissertations (AI9 & AI10)
> Masters Abstracts (AI13)
> Black: Guide to lists of masters theses (1AI1)

9-1   The first of these sources to examine, the Vertical File Index, is one which provides coverage specifically for pamphlet material.   What is a pamphlet?

9-2   UNESCO has established a certain number of pages as the distinction between a "book" and a "pamphlet"; this is indicated in the criteria for listing in PW Weekly Record (see #73).   What is this number?

9-3   Of the bibliographic sources you have examined so far, which have included pamphlets?

9-4   What is a "vertical file?"

9-5   Who is the publisher of the Vertical File Index, and what does this indicate you might expect from the publication?

9-6   What is the arrangement of the Vertical File Index? Is it similar to other Wilson bibliographies or indexes you have examined already? Does it have the three primary types of bibliographic access?

9-7   Looking at one of the recent issues of the Vertical File Index itself, can you tell what its scope is?

9-8   How then can you tell what the criteria for inclusion are?

9-9   Look through a recent few issues of the Vertical File Index to see what type of subject heading is used, and to see what type of material is listed. (Many of the items listed in the VFI do not seem to fall clearly into the category of "pamphlet," nor are the items always cheap or of a minimum number of pages.)

If you were looking through the VFI for inexpensive material for your library collection on the general subject of urban problems, what subject headings might you find such material under?

9-10   Does the Vertical File Index include government publications?

9-11   How often is the Vertical File Index issued?

9-12   When did the Vertical File Index begin publication? Was it always called by that title?

9-13   Why is it useful for you to know that a serial or periodical publication has changed title?

9-14   Is it possible to use the Vertical File Index to identify specific pamphlets? For example, could you use the VFI to locate the publisher and price for David Lowenthal's Environmental Perception and Behavior?

9-15   Where would you find a list of the publications put out by the National Education Association?

9-16   A 20-page pamphlet on the use of teachers' helpers (or non-professional teaching personnel) was issued in 1967. What is its price and where can it be obtained?

9-17   Would you expect this to be listed in BIP, even though it is pamphlet material? Would it have been listed in PW/BPR?

9-18   What do you think would be the primary use or purpose of the Vertical File Index? Why is such a source necessary?

9-19   If you were setting up a pamphlet file or vertical file in a library, what "headings" or subject categories might you use to classify and organize your material?

9-20   The next source is Dissertation Abstracts International. What are dissertations and theses?

9-21   Dissertations and/or theses are another type of publication rarely listed in trade bibliographies. In fact, dissertations and/or theses are rarely actually published. At one time it was considered an important part of a dissertation to have it published and the research it reported therefore available. However, such material is not commercially saleable, and the publication is therefore costly to the student, as well as costly to the libraries which would have to acquire and process hundreds of thousands of dissertations. What is the full title of Dissertation Abstracts International?

9-22   What are "abstracts?" How does Dissertation Abstracts International attempt to meet the problem of availability of dissertation research?

9-23   What is the scope of Dissertation Abstracts International? Does it list all dissertations? Is it limited to dissertations from U.S. universities? Does it include masters theses?

9-24   What is the arrangement of Dissertation Abstracts International?

9-25   How long has it been published? Does it cumulate?

9-26   Is there any complete listing of doctoral dissertations from U.S. universities?

9-27   American Doctoral Dissertations is also published by University Microfilms, the same company which publishes Dissertation Abstracts International. For some time it was published as the last issue of Dissertation Abstracts International, and for those years would probably be bound in with the final or index volume. Although currently it is issued as a separate publication, it may similarly continue to be bound with the index volume. How is American Doctoral Dissertations arranged? Is it the same as Dissertation Abstracts International?

9-28   How is American Doctoral Dissertations compiled?

9-29   American Doctoral Dissertations began in 1955, according to the Winchell annotation. What retrospective coverage exists prior to that time?

9-30   If you wanted to know what dissertations had been done last year in the field of English literature, how would you go about it?

9-31   If you wanted to know if a dissertation had been completed and accepted recently on the subject of Samuel Taylor Coleridge (English poet), how would you find out?

9-32   Who is the author of the dissertation on Coleridge referred to in #9-31? What university granted the degree? In what year? How do you obtain a copy of the dissertation?

9-33   If you wanted to know if any dissertation had ever been done on specific aspects of Coleridge's poetry, how would you find out?

9-34   Could you find a citation for a doctoral dissertation by a specific person?

9-35   Does Dissertation Abstracts International include masters theses? Where can you look to find citations for masters theses?

9-36   How does Masters Abstracts compare to Dissertation Abstracts?

9-37   Masters Abstracts is, so far, a highly selective list of masters theses.   How can you find a more com-
       prehensive list of masters theses on the subject on library science?   (There are two specific places you
       can look for this.)

       Be aware also of sources such as those listed in Section 4 (National Library Catalog and Union List) for
       manuscripts, motion pictures and filmstrips, music and phonorecords, and microfilm.

Section 9

Sources for Miscellaneous Types of Publications

Answers #9/1-9/37

9-1 A: See ALA Glossary.

9-2 A: 48 pages

9-3 A: BIP includes pamphlets if they are listed in
          publishers' catalogs, but does not include
          free materials.
              PW, BPR exclude specifically if under
          49 pages.
              CBI excludes "most pamphlets."
              Retrospective bibliographic sources
          (Sabin, Evans, Shaw/Shoemaker, Roorbach
          Kelly, etc.) do often include pamphlets.
              LC/NUC does include pamphlets, insofar as
          they are acquired, cataloged and reported
          by NUC libraries.
              Serial sources exclude them since they
          are not serials.
              Some of the indexing services (the sub-
          ject-oriented services such as Library
          Literature, Education Index) and PAIS do
          include pamphlets.

9-4 A: See ALA Glossary.

9-5 A: Wilson Company: dictionary arrangement,
          standard subject headings, regular cumula-
          tion, etc.

9-6 A: No, the Vertical File Index is not really
          similar to the other Wilson indexes you
          have looked at. It is not a dictionary (one
          alphabet) arrangement. The basic arrange-
          ment is by subject with a title index. It
          has no author access.

9-7 A: See sub-title: "A subject and title index to
          selected pamphlet material." The scope is
          limited to pamphlets, and it is selective.
          Beyond an additional statement in the
          "Prefatory Note" that "inclusion does not
          constitute a recommendation," the source
          itself gives no further indication of the
          policy or guidelines for selection.

9-8 A: The Winchell annotation (although some
          years old by now) says: "free and inexpensive
          pamphlets, booklets, leaflets and mimeo-
          graphed material considered to be of interest
          to general libraries. Subjects range from
          those suitable for school libraries to
          specialized technical reports." A similar
          statement is found in the pamphlet "Cata-
          loging and Indexing Services" put out by
          the Wilson Company.

9-9 A: Urban renewal, law enforcement, minorities,
          riots, etc.

9-10 A: You can tell this only by looking through it

at the entries. Yes, it does. See
several listed under "Cookery" in the
September 1970 issue, for example.

9-11 A: It is issued monthly. It does not cumulate
          (no cumulation is indicated in the source,
          in the Winchell annotation, in the Wilson
          Company pamphlet noted in the answer to
          #8). The nature of the use of the VFI and
          of the material listed in it is basically
          ephemeral--not generally of enough per-
          manent interest to warrant cumulation, or
          even maintaining a back file at all for
          many libraries.

9-12 A: It began publication in 1935, and was
          previously (to 1955) called the Vertical
          File Service Catalog.

9-13 A: So that if you are searching in back issues
          and you find that you are looking at some-
          thing called Vertical File Service Catalog,
          you won't be confused. Also if you find a
          reference to it in a source published prior
          to 1955, it would be useful to recognize
          it as the currently titled Vertical File
          Index.

9-14 A: Assuming that the title indicated is a
          pamphlet, it may or may not be listed in
          the Vertical File Index. You have no date,
          and since VFI does not cumulate even an-
          nually, you would have to search through
          potentially many issues, under the title,
          until you found it, and even then you
          might not find it because it might not be
          listed. You can use the VFI for such a
          purpose, but it may not be worth the
          effort.

9-15 A: PTLA. You can confirm that the NEA
          catalog is included in PTLA by checking
          the list of publishers in either PTLA or
          BIP. In recent years, PTLA has included
          catalogs or lists from a widening range of
          publishers, associations, organizations,
          societies, etc., which are ordinarily thought
          of as being "non-trade" in nature.

9-16 A: See May 1967 VFI under "Teacher aides"
          (subject approach). The title is "Auxiliary
          school personnel," the price is 50¢, and
          it is available from the National Education
          Association. It is 20 pages long.

9-17 A: Since NEA publications are listed in PTLA/
          BIP (see #15), you would expect it to be
          there if it is still in print. It would
          probably not have been listed in PW/BPR
          since it is under 49 pages.

9-18 A: Its main use is suggestions (along with specific ordering information) of available free and inexpensive material suitable for a pamphlet file or vertical file, from a subject point of view. (It can be used for identification of specific materials, but has great limitations in this respect--it is only a selective list and it has no author access.) A source such as the Vertical File Index is necessary because much of the material it lists is not included in the major bibliographic sources.

9-19 A: Those used in the Vertical File Index would probably be good, since they have been found to be useful and significant for that type of material. The New York Times Thesaurus of Descriptors (see #597) might also be useful, since it is set up for current events material and this is often the basis of many pamphlet collections.

9-20 A: See ALA Glossary. See also Winchell, 8th edition, p. 163-4. Dissertations and theses are presumably based on original investigation and research; they therefore represent much of the current, new research coming out of our universities, and are primary sources for information on such research.

9-21 A: Dissertation Abstracts International; abstracts of dissertations available on microfilm or as xerographic reproductions.

9-22 A: Abstracts, see #559. DAI allows the user, though reading the abstract, to decide if he actually needs or wants a copy of the dissertation; he or the library can then get a copy on microfilm, or a xerographic reproduction from the microfilm. It is a kind of publishing "on demand."

9-23 A: DAI lists only those abstracts which are released to University microfilms and available on microfilm, therefore only the dissertations from those universities which participate in the abstracting/microfilming program. It is not, therefore, a complete listing, although more and more universities are participating in the program and coverage is extensive. Since 1969, when the title changed from Dissertation Abstracts to Dissertation Abstracts International, the scope was extended to include European universities as well as those in the U.S. and Canada. No masters theses are included.

9-24 A: It is published in two sections: A, Humanities and Social Sciences; B, Sciences. Each section is divided into broad subject categories, such as education, fine arts, history, language and literature, music, etc. The entries and abstracts for each dissertation are given under the appropriate subject category. There are keyword title indexes and author indexes in each issue.

9-25 A: DAI has been published since 1935 (with some title changes, see Winchell). The indexes only cumulate annually, with reference back to the main listing in each monthly issue. There is now a Retrospective Index (published in 1970) for vols. 1-29 (1938-68), with subject and author access.

9-26 A: American Doctoral Dissertations (formerly titled Index to American Doctoral Dissertations, and published as part of Dissertation Abstracts).

9-27 A: It is arranged by broad subject categories (fine arts, psychology, etc.) with only an author index. It does not have a specific keyword subject index as Dissertation Abstracts International does.

9-28 A: It is compiled from commencement programs issued by the universities and is therefore somewhat dependent upon the cooperation of these universities. See Introduction to the source itself.

9-29 A: See Winchell, items AI8 and AI9.

9-30 A: Look in each monthly issue of DAI for 1969 or 1970, under the general broad heading of Language and Literature, General, etc. This would give you some of the dissertations. If the annual listing in American Doctoral Dissertations was available for the past year, you could also look there, again under the broad subject heading.

9-31 A: In DAI, use the specific subject (keyword) index, looking under Coleridge. For example, see DAI, section A, November 1970, index under Coleridge, reference to p. 2345-A (Coleridge's meditative poems and his early religious thought...). As in the last question, you could also look in the annual list of American Doctoral Dissertations if available, but there you would have to look under the broad subject heading (Language and Literature) and search through all entries listed to see if any dealt specifically with Coleridge.

9-32 A: The author is William Harley Henry. The dissertation was done at and the degree granted by Johns Hopkins University in 1970. A microfilm copy of the dissertation could be ordered directly from University Microfilms (publishers of Dissertation Abstracts International) for $4.00; a xerographic enlargement for $13.95. The order number is 70-20, 157.

9-33 A: Use the Retrospective Index of DAI, vol. 8 (which includes Literature), look up Literature section, look for Coleridge as a keyword subject in the index itself. You will then have to look up, in the basic volumes of Dissertation Abstracts, the abstracts of those dissertations you might want to further investigate. This will not list all dissertations on the subject; you can in addition search each annual volume of American Doctoral Dissertations under the broad subject heading as you did in #9-31.

9-34 A: Yes, by looking in the Retrospective Index to
          DAI, author volume, and/or by searching
          in each annual volume of American Doctoral
          Dissertations in the author index.

9-35 A: Masters theses are not included in DAI (see
          #9-23).   A source which does list them is
          Masters Abstracts.

9-36 A: The purpose of both sources is the same.
          Both are published by University Microfilms.
          Masters Abstracts is much more selective
          (see Introduction to source).   The arrange-
          ment is similar.

9-37 A: See Black's Guide to Lists of Masters
          Theses.   Also see Winchell under subject:
          Librarianship and Library Resources
          (AB)--General works--Bibliography--Disser-
          tations (item AB10).

Section 10

Bibliographic Records for Other Countries--Great Britain, France, Germany

Questions #10/1-10/103

You have been examining the national bibliographic records for the United States, plus various supplementary sources covering specific types of publications or materials. Presumably, a national bibliography or bibliographic record would include only publications of that nation or country; since it is necessary to look at so many different and varied sources to get coverage for the U.S., the result is a conglomeration of bibliographical publications serving many purposes.

10-1   Of those sources you have looked at so far, which ones include publications other than those published in the United States? Which ones include publications from other countries, foreign language as well as English language?
Book trade sources: BIP, PW/BPR, CBI?
Retrospective: Sabin, Evans, Shaw/Shoemaker, Shoemaker, Kelly, Roorbach, American Catalogue?
LC/NUC?
Serial/periodical lists: Ulrich's, Ayers?
Serial union lists: ULS, NST, Gregory, Brigham?
Serial indexes: Readers' Guide, etc.?
Government publications?

This final set of sources will give you an opportunity to experiment with some foreign language bibliographic material and to test your facility at finding your way about new bibliographic territory. Your facility in dealing with the bibliographic sources for a foreign country, especially in a language which you do not know, should be based on your familiarity with the U.S. bibliographic sources. The basic organization of the material is surprisingly similar from country to country, and it is easy to feel your way bibliographically through a language you do not know since you are not concerned with textual material but rather in looking for basic guidelines, patterns, etc. Looking at the foreign bibliographies is also a useful way to review the organization of bibliographic control in the United States.

10-2   Think carefully over all the sources you have examined so far, using your review charts from each section. What kinds of organizational patterns appear again and again? What kind of information would you look for in foreign bibliographical sources?

The sources to examine, which cover three countries--Great Britain, France and Germany--and two foreign languages--French and German, are as follows:

Great Britain
        British Books in Print (AA512 and 1AA61)
        Paperbacks in Print (AA513)
        Bookseller (AA510 and AA511)
        Whitaker's Cumulative Book List (AA508, AA509)
        The Publisher (see AA506)
        English Catalogue (AA505 and 2AA69)
        British National Bibliography (AA507)
        Pollard and Redgrave: Short-title catalogue (AA498)
        Wing: Short-title catalogue (AA504)
        British Museum: General Catalogue of Printed Books (AA67, AA68, 2AA13)

France
        Biblio (AA472)
        Bibliographie de la France (AA473)
        Librairie francaise, catalogue général des ouvrages en vente/parus en langue francaise (AA474, 2AA66)
        --, Les Livres de l'Annee (AA47a)
        Catalogue général de la librairie francaise (Lorenz) (AA470)

Vicaire: Manuel de l'amateur de livres du XIXe siècle (AA471)
Quérard: La littérature francaise, 1827-49 (AA469)
Quérard: La France littéraire...XVIIIe et XIXe siècles (AA468)
Bibliothèque Nationale. Catalogue général des livres imprimés. Auteurs. (AA72, AA460, 1AA15,
    1AA16, 2AA15, 2AA16).

Germany
    Deutsche Nationalbibliographie (AA483)
    Jahresverzeichnis des Deutschen Schrifttums (AA485)
    Deutsche Buecherverzeichnis (AA486)
    Deutsche Bibliographie (AA487, 1AA60)
    --; Halbjahresverzeichnis (AA488)
    --; Fuenfjahresverzeichnis (AA489)
    Boersenblatt fuer der Deutschen Buchandel, Frankfurt
    Boersenblatt fuer der Deutschen Buchandel, Leipzig
    Heinsius: Allgemeines Buecher-Lexicon (AA478)
    Kayser: Vollstaendiges Buecher-Lexicon (AA479)
    Hinrichs: Fuenfjahrskatalog (AA480)

10-3   Beginning with the British sources lets you practice without a language handicap. What was the first
        specific source or set of sources which you examined for the U.S. bibliographic records? If a similar
        source existed for British books, would you expect it to have a similar title? Does a similar source
        exist for British books?

10-4   Is British Books in Print exactly the same as the U.S. BIP? Does it also have access by publisher and
        by subject as BIP does?

10-5   Is there any subject access at all in British Books in Print?

10-6   Who publishes British Books in Print?

10-7   One of the sources serving as a supplement to BIP is Paperbound Books in Print, limited to paperback
        books but serving essentially the same purpose otherwise as BIP. Is there a similar source for British
        paperbacks?

10-8   If you wanted to purchase an Urdu dictionary (English-Urdu), published in Great Britain, what could you
        find?

10-9   British Books in Print, like BIP, is published annually. The second set of sources you examined of the
        U.S. bibliographic records were weekly/monthly listings (PW Weekly Record, BPR, Forthcoming Books,
        Subject Guide to Forthcoming Books) giving you more current sources/of bibliographical information to
        supplement the annual publication of BIP. These sources are all published by Bowker, which also pub-
        lishes BIP, and they are specifically noted in the introductory material to BIP.
            What do you have which is similar in purpose, scope, arrangement, etc., for British books?

10-10   Whitaker's Cumulative Book List is issued quarterly and annually. Does it cumulate any more often than
        annually? How is it arranged? How long has it been published? See the Winchell annotation and/or go
        to source on the shelves.

10-11   What is the Bookseller/Current Literature/Whitaker's Cumulative Book List sequence similar to in the
        U.S. bibliographic records? Current Literature has ceased publication as of the end of 1970; what essential

feature of the sequence is therefore now missing?

10-12 Another British periodical, similar to both Bookseller and Publishers' Weekly, is The Publisher (formerly British Books, 1959-67; Publishers' Circular, 1837-59), published by The Publishers Circular Ltd., London. Look at the periodical itself, if possible. What is there in this publication which offers any bibliographic information on current books, similar to sources we have for U.S. bibliographic records?

10-13 Does the information in the Publishers' Books of the Month list cumulate in any way?

10-14 How often is the English Catalogue published? How long has it been coming out? How is it arranged?

10-15 So far you have two weekly current sources for British publications: Bookseller, published weekly, cumulating in Whitaker's Cumulative Book List; The Publisher, published monthly, cumulating in the English Catalogue. Both of these sources are trade (i.e., book trade, see Appendix A) lists, compiled by and for the book trade, although useful to librarians. A third current source, mentioned in the introductory matter to British Books in Print (see #10-9), is the British National Bibliography. The BNB is a true national bibliography, not quite like any of the U.S. sources you have studied previously, and therefore you should look at it carefully and in some detail. What organization is responsible for the publication of the BNB?

10-16 What can you tell briefly about the scope and arrangement of BNB from the title page of a recent cumulated volume?

10-17 As far as arrangement is concerned, what is the BNB similar to in the U.S. bibliographic records?

10-18 The material listed in the BNB are those items received by the Agent for Copyright Libraries. Does the U.S. have anything similar to this?

10-19 Are there any exceptions to the publications or the material listed in the BNB? How then does the BNB compare in scope to such current U.S. bibliographic records as PW Weekly Record and BPR?

10-20 How often is BNB published? How does it cumulate?

10-21 What kind of information is given, in the bibliographic citations, about each item listed? How does this compare with other current sources for British publications? What is the basic difference between the BNB listings and the Booklist Publisher/Bookseller listings?

10-22 Can you find some books recently published in Great Britain on the subject of occultism?

10-23 What sources do you have, so far, for retrospective searching for British publications?

10-24 These sources give coverage, to some extent, for the 19th and 20th centuries. By looking in Winchell, you can find other sources giving coverage prior to the 19th century--for example, Lowndes' Bibliographers' Manual of English Literature (published 1858-64) and Watt's Bibliotheca Britannica (published 1824).

Other sources give coverage specifically for the very early printed books. Two of these sources, because they represent a somewhat different approach to retrospective bibliographies, should be looked at carefully: Pollard and Redgrave's Short-title Catalogue, and Wing's Short-title Catalogue. What are the full titles for these two sources? When were they published?

10-25   From the titles, what is the primary difference in scope or coverage between the two works?

10-26   Would you expect to find any books printed in America listed in the Pollard and Redgrave STC? Why or why not? What about the Wing STC?

10-27   Why do you think that 1475 was chosen as the beginning date for the Pollard and Redgrave STC? Why was 1640 chosen as the closing date?

10-28   How are these two sources arranged, and what bibliographical information is given in the citations?

10-29   Why are the Wing and the Pollard and Redgrave bibliographies called "Short-title catalogs"? Where might you go to find the "long titles" if necessary?

10-30   Both the Pollard and Redgrave and Wing STC's give indication of libraries possessing copies. This information is, in fact, the basic purpose behind both bibliographies. The Winchell annotation for the Wing STC states that it is not a "census of copies." What is meant by a "census of copies"? What other term used so far is it similar to? Why is the Wing STC not a census of copies? Is the Pollard and Redgrave STC a census of copies?

10-31   What can you find in Winchell which does claim to be a "census" of early printed books?

10-32   Would you expect to find any "ghosts" (see #306) in the Pollard and Redgrave STC? in the Wing STC?

10-33   How many editions of Shakespeare's The Tragedy of King Richard the Third are listed in the Pollard and Redgrave STC? The first is listed as published in 1597. What libraries have (had) copies? What does "4°" stand for?

10-34   According to the Wing STC, does the Folger Library have a copy of The Lucky Chance by Mrs. Aphra Behn? Are you sure?

10-35   The last source on the list for Great Britain is the General Catalog of Printed Books of the Library of the British Museum (British Museum Catalog). What is the British Museum Library?

10-36   The British Museum Catalog is therefore similar to what U.S. source?

10-37   Is the BM Catalogue just the same as the LC/NUC? Does it serve the same purpose?

10-38   In what way are they similar in scope?

10-39   In what ways are they similar in arrangement?

10-40   Is the British Museum Catalogue published on a current, continuing basis as the LC/NUC is?

10-41   What is there which does give current, continuing, frequent coverage of books which are, in effect, added to the British Museum Library?

10-42   Can you find in the British Museum Catalogue Fraser's Magazine for Town and Country? (It was published in London). When was it published and in how many volumes? Where else might you find the same information? Look there and see if you find the same or any different information from that given in BM Catalogue.

10-43   Is there a union list of serials for Great Britain, comparable to the ULS/NST?

10-44   Are there periodical indexes or indexing services for British periodicals?

10-45   Can you find the author of a book titled Limey: an Englishman joins the gangs, published in the 1930's?

10-46   From your experience with U.S. bibliography thus far, would you expect there might be a bibliographical source dealing with British government publications? If so, what is it, by whom is it published? How is it arranged, and how often does it come out?

10-47   Can you find the ordering information for The Baking of an English Loaf by Elizabeth David, published in 1969 (in England)?

10-48   The Publishers Circular was published under a number of variant titles before it finally changed to British Books in 1959 and to The Publisher in 1967. Where would you look to find specifically what these titles were?

10-49   Eleanor Farjeon (1881-1965) was an Englishwoman who wrote many well-known books for children. When was her book titled The Starry Floor (Verses) first published?

10-50   Where would you look to find what books are in print in Great Britain on urban problems?

         Now move on to the bibliographic records for France. In dealing with these, your problems are complicated only by the fact that you may be working with an unfamiliar language. If you read French, your problems should be minimal. In either case, it would be helpful to find a French-English/English-French dictionary to have handy to look up an occasional word which does not seem clear in context.

10-51   Armed with a dictionary and with your general expectations of patterns, forms, arrangements, etc., from all the bibliographies you have looked at so far, locate and examine the first title on the list of sources for France: Biblio. Look first at the source itself, without turning to the Winchell annotation.

Biblio is a current source. How often is it issued and does it appear to cumulate?

10-52   Look at the introductory statement ("Répertoire bibliographique") in the front of a recent issue or bound volume. What is the scope of Biblio (first two lines following heading)?

10-53   What is the arrangement of Biblio (directly following the two lines describing the scope)?

10-54   So far, what is Biblio similar to, in scope and arrangement, for U.S. bibliography?

10-55   What information will you find in the bibliographic citations in Biblio?

10-56   What is the publisher, paging, and price for La Gastronomie Francaise by Henri Mercier (published early 1960's)?

10-57   With this much information you should be able to use Biblio as effectively as you can any of the U.S. English-language bibliographic sources. Check your information against the Winchell citation. Biblio is, as Winchell notes, a trade bibliography, and one which is easy to use.

Another current French bibliography is the next title on the list, the Bibliographie de la France. This one is much more complex; it serves both as an official list and as a trade list. Read the annotation in Winchell, then look at a recent weekly issue of the Bibliographie de la France. What are the three parts into which the bibliography is divided? Can you find them in the source itself?

10-58   Look first more specifically at the 1st part, or the Bibliographie Officielle. This is the list of publications received through the "Dépot légal" (legal deposit). What is legal deposit? What is the French legal deposit law?

10-59   How is this list (Bibliographie Officielle) arranged, and what kind of information appears to be given in the citations?

10-60   How is the weekly trade listing in the 3rd part, Les Livres de la Semaine, arranged? What information is given?

10-61   Is there any cumulation of Les Livres de la Semaine? See Winchell if this is not clear from the source.

10-62   How does the Bibliographie de la France compare to Biblio?

10-63   To what U.S. bibliographic source does the Bibliographie de la France compare?

10-64   The listings, both official and trade, which appear in the weekly Bibliographie de la France are cumulated annually into the next title on the list: Librairie Francaise, Les Livres de l'Année. How long has this been published and does it cumulate in any way?

10-65   What subject access is there in the yearly cumulations, Les Livres de l'Année?

10-66   If you want to locate a book about Robert Kennedy, in French, published in 1968, but you do not know the author or exact title, how could you find it in Les Livres de l'Année? Could you also find it in Biblio?

10-67   Is there a bibliographic source for France similar to Books in Print and British Books in Print?

10-68   What retrospective coverage do you have so far for French publications?

10-69   What other retrospective sources exist for the 18th, 19th, and early 20th century? See Winchell.

10-70   Does France have/a national library similar to the Library of Congress and the British Museum?

10-71   Does the Bibliothèque Nationale publish a catalog?

10-72   How does the Bibliothèque Nationale catalog compare to that of the Library of Congress and that of the British Museum?

10-73   Since the Bibliothèque Nationale catalog is not yet complete, and many of the early volumes are now badly out of date (see Winchell annotation), what other sources can be used to supplement it for coverage of French publications?

10-74   Does the Bibliothèque Nationale have a subject access? What retrospective subject access is there for French publications?

10-75   What is a characteristic of the Bibliothèque Nationale catalog which limits its use?

10-76   Pontus de Tyard wrote Mantice, ou Discours de la Vérité de divination par astrologie, which was printed anonymously in 1558. What bibliographic information can you find about this title?

10-77   Where would you look to find some recent French publications on librarianship?

10-78   What bibliographic information can you find about Histoire de l'annexion de la Savoie à la France en 1792, by J. Masse, published in 1891-1898?

10-79   Where would you find the publisher and price for a recent book titled Nuts!...La bataille des Ardennes by Michel Georis?

10-80   Exercises grammaticaux by Clément Bouilion was published in Nancy (France) in 1969.   Was this published as part of a series?

Finally, some bibliographic sources for Germany--again, it would be helpful to locate a German-English dictionary to look up an occasional unfamiliar key word.   The German bibliographic sources are highly organized, and once you get the general overall pattern, can be extremely easy to use. The basic problem with current German bibliography comes from the split in Germany after World War II, into East (German Democratic Republic) and West (German Federal Republic).   German bibliographies beginning before this split were mostly issued from Leipzig, the book trade center, now part of East Germany.   Bibliographic sources--official and trade--are still published there.
        After the split, Frankfurt became the book trade center for the German Federal Republic, West Germany, and bibliographic sources--similar in purpose, scope, arrangement, and format to the East German sources--are now issued from Frankfurt.

10-81   Begin by looking at the older East German current bibliography from Leipzig, the Deutsche Nationalbibliographie (Deutsche-German, therefore German national bibliography).   This source is published in two parts or series (reihe): Reihe A, "Neuerscheinungen des Buchhandels" (publications of the book trade) and Reihe B, "Neuerscheinungen ausserhalb des Buchhandels" (publications out of the book trade).   How often is each series or reihe published?   You can tell this from the dates on the issues or from Winchell.

10-82   How are the two series organized?   You should be able to tell this from looking at them, rather than going to Winchell.

10-83   Are there indexes to this basic arrangement?   What kind of indexes are needed?   Is there anything which looks like an index?

10-84   Is there then author/title/specific subject access as well as broad subject groupings?   Could you find a book if you knew only the title?

10-85   How long has the Deutsche Nationalbibliographie been published?   Does it cumulate in any way?   See Winchell.

10-86   How is the Jahresverzeichnis arranged?   (See Winchell or the source itself.)   Does it cumulate?

10-87   How is the Deutsche Buecherverzeichnis arranged?

10-88   Deutsche Bibliographie is the West German current bibliography from Frankfurt.   How is it organized? Use the source itself, not Winchell.

10-89   When did Deutsche Bibliographie begin publication?   Does it cumulate?

10-90   How is the Deutsche Bibliographie Halbjarhresverzeichnis (half-yearly list) arranged?

10-91   Deutsche Nationalbibliographie (East German) also further cumulated into a 5-year list. Is this also true of the Deutsche Bibliographie (West German)?

10-92   How is the five-year cumulation of the Deutsche Bibliographie arranged?

10-93   What is the scope of the Deutsche Bibliographie and the Deutsche Nationalbibliographie?

10-94   Will you find West German publications in the Deutsche Nationalbibliographie? Will you find East German publications in the Deutsche Bibliographie?

10-95   Do the two current sources you have examined so far, Deutsche Nationalbibliographie and Deutsche Bibliographie, seem to be comparable to the trade bibliographies or trade publications that you examined for the United States, Great Britain, and France?

10-96   England, Off the Beaten Track was published in Germany in 1968. What is the author's name, publisher, price?

10-97   What is the publisher and price of Der Knabe aus dem Rosengarten by Elli Otto, published in 1965?

10-98   Is there a Books in Print type source for Germany?

10-99   What retrospective sources do you have so far for Germany?

10-100   What other retrospective sources are available for German publications?

10-101   If possible, look at any one of the three retrospective sources noted in the answer to #10-100. Can you tell, simply by looking at the source itself, approximately what the arrangement is? (Think: what general possibilities do you have for arrangement?)

10-102   Is there a catalog of a national library for Germany, as there is for the United States (LC), Great Britain (BM), and France (BN)?

10-103   In which bibliographies covered so far might you expect to find current Swiss publications?

Section 10

Bibliographic Records for Other Countries--Great Britain, France, Germany

Answers #10/1-10/103

10-1 A: The book trade sources published by Bowker (BIP, etc., PW/BPR) do not include publications from other countries. CBI does, if they are in English.

Of the retrospective sources, most are U.S./American only, except Sabin which includes publications about America published elsewhere.

LC/NUC does list from all countries, all languages (universal).

Ulrich's is international, Ayers is mostly American, some foreign.

ULS and NST, like LC/NUC, are universal. Gregory and Brigham are American only.

The periodical indexes tend to include English-language material, thus covering some British as well as American (see #585).

Government publications sources are U.S. only.

10-2 A: Retrospective and current.
Frequency of publication (weekly, monthly, etc.), and cumulation patterns.
Arrangement: author, title, subject, chronological, geographical; classed subject, alphabetical subject; standard subject headings, keyword in title subject access; necessary indexes
Information in the bibliographic citations (author, title, publisher, date, collation, price, address of publisher or other ordering information, classification numbers, etc.)
Types of publications included or excluded; trade vs. non-trade, for example.
Sources of bibliographic control: government, professional (library), commercial (book trade)
National libraries, copyright laws, etc.

10-3 A: The first set of sources you examined for the U.S. bibliographic records was Books in Print (plus Publishers' Trade List Annual and Subject Guide to Books in Print). Because the title of the source is virtually self-explanatory, you would expect similar sources --that is, sources serving similar purposes-- for other countries, other languages, to have similar titles. Looking at the list of sources to examine for Great Britain, you find British Books in Print, which seems obviously to be the similar source you want. If you look directly in the basic Winchell, you might be somewhat mislead, since until 1965 British Books in Print was called the Reference Catalog of Current Literature (AA512); although you can tell from the annotation that the purpose is essentially the same as Books in Print.

10-4 A: British Books in Print itself is very similar to BIP, with author and title access (in 1969 both author and title lists are in the same volume; in 1970, there are to be two volumes, one for author, one for titles). The bibliographic information about each entry is approximately the same. British Books in Print is now published annually, although this was not always so (see Winchell annotation). There is a full list of publishers with addresses, as in BIP, but British Books in Print has no publisher access such as PTLA (although the annotation in Winchell, AA512), indicates that much earlier in its history, it was-- like PTLA--a collection of publishers' catalogs with separate alphabetical index. Nor does British Books in Print have the same kind of title access as BIP has with Subject Guide to British BIP.

10-5 A: Yes, through title. You have already had cases (see #218-220) where titles could serve as subject access if the first word of the title was a significant subject. You have also had cases (see #571) where the title could serve as subject access by inverting the title so that any significant subject word in the title became the first or filing word. Both of these techniques are used in the title list of British Books in Print to give some title access. See, in the 1969 edition, books on "indexing" or books on the "Channel Islands," as examples of titles serving as subject entries; also under "Europe, Afloat in, Africa learns about, Air power over, Ancient..." as examples of inverted titles serving as subject entries.

10-6 A: British Books in Print is published by J. Whitaker and Sons, Ltd. in London. It is published in the United States by Bowker. (See title page of source.)

10-7 A: Paperbacks in Print; a Reference Catalogue ...in print and on sale..., also published by Whitaker, semi-annually, with classified subject/author-title access.

10-8 A: Since you want to purchase one, you presumably want one in print, and although you do not have an author or title this is a fairly simple one to find through the title list of British Books in Print (see, for example, Urdu-English-Eng. Urdu Dict. Lal, R.N. 48/- Bailey Bros... in 1969 edition).

10-9 A: Look at the introductory material to British

Books in Print ("Guides to British Books and Their Publishers," 1969 edition); you find specifically noted: Bookseller (published weekly and containing a list of British books as they are published, author, title, subject-through-title in a dictionary arrangement, with monthly cumulated list in the last issue of each month), plus Current Literature (monthly, giving a classified--or broad subject --access), plus Whitaker's Cumulative Book List, cumulating quarterly from Bookseller and Current Literature, then annually. All of these are published by the Whitaker Company. (The British National Bibliography is also noted; this will be discussed at some length later.)

10-10 A: It has been cumulating also on a five-year basis. It has been published since 1924. It is arranged, quarterly and in the cumulations, as a classified (broad subjects, such as architecture, art, biography, domestic science, occultism, poetry, etc.) list with author/title/subject-through-title access also.

10-11 A: Bookseller/Current Literature/Whitaker's Cumulative Book List is similar to the PW Weekly Record (weekly, alphabetical main entry list)/BPR (monthly, classified subject list with author/title index)/BPR Cumulative (annual and five-year cumulations of the classified subject list with author/title index) sequence. The loss of Current Literature eliminates the monthly classified subject access. Quarterly and annual classified subject access is still available through Whitaker's Cumulative Book List. A monthly cumulated author/title/subject-through-title list is still available in the Bookseller, the last issue of the month.

10-12 A: The Publisher does not match specifically any U.S. publication. It is published bimonthly (every other month); its main bibliographic feature is a monthly supplement titled Books of the Month, listing paperbacks, separately, then an author index and a title index (with some inverted titles to serve as subjects), giving approximately the same information as in the Bookseller lists. Also there are several additional supplements titled "Previews" which list new and forthcoming books, some on specific areas such as religious, technical, children's; this is like similar supplements in Publishers Weekly, and--along with the forthcoming lists in the Bookseller--gives some author/title/subject coverage similar to Forthcoming Books and Subject Guide to Forthcoming Books.

10-13 A: Yes, into the English Catalogue. (The annotation in Winchell for British Books, former title of The Publisher, gives this information.)

10-14 A: The English Catalog is published annually

with three-year cumulations at present. It has been published since 1801 (see Winchell). It is arranged by author and title only (with of course some subject access through titles).

10-15 A: See title page of any recent cumulated volume or verso of first page of any recent issue: The Council of the British National Bibliography, Ltd., representing the British Museum, The Library Association, The Publishers Association, The Booksellers Association, etc.

10-16 A: Annual volume for 1969:
Scope: new books published in the British Isle, based upon the books received by the Agent for the Copyright Libraries; Arrangement: classified subject according to the Dewey Decimal Classification with author, title, and subject index.

10-17 A: American Book Publishers Record--classed according to Dewey with author, title, specific subject index.

10-18 A: The Catalog for Copyright Entries comes closest, but even it is not really similar. The British law requires deposit of copies of all new books with The British Museum (the national library of Great Britain) and with various other libraries (Copyright Libraries). (See Landau: Encyclopedia of Librarianship, under "legal deposit" for a history of the legal deposit law in Great Britain and comparative laws in other countries.) The United States has no similar law; copies are deposited with the U.S. Copyright Office in order to obtain copyright, and these copies are usually eventually turned over to the Library of Congress, but there is no law requiring copyright or requiring deposit of copies with any libraries for all books.

10-19 A: Only a few items are excluded--see Preface: periodicals (however, the first issues of new periodicals are listed), music, maps, some government publications, publications without a British imprint.
The scope of BNB is much broader than PW/BPR--which excludes all government publications, and serials/periodicals, pamphlets under 49 p., etc.

10-20 A: It is published weekly, with the author/title/ subject indexes cumulating in the last issue of the last month. There are quarterly and annual cumulations, and five-year cumulations.

10-21 A: BNB citations give full cataloging information, plus price, publisher's address for ordering. This is fuller information than is given in the other current British sources. The Bookseller and The Publisher are trade lists; BNB is more library-oriented, although both library and trade organizations are responsible for its publication (see #10-15).

10-22 A: You want recent information with subject access. Whitaker's Cumulative Book List, under classified subject heading, "Occultism," for publications of the past three months or past year; and/or British National Bibliography under Dewey Decimal Classification 133 for past week and month, year.

10-23 A: BNB to 1950; Whitaker's to 1924; English Catalogue to 1801. (You also have CBI to 1928, and LC/NUC all the way back, see #10-1).

10-24 A: Pollard and Redgrave: A short-title catalogue of books printed in England, Scotland and Ireland, and of English books printed abroad, 1475-1640; Wing: Short-title catalogue of books printed in England, Scotland, Ireland, Wales, and British America and of English books printed in other countries, 1641-1700. Pollard and Redgrave was published in 1926 and Wing (in 3 volumes) in 1945-51; neither were compiled at the time which they cover; both were compiled retrospectively.

10-25 A: The dates covered. Pollard and Redgrave: 1475-1640. Wing: 1640-1700. Both include books published in Great Britain and English (language) books printed elsewhere.

10-26 A: No, you wouldn't; since the first printing in America was not until 1638 (see #290), and the Pollard and Redgrave STC covers only to 1640. The Wing STC does include books printed in America (see the title).

10-27 A: 1475 was chosen as the beginning date presumably because the first book in English (The Recuyell of the Histories of Troy, printed by William Caxton in Bruges) was printed at approximately that date. 1640 was chosen as the closing date presumably to match the dividing date of the transcripts of the registers of the London Stationers' Company (see Winchell AA497 and AA503).

10-28 A: Both are arranged alphabetically by author (and other main entries if the author is not known or is not used as the main entry). Generally speaking there is no title access (except for some anonymous entries), no subject access, and few cross-references. Citations include brief bibliographical information and indication of libraries possessing copies. (Library location symbols are explained in the introductory material of each source.)

10-29 A: The titles listed in these bibliographies are "abridged entries" (see introductory material in both sources), meaning that the titles (traditionally lengthy and complex for books of this period) have been shortened or abridged (see "Memoranda" to Pollard and Redgrave, and "Preface" to Wing, specifically "Method of Abridgement" in both). Other bibliographical sources for the period found through Winchell, might give fuller entries--such as

Catalogue of books in the library of the British Museum..to the year 1640 (AA495), Evans and Sabin for American books, several sources listed (Winchell, 8th ed., p. 16-17) as bibliographies of "early and rare books" (Hain, Copinger, Proctor, etc.)

10-30 A: A "census of copies" (not in ALA Glossary) would be a listing of all known copies. It is somewhat similar to a "union list" but even union lists do not always aim at listing all known copies. See Wing Preface under "Number of Copies Listed:" "This is not a census of copies, but only a guide to inform scholars where each book may most conveniently be consulted... Usually only one copy is located in any one city..." etc. The same is true of the Pollard and Redgrave STC (see Preface, p. viii, and "Memoranda," p. xii-xiii), although since books of that period are considerably scarcer, sometimes it does in fact record all known copies of very rare items.

10-31 A: See Winchell, 8th edition, p. 16-17, "Early and Rare Books--Union lists": item AA168, Goff's Incunabula in American libraries; a third census...

10-32 A: Since both STC's aim to list books "copies of which are known to exist--thus a catalogue of the books of which its compilers have been able to locate copies, not a bibliography of books known or believed to have been produced" (see introductory material in both sources), then presumably neither bibliographies would have any ghosts. The "Memoranda" to Pollard and Redgrave, p. xiv, mentions one ghost, of a sort, and the "Preface" to Wing, p. vii, indicates that in fact he was able to examine only 90% of the books listed so that some ghosts may exist.

10-33 A: Pollard and Redgrave, p. 519, under Shakespeare as author, alphabetized as Richard III, bottom of first column, top of second: 8 editions are listed. The first, item 22314, was published in 1597. Libraries holding copies are British Museum, Bodleian, Huntington, Folger, Yale. "4°" means "quarto" (standard abbreviation, see Appendix 1 of the ALA Glossary) signifying the size of the book.

10-34 A: Wing, vol. 1, p. 131, under Behn. WF is the Wing symbol for the Folger Library (see p. xiii); it is not listed in Wing as having a copy, but this does not mean that the Folger does not have a copy, since the Wing list is not a census of copies but only a selected list.

10-35 A: The national library of Great Britain. See Winchell, 8th ed., p. 7, under "Library catalogs."

10-36 A: LC/NUC

10-37 A: No, not exactly. The BM Catalogue is a catalog of holdings of the British Museum Library and only of the British Museum Library. The LC/NUC has never been really a catalog of the holdings of the LC. It was, in earlier series, a catalog or listing of LC printed cards; later it listed holdings for other cooperating libraries as well, and became a union catalog. The BM catalog does not serve to indicate library locations, except the books listed there are presumably available in the collections of the BM Library.

10-38 A: As catalogs of the national libraries of their countries, one of the functions of which is to collect and preserve the literature of the country, both represent extensive and comparatively complete collections of the publications of their country. In addition, they serve as universal bibliographies because they represent extensive collections of materials from all countries, all languages, all periods of time. Both include most types of publications, books plus periodicals, government publications, etc.

10-39 A: Both are arranged basically by main entry (generally author) only, alphabetically, with some but not extensive cross-references; usually no title entry unless the title is the main entry. Both have some subject access through a separate form of publication; for the British Museum subject coverage, see Winchell AA68.

10-40 A: No. The main set in 262 volumes was published from 1955 through 1966, and includes material cataloged through 1955 (therefore imprints through 1955). There is also a 10-year supplement for items cataloged 1956-1965, in 50 volumes, and a set of 5 volumes for the year 1963. Some form of regular additions is planned, but not yet specifically set forth. The BM catalogue is not published in current, monthly, quarterly, annual issues as is the LC/NUC.

10-41 A: The British National Bibliography, since it is a list of books received by the Agent for the Copyright Libraries, of which the British Museum is one, does give current, continuing, frequent coverage of some of the materials added to the BM Library. The current acquisitions of the BM Library are not limited to books received by the Agent for Copyright Libraries; current acquisitions may include older British publications, or current and retrospective publications from any other country. These will not appear in the BNB. The LC/NUC current issues will include, for example, recent publications from Great Britain; the BNB current issues will not include recent publications from the United States.

10-42 A: It is located in the BM Catalogue in vol. 185, p. 338, under Periodical Publications-London. There is a cross-reference from

Fraser's Magazine at the beginning of all the entries for Fraser, vol. 78, column 696. It was published from 1830-69 in 80 volumes and in another series from 1870-82 in 26 volumes.
You could also find this in ULS, where it is listed under Fraser's Magazine; dates and volumes numbering are the same as in BM, although months are given in ULS. In addition ULS gives clearer information on the title changes and indicates what titles superseded it.

10-43 A: See Winchell under Periodicals (AF)--Union Lists (p. 141)--Great Britain, items AF108, 109: British union-catalogue of periodicals...

10-44 A: Yes, many of which are the same ones as for U.S. periodicals. See answer to #585.

10-45 A: The BM Catalogue covers this period, but you need title access, so you must go to the English Catalogue, 1933; the title entry gives the author as Spenser (J.), which is given in the author entry as Spenser (James). Publisher is Longmans.

10-46 A: Yes, you would expect one. See Winchell under Government Publications (AH)--Great Britain (p. 160)--19th and 20th centuries: items AH61, 62, 63: Great Britain. Stationery Office. Catalogue of Government Publications, 1922+. It is published by Her Majesty's Stationery Office (HMSO), equivalent of the U.S. GPO. It comes out monthly and annually and is arranged basically by issuing agency.

10-47 A: BNB, Whitaker's, English Catalogue, CBI would presumably all include the listing. It is in the 1969 cumulative volume of BNB, under author with reference through classification number to the fuller entry in the classed subject section. The price is 2/6, the standard book number is 901794 00 7, the publisher is Elizabeth David, Ltd., 46 Bourne Street, London SWI, England.

10-48 A: ULS and NST. Perhaps also LC/NUC. The Winchell annotation doesn't really list them.)

10-49 A: Since you don't have a date, your first choice would be a source which would bring together in one place as much as possible by this author--here, the British Museum Catalog. In the basic set, this is listed as being published in 1949, and since no earlier publication is listed, it is reasonable to assume that this was the first edition. In the English Catalogue, Whitaker's, BNB, CBI, you would have to search either from beginning to date, or from current volumes back (it could have been a posthumous publication) through many volumes. (LC/NUC might also be a possible source, although you would have to be sure there that you did not find the first U.S. publication which may have been later than the first British publication.) If the title is listed in British Books in Print, the date given would not necessarily be that of the first publication.

10-50 A: Since you want books in print, you would go to the latest British Books in Print which has no full subject access, so you would be limited to finding only those titles which have "urban" in the title (see under Title section of 1969 British Books in Print); you could also look under related words (housing, poverty, city, slums, welfare, etc.; see #535).

You could in addition look in current (this year, last year) issues and cumulations of BNB and Whitaker's Cumulative Book List under appropriate subject classification on the assumption that such recent titles would still be in print. (Once having found the authors and titles, you could also then check against British Books in Print for in-print status).

10-51 A: It is published monthly, which you should be able to tell from the names of the months appearing on the current issues themselves, and it cumulates at least in some way on an annual basis, which you should be able to tell from the dates on the spines of the volumes on the shelves.

10-52 A: "De tous les ouvrages parus en langue francaise dans le monde entier." All the works appearing in the French language in the entire world.

10-53 A: You should immediately recognize the phrase "catalogue-dictionnaire": dictionary catalog. In a single alphabetical list are
1. Auteur (author)
2. Titre (title)
3. Matière (subject)

10-54 A: CBI: all books in English no matter where published; author/title/subject in a single alphabetical list (dictionary catalog)

10-55 A: In the paragraph following that about the dictionary arrangement, you find "une description bibliographique complete: auteur (author), titre complet (complete title), collection (series), nombre de volumes (number of volumes), format (size), nombre de pages (number of pages), illustrations (illustrations), planches (binding), portraits (portraits), prix (price), tirages sur beaux papiers (deluxe editions), date (date), lieu de publication... (place of publication, unless it is Paris), éditeur (publisher).

10-56 A: This can be found in Biblio, by searching the annual cumulated volumes from 1960 until you find it, either under author (more direct) or under title which will refer you to the author entry for full information. It is in Biblio 1963: the publisher is Flammarion; the price is (or was) 2,950 francs, and it has 320 pages.

10-57 A: Be sure you are looking at the Bibliographie itself, not one of the supplementary issues titled "Les Livres du Mois." Issues prior to the second half of 1970 are in a loose form in folders and are hard to handle. If possible, examine a late 1970 or later issue.

The first page headed "Sommaire" (summary of list of contents) shows you three parts:
1st part: Bibliographie Officielle (the official list, publications received through the legal deposit);
2nd part: Chronique (news--i.e., of the book trade, libraries, related items);
3rd part: this should always include "Les Livres de la Semaine" (Books of the week), plus a monthly supplement, "Les Livres du Mois" (Books of the month). It also includes "Annonces" (publishers' advertisements). This 3rd part is the trade or publishers' lists.

10-58 A: See #10-18 on legal deposit. For the legal deposit law in France, see the first page of the Bibliographie Officielle, the note at the bottom, second paragraph which translates roughly as: It is recalled that by the terms of the law of June 21, 1943, amended by the decree of November 21, 1960, deposit must be made first, by the publishers, not later than 48 hours after first being put on sale (deposits made directly to the Administration) and three days before being put on sale (if sent by post) for books, immediately before being put on sale for periodicals; second by printers of finished drawings for books and periodicals.

10-59 A: The list is arranged alphabetically by classed (broad) drawings for subject (i.e., general works, philosophy, religion, social sciences, linguistics, pure sciences, etc.) with an author (auteurs) index. There are sometimes additional special lists such as serials, music, theses, maps (cartes), official or government publications, etc.: materials which would not ordinarily appear in "trade" lists but which would be included in the legal deposits.

The information given in the citations is more or less full cataloging, in recognizable form.

10-60 A: In the same broad subject classification as the Bibliographie Officielle, but with no index. The information given is somewhat briefer than that in the Bibliographie Officielle list.

10-61 A: Les Livres de la Semaine (weekly) is cumulated into Les Livres du Mois (monthly) with author/title indexes. The monthly list is cumulated quarterly (trimestre, semestre), and then annually into Les Livres de l'Année. Books from the Bibliographie Officielle which are not included in Les Livres de la Semaine are also listed in the yearly cumulation.

10-62 A: Bibliographie de la France is published more frequently (weekly) than Biblio (monthly), although in general publications are apt to appear first in Biblio; listings in the Bibliographie Officielle section of Bibliography de la France are careful and full, and are often delayed in appearance.

The Bibliographie Officielle lists only works received through the legal deposit (although this is extensive) but therefore also includes a lot of non-trade type material (music scores, theses, etc.)

Biblio includes French works published elsewhere, and is easier to use.

10-63 A: Bibliographie Officielle, official list from legal deposit, somewhat comparable to U.S. Catalog of Copyright Entries or to LC/NUC. Les Livres de la Semaine, etc., trade list, somewhat comparable to BPR.

10-64 A: Librairie Francaise, Les Livres de l'Année has been published annually since 1933 (except during the war). It cumulates more or less every 10 years into La Librairie Francaise (subtitle varies) (see Winchell AA74 and 2AA66) which was actually first published in 1930. This is arranged only by author and title, with no classed subject list as in Les Livres de l'Année.

10-65 A: Classed subject access as basic arrangement of entries. Also a special index in the front of more recent annual volumes called "Index des mots usuels et des mots vedettes." Mots= words; vedettes= prominent. Therefore this index is similar to what subject approach? <u>Keywords</u> in title.

10-66 A: In Les Livres de l'Année, 1968, in the keyword index in front, under Kennedy, Robert--a reference to page 93 (author: Koch), where you find <u>John Kennedy - M. Luther King - Robert Kennedy. Pour un nouveau monde</u> by Thilo Koch, published by Rencontre, 204 pages, 22,80 francs.

In Biblio, 1968 p. 633, the same book is found under "Kennedy, Robert Francis, 1925-1968" (subject entry), as <u>Pour un nouveau monde. John F. Kennedy, Martin L. King, Robert F. Kennedy,</u> published in Lausanne (Switzerland).

10-67 A: Not yet, although a source to be titled Catalogue de l'Edition Francaise has been announced by Paris Publications of Port Washington, N.Y.

The Librairie Francaise, Catalogue Général des Ouvrages en Vente (see #10-64) at one time may have served a somewhat similar purpose but this is no longer true.

10-68 A: Biblio back to 1933; Bibliographie de la France back to 1811, with annual and 10-year cumulations back to 1930.

10-69 A: Quérard: La France littéraire...XVIII et XIX siècles (AA468)
Quérard: La littérature francaise... 1827-49 (AA469)
Catalogue général de la librairie francaise, 1840-1925 (Lorenz) (AA470)
Vicaire: Manuel de l'amateur de livres...1801-1893 (AA471)

10-70 A: Yes, the Bibliothèque Nationale, see Winchell, 8th edition, p. 7.

10-71 A: Yes, see Winchell, item AA72.

10-72 A: The BN catalog, like that of the BM, is not published on a current monthly basis as is the LC/NUC. The basic set of the BN is still in progress of publication (has been since 1900), and the first five-year supplement (1960-64, see Winchell 1AA16 and 2AA16) has been published.

Like the BM and unlike the LC/NUC, the Bibliothèque Nationale catalog is a catalog of the holdings of the Bibliothèque Nationale. Like BM and LC/NUC, because it collects publications from all countries, all times, as well as the national literature, it serves as a universal bibliography.

Like the LC/NUC and BM, full bibliographical information and notes are given.

Unlike the LC/NUC and the BM, the BN has entries under personal author names only (no titles, no periodicals, no corporate authors, government authors, etc.)

10-73 A: All current and retrospective sources, see answer to #10-68 and #10-69. Also the LC/NUC and the catalog of the British Museum Library.

10-74 A: No, there is no subject access to the BN catalog. There is some subject access through Biblio and Les Livres de l'Année to about 1930, and some through Lorenz (Winchell AA470) from 1925 back to 1840.

10-75 A: The fact that it has only personal author entries, with no title entries for anonymous works, no corporate author entries, no government author entries, etc.

10-76 A: Although it was published anonymously, you do know the author (or presumed author), and you may therefore expect to find it in the Bibliothèque Nationale catalog. It is in vol. 196, p. 526, under author, Tyard (Pontus de). The author's name is given in square brackets in the citation, indicating that it does not appear on the publication. It was printed in Lion by J. de Tournes, in 98 pages; other information is also given, about the title page, etc. Similarly, a citation for this title (with less information) is given in the British Museum catalog (vol. 242, under Tyard).

10-77 A: You have a current source with subject access: Biblio (subject headings like CBI) or Bibliographie de la France (in Bibliographie Officielle and/or Les Livres de la Semaine—both have classed subjects like BPR). Biblio is easier to search in, but publication might be somewhat scattered due to nature of subject headings; publications are more likely to be listed together (under O. Généralities: 00/02... Bibliographie-Bibliotheconomie) in a classed subject approach such as Bibliographie de la France. See #184 on similar problem with BPR and CBI.

10-78 A: Period is late 19th century, which is covered by Bibliographie de la France, Quèrard's La France Litteraire, Lorenz' Catalogue general, somewhat by Vicaire's Manuel (see #10-68 and #10-69), and Bibliothèque Nationale Catalog. This title is located in Lorenz, vol. 15 covering 1891-1899 I-Z, under author Masse, Jules. The title was published in 3 volumes from 1891-1898, the publisher was Allier in Grenoble (France), and it is extracted (taken) from the Bulletin de l'Academie delphinale.

This title is also listed in the Bibliothèque Nationale catalog, vol. 109, p. 241-- the author's name is given as Mases, Jules, but this appears to be a misprint since it is filed as if it were Masse. The same information is given with the addition of the series and volume numbering for the periodical (Bulletin de...).

10-79 A: You want a current source giving ordering information, and you have author or title access. Biblio or Bibliographie de la France (in Bibliographie Officielle or in Les livres de la Semaine/du Mois) should list it and you would have to search from current issues back till you found it. Biblio has less places to search than Bibliographie de la France so is easier. The publisher is Editions France-Empire, the price is 19,20 francs (Biblio, January 1970, p. 48).

10-80 A: You have author, title, date, and want fuller bibliographic information. Your easiest source is probably Biblio, annual cumulated volume for 1969. You can find the full citation under the author, Bouillon, Clément. The series note is given in parentheses following the complete title, and you find that this book publication was indeed published as a part of a series, apparently an unnumbered series: Publications of the Group de Rechaerches et d'Applications Pédagogiques of the Institute d'Anglais of the University of Nancy. It is possible that this title might appear in a library card catalog only under the series, rather than under author. It is also possible that a library might place a standing order to receive all of the publications of this particular institute or organization, rather than ordering each separately by author and title. In either case, to locate or to order, it could be vital to know the series information.

10-81 A: Reihe A is published weekly; Reihe B semi-monthly.

10-82 A: Both are arranged basically in classed or broad subject groups, which are listed on the title pages of each series, such as: Religion (religion), philosophie (philosophy), politik (political science) schoeneliteratur (literature), musik (music), medizin (medicine), etc.

10-83 A: Author and title indexes plus possibly specific subject indexes are needed for a broad subject grouping or classed arrangement. In each issue of both Reihe A and B there is an index in the back, titled "Verfasser (author) und stichwort (catchword) register (index)," plus a "Register der Korporativen verfasser" (Index of corporative authors). Reihe A also has a "Verlagregister" (publisher index).

10-84 A: There is author access. There is also a catchword (or keyword) title access (which you have seen before used also as a specific subject access, for example in British Books in Print.) Thus there is both title and specific subject access, of sorts, combined in the stichwort or catchword index.

10-85 A: It has been published since 1931. It cumulates (since 1945) into the Jahres-verzeichnis des Deutschen Schrifttums (jahresverzeichnis =yearly list). The indexes cumulate quarterly (vierteljahres-register).

10-86 A: The Jahresverzeichnis is in two parts:
1. Titleverzeichnis (which is essentially an author list)
2. Stich-und schlagwortregister (catch-word subject index)
It cumulates into a five-year list: Deutsche Buecherverzeichnis (which has been published since 1911).

10-87 A: Same as the Jahresverzeichnis, see answer to #10-86.

10-88 A: Basically, the Deutsche Bibliographie is organized just like the Deutsche National-bibliographie, so you should be able to figure it out directly from the source. There are three series/reihe: A (trade, issued weekly), B (non-trade, issued semi-monthly), C (karten/maps, issued quarterly). A and B are arranged in the same large subject groups as the Deutsche Nationalbibliographie with author (verfasser) and catchword title (stichwort) indexes.

10-89 A: It began in 1947. The index to Reihe A, the weekly list of in-trade publications, cumulates monthly (monatregister) and quarterly (vierteljahrregister). Reihe B has an annual index. Reihe A and some B and C titles further cumulate into a half-yearly or semi-annual list: Deutsche Bibliographie; halbjahres-verzeichnis (since 1951).

10-90 A: More or less the same as the yearly cumulations of the Deutsche Nationalbibliographie, see answer to #10-86. The catchword title entries (stichwort) are in the first volumes. The schlagwort register in the second volumes is more similar to subject headings.

10-91 A: Yes, it cumulated into Deutsche Bibliographie; Fuenf jahresverzeichnis (five-year list), published since 1945/50.

10-92 A: Same as the half-yearly cumulation of the Deutsche Bibliographie (see #10-90)

10-93 A: All materials published in Germany, and German materials published elsewhere.

10-94 A: Yes to both.

10-95 A: These two sources are really official national bibliographies, rather than trade lists, similar to the British National Bibliography, or the Bibliographie Officielle of the Bibliographie de la France. They are similar in arrangement to BPR but broader in scope, as they list many non-trade (Reihe B) publications usually not listed in BPR or other trade sources.

There are two trade publications similar in format and purpose to Publishers' Weekly, The Publisher, Bookseller, and the Annonces section of Bibliographie de la France: Boersenblatt, published in a West German edition in Frankfurt and an East German edition in Leipzig. Look briefly at a few issues of either or both editions, if possible, and you can see that they contain publishers' advertisements and book news as do the other trade publications.

10-96 A: Deutsche Nationalbibliographie, first quarter of 1969, index (I. Vierteljahresregister) under title, gives a reference to 5,294 (5th heft/part which is Feb. 1, 1969, item 294). The author is Jan F. Finlay, the publisher is Hueber in Muenchen/ Munich. It has 51 S (seiten/pages), and the price is 3.80 marks.

10-97 A: The publisher is Verlag der Karlsruher Bote, the price is (was) 4 dm (deutsche mark). Found in Deutsche Bibliographie, halbjahresverzeichnis, 1965/I "Titie" volume, under author (Otto).

10-98 A: No, not yet, although the Bowker Company has announced distribution of a two volume

work to be titled German Books in Print.

10-99 A: Deutsche Nationalbibliographie back to 1931, with its cumulations: yearly (Jahresverzeichnis) to 1945, five year (Deutsche Buecherverzeichnis) to 1911; Deutsche Bibliographie back to 1947, with its cumulations: half-year (halfjahresverzeichnis) to 1951, five-year (fuenfjahresverzeichnis) to 1945/50.

10-100 A: Those listed in Winchell, under Germany --early, 18th and 19th centuries, such as Heinsius, 1700-1892 (AA478), Kayser, 1750-1910 (AA479), and Hinrichs, 1851-1912 (AA480), etc. You can also use LC/NUC, British Museum catalog, and to some extent perhaps the Bibliotheque Nationale catalog (all are universal bibliographies.).

10-101 A: All are arranged by chronological periods, which you can tell from the dates on the spines. Heinsius has author and catchword titles in one alphabet. Kayser has author and catchword titles in one alphabet, with some separate subject (sach) and catchword subject (schlagwort) indexes. Hinrichs has an author-title list with subject index.

10-102 A: Winchell (8th ed., p. 9) lists three items (AA69, 70, 71), all published by the Preussichen Staatsbliothek (Prussian State Library) in Berlin, but none really up-to-date or currently active. Coverage from these sources is therefore rather sporadic and not really comparable to that obtained through the LC, BM, and BN. Current national library bibliographic activity in Germany is seen in the publications Deutsche Bibliographie and Deutsche Nationalbibliographie.

10-103 A: Biblio if in the French language; CBI if in English; Deutsche Bibliographie and Deutsche Nationalbibliographie if in German.

Section 11

Review

Questions #11/1-11/60

This section is a review of Sections 1-10 of Part I: Basic Bibliographic Sources, covering the basic sources for the U.S. and selected sources from other countries.

In this review, you should follow the same procedure used in Section 3 (Search Strategy and Review): you can either search out the specific answers in the sources, or simplify the process by deciding which source(s) you would use to answer the question, or use a combination of both methods. What you do should depend on how much time you have and how much practice and review you think you need.

Even if you do actually search out the answers, you should still begin by deciding which source or sources to use. Think in terms of the scope of the question (i.e., type of publication, time period covered, etc.) and the scope of the sources available. Think in terms of what information you have, what information you need, what access there is to the various sources available, what information is given in the various sources available. If you find that you are not really sure which source(s) you should choose, and why, then it may be that you need more practice in and use of the sources to clarify your understanding of them. Try searching out the answer to the question in various likely sources, and see if this procedure helps you to compare the usefulness and scope of the sources.

For many of the questions, there may be several possible sources in which you could find the answer. You should try to think of as many possibilities as you can, because you are not likely to be working in a library which will have all of the sources studied in this manual. Remember also that none of the sources are infallible, and a source which seems for every good reason to be the obvious source may, in actual use, not give you the desired information, and you may have to go on to search in other sources.

However, one of the objectives here is to learn to search systematically through the available sources, as opposed to searching aimlessly or frantically. Therefore, in this review section, you should assume that you have available all of the sources studied in the manual, and you should then think in terms of which would be the best or the most likely source to use and why. Think of the basic organization and structure of the bibliographic sources and of bibliographic control as it now exists. (See questions #317-323 of Section 3.)

If you have made the various charts as suggested, you have them to use as an aid. Try to become independent of using the charts as crutches, however. To get away from the feeling that you must memorize the charts, try this approach: first, review the charts (or whatever notes you have) for the overall view, then put the charts to one side and try to answer the questions without referring back to them. Guess, even if you guess wrong. If you are always or frequently guessing wrong, then you may need more review of the charts, or you may, as suggested above, need more use and practice with the sources. Do some of your reviewing in the reference collection, if possible. Just looking at the sources themselves will jog your memory, as it would in an actual working situation. There are intentionally plenty of review questions, and many repeat the same type of problems at intervals, so that you can use them for review as you feel you need them.

11-1   Is the novel Tree of Man by Patrick White still in print?

11-2   What is the title of a recently published biography of playwright Arthur Miller?

11-3   The President's Commission on Obscenity and Pornography was created in 1967 and its report was released in September 1970. Where would you find the price and ordering information for the report?

11-4   Where would you find a list of all the books currently available from the University of Missouri Press?

11-5   Where would you look to find citations for various articles about Edmund Muskie which have appeared in Time, Life, Newsweek, National Review, etc., during the past few years?

11-6   What is the subscription price for Sunset Magazine?

11-7   Where would you find listings of recent pamphlet-type material on summer employment opportunities for high school students?

11-8   Who is the author of a book titled The Value of a Child; or, Motives to the Good Education of Children, published in Philadelphia in 1753?

11-9   Where would you find the Library of Congress classification number for a book by James Pilditch titled Communication by Design, published recently?

11-10   What German language newspapers are published in Chicago?

11-11   What doctoral dissertations, if any, have been written in the past few years in the field of medieval art?

11-12   Who is the publisher of Francois Mauriac's novel La Sagoiun, published in Paris in 1951?

11-13   Can you find the address of Four Winds Press, a U.S. publisher?

11-14   Where would you look to find some information on the current rate and type of casualties in the Vietnam war?

11-15   Where would you find a listing giving both ordering information (price, order number, etc.) and a descriptive annotation for the 1965 Yearbook of Agriculture (published by the U.S. Dept. of Agriculture) titled Consumers All?

11-16   Who is the author of a recently published book titled Vietnam: the Unheard Voices?

11-17   Can you find the authors and titles of some books about education published in the 17th century?

11-18   Is there a paperback edition available of Time Probe; the Sciences in Science Fiction by Arthur Clarke?

11-19   Can you find ordering information for a magazine titled Aging, published by the Department of Health, Education and Welfare?

11-20   Where would you find population statistics on Sacramento, California?

11-21   Where would you find a list of available editions of the poetry of John Donne (English poet, 1573-1631)?

11-22   Where could you borrow back volumes of Studies in American Literature, published in The Hague (Netherlands) since 1964?

11-23   Can you find the subject of a book titled The Authentic Shudder by W. E. Bennett, published in the 1960's?

11-24   Lud is the name of a periodical published by the Polish Society of Ethnology. When did it begin publication? Is it still being published, as far as you can tell?

11-25   Can you find the address of Faber and Faber, a British publisher?

11-26   Where would you find a list of government publications on maps and map reading?

11-27   Where and how would you find the citation (date, paging, volume number, etc.) for an article titled "Our Mylai of 1900; Americans in the Philippine Insurrection," which appeared in Trans-Action in late 1970?

11-28   Are there any books to be published soon on the general subject of ecology, the protection of the environment, air and water pollution, pesticides, etc. ?

11-29   Where would you look to find recent articles of criticism dealing with the poetry of Edmund Spenser (English poet, 1552-1599)?

11-30   Can you find listings for some recent (this year, last year?) phonograph recordings of any of Bruckner's symphonies?

11-31   Can you find the text of President Kennedy's proclamation on the removal of Soviet weapons from Cuba?

11-32   What mystery novels written by Agatha Christie are still in print?

11-33   A filmstrip titled "Morning Noon and Night" was issued in 1968 by Educational Reading Service. Where would you find information about it such as how long, whether in color, subject matter?

11-34   Who is the publisher of John Updike's recent novel Bech?

11-35   What is the subscription price of Elle, a women's magazine published in Paris?

11-36   Who is the publisher of Vengeance of Private Booley by Cyril Jolly, published in England in the 1950's?

11-37   What is the annual subscription rate of the Detroit Free Press?

11-38   Does the book Nineteenth Century Art Glass by Ruth Lee contain any full color illustrations?

11-39   Where would you look to find information on what bibliographies (in English) of Flaubert (a French novelist) are currently available?

11-40   At what university did Frances A. Spurrell complete study for a doctoral degree during the year 1955-56?

11-41   How would you locate some recently published material on racial attitudes?

11-42   Is Beginning Spanish, published by the Odyssey Press, designed for elementary schools, secondary schools, or for colleges?

11-43   From what libraries could you borrow on interlibrary loan a copy of Psychosomatic Music by Alvin Langdon, published in 1960?

11-44   Where would you find titles and information about motion pictures and films (8mm, etc.) on the subject of "communication," issued in the past five years?

11-45   What are the titles of some books published in the 1950's about archaeology?

11-46   What is the organization responsible for publishing the current quarterly journal called Daedalus?

11-47   What is the publisher and price for Economic Aspects of the Welfare State in India by R. Agarwal, published in India in 1967?

11-48   C. E. Lovejoy's The Story of the Thirty-Eighth is a regimental history. With what war is it concerned?

11-49   How would you check to find out if Kate Millett (women's lib) has published anything recently in popular women's magazines such as McCall's, Vogue, Ladies' Home Journal, Mademoiselle, Good Housekeeping, etc. ?

11-50   What is the publisher and price of Stoffdruck, Stoffmalerei und Batik by Jutta Lammer, published in Ravensburg in 1968?

11-51   What libraries on the east coast have copies of a book by Henry Wilson Lockette titled An Inaugural Dissertation on the Warm Bath, published in 1801?

11-52   How would you find out if Red-Wing; or, the Weird Cruiser of Van Dieman's Land by G.S. Raymond, published in 1853, was published in the U.S. or Great Britain?

11-53   How would you find the titles of some books published in the 1960's on the subject of music--including opera, vocal music, musical comedies and reviews, church music, choral music, composers, etc. ?

11-54   Can you find the citation for an interview with Father Daniel Berrigan published in The New Yorker in 1970?

11-55   How would you go about finding as much bibliographical information as possible about a series of religious tracts written by the Reverend Thomas Boston, published in the 1800's?

11-56   Can you find information on the director, screen writers, photographers, film editors, etc. of the Warner Brothers' movie "None But the Brave," released in 1965?

11-57   Guide des Musees Suisses by C. Lapaire was published in Berne, Switzerland, in early 1970. Is this a new edition or just a reprinting of an earlier edition?

11-58   Can you find the birth and death dates of Stewart Culin, the author of a pamphlet titled Chinese Games with Dice and Dominoes, published by the U.S. GPO in Washington, D.C., in 1895?

11-59   If you were searching for periodical articles written about education written in the nineteenth century, where would you look?

11-60   Does Sweden have a national bibliography?

Section 11

Review

Answers #11/1-11/60

11-1 A: Books in Print. The only source which will tell you if a book is in print, except PTLA and you can't use PTLA because you don't know the publisher. You have no reason to think this title is anything but a U.S. publication. However, if you checked in BIP and did not find it listed, you might consider also checking British Books in Print to see if it is still in print in Great Britain.

11-2 A: A recent source with subject access (Miller as subject): Subject Guide to Books in Print and Subject Guide to Forthcoming Books; BPR; CBI. Subject Guide to Forthcoming Books is probably the most likely.

11-3 A: Monthly Catalog of U.S. Government Publications.

11-4 A: PTLA

11-5 A: Periodical indexing service, in this case it should be fairly obvious that these would be in the Readers' Guide. Use Muskie as the subject.

11-6 A: Ulrich's.

11-7 A: Vertical File Index (pamphlet materials with a subject approach).

11-8 A: Evans--covers the period and has title access. Sabin and LC/NUC do not have title access.

11-9 A: PW Weekly Record/BPR give full cataloging information and include LC classification number, and are current. LC/NUC also gives this information--depends on how recently published the title is whether it would be listed there yet.

11-10 A: Ayer's--see separate language listings, or see under Illinois, Chicago.

11-11 A: Dissertation Abstracts International under specific subject heading in Keyword Index, and/or American Doctoral Dissertations under general subject classification of art.

11-12 A: French publication in French, therefore Biblio or Bibliographie de la France (actually Les Livres de l'Annee) which cover the period. Biblio would probably be easier. Remember that it may be necessary to check in the source beyond the date given; i.e., check in 1952 if not found in 1951 volume, etc.

11-13 A: BIP volume 2, PTLA (publishers catalog), CBI.

11-14 A: Current events--New York Times Index. This source would probably give you some information directly. Current periodical articles might also be a source of information, so the Readers' Guide could be used.

11-15 A: Leidy: A Popular Guide to Government Publications, title access through index. Jackson lists the Yearbook of Agriculture (under Agriculture) but gives no specific information on Consumers All. You could also find ordering information in the 1965 Monthly Catalog (using the yearly index to find the citation in one of the monthly issues), but the chances are you would not find a good description of the publication as you do in Leidy.

11-16 A: Recent sources with title access: Books in Print and Forthcoming Books; BPR; CBI. Forthcoming Books is probably the most likely, depending on the time of year. Subject access is also a possible way to search but since the sources are the same in either case (see #11-2), title is probably easier.

11-17 A: Sabin and Evans and LC/NUC cover this period. Only Evans has subject access. Neither Sabin nor LC/NUC has title access except for anonymous publications, so you cannot even get subject-through-title access.

11-18 A: Paperbound Books in Print or BIP.

11-19 A: A government publication, thus in Monthly Catalog of U.S. Government Publications, February issue, alphabetical list of current periodicals. Also possibly in Ulrich's.

11-20 A: Ayer's

11-21 A: Since you want available editions, you want currently in print (not therefore retrospective sources for his lifetime): BIP for those published in the U.S., and British Books in Print for those published in Great Britain.

11-22 A: Union list; NST since that includes titles beginning after 1950.

11-23 A: You have author and title and are trying to find the subject, so you are not interested here in sources which have subject access, only those which are likely to give you in the citation some subject indication.

LC/NUC is probably the best source; listings there give full cataloging information, and you can find the subject from subject tracings on the bottom of the card or from the classification number, just as you can from a card in a library's card catalog. And the source cumulates sufficiently so that you would not have to look in several places to cover the 1960's, as you have the date only generally. BPR Cumulative similarly gives full cataloging information and probably, for the early 1960's, would give at least the classification number. This source only works, of course, for titles published in the 1960's or later, as BPR Cumulative begins with 1960.

Sources such as CBI which have subject access are not really useful for this problem because you cannot find the subject entry for a title unless you already know the subject. Author/title entries do not give the subject unless it is somehow indicated in the title itself. For example, if you wanted to know the subject of The Ample Proposition by John Lehmann, published in 1966, the CBI author entry (CBI, Jan.-July 1967) gives the full title as The Ample Proposition: autobiography 3.

PTLA (by using BIP first to determine publisher) might work, if the publisher's catalog gives some sort of annotation showing subject matter for each item, and if the book is still in print (unless you can go back to out-dated PTLA's).

11-24 A: Ulrich's (if it is currently published and if it is listed there, the beginning date should be given). If not in Ulrich's, then check ULS and NST; those sources will not tell you if it is still being published, however.

11-25 A: British Books in Print or CBI.

11-26 A: Leidy: A Popular Guide to Government Publications, or the U.S. GPO Price List on Maps.

You could also compile a list of your own by going through several issues of the Monthly Catalog of U.S. Government Publications and checking under relevant subjects in the index or issuing agencies.

11-27 A: Periodical indexing service. (Trans-Action is a periodical.) This is indexed in Readers' Guide, which you could guess at if you were familiar with the periodical, or find from Ulrich's, or check in the list in the front of Readers' Guide. You have no author, and RG has no title entries, so you would have to look under the subject (Philippines, not Vietnam).

11-28 A: Subject Guide to Forthcoming Books, check under all relevant subject headings.

11-29 A: Probably Social Science and Humanities Index; sounds too scholarly for Readers' Guide.

11-30 A: LC Catalog of Music and Phonorecords.

11-31 A: The Monthly Catalog of U.S. Government Publications would lead you to whatever has been published by the government. Actually, this might more easily be located through the New York Times Index, since the New York Times is noted for publication of the complete text of such speeches, documents, etc. In either case, it would help to pin the date down to a year for ease in searching.

11-32 A: BIP, and since she is British, also in British Books in Print. You could also check Paperbound Books in Print, and Paperbacks in Print (British).

You would also probably want to check the latest Forthcoming Books, to see if any new reprints or re-issues have been added to what is listed in BIP.

11-33 A: LC Catalog of Motion Pictures and Filmstrips.

11-34 A: BIP, or if too recent for that, then Forthcoming Books.

11-35 A: Ulrich's (international in scope).

11-36 A: British Books in Print only if it is still in print or has been reprinted. Otherwise: CBI, BNB, English Catalogue, Whitaker's Cumulative Book List.

11-37 A: Ayer's (newspaper).

11-38 A: You want a source which gives as full bibliographic information as possible and you do not have a date.

LC/NUC would probably be the best source since it will/should give that information in the citation, and there are probably less places to search for the entire time span. CBI might also give the information. If it happened to have been published since 1960, BPR Cumulative would give the information.

11-39 A: Subject Guide to Books in Print followed by Subject Guide to Forthcoming Books-- looking under Flaubert as the subject. You want "currently available" which has been taken to mean "in print." You need a subject access since you donot know author or title. You could also look in CBI and BPR, both of which are current and have subject access, going back perhaps five years to cover "current," but then you would have to recheck in BIP the titles which you found in CBI and BPR to find if they were still in print.

11-40 A: Dissertation Abstracts International, and/ or American Doctoral Dissertations.

11-41 A: Vague, but sounds like periodical articles. Therefore a periodical indexing service: Readers' Guide, Social Science and

Humanities Index would both do. Also PAIS which would include books, pamphlets, documents, etc. Subject heading(s) might vary, such as "race relations."

Possibly also New York Times Index for information.

11-42 A: Publisher's catalog in PTLA usually gives this type of information. (In this case it doesn't.) El-Hi Textbooks in Print (under Language--Spanish) is another source which in this case does give the information.

11-43 A: LC/NUC--union catalog; since it was published since 1956, it should be listed.

11-44 A: LC Catalog of Motion Pictures and Filmstrips (using subject index).

11-45 A: CBI is the best source here. It has subject access and covers the time period. BPR Cumulative did not begin till 1960 so can't be used. Subject Guide to BIP, current volume, will contain only those 1950 publications which are still in print. You could of course go back to retrospective volumes of Subject Guide to BIP (which began in 1957), searching volumes for 1957, 1958, 1959; however, the 1957/59 volumes will contain more than just 1950 publications and it is not always that easy to tell about the publication dates, BIP, PTLA, and Subject BIP are rarely used for such retrospective searching.

11-46 A: Ulrich's

11-47 A: CBI includes books from other countries if in English. LC/NUC might also have it, might not be so likely to have the price.

11-48 A: This is similar to #11-23; you actually need some subject information but not really through a source which will give you sufficient information in the citation--such as LC/NUC and PW/BPR which give full cataloging information; you can get the information from the subject tracings, possibly from the classification number, possibly from a fuller title if there is one. Here you have no date, so you have to begin from the earliest possible time and work forward or from current dates back. In either case, LC/NUC is probably more likely to yield the title than PW/BPR.

11-49 A: Check Readers' Guide under Millett as author.

11-50 A: German current bibliographies: Deutsche Nationalbibliographie (and cumulations), Deutsche Bibliographie (and cumulations).

11-51 A: Shaw/Shoemaker and Sabin cover the period and give library locations; Shaw/Shoemaker is probably more likely to have it than Sabin, as 1801 is in the "uncertain" territory for inclusion in Sabin. LC/NUC covers the period and may well include a

citation for the book but would not give library locations (other than LC itself) for an 1801 publication yet. The NUC listings begin only with 1956+ imprints; the pre-1956 Imprints are still in progress and not to the L's yet.

11-52 A: The simplest first source to go to is one which will cover both U.S. and British publications: LC/NUC and/or British Museum Catalog. If it is not listed in either of these, then you could check U.S. bibliographies for the period (Kelly), then British bibliographies for the period (English Catalogue), or vice versa.

11-53 A: Sources with subject access which cover the 1960's: BPR Cumulative, CBI, Subject Guide to Books in Print. BPR Cumulative is probably the best for this topic since it will bring all material on music together in the Dewey 780 section, whereas CBI and Subject Guide to BIP, with subject headings, will scatter the material alphabetically (i.e., under music, church music, opera, etc.).

11-54 A: Periodical indexing service, again you can guess Readers' Guide as the most likely. Search Berrigan as subject.

11-55 A: Search all the sources covering the period, under author, cumulating and collating your information as you go. LC/NUC, possibly Sabin, Shaw/Shoemaker, etc.

11-56 A: LC Catalog of Motion Pictures and Filmstrips (in the 1969 catalog, under title).

11-57 A: Swiss publication but in French, so would appear in Biblio. (March 1970 issue lists it as a 2nd revised edition.)

11-58 A: Although this is a government publication, the major bibliographic sources for government publications are not likely to give information such as birth and death dates. Many government publications are listed in the LC/NUC if received and cataloged by either LC or an NUC library, and LC citations, being cataloging cards, do give birth and death dates for authors, especially in early years.

11-59 A: Poole's Index and Nineteenth Century Readers' Guide.

11-60 A: See Winchell.

PART II

BASIC REFERENCE SOURCES

Section 12

Dictionaries

Questions #12/1-12/81

You have examined and used a great many sources so far, but they have all been variations on one type of source: bibliographies. Bibliographical sources are basic to library work, in technical services (acquisitions, book selection, cataloging) as well as in public services (reference work). For libraries particularly, but also for library users, they answer many questions directly (for example, going to Books in Print to find out the price and availability of a specific title). They are also indirect sources (for example, looking under the subject headings in CBI to find out what books have been published on the subject of coin collecting so that one may try to locate and use those books to find out more about coin collecting). Bibliographical sources are probably much less well understood and used by library patrons than the more direct and familiar sources we are used to finding in reference collections.

In the second half of this self-study manual, you will examine several other types of reference sources: dictionaries, encyclopedias, yearbooks, handbooks, etc. The technique of examination and evaluation of a source that you have used with bibliographies is applicable to these other reference/information sources as well.

The first type of source to be taken up in Part II is dictionaries. Everyone is familiar with dictionaries, but probably not sufficiently so to use them as well as possible. The best way to approach dictionaries is to examine one in great detail and then more briefly consider a variety of others in comparison/contrast to the first.

> Webster's Third New International Dictionary (AE8)
> Webster's New International (2nd ed.) (AE7)
> Funk and Wagnalls New Standard Dictionary (AE6)
> Random House Dictionary (1AE2)
>
> Century Dictionary and Cyclopedia (AE4)
> Oxford English Dictionary (AE20, AE21)
> Dictionary of American English (Craigie) (AE80)
>
> American College Dictionary (AE9)
> Funk and Wagnalls Standard College Dictionary (AE10)
> Random House Dictionary, college ed. (2AE1)
> Webster's 7th New Collegiate (AE12)
> Webster's New World Dictionary (AE11)
> New Century Dictionary (AE5)
> Shorter Oxford English Dictionary (AE22)
> American Heritage Dictionary

12-1   Dictionaries are a type of reference source with which you have had some experience in the past. Based on this experience, and any reading which you may have been assigned on this topic, how would you define what a dictionary is? In your own words--that is, do not look up a definition; make up one.

12-2   Now look up a definition in a dictionary (any). Does it differ substantially from your own definition?

12-3   What are some of the common basic elements in the definition above? (Both your own and the one you looked up).

12-4   One of the elements which appears to be basic to any dictionary is the aspect of alphabetical order--its arrangement. How are dictionaries arranged?

12-5   Would it be safe to say that <u>all</u> dictionaries are arranged in this way--in a single alphabetical list?

12-6   If any book or reference source uses the word "dictionary" as part of its title, what does this mean? Can you think of any examples from the sections on bibliographies?

12-7   A basic way to evaluate a reference source is to know how well it fulfills its functions, and to do this, you must first know what its functions are, or should be. Again, based on your past work with diction- aries and/or any preliminary reading you have done, what are some of the functions of dictionaries? What are dictionaries used for?

12-8   Begin your examination of specific dictionaries with the largest unabridged, English, adult, general dic- tionary, which is?

12-9   First, look at the publication as a physical entity; get a quick overall idea of its general format: size, shape, color; number of volumes (i.e., more than one, more than five, etc.), number of pages (i.e., a lot or a few), type of binding, typography, layout, printing: type-set, mimeographed, etc.; easy to read, illustrated, etc.
         This quick physical orientation with a publication soon becomes so automatic and subconscious that it is done indirectly. It can save time and misunderstanding.
         What is the general format of Webster's Third New International Dictionary?

12-10   What is the full title of Webster's 3rd?

12-11   Does the title tell you anything about the scope?

12-12   What information about the imprint is given on the title page? Is a publication or copyright date given?

12-13   Is there an edition statement on the title page of Webster's Third? What does Winchell tell you about the edition of Webster's Third? What is the publication date for Webster's Third, as given in Winchell?

12-14   Why do the publication dates and copyright dates vary (see answer to #12-12)? Why aren't they con- sistently given as 1961?

12-15   What is the importance of the publication date or copyright date?

12-16   What introductory or explanatory material is given in Webster's Third? It is useful to look specifically at each part of the introductory material, rather than simply noting it from the Table of Contents.

12-17   Who are the person or persons responsible for the content of Webster's Third? Who made the decision about what was included, what definitions were used, what pronunciation is given, etc.?

12-18   What connection, if any, does Webster's Third or the Merriam-Webster Company have with Noah Webster and his 17th century dictionary?

12-19   Look up the word "orator" in Webster's Third.   Several meanings are listed.   How do you distinguish between them?   What do the bold face numbers and letters mean?

12-20   Of the two major meanings or senses given for "orator," which seems more currently relevant to you? Is there any indication that the other sense may no longer be relevant?

12-21   How is the word "orator" pronounced?   Is the stress (accent) on the first syllable or second syllable?

12-22   What is the historical derivation (etymology) of the word orator?

12-23   Does the entry in Webster's 3rd give any synonyms for the word "orator?"

12-24   Can you find out who George Eastman is through Webster's 3rd?

12-25   Can you find out where the Styr River is through Webster's 3rd?

12-26   Can you find out anything about the goddess Venus or about the planet Venus through Webster's 3rd?

12-27   What does "zip" in "zip code" stand for?

12-28   How would you address a judge in Great Britain?

12-29   Webster's New International Dictionary, 2nd edition, which would appear to be superseded by the Third, is still listed as a major item in Winchell.   Why is this?   (See Winchell annotation to Third.)

12-30   When was Webster's 2nd edition first published?   (See Winchell.)

12-31   What are the major differences between Webster's 2nd and 3rd editions?   (Use Winchell annotation.)

12-32   Look at the entry for "orator" in Webster's 2nd.   How does it differ from that in Webster's 3rd?

12-33   Can you find information on George Eastman, the Styr River, the goddess Venus, and the planet Venus through Webster's 2nd?   If so, where?

12-34   Can you find what ZIP in "zip code" stands for in Webster's 2nd?   Why or why not?

12-35   Another major full-sized or comprehensive dictionary is Funk and Wagnalls New Standard Dictionary.
         How does the Funk and Wagnalls dictionary compare to Webster's 2nd and 3rd in size? (See Winchell
         or see prefaces to all sources).

12-36   How current is the Funk and Wagnalls New Standard Dictionary? (See Winchell annotation.   See also
         the copyright date on the title page or verso of title page of the specific copy you are able to examine.)

12-37   Does the arrangement of the Funk and Wagnalls dictionary differ from Webster's 2nd?   Does the arrange-
         ment and scope of the Funk and Wagnalls dictionary differ from Webster's 3rd?

12-38   Does the arrangement of the definitions in the entries of the Funk and Wagnalls dictionary differ from
         the Merriam-Webster (Webster's 2nd and 3rd editions) dictionaries?   Look up entry for "orator."

12-39   Does the pronunciation guide for the Funk and Wagnalls dictionary differ from that in the Merriam-
         Webster dictionaries?   Look up "orator."

12-40   The Webster's New International Dictionaries published by the Merriam-Webster Company and the Funk
         and Wagnalls New Standard Dictionary have long publishing histories.   A much newer work is the Random
         House Dictionary.   When was it first published?   How would you know if it is being revised or changed
         from time to time since this first publication date?

12-41   Is the Random House Dictionary comparable in size to those you have already examined?

12-42   What material is included in the Random House Dictionary which is not included in the other compre-
         hensive, unabridged dictionaries you have examined?

12-43   Of the four dictionaries examined so far (Webster's 2nd, Webster's 3rd, Funk and Wagnalls, and
         Random House), which one would seem most likely to contain a definition for the current usage of the
         word "hippie"?   Which one does?

12-44   Is the Webster's 2nd edition still available for purchase?   How would you find out?

12-45   Of the three major dictionaries examined which are still available for purchase--Webster's 3rd, Funk
         and Wagnalls, Random House--which would seem to be most useful for home purchase (as opposed to
         library purchase)? Why?

12-46   What does the word "obsolete" mean specifically as used in dictionaries?

12-47   In general, would you expect to find obsolete words in the major comprehensive dictionaries that you have
         examined?   Why or why not?

12-48   What sources are there which would cover older, obsolete words now no longer listed in the currently published dictionaries?

12-49   The next source on the list of major English dictionaries is one of those no longer published--The Century Dictionary and Cyclopedia. When was it published? (See Winchell or see title page of source.)

12-50   How does the Century Dictionary and Cyclopedia differ from the other major dictionaries you have examined?

12-51   The Century Dictionary was published in the United States. Another older dictionary with historical use was published in England: the New English Dictionary or Oxford English Dictionary, edited by Sir James Murray. What is the difference between the New English Dictionary (N.E.D.) and the Oxford English Dictionary (O.E.D.)? (See Winchell annotation).

12-52   Does the OED claim to be a complete listing of all known words?

12-53   What would be the principal use of the OED in comparison to the major unabridged dictionaries you have examined?

12-54   Can you find, in the OED, the meaning of the word "alderdom"? What is the exact reference or citation for the first quotation listed for this word?

12-55   Since the OED does not claim to be complete, are there other sources which can be used to supplement it? For example, what about a dictionary on historical principles for American English?

12-56   Of all the dictionaries you have looked at so far, what is one common characteristic which might be construed as limiting their use in certain situations?

12-57   The third group of dictionaries on the list to be examined are of a more portable type, commonly called "desk" dictionaries, or "college" dictionaries. The characteristic common to all of those on the list is their size, and the corrolated fact that they are therefore more selective in their entries than the unabridged or comprehensive dictionaries. Look at the entries and annotations for these dictionaries in Winchell. Can you get any clues for quick identification of the differences or variations in these "desk-sized" dictionaries?

12-58   Webster's Seventh New Collegiate Dictionary is published by the Merriam Company and based on Webster's Third New International. Is there any way in which the desk dictionary varies from the unabridged?

12-59   Is the Webster's New World Dictionary of the American Language related to Webster's 3rd New International, or to the original Noah Webster's dictionary?

12-60   Is the use of the word Webster's in a title therefore meaningful for the reputation of the dictionary?

12-61   Although not related to the Merriam-Webster Company, the Webster's New World Dictionary is a very reputable dictionary. How is it arranged? What is the order of the definitions? Does it include proper names, etc. ?

12-62   Do you think it is necessary to remember which dictionaries give historical meanings first and which give common meanings first? If not, what do you think you should remember?

12-63   Is the American College Dictionary related to any of the major unabridged dictionaries?

12-64   The last of the desk dictionaries listed is the American Heritage Dictionary, which is not yet included in Winchell. It is a good one, therefore, to practice on without having the Winchell annotation as an aid. Look at the dictionary itself. When was it published, who is the publisher, and what is the size (word count) in comparison to the other desk dictionaries?

12-65   In regard to scope, what material is included besides the basic word list?

12-66   How is the dictionary arranged? What is the order of the definitions?

12-67   Generally speaking, how does the American Heritage Dictionary differ from the other dictionaries, desk size or comprehensive?

12-68   Most of the dictionaries you have looked at are specifically of American origin, as opposed to British, although of course the English language is common to both countries with some variations. Which of those dictionaries you have examined are of British origin, if any?

12-69   Presumably there are dictionaries of the English language published in Great Britain, comparable in size and scope to those American dictionaries you have examined. Where would you look to find information on them? What are the titles of some British dictionaries?

         The following questions to the end of this section are search-type questions covering all of the dictionaries you have examined so far. It is not as easy with these sources as it was with the bibliographic records to decide clearly which specific source /title will best answer the question, or be most likely to contain the answer.
         Therefore, your best use of these questions is probably to search out the actual answers in the sources, using a variety of the dictionaries available to you--both unabridged /comprehensive and desk /college sizes. For example, in the few brief questions covering the desk /college dictionaries, you did not really look carefully or in detail at any of them; this is an opportunity to use them comparatively. For most of the questions, try to find the answer in at least two sources, or more if you have time, and compare ease of search and information given. The more sources you can check in for comparison, the more feeling you will get for differences and variations in the dictionaries.

12-70   What is the preferred spelling of the word "judgement"?

12-71   Does the adjective simon-pure have anything to do with Simon Peter in the Bible?

12-72   What is a stroboscope?

12-73   What is the correct pronunciation of the word "hegira"?   For this one, especially if you are one of those who is confused by the pronunciation scheme used in dictionaries and further confused by the presumable variations in such schemes, you might find it most helpful to use this word to check the pronunciations in several dictionaries.   Copy down one under the other the full phonetic spellings given in each dictionary; then you can easily look at them in comparison.   Try Webster's 3rd unabridged, Funk and Wagnall's unabridged, and Random House.   Then you might go further to try Webster's New World, American College Dictionary, and American Heritage of the desk size.   Note also where you have to look in each dictionary to find the meaning of the various phonetic symbols used.

12-74   Can you find a use of the word "librarianess"?

12-75   In what dictionaries can you find the meaning of the word "psychedelic"?

12-76   What is another more common word for "anaphylaxis"?

12-77   What is the first recorded usage of the word "lazy-bones" in the English language?   (Give full citation of author and title).

12-78   Where is the island of Nauru?   What country has administrative control over it?   Would you expect to find this information in all of the dictionaries?   Compare the entry in the Random House and the ACD.

12-79   What is a manticore, and can you find a picture of one?

12-80   Can you find out who wrote From Here to Eternity through the dictionaries?

12-81   What is the origin of the word "kaput" (as in finished, destroyed, kaput)?

Section 12

Dictionaries

Answers #12/1-12/81

12-1 A: Your definition should probably be something along the line of: a list of words
in alphabetical order giving definitions,
etc. One of the simplest definitions of a
dictionary is: a wordbook.

12-2 A: Probably it will not. For example, see
"dictionary" as defined in Webster's Third
New International Dictionary.

12-3 A: Basic common elements in defining a dictionary seem to be:
    list of words
    arranged in alphabetical order
    giving definitions, etc...

12-4 A: In a single alphabetical list.

12-5 A: Yes, probably.

12-6 A: Arranged in a single alphabetical list.
Sabin's Dictionary of Books Relating to
America... (a list of books alphabetically
arranged).

12-7 A: Definitions (meanings, synonyms, antonyms,
    homonyms); specifically for foreign
    words, abbreviations, signs, symbols,
    names, places;
Usage (slang, dialect, colloquial, idiom,
    substandard, nonstandard);
Etymology (derivation);
Orthography (spelling), syllabication;
Pronunciation;
Morphology, syntax, grammar.
(If you do not know the meaning of any of
the above terms, look them up in any
dictionary.)

12-8 A: Webster's Third New International Dictionary of the English Language, the first
title on the list.

12-9 A: In one very large and unwieldly volume,
regular binding, regular printing, some
scattered illustrations.

12-10 A: Webster's Third New International Dictionary of the English Language, unabridged.
(See title page).

12-11 A: It tells you mainly that it is a dictionary
of the English language. Third, new,
international, and unabridged should all
have some significance but it is not clear
yet just what they are.

12-12 A: Publisher (G. and C. Merriam Company,
    Publishers) and place (Springfield, Mass.,
    U.S.A.

Copyright date(s) are given on the verso
    of the title page (date varies).
Publication date is sometimes given on
    the title page (date varies). The
    copyright and publication dates will
    vary according to the date of purchase
    of the specific copy you are looking at.

12-13 A: Only the word "Third" in the title. See
Winchell annotation, first paragraph, about
the edition. Actually, the "Third" is not
really a new edition, based on the
"Second," but rather an entirely new publication. The date for the Third, given
in Winchell, is 1961.

12-14 A: 1961 is the date of the first publication/
printing of the Third. Later publication
and/or copyright dates are for later
printings. Presumably whenever new or
changed material is added to the publication, it is newly copyrighted. A copyright date later than 1961 (first publication
of the Third) shows that some new material has, presumably, been added since
1961. See Winchell annotation under
Webster's 2nd (AE7), first paragraph, for
comment on this.

12-15 A: It tells you, to some degree, how up to
date or how current this source is. You
can't assume that a source with a 1969
copyright date is current to that time, but
you can assume that one with a copyright
date of 1950 is not going to include information from the 1960's.

12-16 A: The Table of Contents follows the title
page, and lists all introductory material.
Pages 5a through 64a contain introductory
material, including an explanatory chart
and notes, pronunciation guide, list of abbreviations, etc. All of this material is
basic in using and understanding the dictionary. Obviously you can't read through
all of it now, but at least look briefly at
each section to know what it includes.

12-17 A: Editor in chief Philip Babcock Gove and
the Merriam-Webster Editorial Staff (see
title page). Also see Merriam-Webster
Editorial staff listed (p. 8a-10a) and
Outside Consultants listed (10a-14a).

12-18 A: See first paragraph of the Preface, p. 6a.

12-19 A: Bold face numbers and letters are "sense
numbers" and "sense letters"--see "Explanatory Chart," which indicates you
should look under item 12 in "Explanatory

Notes" for fuller explanation. For
"orator," there are then two major
senses, the first of which has two coordinated or related subsenses, and the
second of which has three coordinated
or related subsenses.

12-20 A: The second: a public speaker, etc. The
first sense, advocate or pleader, is
labeled obs. (obsolete, see abbreviations).

12-21 A: Pronunciation is given at the beginning of
the entry, between "reversed virgules"
(reversed slashes). Symbols are explained
on p. 32a of the introductory material
(Merriam-Webster Pronunciation Symbols).
The basic pronunciation is given, with what
would appear to be four variations, none
of which indicate the major or primary
stress on the second syllable. Make the
effort now to try to figure out the pronunciation using the symbols as given; you
may have to do it some day with a patron
hovering near.

12-22 A: Etymology is given following the pronunciation and preceding the definition, in square
brackets (from a Middle English word
which is from Middle French or Latin.)

12-23 A: No, it doesn't. Synonyms would be
specifically indicated by the use of the
abbreviation "syn" followed by a see
reference (as an example of this, look at
the entry for "comatose") or by a "synonymy",
a brief paragraph discriminating between
synonymous words (as an example of this,
look at the entry for "abjure"). See section
18 of the Explanatory Notes, or under
"synonymous cross-reference," etc., in
right hand column of Explanatory Chart.

12-24 A: No, there are no biographical entries in
Webster's 3rd, either directly in the main
list or in a separate appendix.

12-25 A: No, there are no geographical place entries
in Webster's 3rd, either directly in the
main list or in a separate appendix.

12-26 A: Not directly, as there is no entry for
Venus, the goddess. However, you can
find out through the etymology under the
noun "venus" that the word derives from
the Roman goddess of love, or from the
2nd planet from the sun.

12-27 A: See entry for zip code in Webster's 3rd
(copyright 1966), Addenda Section (p. 55a).

12-28 A: See "Forms of Address" in introductory
material, p. 51a-54a (Webster's 3rd, copyright 1966).

12-29 A: As the Winchell annotation to Webster's
Third indicates, there have been varying
opinions on the 3rd edition of Webster's,
and libraries have often chosen to retain
and use the older editions as well as

(sometimes in preference to) the new one.

12-30 A: 1934 (see annotation; publication date in the
citation is given as 1961).

12-31 A: Scope: word total reduced from 2nd to 3rd,
meaning that since new words were added,
many older words have been dropped;
gazetteer and biographical information
dropped; proper nouns dropped;
etymologies and pronunciations expanded.
Arrangement: abbreviations, etc., included
in main alphabet in 3rd rather than
separate appendices.
W3 stresses current usage (as does W2, but
1961 is considerably more current than 1934)
and has dropped most of the qualifying labels
(colloquial, vulgar, etc.) which users of
W2 had come to rely on for indication of
acceptability or correctness.

12-32 A: Typography and arrangement of entry is
somewhat different; W2 may seem clearer.
Pronunciation: W2 gives only one variation,
as opposed to several variations in W3.
Oldest meaning is still given first, but
other meanings are specially labeled as
"law" or "Eng. Univ." Etymology similar
but expanded in W3.

12-33 A: Yes to all. Eastman in A Pronouncing Biographical Dictionary in appendices; Styr
River in A Pronouncing Gazetteer in appendices; Venus in main alphabetical list
under Venus (capitalized), goddess meaning
no. 1, planet meaning no. 7.

12-34 A: No. Too recent.

12-35 A: F&W: 450,000 words
W2:   600,000 words
W3:   450,000 words

12-36 A: Thorough revision published in 1913 and
changed periodically with new issues or reprints (Winchell). Copyright dates on verso
of title page reflect revisions or changes.

12-37 A: In F&W, all entries, including proper names
are in major alphabetical list rather than in
appendices in back as in W2. F&W includes
proper names (biographical, geographical)
which W3 does not, but the arrangement is
similar to W3, since all entries are included in the major alphabetical list.

12-38 A: Yes. F&W lists current, common, present
day meaning first. Merriam-Webster dictionaries list historical or oldest meaning
first.

12-39 A: F&W gives two pronunciation guides, no. 1
is called the "Revised Scientific (or National
Education Association) Alphabet"; no. 2 is
the "text book key" (use of diacritical marks,
similar to that used by Merriam Webster).

12-40 A: 1966 (see Winchell entry). Later copyright
dates in individual copies would indicate

changes or revisions of material.

12-41 A: Random House 260,000+ entries. Compare
           to answer for #12-35. It is approximately
           half the size of the other so-called "un-
           abridged," or comprehensive dictionaries
           you have looked at.

12-42 A: See Table of Contents or Winchell annota-
           tion. Foreign word lists, atlas, list of
           reference books; various lists of dates,
           presidents, continents, ocean deeps, states,
           parks, air distances, lakes, waterfalls,
           islands, deserts, volcanoes, etc.

12-43 A: Random House is the most recent. None
           of them include it (as of 1966 copyright in
           W3 and 1967 copyright in Random House).

12-44 A: Available meaning "in print"; therefore
           look it up in BIP, or in the Merriam Com-
           pany catalog in PTLA. It is no longer
           listed, therefore not available new (al-
           though second-hand or used copies may be
           found).

12-45 A: Random House, for all its additional "en-
           cyclopedic" type information. (See
           answer to #12-42.)

12-46 A: Generally it means no longer current, no
           longer used, out of date. Specifically,
           see Webster's 3rd, Explanatory Notes,
           Section 8 on "Status Labels": obs, or
           obsolete means no evidence of standard
           use since 1755.

12-47 A: These dictionaries reflect current word
           usage. Although they are comprehensive,
           they are still limited in size, and do not
           claim to include all words ever used.
           When new words are included, older or
           obsolete words must be dropped. (See
           #12-31).

12-48 A: Older editions of the current dictionaries.
           For example, many obsolete words not
           listed in Webster's 3rd would be listed
           in Webster's 2nd. Also in the older dic-
           tionaries no longer published.

12-49 A: The latest edition listed in Winchell is
           that revised and enlarged in 1911, in 12
           volumes. (Earlier editions may be found
           in some libraries.)

12-50 A: Size (much larger), date of publication
           (older), many quotations, full etymologies,
           encyclopedic type information (for ex-
           amples, see entries under "pearl" or
           under "Cuckoo").

12-51 A: The NED was published in 10 volumes plus
           supplement in 1888-1933. The OED is a
           reprint, somewhat different in size, in 12
           volumes and supplement, with some correc-
           tions made. The more common name for
           the set is now Oxford English Dictionary
           or OED.

12-52 A: See Winchell annotation for NED. No, it
           is still selective.

12-53 A: Historical background, etymologies,
           derivations fuller than in other dictionaries;
           older obsolete words excluded from cur-
           rent dictionaries; some colloquial or slang
           words with full historical background when
           included, etc.

12-54 A: Found in OED directly under "alderdom,"
           indicating obsolete, meaning "lordship,
           chief authority." The first quotation listed
           is c950 (the date), Lindisf. Gosp., Luke
           XIX.20. To find the exact reference or
           citation for "Lindisf. Gosp.", you look in
           the last volume of the set (vol. 13 of the
           1933 set) in the "List of Books Quoted in
           OED."

12-55 A: The annotation for NED in Winchell lists
           other similar dictionaries, including the
           Dictionary of American English edited by
           Craigie and Hulbert, which is also listed
           and annotated in Winchell under "regional
           dictionaries."

12-56 A: Size. All are large, unwieldy, not very
           portable.

12-57 A: Several are based on the larger unabridged
           dictionaries, and will therefore follow the
           "parent" dictionary in style, arrangement,
           etc.

12-58 A: The Webster's 7th New Collegiate lists
           abbreviations, signs, symbols, etc., in
           an appendix rather than in the main list
           as in W3. Webster's 7th includes
           separate lists of biographical names and
           geographical names, which W3 does not
           include at all.
                 Definition order, pronunciation symbols,
           etymologies, and general standards for
           inclusion and usage will be the same as
           in the unabridged.

12-59 A: No, it is published by World Publishing
           Company; according to the Winchell anno-
           tation, not based on any existing dic-
           tionaries.

12-60 A: Any dictionary can be called a "Webster's"
           and many are. The word does not always
           indicate a connection with the original
           Webster's or with the company which
           currently publishes the unabridged Web-
           ster's 3rd.

12-61 A: All entries in one alphabet, including
           proper names and places. Definitions
           give oldest meaning first, as do the
           Merriam-Webster dictionaries.

12-62 A: It is helpful but not necessary to remem-
           ber which dictionaries do which. What
           you must remember is that they do not
           all do the same thing.

12-63 A: No, not really. However, the entry in Winchell under the Random House Dictionary indicated that that dictionary, a later work than the ACD, nevertheless had many characteristics similar to the ACD.

12-64 A: First copyright date is 1969, published by the American Heritage Publishing Company and Houghton Mifflin Company. The word count is not given in the introductory material as it was in the other dictionaries (advertising puts it at 155,000--similar to Webster's 7th at 130,000, Random House college ed. at 155,000, etc.)

12-65 A: Special articles on language and usage, etc., in the introductory materials; appendices on Indo-European languages including a major list of roots (derivations, etymologies) of indo-european words. Lots of illustrations. No atlas, foreign language word lists, etc., as in Random House.

12-66 A: All entries in one alphabetical list (including proper names, place names). The order of definition is a "synchronic semantic analysis" (see p. xlvii, "Order of Definitions," under "Guide to the Dictionary"); the only thing about this which is really clear is that it is not a historical order.

12-67 A: It differs most in looks--typography, page lay-out, readability, illustrations, etc. It is also more up-to-date, both because it is the most recent to be published but also because it sets out to be really up-to-date. See if the American Heritage has a definition for "hippie." (It does; so does the Random House college edition.)

12-68 A: OED

12-69 A: Look in Winchell under "Language Dictionaries--English Language--English" (see also Winchell's comments, 8th ed., p. 92 under "English Language" on comparisons between American-English and British-English dictionaries). Some titles: Cassell's English Dictionary; Concise Oxford Dictionary, etc.

12-70 A: Most dictionaries list "judgment" first with "judgement" second or at the end of the entry or not at all. (See W3 and F&W unabridged; see Random House--lists judgment only; see Webster's New World, for example.)

12-71 A: No, it is from a character in a play. See W3, Webster's New World, etc.

12-72 A: Most dictionaries have definitions. Random House is quite extensive. American Heritage has definition and illustration of one plus two stroboscopic photographs.

12-73 A: W3, F&W, RH all list two pronunciations, the first with the stress on the first syllable, the second with the stress on the middle syllable. F&W gives two entirely different phonetic respellings (see #12-39). In W3, you must turn to the end-paper for the phonetic key, but you find there all the vowel and consonant sounds plus explanations of stress signs, etc. F&W gives at the top of each page the keys for both respellings, including consonants. RH gives at the bottom of the right page the symbols for the vowels but you must turn to the end paper for the full key including consonants.

12-74 A: OED, under "Librarian." (1862 Trollope quote given).

12-75 A: American Heritage. Random House, Webster's 3rd (c.1966) in Addenda. You should recognize this as a word of recent origin, therefore more likely to be contained in the dictionaries most recently revised, or in those dictionaries which claim (as do American Heritage and Random House, for example) to be most "with it."

12-76 A: W3, RH, ACD, W New World all give definitions but do not give another more common word. F&W gives the definition for anaphylaxis as part of the definition for its opposite word, prophylaxis, with a cross-reference from anaphylaxis. American Heritage gives a similar definition to the others and further gives "allergy" as part of the definition. (The fact that "allergy" is not used as part of the definition in any of the other dictionaries might make one wonder how valid it really is, medically speaking, as a synonym for the word anaphylaxis.)

12-77 A: OED, under "lazy-bones"; date 1592, author G. Harvey, title Pierce's Super. (See last volume for full citation.) Other dictionaries would probably include the word "lazy-bones" and might give a quotation showing usage, but you want the first recorded usage, and this is a piece of information which you know specifically you should find in the OED, therefore you might as well go directly there (assuming that you have access to the OED).

12-78 A: You would generally expect to find it in all of them except W3 which does not include people- or place-names. It is not listed in Funk and Wagnalls unabridged. It is included in W2, in the separate list in the back. Random House includes it. ACD and Webster's New World also include it. All definitions indicate that it is in the Pacific, some give more specific locations than others (i.e., RH: "near equator"; W2: "26 m. S. of the equator"). All indicate that the former name was Pleasant Island, and W2 in addition says that it has phosphate deposits. W2 says that it is a jointly held trust territory of Britain, New

Zealand, and Australia; RH says it is ad-
ministered by Australia. RH has the virtue
of being more up-to date than W2, but it may
also just be less complete. The RH and
ACD definitions are virtually the same (see
#12-63).

12-79 A: W3, W2, F&W unabridged have definitions
but no picture. Random House doesn't have.
American Heritage has with an illustration.

12-80 A: Yes, in Random House, under From Here...

12-81 A: A brief indication of the origin/derivation/
etymology is given in the dictionaries which
include the word: W3 indicates it is German,
from the French; Webster's New World indicates it is German and came into English
through soldiers' slang; American Heritage
indicates it is German (see full etymology
in the Appendix). It is not included in the
OED.

Section 13

Supplementary Language Sources

Questions #13/1-13/85

13-1   In the previous section you examined and compared the major unabridged/comprehensive English language dictionaries, plus to some extent the "desk-size" versions, in regard to their scope and arrangement, and specifically in regard to the way each dictionary handled or treated the various types of information commonly found in dictionaries. What types or kinds of information do you expect to find in dictionaries?

The next set of sources to be examined also cover some of these same kinds of information. These next sources, however, are limited to some specific aspect of word study--such as synonyms, slang, usage, abbreviations, etc.--and for that particular aspect, they can usually be expected to provide additional and more thorough information than can be found in even the major dictionaries. Most of these sources are self-explanatory in scope and arrangement, and can be looked at quickly for general comparison and for the basic purpose of getting an overall picture of the available sources. However, all will repay more thorough study and use than they will be given in this manual. If your time is not too limited, it would be both useful and revealing to read the prefaces to these sources.

Fowler. Dictionary of Modern English Usage. (AE44)
Evans. Dictionary of Contemporary American Usage (AE43)
Follett. Modern American Usage: a Guide (1AE9)

Webster's New Dictionary of Synonyms (2AE12, AE79)
Roget's International Thesaurus (AE77)
Lewis. New Roget's Thesaurus of English in Dictionary Form

Wentworth and Flexner. Dictionary of American Slang (2AE9, AE72)
Berrey and Van den Bark. American Thesaurus of Slang (AE65)
Partridge. Dictionary of Slang and Unconventional English (2AE7, AE67)

Mathews. Dictionary of Americanisms (AE81)

De Sola. Abbreviations Dictionary (2AE2, AE27)
Acronyms and Initialisms Dictionary (Gale) (1AE53, AE79)

NBC Handbook of Pronunciation (AE56)

Wood's Unabridged Rhyming Dictionary (AE62)

13-2   Of all the kinds of information found in dictionaries, which do you think is most likely to prove controversial? For which type of information are you more likely to need to refer further, for additional information or to other "authorities"? Think of this particularly as it relates to the Webster's Third and Webster's Second controversy (see questions #12-29 and #12-31 and any reading you have done).

13-3   The first of the supplementary sources to be considered deal with this problem area of usage, the way in which words are used. There are several of these: see Winchell's section on "Idioms and Usage" (8th ed., p. 97) following American and English dictionaries. Part of the problem with usage is whether it is defined as "the way words are used" or "the way words should be used." These books may reflect to a great extent the personality and views of their authors, and may come to have almost a personality themselves. Getting the flavor of this "personality" is one of the best ways to distinguish between the various usage books available. One of the oldest, most well known, and perhaps most personified is Fowler's A Dictionary of Modern English Usage. The edition cited in Winchell is the second edition, published in 1965. Was Fowler himself responsible for the second edition? When was the first edition published?

13-4   What is the basic arrangement of Fowler? Is it similar in arrangement to the dictionaries?

13-5   Does Fowler cover only usage? Are other areas of word study covered as well?

13-6   Is Fowler more concerned with British English than with American English? How would you find out?

13-7   If time permits, read the preface to the Revised Edition (p. iii-x) of Fowler which will give you some feeling for Fowler himself as a person as well as the place his book has assumed in this field. In addition and/or otherwise, reading some of the entries themselves is revealing. For some shorter Fowlerisms, see for example: I.Q.; iron out; hiccup; subtopia; Santa Claus; battered ornaments; fissionable; foreign danger... and for Women's Lib, see the various entries under "female" through "feminineness...".

        Another usage book which can profitably be compared to Fowler is Evans' A Dictionary of Contemporary American Usage. What is one major way in which Evans is obviously dissimilar to Fowler?

13-8   How does the arrangement of Evans compare with Fowler?

13-9   Would you expect Evans to include the same entries as Fowler does? That is, can you find everything in Evans that you can find in Fowler, and vice-versa?

13-10   To get some of the personal "flavor" of Evans, see such entries as: live audience; dog's life, lead a; ruination; square; flash in the pan; profession...

        How would you find out where Evans stands on the usage controversy--whether his comments are apt to be more or less or similarly "permissible" than Fowler?

13-11   What is the difference between infer and imply? Can they be used interchangeably? Compare Fowler and Evans.

13-12   Another usage source listed in Winchell is Nicholson's A Dictionary of American-English Usage. How does it relate to the two sources you have just looked at?

13-13   Is there a reference book which explains American English to Britishers? How would a Britisher find out that "gas" in American means "petrol"?

13-14   Modern American Usage; A Guide, by Follett, is listed in the first supplement to Winchell (8th ed.). How can this be compared quickly to the other sources you have seen?

13-15   Another kind of information for which dictionaries are frequently used is to find synonyms, antonyms, homonyms. What is meant by synonym, synonymy, antonym, homonym?

13-16   Again, there are several sources which list and discuss synonyms; see in Winchell, 8th ed., p. 99, under "Synonyms and antonyms." Two of these--Webster's and Roget's--can be looked at comparatively. Look at Webster's New Dictionary of Synonyms first. Does the use of the word "Webster's" have any particular significance? What else can you look for which might be more significant?

13-17   What is the arrangement of Webster's synonym dictionary?

13-18   Does Webster's simply give a list of synonymous words for each entry? For example, see under discrimination and under discuss. Where would you look to find an exact indication of the use of the word "acumen" as compared to discrimination?

13-19   What are "analogous words" as used in the Webster dictionary of synonyms?

13-20   What are some words which can be used in place of "luxurious"?

13-21   Another well-known synonym book which can be compared to Webster's is Roget's International Thesaurus. Actually, there are several synonym books which use Roget in the title somewhat as Webster is used for dictionaries; look specifically at the one titled Roget's International Thesaurus, published by Crowell (item AE77 in Winchell). What is the basic, most obvious way in which the Roget differs from the Webster's?

13-22   What is the basic arrangement of Roget's? Is it similar to the dictionaries? Is it similar to anything you have examined in the bibliographies?

13-23   Who is responsible for the classed arrangement of words found in Roget's? What is the idea behind it? Can you see any advantages of it in use over the strict alphabetical arrangement of Webster's?

13-24   How does the Roget arrangement deal with antonyms?

13-25   What does "thesaurus" (used in the title of Roget) mean?

13-26   Can you use Roget's to find simple synonyms, such as "other words for luxurious" as in #13-20?

13-27   If you wanted to know if the word "babel" could be used as exactly synonymous with the word "hullabaloo," would it be better to look in Webster's or Roget's? Try both if in doubt.

13-28   If you were looking for a list of various noun words used for demons or evil spirits, would you find Webster's or Roget's more helpful? If in doubt, try both.

13-29   If you were trying to remember a word similar to "derogatory," which you couldn't quite recall to mind but needed only to see it to jog your memory, would it be better to look in Webster's or Roget's?

13-30   What type of person might find Roget's more easily used, perhaps even more useful, than Webster's?

13-31   A source not yet listed in Winchell is the New Roget's Thesaurus of the English Language in Dictionary
         Form, edited by Norman Lewis. By looking at the source itself, what can you tell about its scope and
         arrangement in comparison to the other two synonym books you have just examined? How does it com-
         pare in its treatment of "demon"?

13-32   Would you expect to find synonym discrimination in the usage books?

13-33   Another popular type of supplementary word sources are those related to slang, and again there are
         many sources to choose from.   Two of these--Berrey and Van den Bark's American Thesaurus of Slang,
         and Wentworth and Flexner's Dictionary of American Slang--can be compared much as the Webster's
         and Roget's synonym books were. Looking at the titles alone, what can you immediately say about the
         probable difference in the two sources? Look quickly at both sources and see if your supposition is true.

13-34   What is slang? What is the difference between slang, colloquialisms, dialects, jargon, and argot?

13-35   On what basis were the slang terms included in Wentworth and Flexner?

13-36   What is a lounge lizard?

13-37   What does "cool" mean, as in losing your cool?

13-38   How is the American Thesaurus of Slang (Berrey and Van den Bark) best used? What are the ad-
         vantages and disadvantages arising from its arrangement?

13-39   What are some slang terms having to do with writing and publishing?

13-40   If you were reading, or perhaps even writing, a story about boxing, which included lots of slang words,
         which of these two sources might be the best approach to clarify the terms? What, for example, is
         meant by the phrase "cutting paper dolls"?

13-41   Can you find definitions for "soul," "soul food," "soul brother"? What about "right on"?

13-42   Both the American Thesaurus of Slang and the Dictionary of American Slang are specifically related to
         American usage. A Dictionary of Slang and Unconventional English by Eric Partridge is a good one for
         basically British slang usage. How recently has it been up-dated, and how?

13-43   Does Partridge include anything except slang terms? Does he restrict himself to British slang terms?

13-44   Do the entries in Partridge seem to give any different type of or fuller information than that given in
         Wentworth and Flexner? See entry for "grit," for example.

13-45   Does the Oxford English Dictionary (OED) include slang terms? Is there then an overlapping between the OED and Partridge? Would you expect to find in OED everything that is in Partridge?

13-46   Eric Partridge is one of our most prolific writers on words. Where would you find titles of other word books, dictionaries, etc., which he has written and compiled?

13-47   A specialized word information source somewhat similar to the slang sources are lists or dictionaries of regional and dialect variations in languages. What is meant by regional and dialect variations?

13-48   What sources have you looked at previously which would include this information?

13-49   Apparently in the sense that American English can be considered a regional variation of British English, Winchell has listed Craigie's Dictionary of American English under "Regional and dialect" sources (8th ed., p. 100). Another major source also listed there is A Dictionary of Americanisms on Historical Principles by Mitford Mathews. What is the difference in scope between Craigie and Mathews? What is meant by "Americanisms" as used in the Mathews' title?

13-50   How does Mathews differ from Craigie other than being more limited in scope? Does Mathews simply "abridge" Craigie, in a way, or does it add new material specifically to its own scope?

13-51   What is the purpose of Mathews' Dictionary of Americanisms? See preface.

13-52   According to Mathews, what is the origin of the word "filibuster"? How long ago was it first used? Does the fact that it appears in Mathews mean that the word is unknown in British English? How would you find out if it is or has been used in British English?

13-53   Next on the list to be examined are two examples of sources specifically devoted to abbreviations. The first, Abbreviations Dictionary by De Sola, is one of the most recent to be published. Do you think currency is important for abbreviations?

13-54   What is the scope and arrangement of the De Sola Abbreviation Dictionary?

13-55   What are acronyms?

13-56   The second example of an abbreviation source is specifically for those alphabetic designations: Acronyms and Initialisms Dictionary, 2nd ed., published by Gale Research Company. What fields does it attempt to cover?

13-57   How then does the Gale Research Company's Acronyms and Initialisms Dictionary differ in scope from the De Sola dictionary?

13-58   Does it differ in arrangement?

13-59   What is "id." (in footnotes) an abbreviation for, and what specifically does it mean? Would you expect to find this in both of the abbreviations sources?

13-60   What is ALA an abbreviation for besides American Library Association?

13-61   What does "flak" stand for?

13-62   What does CARE stand for? It has changed its name to reflect its extended coverage, but the letters remain the same. What was the earlier name?

13-63   Pronunciation of words--whether standard, slang, regional, etc.--is usually given in the sources in which they are listed (the major exception being the synonym books). There are also a few specialized sources for pronunciation. Of those listed in Winchell, look specifically at the NBC Handbook of Pronunciation. What does NBC stand for in the title and what does that tell you?

13-64   Does the NBC Handbook attempt to list a variety of pronunciations for every word listed, showing regional variations, etc.? What is the standard used for the pronunciations listed?

13-65   The NBC Handbook lists 20,000 words--obviously a limited number. How were these words chosen?

13-66   Look up the pronunciation of the word "Hegira" (see #12-73) in the NBC Handbook of Pronunciation. How does it differ from that which you found in the dictionaries?

13-67   Of the other pronunciation sources listed in Winchell, do any attempt to give U.S. regional variations?

13-68   A final type of supplementary word source is the rhyming dictionaries. The information found in these sources cannot easily be found in dictionaries as well. There are several rhyming dictionaries or handbooks listed in Winchell (8th ed., p. 98, under "Rhymes"). Look at the Winchell annotations and at one or two of the books themselves. In what way do these rhyming dictionaries vary in arrangement from regular dictionaries?

13-69   If you wanted to find a rhyme for the word "librarian," in Wood's, how would you locate it?

13-70   What other information besides lists of rhyming words is often found in such sources?

The next several questions to the end of the section cover the supplementary sources examined in this section, and the dictionaries from the previous section. You can use these questions as review, deciding which of the possible sources would best answer the question. Or you can use them as additional opportunities to use and compare the sources you have examined. As you did with the dictionary questions, try to look up some of the questions in more than one source, and compare answers.

13-71   You are writing a report and you need a word which is similar to "ensuing" but that isn't quite the word you want to use. What other possibilities are there?

13-72   What is the correct abbreviation for kilogram?

13-73   Who is Theodore Roethke?

13-74   What does the Australian slang phrase "put the nips into" mean?

13-75   What is a word which means the opposite of "reprehend"?

13-76   If someone offered to sell you a hand of herrings, how many fish would you expect to receive?

13-77   If someone complained to you that the word "finalize" is in Webster's Third but he still didn't understand when it should be used, how could you help him?

13-78   Can you find some words which are used to express the idea of color, particularly yellowness and orangeness?

13-79   A line from Chaucer (English poet, 1340?-1400) reads: "But thynne, it lay, by colpons oon and oon." What does "colpons" mean?

13-80   Who or what is Barnaby Rudge?

13-81   Anapests, iambs, and spondees are metrical patterns for scanning poetry. What do they mean; how are they used?

13-82   Can you find definitions for laser, quasar, and/or pulsar?

13-83   What is the origin of the term "Podunk," as in "Oh, I don't know, he comes from Podunk some-where..."?

13-84   Why is "squirrel" sometimes used as a slang word for psychiatrist?

13-85   Is it really considered bad grammar to use "like" in place of "as" ("like" as a conjunction, as in "like a cigarette should")?

Section 13

Supplementary Language Sources

Answers #13/1-13/85

13-1 A: This is the same answer as that to question #12-27, what are dictionaries used for.

13-2 A: Probably the area of usage ("usage" as defined by W3: "habitual or customary practice or use...the way in which words or phrases are actually used...generally or among a community of persons...")

13-3 A: 2nd ed., revised by Sir Ernest Gowers (Fowler died in 1933); first edition published in 1926 (see Winchell citation and annotation, or see title page and verso of title page of source).

13-4 A: The arrangement is alphabetical by word entries; this is similar to dictionaries, of course, but the individual entries are generally much longer and more discursive than dictionary entries; some in fact are almost essay length (see "elegant variations").

13-5 A: See "Classified Guide to the Dictionary," p. xv-xx, which appears in the 2nd edition only, and which indicates that most of the articles fall under "usage" but there are also some on pronunciation, punctuation, word formation, spelling, etc.

13-6 A: The Winchell annotation doesn't really say, and probably the easiest way to decide without reading the entire preface is by the fact that it is a British publication (publisher: Oxford University Press in Oxford, England, with offices also in New York, etc.)

13-7 A: Evans is American usage (see title, Winchell annotation, preface to source) and Fowler is British (see #13-6). Evans is published by an American publisher (specifically Random House, New York).

13-8 A: The same, basically: alphabetically by word entry with entries themselves being often discursive.

13-9 A: Not really, since both are basically personal compilations; although it is surprising that so many comparable entries are found.

13-10 A: The Winchell annotation doesn't really give any clues. Reading the preface should be of some help. Looking up controversial problems in both sources and comparing results should give even further clues.

13-11 A: Fowler (entry: infer) would maintain the distinction; Evans (entry: imply) is somewhat more permissive to the loss of distinction between the two words.

13-12 A: From the full title alone, as given in Winchell or on the title page of the source, it should be clear that Nicholson is an American version of Fowler.

13-13 A: To a certain extent, these things can be found out through the sources you have already examined--the dictionaries themselves often give the British equivalent for an American term (see W3 under "gas"), and the usage books often give such distinctions (see Evans under "gas"). A source which exists to serve this specific purpose is item AE46 in Winchell, included with the "idioms and usage" books: Horwill's Dictionary of Modern American Usage.

13-14 A: Like Evans, it is American usage. Evans was published in 1957; Follett, having been published in 1966, may reflect more current usage than Evans. Also, having seen the personal quality of Evans and Fowler, one can expect Follett to reflect some of the opinions and idiosyncracies of its author (in this case, authors); comparing entries, as in #13-11, may show some differences. Compare what Follett has to say on the infer/imply question.

13-15 A: Synonym: meaning the same.
Synonymy: the study of synonyms, a list of synonyms.
Antonyms: meaning the opposite.
Homonyms: having the same pronunciation, but different meanings.

13-16 A: The use of the word Webster's, used by itself, does not have any significance (see #12-60); however, you can look for the name of the publisher which might be more significant--in this case it is Merriam Company which also publishes Webster's Third unabridged.

13-17 A: Again, from the title itself, you can assume that it would be alphabetically, and a quick glance through the source itself confirms this.

13-18 A: Under discrimination, three groups of words are listed: synonyms; analogous words; contrasted words. In each group, the starred word should be referred to for a fuller discussion (i.e., discrimination) of the exact use of the words. To find the more exact use of acumen as compared to discrimination, see under "discernment." The entry for "discuss," following that for "discrimination," is an example of a discriminated article or entry. These are similar to but generally longer than the synonymies found in Webster's Third unabridged (see #12-23). See the subtitle of Webster's New Dictionary of Synonyms; a Dictionary of Discriminated Synonyms... See also the W̲i̲n̲c̲h̲e̲l̲l̲ annotation, to some extent. The fullest and best explanation of the way the source works would of course be found in the preface or other introductory matter; for this, the "Explanatory Notes" on p. 32a (c.1968 ed.) are sufficient. The preface is more detailed. If time permits, reading the "Introductory Matter" (p. 5a-31a of this source is an excellent way to get background on the use and importance of synonyms, etc. Another somewhat shorter approach is to read what Evans and Fowler have to say on the subject (entry: synonyms).

13-19 A: See "Introductory Matter" under "Analogous and Contrasted Words," p. 30a-31a.

13-20 A: In Webster's, under luxurious, are listed sumptuous, opulent, etc.

13-21 A: Basically, in arrangement.

13-22 A: The basic arrangement of Roget's is not alphabetical as in the dictionaries but rather a classified arrangement, similar to the classed or classified subject arrangement in such bibliographies as American Book Publishers Record. It is not exactly similar; that is, the classification scheme does not follow Dewey, for example, but the principle of arrangement is the same.

13-23 A: The classed arrangement of Roget's was thought up by Roget himself, the purpose being to show what words could be used to convey an idea, thus the arrangement of words classed according to the idea they express. He based it on the general system of classification used in natural history. (See "Peter Roget's Introduction" in introductory matter of the 1̲9̲4̲6̲ edition. See also p. 14a-15a of the Introductory Matter of Webster's New Dictionary of Synonyms.) An advantage of Roget's arrangement is that, like any classed arrangement, it brings together in one place all related words rather than scattering them alphabetically. See, for example, category "792. Thief" in Roget's. Listed in that section are many similar although not necessarily synonymous words related to "thief," including slang terms, foreign words, literary allusions (although with no explanations), names, etc.

13-24 A: See for example, category 518, intelligibility,

followed by category 519, somewhat antonymous words under unintelligibility.

13-25 A: Treasury or storehouse, hence a book containing a store of words, a dictionary; or especially a book of classified synonyms (Webster's New World). Thus, the use of "thesaurus" in a title can often mean a basic classed arrangement of words like Roget's.

13-26 A: Yes, by looking in the alphabetical list in the back, which refers you, under luxurious, to the various categories or sections in which similar/related words will be found. It necessitates more looking back and forth than Webster's, but can be done.

13-27 A: Roget's only lists the words, does not try to distinguish or discriminate between them. Webster's under "din" (both babel and hullabaloo indicate the discriminatory discussion will be found under "din"), discusses the exact differences. In this case Webster's might be more useful. A dictionary would also probably be more useful than Roget's.

13-28 A: Here is where Roget's is useful. Demon, in the alphabetical index, refers you to several categories, each of which gives useful lists of related words; one of which (evil spirit) gives you specifically the list you want, another of which (familiar spirit) gives you a somewhat antonymous list. Demon is not listed in Webster's.

13-29 A: Since this isn't a case of needing careful discrimination between words, either Webster's or Roget's would do the job. A dictionary might also do it. Since Roget's tends, by virtue of its arrangement, to list more related words than either Webster's or a dictionary, it might be more likely to be helpful--depending how close in meaning your elusive word comes to "derogatory." Roget's lists more "analogous" (see #13-19) than strictly synonymous words.

13-30 A: Roget's lists lots of synonymous and analogous and related words, with no clear distinction between them. Writers or others who use words frequently and are already basically knowledgeable about them can use Roget's more easily because in most cases they are searching for a word which they are already familiar with but can't quite recall to mind (as in #13-29) and they do not need to be so dependent upon the discriminatory articles which are an important part of Webster's. Those who are less certain, less knowledgeable about words would generally find Webster's more helpful and Roget's just confusing.

13-31 A: It is based on Roget's and would presumably therefore be similar to Roget's in scope, but the arrangement--dictionary form--is similar to Webster's. The title, including as it does both "thesaurus" (see #13-25) and "dictionary form," is something of a contradiction in terms. The Lewis book is itself based on an earlier re-arrangement of Roget made by Mawson. A glance through the book will show that to a limited extent the "categories" or lists of words related to an idea have been retained. Demon, in the alphabetical list, refers you to "devil" as the category; the category "devil," found also in the alphabetical list, gives related words, less than the regular Roget's, but more than Webster's.

13-32 A: Yes, since this often is in fact a problem of correct or common usage. See Fowler on "foam; froth" and "flurried; flustered; fluttered." See Evans on "reticent, secretive, taciturn, laconic."

13-33 A: One is called a "thesaurus," the other a "dictionary;" presumably the main difference will be in arrangement--the thesaurus classed like Roget (see #13-25) and the dictionary alphabetical. The sources themselves bear out this difference.

13-34 A: See definitions in Webster's Third unabridged, or in Preface of Wentworth and Flexner Dictionary of American Slang. (The entire preface is good reading, if time permits.)

13-35 A: See first paragraph of "Explanatory Notes."

13-36 A: See Wentworth and Flexner: a ladies' man, etc.

13-37 A: Wentworth and Flexner, supplement, under cool.

13-38 A: Berrey and Van den Bark is based generally on the Roget classed arrangement of words (see "Explanation" in front matter). As such, it has most of the same advantages and disadvantages of the Roget arrangement. Slang terms are only listed, not always clearly defined. Individual words or phrases can be found through the index with reference to the classed arrangement. Similar and related terms are brought together in broad and often useful groupings.

13-39 A: Basically, this can be found only through the Berrey and Van den Bark thesaurus approach--see various categories 518-526: Journalism, writing, publishing.

13-40 A: The thesaurus (Berrey and Van den Berk) has a long list of related slang words about boxing. This would bring all the terms together in one place. Many of the terms could be found, alphabetically, in the dictionary (Wentworth and Flexner), and a clearer statement of meaning might be given. In this case, you might find it useful to use both sources together. The phrase "cutting paper dolls" is listed

in Wentworth but with no meaning given that relates to boxing. If you looked in Berrey under the category of boxing, you would have to check through all the many lists of words till you found "Cutting paper dolls" under "punch-drunk," dazed. You could also look it up alphabetically in the index which refers you to the specific section on Boxing--Punch-drunk.

13-41 A: Soul, soul food, soul brother are all listed in the Wentworth and Flexner supplement. Right on is too recent to be included. It seems pointless to look for any of them in Berrey and Van den Bark since its last copyright date is 1953.

13-42 A: 6th edition, 1967; the supplement or second half of the work has been revised, the first part left unchanged. (Winchell, 2nd supplement).

13-43 A: He includes colloquialisms, catch-phrases, solecisms, catachreses, nicknames, vulgarisms, and such Americanisms as have been naturalized (see sub-title or Winchell annotation). Australian and New Zealand slang is also included, although not so clearly noted in the prefatory matter.

13-44 A: Perhaps more etymology, derivation, quotes, historical and now obsolete terms. In general, Partridge seems to have more of the historical aspect of slang than Wentworth and Flexner.

13-45 A: The OED does include some slang terms. Actually, Partridge is more inclusive, broader in scope, for slang, than even the great OED. See Preface (of 1936 edition) in which he compares relevant terms and claims to include all slang, etc., terms from the OED plus about 35% more.

13-46 A: See Winchell, same section as the Dictionary of Slang; several titles following, on underworld words, for example. Also in Winchell index under Partridge, you are referred to two etymological dictionaries. A publisher's list opposite the title page in the New York, Macmillan, c1967 edition of the Dictionary lists several varied titles.

13-47 A: See Webster's Third unabridged, or check your answer to #13-34.

13-48 A: The OED for basically British English, and the Dictionary of American English (Craigie) for American English. To some extent it is also included in any dictionary.

13-49 A: "Americanisms" is used to mean "a word or expression that originated in the United States...." (see Winchell annotation or preface of source). The Craigie dictionary is less limited in scope, including "not only words...of American origin...but also every word denoting something which has a real connection with the development of the country and the history of its people."

13-50 A: In the first place, Mathews was published in 1951 including material up to the time of publication (see Winchell annotation), and Craigie, published 1936-44, covers only to the end of the 19th century (see Winchell annotations). Mathews also attempted to refine and build upon the material in Craigie, in some cases new evidence leading to new conclusions.

13-51 A: The purpose is to treat such words historically. Note that the OED, Craigie's Dictionary of American English, and Mathews are all built on "historical principles."

13-52 A: The origin is from the Spanish; quotes are given as early as 1850's. Its appearance in Mathews does not limit its use to America; it means that it first came into use, in that specific sense, in America. It may since have become used in Great Britain, it may have come into British English via some other route or with some other meaning. Checking in the OED or any of the British dictionaries should indicate if it is commonly known in Great Britain.

13-53 A: Probably more so than in any other aspect of word study except possibly slang. New abbreviations come into use every day, and keeping up with them and identifying them are often almost impossible.

13-54 A: Arrangement is alphabetical; scope is "abbreviations, acronyms, anonyms, contractions," etc., as listed on the title page. Note also the special lists of signs and symbols such as "chemical element symbols, international civil aircraft markings, etc." also listed on the title page.

13-55 A: Words formed from the initial letters of other words, such as "radar" from Radio Detection and Ranging.

13-56 A: See list on title page: aerospace, associations, etc.

13-57 A: It includes only acronyms, and to avoid technical quibbles over what specifically are acronyms and what are not, also includes initialisms (see preface under "Editorial Policies," p. 10.) Its scope is therefore more limited than De Sola but is apt to include more material in depth on the specified type of abbreviation to which it is limited.

13-58 A: No.

13-59 A: Abbreviation for idem, which is Latin and means "the same." (De Sola, p. 134.) Since it is not really an acronym or initia-

lism, but clearly an abbreviation, it should not be listed in the Acronym Dictionary. It would probably be in any standard dictionary, however.

13-60 A: American Latvian Association and American Legion Auxiliary, among others. (See both De Sola and Acronyms)

13-61 A: Fliegerabwehrkanone, etc.--the German word for antiaircraft gun, used for antiaircraft fire (also Fondest Love and Kisses, according to Acronyms). The Acronym Dictionary gives somewhat more information here.

13-62 A: Cooperative for American Relief Everywhere is listed in both De Sola and the Acronym Dictionary. Only the Acronym Dictionary lists earlier names as well.

13-63 A: NBC stands for National Broadcasting Company, and indicates that the pronunciations given therein are likely to be in some way approved by or used by NBC announcers; it should also indicate an attempt to cover material--such as names and places--which might frequently appear in the news.

13-64 A: See "Standards of American Pronunciation" in the introductory matter. It attempts to record the pronunciations used by educated persons in the greater part of the U.S.-- that is "General American" pronunciation. Only one pronunciation is given and that is chosen more or less arbitrarily.

13-65 A: See "Standards of American Pronunciation," bottom of p. ix.

13-66 A: NBC Handbook gives two pronunciations: one in "respelling" and one in the International Phonetic Alphabet (IPA). The "respelling" (hi JIGH ruh) pronunciation is probably much easier to use than the dictionary diacritical markings, unless you are very familiar with those. It might be helpful regarding pronunciation notations in general to read the section titled "Ways of Noting Pronunciation" in the "Standards of American Pronunciation" in the front matter of the NBC Handbook.

13-67 A: Kenyon and Knott: A Pronouncing Dictionary of American English (Winchell AE55) does, for example.

13-68 A: The arrangement is not alphabetical by the first letter of the word as in dictionaries. In fact the approach is almost backwards. Words are grouped by the rhyming syllables --the last, last two, last three, etc., syllables of the words. Sometimes they are arranged alphabetically within these groupings. Wood's Unabridged Rhyming Dictionary (Winchell AE62), for example, is grouped in single, double, triple rhymes and arranged within those groups strictly by phonetics or sound, rather than spelling.

13-69 A: If you wanted to rhyme the last three syllables, you would look in the "triple rhymes" section, words accented on the second syllable from the last, (beginning p. 809 of c.1943 edition); then under the phonetic equivalent of the last three syllables of "librarian"--ar-i-an--under which you find such possibilities as antiquarian, grammarian, barbarian, humanitarian,...

13-70 A: General information on poetry, forms, definitions, mechanics, etc.

13-71 A: A synonym book (Webster's or Roget's) would be useful; or any dictionary might also be helpful, depending on how extensively it lists synonyms for the specific word. In all you would start under "ensuing," following up other possibilities which are mentioned under that word. In both Webster's Third unabridged and Webster's synonym dictionary you would have to look under "ensue"; in Roget's you can actually look under "ensuing." Suppose that the actual word which you vaguely had in mind was "resultant," even though that may not be strictly synonymous with ensuing. In this case Roget's would have given you your word immediately, just in the index alone.

13-72 A: This is a somewhat different approach to the abbreviation problem than can be solved with the abbreviation dictionaries. It would be easiest to go to a dictionary and look under "kilograms" to find the abbreviation. You could also guess that the abbreviation might be "kg" and look in an abbreviation list to see if you were correct, but this is essentially a backwards approach, and not really necessary.

13-73 A: An American poet who died in 1963, and whose importance is apparently too recent to get him into either the Funk and Wagnall unabridged or Webster's 2nd unabridged (did you check in the Third? Why?), but Random House Dictionary lists him, in the regular alphabetical order.

13-74 A: Slang, and specifically Australian, which leaves out the Dictionary of American Slang and the Thesaurus of American Slang, and therefore leaves Partridge's Dictionary of Slang. You might also try the OED on a guess, but it isn't there. Partridge lists it under "nips in(to), put the."

13-75 A: You want an antonym, which are sometimes given in the dictionaries, perhaps more often given in the synonym books. Webster's Third, Funk and Wagnalls, Random House give synonyms, no antonyms for reprehend. Webster's synonym dictionary gives synonyms but no antonyms for reprehend. Roget's index leads you to the category of "Disapprobation" (967), followed by the generally

opposite category of "Approbation" under which you find approve, sanction, accept, etc., which will probably suit your needs.

13-76 A: Webster's Third unabridged (and Second) both list under definitions for "hand"; five articles of the same kind sold together. Not listed in Funk and Wagnalls unabridged nor in Random House.

13-77 A: Probably the best thing to do is to go to a usage book. Finalize is listed in Webster's Third (but not in the Second) with no usage label to indicate its acceptance in formal writing, etc. Neither Evans nor Follett deals with the word; Fowler, rather surprisingly, says that there are a "few occasions when it is an improvement on completed or finished."

13-78 A: This is a case where Roget's is probably the most helpful source, looking directly under the category for Color, and the various more specific categories (i.e., orangeness) following. Webster's synonym dictionary and Webster's Third unabridged are no help.

13-79 A: OED (you could of course also check unabridged dictionaries, since you don't know for sure that the word is not in current usage, but it seems more reasonable to go directly to the historical source). Under "colpon," you find that the word is a variant of "culpon," being obsolete, meaning "cut, piece." Further information is given in the main entry under "culpon," including the quote from Chaucer. Century Dictionary lists only under "culpons" with no cross-reference from "colpons."

13-80 A: Webster's Third would not have it as it is a name; Funk and Wagnalls unabridged and Random House do not have it. It is listed in Webster's Second Unabridged under Barnaby (not Rudge, although there is a cross-reference from Rudge, Barnaby to Barnaby Rudge at the bottom of the page-- underneath the line--on which Rudge would appear).

13-81 A: You could look each up separately in any dictionary. A better way would be to turn to one of the rhyming dictionaries (Wood's, for example) which includes discussion of versification and scansion to find more detailed and comparative information.

13-82 A: All are relatively recent terms. Webster's Third unabridged lists laser only (Addenda, c.1966 edition). Random House lists laser and quasar. American Heritage lists all three. Another source which might not immediately occur to you as a possibility is abbreviation books, on the assumption that these words are acronyms of some sort (like radar). The Acronyms and Initialisms Dictionary lists only quasar; De Sola lists lasar and quasar.

13-83 A: Webster's Third unabridged, Webster's
           New World list it as from a village of
           that name in Massachusetts or Connecticut.
           Dictionary of American English (Craigie)
           further identifies it as of Algonquian Indian
           origin.   Not in OED.

13-84 A: Wentworth and Flexner, under squirrel,
           noun, meaning 2: that is, one who examines
           "nuts."

13-85 A: Webster's Third lists the use of like as a
           conjunction as acceptable.   If you prefer
           not to take the word of Webster's Third,
           Eisenhower, Art Linkletter, and the Winston
           Company, you can go on to the usage book
           for further discussion.   Fowler says it is
           generally condemned as vulgar, and has
           colloquial use in the U.S.; Follett says it
           cannot be used in place of "as." Evans is
           more permissive, says it is an established
           function, and points out historical and literary
           precedent (quotes from Keats being, pre-
           sumably, more acceptable to the prescriptive
           grammarians than quotes from Art Linkletter).

Section 14a

Encyclopedias

Questions #14/1-14/112

14-1   If you wanted to find the definition of "communism," you would look it up in a dictionary.   If you wanted
        to find out the historical development of Communism, would you expect to find this in a dictionary?   What
        type of reference source would give you this information?

        The next set of sources to be examined are:

                        Encyclopedia Americana (AD1)
                        Encyclopaedia Britannica (AD2)
                        Collier's Encyclopedia (AD4)

                        Columbia Encyclopedia (AD5, 1AD1a)
                        Lincoln Library (AD6)

                        Compton's Pictured Encyclopedia (AD14)
                        World Book Encyclopedia (AD16)

                        Encyclopedia International (AD15)
                        Grolier Universal Encyclopedia
                        American Peoples Encyclopedia
                        Britannica Junior (AD13)

                        Subscription Books Bulletin Reviews (AA309a)
                        General Encyclopedias in Print (see annotation to 2AD4)

14-2   What is an encyclopedia?   How would you define the term?

        Just as an encyclopedia itself is a vast undertaking, so is the specific examination and evaluation of any
        specific encyclopedia.   For real evaluation, one must rely on the published reviews and comments of
        experts.   A feeling for the general usefulness of encyclopedias, perhaps more so than in any other type
        of reference source, must come from continued and daily use in a reference or research situation.   How-
        ever, there are several specific points on which you can compare and contrast the encyclopedias and
        which may help you get a general idea of the types of information which can be found through encyclo-
        pedias, and the most efficient ways of using them.

        As with other reference sources, you should look first at the basic physical bibliographical facts about the
        source: full title, publisher, copyright date or edition of the set you are examining, number of volumes,
        etc.

        Then, as with the other reference sources, you can go on to determine general scope and arrangement,
        and you can check for specific types or kinds of information included (illustrations, maps, bibliographical
        references, etc.).

14-3   The first three encyclopedias listed to examine are the major well-known American adult encyclopedias:
        Americana, Britannica and Colliers.   All are listed in Winchell's section on encyclopedias under "Amer-
        ican and English."   It is probably easiest to examine all three together and comparatively, checking
        against the Winchell annotations and remembering that any of the specific comments in Winchell may now
        be outdated.   Look first at the Americana.
            What is the full title, and what is the publisher?

14-4   Be sure to note the date of the edition or set of the specific set which you are examining.   Where would
        you expect to find this date?   What does the date indicate to you?

14-5   Do the encyclopedia publishing companies come out with completely new and revised editions every year?
        How do they make provisions for revising or up-dating the material in the encyclopedias?   (See Winchell.)

14-6   Does the Encyclopedia Americana use the "continuous revision" policy?   How can you tell?

14-7   Can you tell what material is changed or revised each year?

14-8   What introductory or prefatory matter is included?

14-9   Is there anything in the introductory matter which tells you how to use the encyclopedia?

14-10   What is the publishing history of the Americana?   When was it first published?   When was the last major
        complete revision?

14-11   How many volumes are there to the set?

14-12   What is the basic arrangement of the set?   What can you tell from the spines of the volume?

14-13   With encyclopedias, it is not really sufficient to say that the arrangement is alphabetical.   So much in-
        formation is included that it is also necessary to know how it can be found alphabetically and to what
        depth it is discussed.   Considering the type and depth of information found in encyclopedias, what are the
        possibilities for arrangement of material?   Look, for example, in vol. 1 of the Americana under Alaska
        and Adak.

14-14   Are the articles or entries in the Americana mostly short or long?

14-15   The arrangement of the Americana is alphabetical, with a mixture of long and short articles.   If you want-
        ed to locate in the Americana information on The Maid's Tragedy, a 15th-century English play by Beaumont
        and Fletcher, would you look under Maid's Tragedy, under Beaumont, under Fletcher, under English
        literature, English drama, drama, fifteenth-century drama? ·

14-16   Does the Americana have a separate article on German Shepherd dogs?

14-17   If you were looking in the Americana for information on educational psychology, for which there is a
        separate article, how could you be sure that all the pertinent information you might find helpful would be
        included in that article?   How could you find out where else in the set you might find pertinent informa-
        tion?

14-18   Is there any way in which you can judge the relative authority and accuracy of the articles in the Americana? For example, who wrote the article on Air Pollution and what are his qualifications for doing so?

14-19   Are all articles signed?

14-20   There is a list of contributors in the introductory matter of vol. 1. Does this give you additional information to that found at the end of the articles? The list of contributors may seem impressive. Can you actually tell to what specific topic they made some contribution?

14-21   Would you expect to find maps in the encyclopedia? Where are they found in the Americana? What company is responsible for the maps in the Americana? Can you tell how recent the maps are?

14-22   What other kinds of illustrations or graphic material do you find in the Americana? Do you think this illustrative material is important?

14-23   Do the encyclopedias give you access to any further information, beyond the scope of their contents? For example, if you had read the article on Air Pollution in the Americana, and wanted further information on the subject, what can you find in the Americana to help you?

14-24   These "bibliographies" (lists of further references is perhaps a more accurate term than bibliographies) are very important in the proper use of encyclopedias. It is too easy to think that all information is contained in the encyclopedia, or that the encyclopedia is really the only necessary source you need to refer to for information. Does the Americana have bibliographies for all articles? Is the information given in the bibliographies complete? Do the bibliographies list foreign works, or only English language materials? How do you tell if the bibliographies are up to date?

14-25   If you looked in the Americana to find further information on Hejira, could you also find out how to pronounce it at the same time?

14-26   So far, the questions you have been answering about the Americana have dealt with specific items for which there are reasonably clear answers. You have considered the basic arrangement of the encyclopedia, the general authority of its contributors, and the general way in which it is revised or kept up to date. The only way in which you have dealt with the problem of "scope" is by looking for specific kinds of information or features such as bibliographies, maps, illustrations, pronunciations, etc. In a very general and obvious sense, what is the "scope" of an encyclopedia?

14-27   Considering the scope of an encyclopedia to be "all knowledge" is pretty overwhelming. Can this be narrowed down in any way? What is the purpose of a modern encyclopedia? Is the purpose of an encyclopedia to provide highly technical, specialized information to a person already an expert in the field? Should an encyclopedia article on nuclear physics be written in such a way that it can be understood only by a nuclear physicist? Should it be written in such a way that it can be understood by an eighth-grade student? Should an article on musical harmony be written in such a way that it can be understood only by a musicologist? Should it be written in such a way that it can be understood by a nuclear physicist? At what audience or level is an encyclopedia aimed?

14-28   What is the audience at which the Americana is aimed? Where would you expect to find this information?

14-29   From young students through adults is still a very broad range.   In general, do you think that young students would understand the material in the Americana?   What is one way in which you could try to test this (short of finding a young student and asking him)?

14-30   Is there any other way in which the scope of an encyclopedia can be narrowed down?   Consider the country (and/or language) of publication.

14-31   Is the Americana noted for any special aspects or strong points?   (See Winchell).

14-32   The next major encyclopedia to be examined is the Encyclopaedia Britannica.   Who is the publisher, how many volumes are there in the set, and what is the revision policy?   Be sure to note the copyright date or "edition" of the set at which you are looking.

14-33   At what audience is the Britannica aimed?   What is the general level of writing, of the presentation of material?

14-34   The Britannica has long had a reputation as the most scholarly, most technical, most advanced of the encyclopedias, but the trend with recent revisions has been more to the popular level, more in competition with the nonspecialist level of the Americana.   What can you do to test this?

14-35   Is there anything in the introductory material which tells you how to use the encyclopedia, and discusses scope, arrangement, special features, etc.?

14-36   How does the arrangement of the Britannica compare with that of the Americana?   Consider the index also.

14-37   How does the Britannica's article on Africa compare with that in the Americana?   Can you find any information on Adak in the Britannica?

14-38   Does the Britannica have an article on air pollution?   Can you find any information in the Britannica on air pollution?

14-39   Who is the author of the article on "aluminum" in the Britannica?

14-40   Look at some of the bibliographies in the Britannica.   How do they differ from those in the Americana?

14-41   Where are the maps in the Britannica?   Who makes the maps?   Are they dated?

14-42   The Britannica is also generally cited as the longest of the three major encyclopedias in terms of words; yet it has only 24 volumes in comparison to Americana's 30.   How do you account for this?

14-43   Does the Winchell annotation give you any further clues to any specific differences in the scope of Britannica as compared to the other encyclopedias?

14-44   The third major encyclopedia is Collier's. Who is the publisher? How many volumes? What is the revision policy? Note date of the set.

14-45   How does Collier's differ from the other two encyclopedias (Americana, Britannica) in regard to scope, audience or level?

14-46   Does Collier's differ from the Americana and Britannica in regard to arrangement?

14-47   Can you find through Collier's a list of further reading on the subject of air pollution?

14-48   Why are the bibliographies in Collier's arranged in this fashion, rather than following the articles as in the other encyclopedias? What are the advantages and disadvantages of such an arrangement?

14-49   The items in the bibliographies--see History: The Ancient World, for example--are not listed alphabetically following the subject heading. On what basis are they listed?

14-50   How are the bibliographies in Collier's arranged, and how do you find one on air pollution?

14-51   How do the maps and other illustrative matter in Collier's compare to the other encyclopedias?

14-52   Who wrote the article on Africa in Collier's and what are his qualifications for doing so?

14-53   You have examined and compared, briefly, the three major adult encyclopedias. In general, how did they differ? What kinds of comparative statements can you make about their scope, arrangement, special features, etc.?

14-54   Look specifically at the articles on libraries in all three encyclopedias and compare them. Is the access similar for all (direct or through the index)? Is the length similar? Is the structure similar? What about illustrations? Which of them discuss librarianship itself? Which give information about education, certification, degree requirements, etc.? Which give the most information about foreign libraries and library systems? Do any of them give basic information to help someone use the library (the card catalog, the reference sources, etc.)?

14-55   If you wanted to find, through the encyclopedia, an outline of the Dewey Decimal classification scheme, how would you locate it?

14-56   Using these three encyclopedias, can you find a picture of Canterbury Cathedral (in England)? How did you go about searching for it? How did you locate it?

14-57   Using the indexes only, can you find out who Jean Arp was?   Can you find out when he lived and what he was noted for?   Compare all three encyclopedias.

14-58   When and how is St. Nicholas' Day celebrated in various countries?   What is its historical significance? Try all three encyclopedias and compare results.

14-59   How do you read the symbols on a weather map?   Try all three and compare.   What is your best approach to this?   If you looked directly for an article on "Weather" or "Weather maps," what would you find?

14-60   In which of these three encyclopedias could you find the titles of some books on chemistry suitable for high school students?

14-61   If, after hearing about present day problems of the American Indian as a minority group, you wanted to "get some background information" on various Indian tribes, where they were originally located, something about their languages, their customs, the relationships between the tribes, their current status, etc., to what type of source would you go?   How would you use this source?

14-62   Why is it useful (or necessary) for a library to have more than one encyclopedia?

14-63   What is the importance of the index in using encyclopedias?

14-64   The best use of an encyclopedia is probably for general information or background questions, such as those on the celebration of St. Nicholas' Day, the symbols on a weather map, the background information on American Indian tribes.   However, encyclopedias are also used extensively for locating "facts" or illustrations, for quick answers to specific questions, etc.   For these uses, the index of an encyclopedia is indispensible, since it is generally the only access you have to specific information.

How does the use of an encyclopedia differ from the use of a dictionary in regard to arrangement?   Both are arranged alphabetically, but the dictionary does not need to have an index?   Why not?   Does it have anything to do with the kind of information they give?

14-65   Does the information given in encyclopedias overlap that in dictionaries?   How?   Could you find out who Jean Arp was through the dictionary?   Could you find out when St. Nicholas' Day is celebrated through the dictionary?

14-66   The next two encyclopedias on the list represent a form which seems to fall half-way between the dictionary and the encyclopedia: the "one-volume" encyclopedia.   Look at the Preface to the Columbia Encyclopedia.   What is the purpose of such a single-volume encyclopedia?   What is it trying to do?   How does it differ from a dictionary?   from a regular encyclopedia?

14-67   What does the Preface tell you about the scope of the work?   Any special aspects covered?

14-68   What is the arrangement of the Columbia Encyclopedia?   Is there an index?   Is an index needed?

14-69   Does the Columbia Encyclopedia contain such special features as maps, illustrations, bibliographies, pronunciation guides, etc., as the regular encyclopedias do?

14-70   What is the major obvious way in which the Lincoln Library differs from the Columbia Encyclopedia?

14-71   How does this compare to other sources you have examined previously? What are the advantages and disadvantages to these two types of arrangements?

14-72   Did Roget's Thesaurus and the slang thesaurus have indexes? Does the Lincoln Library have an index? Why is an index needed?

14-73   Using either of the single-volume encyclopedias (Columbia and Lincoln Library) can you find out what Jean Arp is noted for? Can you find the location of Adak, Alaska?

14-74   In which of these two single-volume encyclopedias would you expect to find a "background" type article on mineralogy, discussing its relationship to geology, with lists and descriptions of various rocks and stones, possibly with illustrations? Could you find the definitions, etc., of the various rocks and stones through the other encyclopedia?

14-75   Can you find some background material on American Indians?

14-76   How do the revision policies for the Columbia Encyclopedia and The Lincoln Library compare?

14-77   One of the ways in which encyclopedias differ is in level: reading level, level of understandability, etc. (See #14-28, 14-33, 14-45, 14-53). All of the encyclopedias you have examined so far have been basically adult level, with one exception. Which of the encyclopedias you have looked at seems to be aimed at a younger audience?

         The next two encyclopedias on your list to examine are examples of sets designed specifically for children and/or young people (in Winchell, listed as "juvenile" as opposed to adult).

14-78   Look first at Compton's Pictured Encyclopedia. What is the basic information you need to know about it: publisher, number of volumes, revision policy, date of set you are looking at?

14-79   According to the preface of the set itself, what is the general grade level or reading level aimed at by Compton's?

14-80   What is the basic arrangement of Compton's? Does it differ in any way from the adult encyclopedias you examined?

14-81   Is there an index at all? Is it the same as the other indexes? Does this have any effect on the basic arrangement of the set?

14-82   What is the theory behind this particular type of indexing arrangement?

14-83   Can you find, through Compton's, who Jean Arp was and what he was noted for?

14-84   How does the Compton's article on libraries compare with those in the adult encyclopedias?

14-85   The other children's or juvenile encyclopedia to be examined is the World Book Encyclopedia.   Note the publisher, the number of volumes, revision policy, and date of the set you are examining.   What is the general grade level or reading level aimed at by this set?

14-86   Does the arrangement of the World Book differ in any way from the other sets you have examined?   Can you find anything about Adak, Alaska or Jean Arp through the World Book?   Can you find anything about the location of the Arfura Sea?

14-87   Does the lack of an index have any effect on the arrangement of the set itself?

14-88   Is there anything which gives you an alternative approach to the World Book alphabetical arrangement? See Winchell annotation.

14-89   Can you find, in the World Book, a broad general background on the American Indian, such as you looked for in the adult encyclopedias in #14-61?

14-90   Since Compton's and World Book are encyclopedias designed primarily for children, what would this lead you to assume about the illustrations, maps, other graphic material?   Is your assumption borne out by examination?

14-91   What can you determine about the authority behind the articles in Compton's and World Book?   Would you expect the same authority as with the adult encyclopedias?

14-92   Where could you find a short list of books on chemistry for a junior high school student?

14-93   If you were a very unscientific type, and you wanted to know in a general way what lasers are and how they work, where might you go for an introductory article?

14-94   Should the use of the children's or juvenile level encyclopedias be limited to school libraries or children's collections?   Would it be useful for an adult reference collection to have a juvenile level encyclopedia as well as the adult level?

14-95   Besides the obvious one of reading level, does the approach of the children's encyclopedias differ from the adult encyclopedias in any major way?

14-96   Do you think that this difference in index approach has any special usefulness for the children's ency-
          clopedias?

14-97   There are two other "juvenile" encyclopedias listed in the basic volume of Winchell: Britannica Junior
          and Encyclopedia International. Looking at the Winchell annotations, is there any difference in the age
          or reading level aimed at by these two sets? How do they compare to Compton's and World Book?

          The Encyclopedia International, published by Grolier (and an abridged, cheaper version called Grolier
          Universal), and the American Peoples Encyclopedia, also published by Grolier, are sets which fall--in
          reading level--somewhat between the general college level of the three major sets (Americana, Britannica,
          Collier's) and the school level of the children's sets. They have been set up as "popular" encyclopedias,
          aimed at the mass audience, aimed perhaps at the high school graduate who might not feel comfortable
          with the Big Three. They also tend to be less expensive than the Big Three. If you have access to
          either of these sets, or both, examine one of the sets comparatively to those encyclopedias you have
          looked at already, using the same type of questions and problems.

14-98   The encyclopedias you have examined in this section have been only the major and well-known titles.
          There are others. How would you judge the relative worth of a lesser-known encyclopedia, or a newly
          published encyclopedia?

14-99   What are "subscription books"?

14-100   Another published source which gives some basic factual information about all of the available encyclo-
          pedias is the last source on your list, General Encyclopedias in Print, compiled by J. P. Walsh and
          issued annually. What kind of factual information is given in this listing?

14-101   Winchell does not have a separate listing for this source but does note it in the annotation to Walsh's
          Anglo-American General Encyclopedias (2AD4), a similar listing but with more historical information.
          What does the Winchell annotation indicate as the primary use, to librarians, of General Encyclopedias
          in Print?

14-102   One major difference in encyclopedias, although not so evident so far, is price. Where would you look
          to find the prices for these encyclopedias? Would you expect to find them listed in BIP/PTLA? Would
          you expect to find new printings, etc., listed in such sources as CBI, BPR, etc.?

14-103   Where would you find the prices, then, if not in BIP, etc.?

          The following questions are to be used for review, drawing on sources from the dictionary, supplementary
          language and encyclopedia sections. For some, where it is not clear what source would give the best
          answer, a check in more than one source, or in more than one type of source, will help you gain fa-
          miliarity with using the sources to best advantage.

14-104   Who is John Rolfe? When did he live?

14-105   What are the names of the various figures in figure skating?

14-106   In the section on dictionaries, you found a definition of "stroboscope." If someone wanted to understand how a stroboscope worked, where would you look?

14-107   What can you find out about the word "hello"? Is it mainly an American usage? Is it also used in Great Britain? How did it originate? What other forms does it have?

14-108   What is the art of falconry? Is a falcon the same as a hawk? Is there any current interest in falconry? Where? How do you train the falcon?

14-109   What time is "five bells," ship's time?

14-110   Where would you look to find some general information on folk music, how it got started, some of the well-known singers, names of some of the songs, something about folk music in other countries?

14-111   Specifically, what does a student mean when he refers to a class or an assignment as "mickey mouse"?

14-112   Can you locate Hainan on a map? Where is it? What is it?

Section 14a

Encyclopedias

Answers #14/1-14/112

14-1 A: This is highly unlikely to be given in a comparatively brief dictionary definition. The type of reference source which would probably give you the information is an encyclopedia.

14-2 A: See Webster's Third Unabridged or the ALA Glossary.

14-3 A: Full title: The Encyclopedia Americana, International Edition. Publisher is listed on the title page as Americana Corporation (now owned by Grolier Corporation).

14-4 A: The date would appear probably on the verso of the title page, as a copyright date (e.g., "Copyright© 1967 by Americana Corporation). There will probably be a series of dates; the latest date given is the last date on which any new or revised material has been added to the set. This date will vary according to the time at which your set was purchased. (A new set purchased in 1968 should have a copyright date of 1967 or 1968). See #12-12 through 12-16 for the same situation in regard to dictionaries.

14-5 A: Winchell, 8th ed., p. 81, under "Encyclopedias," discusses the "continuous revision" policy for bringing encyclopedia sets up to date.

14-6 A: Yes, it does. Check the Winchell annotation. Also the yearly copyright dates on the verso of the title page indicate that new material was added or changed each year, which is a fairly safe indication of a continuous revision policy.

14-7 A: No, you can't (except by tedious detailed checking of dates, statistics, etc., from one year's printing to the next). That is, there is no way in which new or revised material is clearly designated or separated from other older unchanged material.

14-8 A: See volume 1: Preface, Editorial Staff, contributors, key to pronunciation, abbreviations--much the same as in the dictionaries.

14-9 A: Nothing specifically so titled. However, there is material in the Preface ("arrangement of contents," "special features," etc.) which would be helpful.

14-10 A: See the Preface or see the Winchell annotation.

14-11 A: 30 volumes. This seems to remain constant with each year's printing. (Page numbering, however, may be very inconsistent due to the requirements of the revisions--see Preface under "Arrangement of Contents.")

14-12 A: Basic arrangement is alphabetical. The last volume, vol. 30, is an index.

14-13 A: The choice is basically between a separate short entry for each specific subject (as in dictionaries) and a long entry or article bringing many smaller subjects together under a more collective entry. Adak is a short entry, for a place name in Alaska, giving more information than would probably be found in a dictionary entry, but still brief, as compared to the longer collective-type article for Alaska.

14-14 A: There is a mixture. In vol. 1, see the article on Africa which is really a good-sized pamphlet, see also the article on Alaska (shorter than Africa), on adult education (moderate length), and on alkali (fairly short), etc.

14-15 A: Probably the simplest thing to do would be to look in the index under Maid's Tragedy and find that it is on p. 417 of volume 3, which happens to be the article on Beaumont and Fletcher (1967 edition).

14-16 A: You could look directly under German Shepherd dogs in the volume covering that alphabetical entry, or you could look in the index under the same entry where you would find the words in capital letters, indicating that there is a separate article on it, plus three other references, including one to an illustration which is not part of the separate article on German Shepherd dogs.

14-17 A: Some of the articles have cross-references within them to other articles in the set. The index also gives references: under the entry "educational psychology" in the index, you are referred to the main entry plus several other related entries such as "Learning, psychology of."

14-18 A: The name of the author and his position is given at the end of the article (Arthur J. Benline, Commissioner, Dept. of Air Pollution Control, NYC: 1967 Americana). It is not clear from this, of course, when Mr. Benline was commissioner...

14-19 A: No, many of the smaller ones are not.

14-20 A: Their full titles are given, and this is not always included in the reference at the end of the articles. Also a note is made for each showing--sometimes rather generally--what articles they contributed to or helped with.

14-21 A: Yes, you would expect to find maps, since the kind of visual information maps give is important to an understanding of many areas or topics. They are found throughout the articles in the Americana, for example, in the articles on Alaska and Africa. The Hammond Company is responsible for the maps (see copyright note on the maps themselves, or see the Preface). No dates are indicated on the maps.

14-22 A: Pictures, photographs, drawings--both color and black and white; maps, charts, technical drawings. Again, this kind of visual information is helpful to an understanding of the material presented--in illustrating certain points, in clarifying technical material, etc. Also it adds a great deal to the general attractiveness of the presentation.

14-23 A: A short "bibliography" is at the end of the article on air pollution, indicating books on the subject which you might read.

14-24 A: Not all of the articles in the Americana have bibliographies. Author, title, place of publisher and date of publication are given. Publisher and paging are not given. All bibliographies seem to include only English language materials. You can tell to some extent, by the dates of publication, how up-to-date the bibliography is. The list of books following the article on Air Pollution in the 1967 Americana lists three 1965 books. Some bibliographies are more up-to-date than others (see Winchell annotation).

14-25 A: Americana gives pronunciations for the entry words; the key (diacritical markings) used is given in the front matter of volume 1. If you looked up Hejira in the H volume, you would not find anything (1967 printing); if you looked up Hejira in the index, you would find a see-reference to Hegira. (Hejira is the second of the spellings given in most of the dictionaries.) In the index under Hegira, you would find a reference to the main entry for it plus other references; the main entry for Hegira indicates the spelling. This is another indication of the usefulness of the index, for cross-references which may not be given in the main volumes.

14-26 A: For the general encyclopedia, as opposed to subject or special encyclopedias, the scope is "all knowledge" (see definitions from your answer to #14-2).

14-27 A: The major meaningful distinction between available encyclopedias, and the major problem in using encyclopedias, lie in this area--the audience at which the encyclopedia is aimed, the level at which the material is presented. Both the virtues and sins of encyclopedias lie in their trying to be all things to all people. The major modern encyclopedias seem to have settled for the non-specialist, but even here there are varying levels of education: the elementary school student, the high school student, the high school graduate, the college student, the college graduate, etc.

14-28 A: You could get it from the Winchell annotation (which, actually, is no more specific than "for general use"). You could also find it in the Preface. The preface of the 1967 "edition" states that the Americana is "intended to serve as a bridge between the world of the specialists and the world of the general reader...serves a wide range of readers. The young student... Teachers, librarians, and adults in other fields...for which they have no advanced training."

14-29 A: You could try to select a reasonably technical subject on which you had no knowledge whatsoever, read the article for it, and see how well you understand it. For the student, it depends on how young and how bright he is, of course.

14-30 A: Although most of the encyclopedias are regarded as international in scope, it is inevitable that the material included will reflect the country in which it is published. For example, although the Americana has a lengthy article on Africa itself, compare the size of the article on Alaska with the article on Nigeria, one of the countries in Africa.

14-31 A: See Winchell annotation--strong on information for American towns and cities, for evaluation of books, operas, works of art, etc.

14-32 A: Publisher: Encyclopedia Britannica, Inc. (title page).
Number of volumes: 24 (set itself, and Winchell).
Revision policy: continuous revision (Winchell annotation; the verso of the title page of the 1969 edition gives only one copyright date, the most recent, and it is perhaps not clear from this that a continuous revision policy is in effect).

14-33 A: The Winchell annotation does not really say, except to indicate that earlier editions at least were "very scholarly." The Britannica itself is also rather circumspect; the Editor's Preface of the 1969 edition indicates vaguely that "All...seek...to serve an ever widening public."

14-34 A: As it was suggested in #14-29, you can find

an article on a technical subject of which you have no knowledge, read it, and see how well you understand this. You can then check the same subject in the other major encyclopedias for comparison.

14-35 A: One page (in the 1969 edition) titled "How to Use Britannica" and which is concerned mostly with the specific alphabetical arrangement.

14-36 A: The Britannica is also alphabetical. There are some short entries, but apparently less than in the Americana; most of the articles are of some length. (If you have access to an earlier 9th or even 11th edition of the Britannica, look at its general arrangement, and you can see more clearly the concept of long monographic-type articles on large subjects, as compared to the more current practice of breaking down into smaller subjects.) The index is in the last volume; like the Americana, it shows main entries plus references to other places in the set where material on the subject may be found.

14-37 A: The article on Alaska seems shorter in the Britannica, certainly with less colored illustrations, maps, etc. There is no separate article in the Britannica on Adak, but it is listed in the index, a reference to information with another article.

14-38 A: No article on air pollution (1969 edition). Index has nothing under air pollution, but indicates a main article and several references for Pollution, Environmental, and references under that to "air."

14-39 A: F.C.F. (1969 edition). You have to refer to the index volume to the list of contributors to find the name (and position) of F.C.F.

14-40 A: They are frequently quite long; they often include foreign language publications; the citations are briefer, giving author, title, date, but no publisher.

14-41 A: The major maps are in the index volume in a separate section called "Atlas." This section also contains an index to the maps, or to the atlas. There are some small maps scattered throughout the text. Some of the maps are from Rand McNally; others, unmarked, presumably are Encyclopaedia Britannica maps. The maps are not dated.

14-42 A: More pages per volume, also less illustrations; and the general page lay-out of the Americana, while attractive, is sometimes space-consuming.

14-43 A: "Still reflects traces of its British origins... in the relative length of treatment of many British topics."

14-44 A: Crowell Collier and Macmillan (title page). 24 volumes. Continuous revision (Winchell).

14-45 A: See Preface under "Scope": "...essential content of the curricula of colleges and secondary schools, as well as the upper grades... in depth for the nonspecialist, but included, too... desired by the professional in the field." Winchell annotation indicates that the level is college, but not as advanced as Americana and Britannica.

14-46 A: Very similar: alphabetically with an index in the last volume. Like the other encyclopedias, the index is detailed, showing main entries plus references to other sources of information in the set, and entries for subjects not treated as separate entries. The articles are mostly long, although there are some short entries.

14-47 A: Bibliographies are not with the article itself, as in Britannica and Americana. In Collier's, the bibliographies are all listed in the Bibliography and Index volume.

14-48 A: See "How to use the Bibliography" in the last volume.

14-49 A: See "How to use the Bibliography." They are listed more or less in increasing order of difficulty.

14-50 A: The bibliographies in the last volume are arranged in a general classed order, with an alphabetical subject guide at the beginning. Air pollution is too specific to be included in that list, but the index includes references to the bibliographies as well as to items in the set itself. The index entry for air pollution (1966 edition) lists Bib. in vol. 24, p. 147, item 241. There is one title listed (as compared to 6 in the 1967 Americana.).

14-51 A: Maps are scattered throughout, as in Americana, unlike Britannica. Illustrations are similar to Americana, more than in Britannica, more in color.

14-52 A: In Collier's the full name of the author is given following the article, but not his position. Contributors with their positions are listed in the front of volume 1.

14-53 A: In general, the three encyclopedias differ mainly in detail (i.e., location of maps, extent of illustrations, location of bibliographies, location of names of authors of articles, etc.). In arrangement they are very similar. All include both long and short articles; the Americana perhaps has more short articles than the others, the Britannica perhaps still tends to stress the longer article. All indexes are similar in detail and use. They are similar in scope, U. S. products, with the Britannica perhaps retaining some British bent, the Americana being perhaps stronger on American geographical items. In theory, they differ in level, although not always noticeably: the Britannica is still generally considered at the most advanced level, followed by the Americana, with Collier's at a college level perhaps not so advanced as the other two, certainly useable at a high school level for most students. In sum: the three encyclopedias are strikingly similar, and getting more so each year.

14-54 A: All three have a major full-length article on libraries (Britannica is titled "Library"). Access is direct but can also be located through the index plus other references not in the articles themselves. Both Britannica and Americana have long bibliographies. (Collier's of course is not with the article but is presumably in the Bibliography volume.)

Britannica and Americana give short outlines at the beginning of the articles, so that the content and structure are easily seen; Collier's does not.

Britannica seems to have the most information on foreign libraries, and also has the least illustrations.

Americana seems to have the most information on the profession of librarianship, educational requirements, etc. (None have separate articles on "librarianship.")

The best information on how to use a library is probably given in Collier's article called "Library Research and Reports," following the articles on Libraries and Library Association.

14-55 A: If you looked through the articles on "Libraries" which you have just examined, you would find that only the one in Collier's outlines the scheme to any degree. The Americana article lists only the major classes. If you checked the Indexes, you would find that none of the encyclopedias have articles on the Dewey Decimal scheme (although all have short articles on Melvil Dewey, none of which give an outline for the classification scheme). All have references under Dewey Decimal Classification, Americana and Collier's only to the articles on Libraries or on Dewey himself. The Britannica also has a reference to the article on Information Processing, which does include a listing of the general classes of Dewey plus an example of some breakdowns.

14-56 A: All three encyclopedias will indicate illustrations through the index (although it is not clear that they index absolutely all illustrations). Therefore it would seem reasonable to turn to the index first. All three list Canterbury Cathedral in the index, Americana and Collier's as such and Britannica as a subdivision under Canterbury. Collier's has an article on Canterbury

Cathedral (indicated by typeface for entry), and the index indicates a reference for an illustration contained in that article (which is only a small portion of the west side). The others do not have articles on Canterbury Cathedral. Americana indicates a reference for an illustration (in the article on Crypts, and illustrates only the crypt.) Britannica has several scattered references for the Cathedral, none for illustrations. Looking in the Britannica article for the city of Canterbury, you can find a floor plan for the cathedral, no picture. (Americana 1967, Britannica 1969, Collier's 1966).

14-57 A: The indexes in all three indicate that he was an artist. Britannica gives only that much, Collier's says he was a French artist, Americana says he was an Alsatian artist and poet. You would have to look further to find when he lived and what he was noted for. Collier's and Americana both have articles on Arp, plus other references. Britannica has no article but lists several references in scattered volumes. (Americana 1967, Britannica 1969, Collier's 1966).

14-58 A: Search in the indexes under St. as if it were spelled "Saint."

Americana has a reference (no article indicated) for St. Nicholas Day, which turns out to be in the article for "Nicholas, Saint"; gives history but not much on when and how it is currently celebrated.

Collier's index lists as such, has no article, but a reference which is found in the article on "Santa Claus." This is quite good on when and how celebrated, with some history, and good comparison to the more American custom of Santa Claus.

Britannica has no index entry for St. Nicholas Day; one of the references for Saint Nicholas looks promising but turns out to be a town in Belgium. However, in the index under Nicholas, Saint, there is a reference to the article on Nicholas, Saint, which gives some of the information you need but not as much as you find in the other two. (Americana and Collier indexes both have references from Nicholas, Saint, to the articles on which you will find information on St. Nicholas' Day.) (Americana 1967, Britannica 1969, Collier's 1966).

14-59 A: Direct access: none have articles on "weather maps" as such. Americana and Collier's have articles on "weather" and on "meteorology" (meteorology being the science of or study of the atmosphere or weather). Britannica has an article on meteorology, nothing on weather, no cross-reference from weather to meteorology in the main alphabetical arrangement; however, Britannica does have an article on "weather forecasting" which does include references to meteorology. Americana has a reference in the main alphabetical arrangement for "weather maps" with cross-references to meteorology and weather forecasting.

Index: All have references under weather maps, although Britannica's is a cross-reference to "Synoptic weather charts," for which there is an article (but it is short, has no pictures, maps, indication of symbols, etc.)

On this one, it becomes necessary to follow through all the references and possibilities to find something suitable, although, of course, you may be lucky and hit an answer before you have followed up all possibilities.

The Americana index reference on weather maps is to the article on meteorology, which has a section on weather maps, with no pictures, no maps, no symbols, etc.

Collier's index references on weather maps include one for a map and one for an illustration, both of which are in the long article on Meteorology and Climate, and which do include a picture of a weather map with some symbols indicated on the picture of the map. The article on weather only mentions maps, gives no symbols, pictures, or cross-references.

Britannica's index references on synoptic weather charts (cross-referenced from weather maps) lists the article on that topic (which is short, has no pictures, maps, symbols, etc.); one of the other two references leads you to the article on "weather forecasting," where a fuller graphic description of the symbols, with pictures of maps, charts, etc., is found. (Americana 1967, Britannica 1969, Collier's 1966).

14-60 A: Collier's "Bibliography" in the index volume specifically lists books in order of increasing difficulty, so presumably titles coming first in their list on chemistry might be suitable for high school students. Level of reading/difficulty is not so clear for the bibliographic references in the other two encyclopedias.

14-61 A: An encyclopedia would probably be the best source for this very general non-specific background information. Turning directly to the main article on Indians (being aware of the possibilities for variation, such as American Indian, South American Indian, etc.) would probably be satisfactory; however, turning first to the index might give you a general idea of how the material was located--for example, whether there was a major article on Indians, whether material on specific tribes or for specific locations would be located in separate articles, etc. If after or during your reading of the main article you wanted more specific information or facts, you could make use of the index. Finally, the encyclopedia article should give you some

additional or further reading through the bibliographic references.

14-62 A: Information varies from encyclopedia to encyclopedia--in depth, in currency, in level, in access; it also varies factually. The more encyclopedias a library can have available, the more possibilities there are for locating hard-to-find information, and for double-checking information.

14-63 A: Most of the encyclopedias themselves stress that the index should be the first place you should look. The advantage of the index is to cover all possibilities. Specific information may not always be located in the article in which you think it should be. If you want general information, it is probably sufficient to go directly to the article itself; if you want specific information, it is probably necessary to work through the index.

14-64 A: The entries in the dictionary are so specific that no index is necessary to get at all the information they offer, although some cross-referencing is necessary in dictionaries. Even though the trend in modern encyclopedias is away from the very broad, all-encompassing survey articles toward more specific shorter articles, the specificity of an encyclopedia can never be as great as that in a dictionary. A dictionary is concerned with words (which can be specific) rather than with ideas (which cannot be so specific).

14-65 A: The dictionaries contain much factual, quick answer type of information, especially for names of people and places, and some things, events, etc. Information given is usually very brief, but may be sufficient for many needs.

14-66 A: "Compact form, ready reference, simple and accurate information to the ordinary reader...offers no definitions...rapid check on dates, bibliographies, accepted spellings of names...guide to essential facts and enough information to help him to pursue further his search for knowledge..." etc. "Essentially The Columbia Encyclopedia offers first aid to all readers, specialist and nonspecialist alike."

14-67 A: "Preoccupation with American interests and American topics." Also extensive coverage of the King James version of the Bible.

14-68 A: Alphabetical, very short specific topics. No index needed because of the specific topics (although it may be remembered that facts and details will appear in even these short entries for which there is no direct access).

14-69 A: Yes, all these features are included, but obviously to a lesser extent.

14-70 A: In arrangement: Lincoln Library is "classed," with information on major topics such as government, fine arts, etc., brought together rather than scattered alphabetically.

14-71 A: For example, this is comparable to the alphabetical arrangement of Webster's Dictionary of Synonyms, as compared to the classed arrangement of Roget's International Thesaurus. (Or the dictionary of slang, and the thesaurus of slang.) For advantages, etc., see answer to #13-23. Better yet, see the Preface to the Lincoln Library.

14-72 A: All have indexes. The indexes are needed to provide specific access to names, places, subjects, etc. See "Index" preceding the index itself in the Lincoln Library, which discusses the use and value of an index in this type of arrangement.

14-73 A: Both are in Columbia (under Arp, and Adak); information given is not extensive but is adequate. Neither is in Lincoln Library, either in the index, or in the bibliographical and geographical sections.

14-74 A: This would be in the Lincoln Library (in major section on Science, following Geology--see Contents page). Each of the rocks, stones, gems, listed would probably also be listed and described in the Columbia Encyclopedia, but you would have to know the name of the rock or gem to find it.

14-75 A: Columbia has no article, even a brief one, on the American Indians. However, it does have short articles on such aspects as Indian music, Indian art, etc. And there are short articles on specific tribes, such as Hopi.
　　Lincoln Library has a moderately long section on American Indians (in the major section on History--Peoples of the World); this is not too clear from the Contents page, but the index under Indians gives enough references to this general area to make you suspect it is a long article, plus other scattered references.

14-76 A: Columbia is revised periodically with new editions (see Winchell annotation); Lincoln Library is revised with each new printing (continuous revision) (see title page and/or Winchell annotation).

14-77 A: Lincoln Library. (All of the adult level encyclopedias can be used on a high school level, depending on the abilities of the student, etc.) Lincoln Library is not specifically a children's encyclopedia, but it is set up to be useful in schools and with children.

14-78 A: Publisher: Compton Co., Division of Encyclopedia Britannica (title page); Number of volumes: 15; Revision policy: continuous (see verso of title page, or Winchell annotation); Date of set you are examining will vary--see verso of title page for last date.

14-79 A: Children and young people. "All articles are written at the lowest reading level that can effectively give the needed information. For those topics which are studied at more than one grade level, the more advanced material is put later in the article." Material for adults to use in helping children is also given. Winchell annotation says "upper elementary and high school."

14-80 A: Basic arrangement is alphabetical. Length of article is moderate to long. There is no index in the last volume as with the three adult encyclopedias you looked at.

14-81 A: Each volume has its own index in the back of the volume, with the alphabetical designation being basically the same as that of the volume in which it is contained. It is called a Fact-Index, and is really more than an index. There are entries for articles in the encyclopedia and references to other articles (in other volumes) in which further information may be found, as in the adult encyclopedias. There are also entries which give a brief definition or description of the item (facts), and these may or may not have references to appearances in the encyclopedia itself. The index thus serves as a ready-reference or quick reference source. What Compton's has done is to take the very short articles which the adult encyclopedias have included in the main body of the arrangement, and move them to the back of the volume interfiled with the index entries. Thus the articles in the main part of the set tend to be longer, broader, bringing related facts together.

14-82 A: See "Editor's Preface," under "How Compton's is Arranged."

14-83 A: Fact-index (first volume) under Arp lists Arp, Hans or Jean, gives dates, says he was a "German sculptor, painter and poet, born Strasbourg, Alsace (now France); best known as surrealist painter and founder of Dadaism." No reference is given to an appearance in the encyclopedia itself. A brief explanation of Dadaism is found in the Fact-Index for the volume covering D. (Compton's 1968).

14-84 A: There are several articles on libraries, beginning with "Libraries--Storehouses of Man's Knowledge." That article has a small inset called "Fact Finder for Library Articles" giving references to the major articles on Libraries found in that volume, other related articles (such as Bibliography), and reminds you of the Fact-Index. The article gives the main classes for the Dewey Decimal System with an example of further subdivisions. There is some history, some information about foreign libraries, some information about how librarians are trained, etc.

14-85 A: Publisher is Field Enterprises. Volumes is 20. Continuous revision policy. Date of set will vary. Age level is in the Preface, under "The Audience World Book serves": "all members of the family; students in elementary schools, in junior high schools, and in senior high schools..." Also adults.

14-86 A: The basic arrangement of World Book is alphabetical, with short specific entries. There are some longish articles (see those on the states, such as Alaska, for example, or "astronomy"). There is no index. There are lots of cross-references within the set in the main alphabetical entries; there is a reference under Arfura Sea to the map of Australia. There are no entries or references for Adak or Arp. (1969 edition)

14-87 A: It means that in order to be useable, the entries in the set itself must be quite specific and there must be sufficient cross-references. Despite the lack of an index, the World Book is highly useable as a fact-finding source.

14-88 A: The Reading and Study Guide noted in the Winchell annotation which gives you a classed approach, somewhat in the order of the Lincoln Library approach, only here the classed approach is the reference to the main body of information. Most of the classed arrangements you have seen so far (Lincoln Library, thesauri of slang and synonyms, American Book Publishing Record bibliography) have had the main body of information in a classed arrangement with the alphabetical, specific access in the index.

14-89 A: Contrary to what you might expect from the World Book stress on short specific articles, there is a long broad background article on Indians, American. The end of the article also lists related articles, as well as an outline of the major article itself and a short bibliography. You could also refer to the Reading and Study Guide for references to specific aspects, such as Family Life of the Indians, etc.

14-90 A: Most educational materials designed for the modern child are highly illustrated with pictures, maps, graphs, charts--all kinds of visual materials which will interest the child and aid in the learning process. The children's encyclopedias are replete with visual aids of all kinds. See for example the set of overlays in Compton's article on "anatomy."

14-91 A: Articles are not signed in Compton's but a list of contributors with general subject areas is given in volume 1. Articles are signed in World Book, usually only with names;

names and titles and articles are identified in the introductory matter in volume 1. Even though these encyclopedias are designed for children, you would expect the same authority and accuracy behind the information as you would with the adult encyclopedias.

14-92 A: Both World Book and Compton's include bibliographies but neither do as consistently as the adult encyclopedias. World Book (1969) does not have any bibliographic references in its article on chemistry, but does in its article on astronomy. Compton's (1968) has bibliographic references for both chemistry and astronomy. Both divide their references into "books for younger readers" and "books for older readers."

14-93 A: Depending on how unscientific you really are and how much you really want to know, you might find the articles in the three major encyclopedias helpful; but you might also find that a more simplified version in one of the juvenile encyclopedias would be even more helpful. Compton's (1968) has no main articles but has a definition in the Fact-Index plus references to other articles. World Book (1969) has a good article with many illustrations, and information on what a laser is, and what they are used for, how they work, and some history.

14-94 A: Many adults would find the more simplified material and plentiful illustrations helpful for certain topics.

14-95 A: Neither Compton's nor World Book has the same kind of index approach that the adult sets have. World Book has none at all, with specificity available through cross-references and very short articles. Compton's spreads the index throughout the set and combines it with short specific fact articles.

14-96 A: Claims are made that children find it difficult to use the more traditional index approach. Counter claims are made that the lack of the traditional index approach in the children's encyclopedias does not prepare or train them to use the adult encyclopedias properly.

14-97 A: Britannica Junior: elementary and junior high school
Encyclopedia International: high school and family
Britannica Junior is therefore somewhat lower in level than Compton's and World Book; Encyclopedia International is somewhat higher in level.

14-98 A: See comments in Winchell, 8th ed., p. 81-82. Published reviews are probably the best source of information on new or unknown encyclopedias; Winchell specifically notes those appearing in the American Library

Association's Booklist (Winchell item AA273) and the cumulated reviews in Subscription Books Bulletin Reviews (AA309a). Look at a recent volume of Subscription Books Bulletin Reviews and read at least one of the reviews of a not-recommended encyclopedia, to get an idea of the usefulness and thoroughness of these reviews (check at the end of the review for the general recommendation). Wilson also gives a thorough outline for testing and examining an encyclopedia, much of which you have already been doing in the previous questions.

14-99 A: See ALA Glossary.

14-100 A: General information on choosing an encyclopedia, some bibliographic references; specific information on the sets listed includes publisher, size, cost, age level, arrangement, etc., plus references to reviews in SBB. Some of the information is comparatively rated.

14-101 A: Both Anglo-American General Encyclopedias and the annual General Encyclopedias in Print listings are useful to give a wide range of information on encyclopedias to library patrons who request advice and recommendations on purchasing encyclopedias.

14-102 A: Since encyclopedias are considered as "subscription books" (see #14-99) and therefore non-trade, they are not likely to be listed in BIP, BPR, CBI, etc. They are occasionally listed in some of these sources but prices are not always given, or not given consistently. Usually there is an indication that you must contact the publisher for the price.

14-103 A: Writing to the publisher is one solution. Checking prices given in General Encyclopedias in Print is another (however, see the note in the introductory information about the variation in quoted prices). Current reviews by the Reference and Subscription Books Reviews Committee published in Booklist (see answer to #14-98) also give prices.

14-104 A: Some of the dictionaries will tell you briefly that he was the husband of Pocahontas, and an English colonist, and give dates (Webster's 2nd unabridged, Webster's 7th in biographical lists; Random House in main list). The encyclopedias will have further information: World Book, Americana, Collier's all have articles on Rolfe, of varying length.

14-105 A: Dictionaries don't really get you anywhere in this, which is not surprising because this is really more "background information" than definitions. If you knew the names of the figures and looked up each in the dictionary for a definition, that might prove more successful. Encyclopedias are better; most under "Ice Skating" rather than "figure skating." World Book and Collier's give some names and illustrations; the most complete list seems to be in Britannica, curiously enough.

14-106 A: Encyclopedias

14-107 A: This is more of a "word" problem than an encyclopedia problem. Unabridged dictionaries don't give much on origin and forms. Usage books--Evans and particularly Fowler--are very helpful. OED and Dictionary of American English are other possible sources.

14-108 A: Dictionaries will define falcons and falconry. Beyond that you have to go to encyclopedias. Britannica has a good article.

14-109 A: Partly a problem in guessing the entry. Webster's 3rd lists under "bells." World Book article on "Ships and Shipping" gives the information under "nautical terms." The DeSola abbreviations dictionary has a special list of ship's bell time signals, especially noted on the title page; one of these odd things found in odd places.

14-110 A: Encyclopedias--you might have to look in more than one to find all the information you needed.

14-111 A: Presumably a slang term, therefore a slang dictionary (Wentworth and Flexner lists, in Supplement) or perhaps a regular dictionary (Random House lists).

14-112 A: Any source with maps detailed enough to show it. Of the dictionaries Random House has maps in the back with a special index, and it is listed there. Most of the encyclopedias should have it. With Britannica you would have to look it up in the special atlas index (in last volume); in Collier's and Americana you would look in the regular index for a map reference.

Section 14b

Supplement: Foreign Encyclopedias

Questions #14/113-14/136

14-113   The encyclopedias you have examined so far in this section have all been American publications, and of
course in the English language. Although their scope is certainly universal and international, there is
inevitably a stronger coverage of minor American people, places, institutions, arts, events, etc., as
compared to those of other countries. Similarly, an encyclopedia published in another country will inevitably tend to stress minor topics relating to that country. In addition, some of the foreign encyclopedias are especially noted for superior coverage in certain areas, such as illustrations, literature, etc.
Winchell lists several "foreign" encyclopedias following the section for English language encyclopedias.
What does Winchell indicate as the use of such foreign language encyclopedias?

Because the foreign encyclopedias can prove so helpful beyond the American sets which you have the most
access to, you should have some experience, even if briefly, in using them. The following titles are
some of the major British, French, German, Italian, and Spanish encyclopedias, selected from Winchell
(the basic set and first two supplements). The first title, Chambers's Encyclopedia, is British and is
included here with the foreign encyclopedias rather than with the "English language" sets as in Winchell.

British
     Chambers's Encyclopedia (2AD1, AD3)

French
     La Grande encyclopédie (1886-1902) (AD27)
     Larousse. Grand dictionnaire universel du XIXe siècle français (1865-1907?) (AD28)
     Grand Larousse encyclopédique en dix volumes   (1960-64); Supplement (1968) (AD31, 2AD8)
     Encyclopaedia universalis.   (1968+, in progress) (2AD7)

German
     Brockhaus Enzyklopaedia (1966+, in progress) (1AD8, 2AD9)
     Brockhaus' Konversations-Lexikon; Der Grosse Brockhaus (16th ed., 1952-60 or earlier) (AD34)
     Meyers neues Lexikon (1961+, in progress) (AD38)
     Meyers Konversations-Lexikon (earlier editions of Meyers neues Lexikon, see Winchell AD338
        annotation)

Italian
     Enciclopedia Italiana di scienze, lettere ed arti (1929-37, with supplements to 1961) (AD48)

Spanish
     Enciclopedia universal illustrada europeo-americana (Espasa) (1905-33, with supplements) (AD68)

14-114   Rather than going through each of these titles individually, to check scope and arrangement, it will be
less time consuming to treat all of them as a group. Just by looking at the titles as listed and looking
briefly at the citations and annotations in Winchell, you should be able to see that there are well-known
"names" of foreign encyclopedias, in each country, as we have in the United States with "Britannica,"
"Americana," etc. What is the name of one of the major encyclopedia publishers in France? in Germany?

14-115   Can you tell, from looking at the Winchell citations and annotations, anything about the general revision
policies for foreign encyclopedias? Are they similar to American encyclopedias in this respect?

14-116   Some of the foreign encyclopedias listed are actually quite old: La Grande Encyclopédie and the Larousse
Grand Dictionnaire Universal du XIXe Siècle Français, for example. What is the point of considering
these encyclopedias at all? Are they not so out-of-date by now as to have lost their basic usefulness?

14-117   Are these the only French encyclopedias?   Is there anything more current?

14-118   Another characteristic of the foreign encyclopedias is that they are not published all at once but rather
as each volume is finished, and the publication may go on for an exceedingly long period of time. With
some of them, the earlier volumes may be out of date before the final volumes are published.   Is there
any particular way in which some of these old but basic sets are up-dated?   For example, look at the
Italian and Spanish encyclopedias on the list.

14-119   Can you tell, from the Winchell annotations, any major differences between the Brockhaus encyclopedias
and the Meyers encyclopedias?

The following questions are to be answered from the foreign encyclopedias.   The first few are to be
answered by using the specific encyclopedia noted.   The others may be answered from any of the sets,
although it is likely from the nature of the material that one of the sets is more apt to have the answers;
if you do not have access to all of the encyclopedias listed, use those which you do have.   Some practice
with the foreign encyclopedias is especially helpful in fixing their existence in your mind and in helping
you to overcome any reluctance to use foreign language material.   If you have time, checking some of the
problems against one or more of the American encyclopedias would also be useful.

14-120   Can you find, in Chambers's Encyclopedia, some information on Finsbury?

14-121   Can you locate the article on Joan of Arc in La Grande Encyclopédie (Winchell AD27)?   How did you find
it?   Who wrote it?

14-122   For comparison, find the article on Joan of Arc in the Grand Dictionnaire Universel du XIXe Siècle
Français (Larousse).   Is it entered the same way?   Is the article signed?

14-123   Where would you be most likely to find an illustrated article on Alhambra, a palace of the Moorish
Kings?

14-124   Can you find in the Enciclopedia Italiana some pictures of the cathedral in Aix-la-Chappelle?

14-125   The Brockhaus' Konversations-Lexikon and the Meyers Konversations-Lexikon are both old enough that
they are printed in Gothic script, and are therefore difficult to use if you do not recognize letters in the
Gothic script.   However, for some things they are not impossible.   Can you find an article on the city
of Stuttgart in each of these encyclopedias, and make any general comparisons on what is included in each
article?

14-126   Where can you find a recent picture of the Brandenburg Gate in Berlin?

14-127   Can you find a list or a map or something which shows the location of the present day estates of the
Duchy of Lancaster?   What is a duchy?   Where or what is Lancaster?

14-128   Where would you find a long article with a lot of illustrations on the city of Rome?

14-129   If you wanted to find illustrations of the various headdresses customarily worn in the provinces of France, where would you look and how would you go about it?

14-130   Can you find a portrait or picture of Mariano Chacel y Gonzales, Spanish poet and dramatist of the 19th century, also some of the names of his plays?

14-131   Where would you look to find a bibliography of and about Georg Hegel, a German philosopher (1770-1831)?

14-132   Leon Duvauchel is a minor French poet born in 1850. Where would you find a list of some of his publications?

14-133   Can you find a colored reproduction of El Greco's painting of San Lorenzo? Where can the painting itself be seen?

14-134   Can you find a picture of the Piazza Garibaldi in Parma?

14-135   If you were looking for a portrait of Stalin, you would probably expect from the previous questions that you might be likely to find it in a Russian encyclopedia (although for someone as well-known as Stalin, it would also be likely to be found in American or other encyclopedias). Is there a Russian encyclopedia? Can you find a picture of Stalin in it?

14-136   Even if you did not know the Cyrillic alphabet, and you absolutely had to find the picture of Stalin in the Russian encyclopedia, how could you set about it?

Section 14b

Supplement: Foreign Encyclopedias

Answers #14/113-14/136

14-113 A: See Winchell, 8th ed., p. 85-86, specially on p. 86 for "three main types of questions." Read all the introductory comments in Winchell on foreign encyclopedias.

14-114 A: In France, Larousse is a well-known encyclopedia publisher. Brockhaus is one for Germany. Often, these publishers are known for dictionaries as well, as you can see by checking the foreign language dictionaries section in Winchell.

14-115 A: Foreign encyclopedias have not yet really taken over the American procedures of continuous revision. They still tend to be published in major new revisions. For example, the Brockhaus Enzyklopaedie (1ADB, 2AD9) is a new (17th) edition, with a new title, of the Brockhaus' Konversations-Lexikon; der Grosse Brockhaus (AD34). The Meyers neues Lexikon is similarly a new revised edition of the Meyers Konversations-Lexikon.

14-116 A: See Winchell annotations for both titles. Like the famous scholarly early editions of the Britannica, these sets are still useful for their authority and thoroughness on topics for which currency is not so important.

14-117 A: There is a more recent (1960's) Larousse (AD31), and the Encyclopaedia Universalis, now in process of being published.

14-118 A: Some of the foreign encyclopedias are updated with supplements. Both the Encyclopedia Italiana and Espasa have been up-dated with supplements to the 1960's.

14-119 A: Brockhaus, published in Wiesbaden, is now West German; Meyers, published in Leipzig, is now East German. See comment in Winchell annotation on Meyers (AD38) that it reflects the East German political orientation. (Remember the same split with bibliographies in Section 10).

14-120 A: Check entry for Finsbury in the index, as you would in any of the other encyclopedias, which refers you to the article for "London." Finsbury is a borough of London.

14-121 A: Remember that "Joan of Arc" is an English language version and you are looking in a French encyclopedia (see Winchell's comments on use of foreign encyclopedias, p. 86). There is no index, so you have to check in the main alphabetical listing and hope for cross-references. American dictionaries and encyclopedias tend to enter

Joan of Arc under Joan, and if you searched this way in the French encyclopedia, you would have to realize that the French form of Joan is "Jeanne." There is a reference from "Jeanne d'Arc" to "Arc (Jeanne d')." (If you did not know the French form of Joan, you could look up Joan of Arc in a dictionary giving biographical information, and you would probably find the French form of the name also given. See Random House Dictionary, for example.) If you looked directly under "Arc," you would probably spot the entry for "Arc (Jeanne d')" and recognize it as what you are searching for.

The author of the article, Maxime Petit, is indicated, as it is in the American encyclopedias, at the end of the article.

14-122 A: It is entered in Larousse under "Darc (Jeanne)" but there is a reference from "Arc (Jeanne d')." The article is not signed.

14-123 A: Spanish encyclopedia: Espasa (Winchell AD68). (If you did not already know, or could not tell from the question, that the palace of Alhambra is located in the city of Granada, Spain, you could have looked it up in another source, such as a dictionary which gives geographical information, or a one-volume encyclopedia, or any encyclopedia through the index.) Located directly under Alhambra. You would probably find information, possibly even full articles, on Alhambra in American encyclopedias. The chances of finding a number of illustrations might be better in a Spanish encyclopedia.

14-124 A: Look in index under Aix-la-Chapelle which refers you to the article on Aquisgrana (in vol. 3, p. 812e). Aquisgrana is the Italian name for Aix-la-Chapelle which is the French name for Aachen in Germany.

14-125 A: Both have articles entered under Stuttgart. Both have maps. Brockhaus has the longer article with illustrations also. (Brockhaus 1928 edition; Meyers 1924 edition).

14-126 A: Brockhaus Enzyklopaedia, article on Berlin. Picture of Brandenburger Tor (1961). (If you are not sure that the Brandenburger Tor is what you want, check the word "tor" in a German-English dictionary--for example, Winchell AE274--to find that tor means gate.)

14-127 A: A "duchy" can probably be explained by any dictionary; Lancaster, in relation to the term Duchy, might also be explained by a dictionary (i.e., the American College Dictionary). Having then found, if you did not know already, that the Duchy of Lancaster is the territory ruled or held by one of the English royal houses, you could proceed to Chambers's, the British encyclopedia, checking under Lancaster, where you would find an extensive article including a map showing the present day estates of the duchy.

14-128 A: The Enciclopedia Italiana, which besides being Italian and therefore a good source of coverage for an Italian city, is also noted for its long articles and many illustrations. The entry would be "Roma," the Italian name.

14-129 A: If you are going to search in a French encyclopedia, you would want to go first to an English-French dictionary (Winchell AE232, for example) to find the French word for "headdress," which is "coiffe." Checking under the entry "coiffe" in the French encyclopedias, you could find an illustrated article in, for example, the Grand Larousse Encyclopédique en Dix Volumes.

14-130 A: In Espasa (the Spanish encyclopedia), under Chacel y Gonzalez, Mariano. In the Spanish alphabet, "Ch" is considered as a separate letter following "C", therefore entries beginning with "Ch" will follow those beginning with "Cz." This is noted in the Winchell comments on foreign encyclopedias, 8th ed., p. 86 (see #14-113).

14-131 A: The article on Hegel in the Brockhaus Enzyklopaedie gives an extensive bibliography. American encyclopedias should also give some listings; Britannica does, for example.

14-132 A: Some of the retrospective French bibliographies (see Section 10), and also in the French encyclopedias--see La Grande Encyclopédie for example, under Duvauchel.

14-133 A: El Greco is a Spanish painter, born in Greece (Crete, actually). Espasa encyclopedia, under "Greco (el)" gives a cross reference to see ("v.") the entry Theotocopuli (Domingo), his correct name. If you had known his correct name to begin with, you could have looked directly under that, but it wasn't necessary in this case. If you hadn't known his correct name, and there was no cross-reference from El Greco, you could have looked up the correct name in some other source, such as a dictionary which gives biographical information, or an American encyclopedia. The article on Theotocopuli (Domingo) gives reproductions, both colored and black and white, of several of his paintings, including that of San Lorenzo. The illustration itself notes in the title line that it hangs in the Museo del Prado in Madrid.

14-134 A: Parma is a city in Italy. The Enciclopedia Italiana (Winchell AD48) has a picture of the Piazza Garibaldi in the article on Parma, in Appendice III, volume 2.

14-135 A: The Russian encyclopedia is the Bol'shaia Sovetskaia Entsiklopediia (Winchell AD59). The encyclopedia is in Russian, of course, and also in the Cyrillic alphabetic, and the guide-letters on the spines of the volumes are also in the Cyrillic alphabet. So unless you happen to know the Cyrillic alphabet, you probably cannot even find the entry for Stalin or even the volume in which it might be.

14-136 A: Find some sources which would give the characters of the Cyrillic alphabet and their transliteration into roman letters. Webster's Third unabridged, for example, has an alphabet table (listed under Index to Tables, on the Contents page) which includes Russian or Cyrillic. You could then transliterate (or change) the roman letters of STALIN to the Russian or Cyrillic characters of СТАЛИН, note that the Cyrillic character "С" is alphabetized between "Р" and "Т," find the volume of the Russian encyclopedia covering "С," find the entry for Stalin as written above, and find the picture. The entry for Stalin, and the picture itself for that matter, are sufficiently large that you cannot miss it. (Vol. 40, between p. 422-423 of the copyright 1957 edition).

Section 15

Yearbooks and Almanacs

Questions #15/1-15/90

15-1   If you wanted to find the name of the winner of the Nobel Prize in Medicine for 1970, would you expect to find it in an encyclopedia? If you wanted to see what the developments were last year in the American Indians' struggle for equal rights, would you expect to find it in an encyclopedia? If you wanted to know what is the longest bridge in the world, would you expect to find it in an encyclopedia?

15-2   What two ways are used to keep encyclopedia sets up to date and current? One way has already been discussed.

There are many annual or yearly publications, including the encyclopedia yearbooks, which give extensive coverage of current information. These yearbooks and almanacs, a special form of yearbook, are the next set of sources to be examined, as follows:

           Americana Annual (AD8)
           Britannica Book of the Year (AD9)
           Collier's Year Book (AD11)
           World Book Year Book (see AD16)
           Annual Register; World Events (DA50)
           Facts on File (DA51)
           Keesing's Contemporary Archives (DA52)
           World Almanac (CG55)
           Information Please Almanac (CG47)
           New York Times Encyclopedic Almanac
           Whitaker's Almanac (CG109)
           Statesman's Year-Book (CG29)

15-3   One of the first problems is that of terminology. For example, the yearbooks of the three major encyclopedias are titled: Americana Annual, Britannica Book of the Year, and Collier's Year Book. What is a yearbook or an annual?

15-4   The word yearbook will be used in this manual as a general term, rather than annual. Look at the yearbooks of the Americana, Britannica, and Collier's together and comparatively. Look at the volumes which cover the events of 1969. Checking the information on the spines and on the title pages, are you sure that you have the 1969 volumes for each? Is there any variation in the way the date is designated?

15-5   Where would be the best place to look to see quickly any variations in the scope and arrangement of the three yearbooks?

15-6   From the Table of Contents of each, does there appear to be any variation in presentation and content among the three yearbooks?

15-7   Looking at the Table of Contents for each, and then looking through the books themselves at their general arrangement, do you see any basic similarities in scope and/or arrangement? What items are included in all of them? Are these items presented in the same general way?

15-8   The main section or main body of each of the yearbooks is an alphabetical arrangement of various short articles on events of the year. Would you expect that there would be an article, in the yearbook, to correspond with each of the articles in the main set of the encyclopedia?

15-9   Are the articles in the yearbooks for very specific topics (i.e., Woodstock Music and Art Fair) or more general (i.e., music)? What access do you have for specific topics such as Woodstock?

15-10   Would you expect the articles included in the yearbooks to be exactly the same in each of the three? Do all three have articles on education, libraries, art, etc.? Do all three have articles on some of the major issues of 1969, such as crime, consumer affairs, conservation, nutrition, pollution, population, poverty?

15-11   1969 was the year of the "Tate murders" in Los Angeles. How would you find information on them in the yearbooks?

15-12   What prominent people died during the year 1969? Are deaths listed separately in some way, or must you check the index?

15-13   How can you determine the authority behind the various articles in the encyclopedia yearbooks?

15-14   Do the encyclopedia yearbooks provide bibliographical references for further reading, as the encyclopedias themselves do? For example, the 1970 (i.e., 1969) Collier's Year Book contains a very interesting special article on "Learning before School." Does the article suggest any possibilities for other articles or books on education in early childhood?

15-15   Using the encyclopedia yearbooks, can you find who won the Nobel prize for Medicine in 1969? Can you find through the 1969 yearbooks who won the Nobel Prize for Medicine in 1960? Do the yearbooks attempt to include retrospective or historical information? Are the indexes retrospective in any way?

15-16   Look at the 1970 yearbook from World Book, one of the two children's encyclopedias you examined. Do the yearbooks for the children's encyclopedias appear to differ in any major way from those for the adult encyclopedias?

15-17   Are the encyclopedia yearbooks indexed in the basic sets themselves? If you had a 1969 printing or edition of the Britannica, would the index include references to the 1968 or 1967 yearbooks?

15-18   Would a 1969 printing or edition of an encyclopedia completely supersede earlier yearbooks? Is there any value to the old yearbooks? Where would you look if you wanted to find out the developments in medicine in 1964?

15-19   Are the encyclopedia yearbooks limited in coverage to the United States?

15-20   If you needed a survey of current events similar to the encyclopedia yearbooks, which stressed events in Great Britain, what would you look for? Where would you look?

15-21 What is the full title of the Annual Register, and where is it published? How often is it published? Is the date of coverage clear, or is there apt to be some confusion as with the encyclopedia yearbooks?

15-22 Does the Annual Register have any connection with some other publication such as an encyclopedia? Is it an annual supplement to something?

15-23 In what section of Winchell is the Annual Register listed? Is it listed as a general reference work?

15-24 How does the Annual Register differ in scope and arrangement from the encyclopedia yearbooks you have examined?

15-25 In the summer of 1969, some major changes were proposed for BBC radio, and similarly for commercial television in Great Britain. What were some of the political comments on these changes?

15-26 One of the values of such current surveys as the encyclopedia annuals and the Annual Register is that they give statements of contemporary (e.g., of the same date or time) opinion or viewpoint on historical events. If you wanted a source which would give you, literally, an 1864 viewpoint of the American Civil War, not a 1970 viewpoint, where could you look?

15-27 In the previous question, you wanted contemporary viewpoints of the Civil War. In question #15-15 you wanted the name of the winner of the Nobel Prize in Medicine in 1969. What other sources have you had previously in which you could also answer both these questions, possibly in even more detail than through the annual survey type of sources?

15-28 The New York Times Index was examined earlier as a bibliographical source; that is, basically as an access to articles appearing specifically in the New York Times or to some extent in any newspaper through the date. It was noted then that the NY Times Index provides not only an index to the newspaper but a summary or abstract of the news itself. Could you find, through the New York Times Index, a survey of the developments in medicine in 1964 (see #15-18)?

15-29 If you wanted to find out who won the Nobel Prize for Medicine for this year (assuming that it has actually been awarded by the time you are at this point), could you find it out through the encyclopedia yearbooks? Where would you have to look?

15-30 Winchell lists two other sources as "Annual and current surveys" along with the Annual Register (see 8th ed., p. 467). Both of these, Facts on File and Keesing's Contemporary Archives, are perhaps more similar to the New York Times Index than they are to the Annual Register. What is the full title of Facts on File, and where is it published? How often does it appear?

15-31 Is there anything in Facts on File itself which tells you how to use it?

15-32 How does Facts on File differ from the New York Times Index?

15-33   Early in 1971, Ralph Nader announced the formation of a new action organization for high school students. What is the name of this group, and what else can you find out about it?

15-34   Does the scope of Facts on File differ from the New York Times Index?

15-35   Could you tell, through Facts on File, specifically what The Toronto Globe and Mail had to say about rioting in Northern Ireland in the summer of 1970?

15-36   In 1970, Thor Heyerdahl, Norwegian explorer, crossed the Atlantic Ocean in a papyrus boat, Ra II. What are the dates on which he set out and on which he completed the trip. Could you find this as easily through the New York Times Index for 1970? What were the names of the crew members?

15-37   The New York Times Index is issued twice a month, and until the cumulated annual volume is published, it is necessary to check each issue in a search for information. Is this also true with Facts on File?

15-38   Facts on File seems most valuable as a very current (weekly) source of information on very recent events. Does it also provide a yearly survey of events or activities as the Annual Register or the encyclopedia yearbooks do?

15-39   How far back can Facts on File be used as a retrospective searching source?

15-40   Somewhat comparable to Facts on File is Keesing's Contemporary Archives. Where is it published, how often is it issued, and how far back does it go?

15-41   In use, Keesing's is similar to Facts on File. In coverage or scope, it is somewhat different. What can you assume might be one obvious difference in coverage?

15-42   In the summer of 1969, the third most sacred Islamic shrine, located in Jerusalem, was set on fire. An Australian named Denis Rohan was arrested and tried for setting the fire. Can you find in Keesing's the digests of the arrest and trial of Rohan?

15-43   Look up the same information in Facts on File; how does the information given and the ease of access compare to Keesing's?

15-44   Does Keesing's provide the same kind of annual survey as Facts on File does (see # 15-38)?

15-45   How do the annual summaries of news events differ from the annual summaries of the encyclopedia yearbooks? Is there any difference in arrangement? Is there any difference in point of view, in perspective, in interpretation of material?

15-46   Do you see any difference in the ways in which these two types of annual summaries can or should be used?

15-47   Facts on File and Keesing's, and to some extent the Annual Register, would seem obviously to be of most importance as sources of current information. Why are they listed in Winchell under "History and Area Studies"?

15-48   Another yearbook-type of source are the almanacs. These have many of the features of the annual surveys you have been examining, with some special aspects. What is an almanac?

15-49   Probably the easiest way to see what an almanac really is is to look at one closely. The first on your list, the World Almanac, is also one of the oldest. When was it first published?

15-50   What is the arrangement of the World Almanac? Is it similar to the encyclopedia yearbooks?

15-51   What kind of specific subject access do you have? How would you find out, for example, that the list of "flowers of the month" is on p. 70 between marriage information and grounds for divorce?

15-52   Because of the nature of the material they contain, and because of the indexing, almanacs are very useful for answering factual questions. How many of the following "facts" can you ascertain from the 1971 World Almanac:
a.   the number of calories in a bagel?
b.   the name of the inventor of the sliderule?
c.   the zip code of Opp, Alabama?
d.   the address of the National Hay Fever Relief Association?
e.   the birthday of Beatle Paul McCartney?
f.   the 1950 winners of the Stanley Cup (hockey)?
g.   the name of the President whose portrait appears on a $500 bill?
h.   the magazine with the largest circulation in the United States?
i.   the westernmost point of the United States?
j.   the number of people in Calaveras County, California, who voted for Richard Nixon in the 1968 presidential election?

15-53   The almanacs are useful for other kinds of information also. How many of the following things can you locate in the 1971 World Almanac:
a.   how to obtain a passport?
b.   how to give mouth-to-mouth resuscitation?
c.   how to become an American citizen?
d.   U.S. parcel post rates?
e.   a table of metric weights and measures?
f.   the U.S. federal income tax law?
g.   how to apply for a patent?
h.   the copyright law of the U.S.?

10-54   Can you find, through the 1971 World Almanac, any information on:
a.   Thor Heyerdahl's 1970 crossing of the Atlantic Ocean in a papyrus boat?
b.   who won the Nobel Prize for medicine in 1970?
c.   a survey of developments in medicine in 1970?
d.   a list of people who died during 1970?

10-55   What is the real key to locating information in the almanacs?

10-56   From questions #15-52, 15-53, and 15-54, how does the scope of World Almanac differ from the encyclopedia yearbooks? Does the almanac include any features found in the encyclopedia yearbooks? Does the almanac include current--e.g., up-to-date--information? Does the almanac include retrospective information (which the encyclopedia yearbooks do not)? Does the almanac include basic standard information such as you might expect to find in an encyclopedia itself?

15-57   Some of the information included in the almanacs is basic or standard information probably also found in other sources--such as citizenship laws, first aid, geographical locations (westernmost point of U.S.), zip codes, addresses, etc. Is there any difference in the information found in the almanacs and that found in the encyclopedias? For example, on the question about the westernmost point of the United States, would the answer be the same in a 1957 printing of an encyclopedia as it would be in a 1958 almanac or 1959 almanac?

15-58   How does the Information Please Almanac compare to the World Almanac?

15-59   The Information Please Almanac does not have quite the long history of the World Almanac. When was it first published?

15-60   An even newer almanac is the New York Times Encyclopedic Almanac, first published in 1970 and not yet listed in Winchell. How does it compare to the World Almanac and the Information Please Almanac?

15-61   The last almanac listed to examine is Whitaker's Almanack. Where is it published and what does this tell you about its scope in comparison to the other three?

15-62   How does Whitaker's compare with the American almanacs in arrangement?

15-63   Is there any way in which you can check the authority of the information given in the almanacs, or must you just take it on faith? Are sources given?

15-64   You examined the 1970 (covering 1969) volumes of the encyclopedia yearbooks, and the 1971 (covering 1970) volumes of the almanacs. Is this a fair comparison?

15-65   What are the latest population figures you can find for Tokyo? Do these figures represent the city-proper or the total urban area? Compare World Almanac, Information Please Almanac, and New York Times Encyclopedic Almanac.

15-66   What are the number of illegitimate births in the United States? What is the latest year for which you can obtain figures? What is the source of these figures? Are these figures based on accurate records? How are the figures obtained? Compare World Almanac and New York Times Encyclopedic Almanac.

15-67   Where can you find a list of endangered animal species of the world?

15-68   How many Presidential libraries are there in the U.S. Where are they?

15-69   Can you find a discussion of current income tax laws and rates in England?

15-70   In what year was Orville Wright named to the Aviation Hall of Fame? In what year did the Wright Brothers make the first airplane flight? If you wanted a source which would give you some contemporary comments on that first airplane flight, where would you look? Can you be sure that such a source would actually have information on that first flight?

15-71   If you wanted to find a list of the addresses of the Foreign Consuls in Canada, where would you look?

15-72   Where would you check to find the prices for sources such as the World Almanac, Whitaker's Almanack, Britannica Book of the Year? These appear annually; would they be listed in Ulrich's International Periodical Directory? What about Facts on File?

15-73   What do you see as the major uses of the yearbooks as compared to the uses of the encyclopedias?

The yearbooks, including the almanacs, which you have examined so far have been very broad in scope, general in coverage. There are many yearbooks or annual publications which specialize in certain fields of coverage. Some of these are related to specific subject fields, such as science (there is a special yearbook on science to supplement the World Book Encyclopedia) or more specifically, agriculture (the Yearbook of Agriculture published by the U.S. Government Printing Office and noted in question #11-15).

Others have wider subject coverage but include only certain types of information. The last title on your list in this section, the Statesman's Year-Book, is an example of a yearbook which might be said to represent subject coverage: e.g., government. However, it is one of the most generally useful sources in any library and the information it includes actually covers an extremely broad scope.

15-74   What is the full title of the Statesman's Year-Book, and where is it published?

15-75   The date given on the volume itself is a double one: 1970-71, for example. Does this mean that it is published every other year? How often is it published?

15-76   How is the Statesman's Year-Book arranged?

15-77   Does the arrangement of the Statesman's Year-Book tell you anything about its scope?

Much of the information given in the Statesman's Year-Book may also be found in some form in the almanacs and encyclopedia yearbooks. It is perhaps then the more straight-forward arrangement by country which makes the Statesman's Year-Book so generally useful.

15-78   What information is given in the Statesman's Year-Book? What information can you find out about Denmark, for example?

15-79   What is the present name of the African country of Nyasaland? Is it part of the British Commonwealth? When did it become independent? Where could you find further information on its history?

15-80   Is the population figure for Tokyo given in the Statesman's Year-Book 1970/71 any different than those which you found in the almanacs (question #15-65)?

15-81   Is there an airfield in the country of Sikkim?

          These last questions can be used as review for the sources examined so far in sections 12, 13, 14, and 15.

15-82   Can you find what the signal is for the letter "K" in the Morse Code? What is the difference between Morse Code used in the United States and Canada, and International or Continental Morse Code?

15-83   How many royal babies were born in England in 1964?

15-84   When is the next Year of the Snake according to the Chinese calendar?

15-85   What does I.Q. mean? What tests are used to determine it?

15-86   What were some of the major American novels published in 1969? What kind of critical acclaim did they receive?

15-87   How do you pronounce the word "eleemosynary"?

15-88   For what crimes may capital punishment be imposed in the Soviet Union?

15-89   Where would you find information about specific activities on Earth Day, 1970?

15-90   What is the currency used in Cambodia and what is its exchange rate with U.S. dollars? If you needed absolutely up-to-the-minute information on this question, what could you do?

Section 15

Yearbooks and Almanacs

Answers #15/1-15/90

15-1 A: Some facts on all these topics would probably
           be found in any of the encyclopedias. It
           would depend on how recent a printing you
           had, and how thoroughly it had been brought
           up to date or revised, whether or not you
           would find the recent material you desire on the
           Nobel Prize and the Indians. The informa-
           tion on bridges may not seem, at first, as such
           a necessity for current information, but in
           fact, since bridge building is going on all the
           time, such statistics will change and current
           information is necessary.

15-2 A: Continuous revision (see #14-5), and ency-
           clopedia annuals or yearbooks (see Winchell,
           8th edition, p. 83, section V.B. of the out-
           line for examining encyclopedias, and the
           section "Encyclopedia annuals" following the
           citations for American and English encyclo-
           pedias).

15-3 A: The ALA Glossary defines both, and the
           definitions are similar. Webster's Third
           unabridged defines both, and the defini-
           tions are similar. The key ideas are that
           they are published once a year, and that
           they cover current information, events or
           developments, either generally or in a
           special field.

15-4 A: The date of a yearbook is often the date
           of the year in which it is issued, not the
           year which it covers. A yearbook issued
           in 1969 could not yet cover all the events
           of 1969, so the 1969 volume will, in most
           cases, actually cover the year 1968. If
           you want the yearbook covering events of
           1969, then you will probably want the
           1970 volume. For example, the Americana
           yearbook covering 1969 is labeled, on the
           spine, 1970 annual. The title page gives
           the title as "The Americana Annual, 1970,
           an encyclopedia of the events of 1969."
           Similarly the Britannica Yearbook cover-
           ing 1969 is labeled, on the spine, 1970,
           although there is also an indication that it
           covers "Events of 1968" (if this vital piece
           of information has not been obliterated by
           the library's call number...). The title
           page indicates only "Britannica Book of the
           Year 1970." Collier's 1970 yearbook says,
           in the middle of the spine, that it covers
           the year 1969, and at the bottom of the
           spine that it is "1970." The title page
           says "1970 Year Book covering the year
           1969." This same problem is relevant
           to all of the yearbooks, annuals, almanacs,
           etc.

15-5 A: The Table of Contents.

15-6 A: Yes, there is variation, although it is not
           as much as it may seem. The Table of
           Contents pages for Collier's and Britannica
           are more detailed than Americana; but
           Americana has in addition a "Classified
           Listing of Articles."

15-7 A: All three contain a brief chronology (listed
           in chronological order) of the main events
           of the year. (Americana: Chronology;
           Britannica: Chronology; Collier's: Calendar
           of News Events).

           All three have some special or feature
           articles on major events of the year
           (Americana: Special Report; Britannica:
           Feature Article and Special Reports;
           Collier's: Special Articles). Americana
           appears to have less of these than the
           other two (at least for 1969). Obviously,
           the major event of 1969 was the moon
           landings. Other years might show more
           variation in the choice of items to be so
           featured.

           All three have, as the main body of the
           book, a selection of moderately short
           articles, arranged alphabetically, covering
           in more detail the events of the year
           (Americana: Review of the Year; Britan-
           nica: Book of the Year; Collier's: The
           Year in Review).

15-8 A: The articles in the yearbook do not attempt
           to correspond with the articles in the main
           sets, since they are only for current cover-
           age and there may be no current activity
           in all of the areas covered in the main sets.
           For example, it is highly unlikely that
           there would be any reason to have coverage
           in the yearbooks on St. Nicholas' Day.

15-9 A: Most of the articles are of a general
           nature, such as "Music." Specific items
           can be found through the indexes. Amer-
           icana and Collier's list Woodstock in the
           index with references to the article on
           "music."

15-10 A: Common topics such as education, art,
           music, libraries, sports, etc., are
           usually consistently covered by all three.
           Some of the new ideas will not be as con-
           sistently covered in all three, although this
           is sometimes more a matter of arrange-
           ment than of judgment or choice of ma-
           terial. For example, Collier's does not
           have an article on pollution in the alpha-
           betical section, but does have a special
           article on "Man in his Environment," and
           several references in the index under
           "pollution."

15-11 A: Specific item, check <u>index</u> under Tate
           (actually Tate, Sharon).   For example,
           Americana has references to the articles
           on "Crime" and on "Los Angeles."

15-12 A: Britannica and Collier's both have articles
           in the alphabetical section titled
           "Obituaries," in which such a list is
           given.
               Americana has a separate article,
           outside of the alphabetical section but
           noted in the Contents, titled "Necrology,"
           giving such a list.
               (President Eisenhower, Ho Chi Minh,
           and Judy Garland died in 1969, among
           others).

15-13 A: The same way as in the basic sets them-
           selves; signed articles, and lists of con-
           tributors in the source itself.   All three
           yearbooks have lists of contributors.

15-14 A: The specific article referred to in the
           Collier's 1970 Year Book does not have
           additional/references. (However, the
           special article on Italy, preceding it,
           does have some references.)   The article
           on "Learning Before School," as do the
           other special articles, has an inset p.
           34) giving references to other articles
           <u>in the basic set of Collier's.</u>   Some of
           the articles in the Britannica yearbook
           have short listings of pertinent Encyclo-
           paedia Britannica films.

15-15 A: Americana and Collier's have articles on
           the Nobel Prizes which list the winners in
           medicine among others.   Both also have
           separate articles on "Prizes and Awards";
           Collier's includes the Nobel Prizes in
           this listing also; Americana does not.
               All of the yearbooks list only the 1969
           (or whatever the year is) winners.   You
           cannot find out the 1960 winners through the
           yearbooks.   None of the yearbooks attempt
           to include retrospective information unless
           it is really pertinent in some way to the
           material discussed.   The indexes are not
           retrospective either;   that is, they index
           only the volume of which they are a part,
           they do not index past yearbooks.   The
           Britannica indexes do include retrospective
           indexing for deaths or obituaries.

15-16 A: Other than reading/comprehension level,
           no.   The children's yearbooks tend to be
           lavishly illustrated (see the 1970 World
           Book Year Book illustrated section on
           Australia).   They include a chronology of
           events, an alphabetically-arranged section
           of articles on various topics (the to-be-
           expected areas such as education, sports,
           art, etc., and some of more current
           interest such as conservation), and special
           articles or reports. (Some of these are of
           obvious appeal to children, such as the
           1970 World Book Year Book's reports on
           zoos and Charlie Brown.)
               Note that the World Book Year Book is

indexed, unlike the set itself (and that
the index is retrospective: the 1970 index
covers 1966-69).

15-17 A: No.   Actually, the encyclopedia yearbooks
           are quite independent of the encyclopedias,
           and can be purchased and used quite satis-
           factorily as entirely separate publications.
           Nor is it <u>necessary</u>, in using the encyclo-
           pedias themselves, to have the yearbooks.
           It is only necessary to realize that, even
           with continuous revision, the encyclopedias
           will not be and cannot be entirely up-to-
           date in all respects and <u>some</u> more current
           sources must be referred to for current
           information.

15-18 A: Presumably some of the current material
           appearing in the yearbooks would be ab-
           sorbed into the basic set from time to
           time with continuous revision.   However,
           coverage of current topics in the yearbooks
           is more in depth for that particular year
           than you would find for it in the basic set,
           even at a later date.   Also, coverage of
           topics in the basic sets is not usually set
           up on a year-by-year basis so it might
           be quite difficult, even from an entirely
           up-to-date article, to determine exactly
           what the developments were during a spe-
           cific year.

15-19 A: No, the scope is international.   In fact,
           many of the articles in the main alphabetical
           listings in the yearbooks are specifically on
           other countries--Australia, Canada, Japan,
           etc.--giving surveys of the major important
           events of the year in those countries.
           However, as with the encyclopedias them-
           selves, stronger, more thorough coverage
           will be given to the United States.

15-20 A: Conclude that there might be a yearbook
           for the British encyclopedias and check
           Winchell to find out.   Winchell does list a
           yearbook for the Chambers's Encyclopedia
           (AD10) but it is not clear that this is still
           being published.   Another source which is
           very similar to the encyclopedia yearbooks
           and which does have British emphasis is
           the next title on your list: the Annual
           Register; World Events.

15-21 A: Title page: Annual Register; World Events
           of 1969.   Published by Longmans in London,
           in 1970.   It is published annually.   The
           date of coverage (for example, 1969) is
           clearly indicated on the spine and on the
           title page as part of the title itself.   How-
           ever, the volume is published in the year
           following the year it covers (for example,
           the 1969 volume is published in 1970 as
           indicated on the title page, and copyright
           in 1970 as indicated on the verso of the
           title page).

15-22 A: No, it is an independent publication. You
           would probably have to go to the Winchell
           annotation to find any history or background
           of the source.

15-23 A: It is not listed under "A: General Reference Works" but rather under "D: History and Area Studies." This is the first of the major sources you have looked at which is classified in a subject field in Winchell (except for a few of the subject-oriented periodical indexes noted in Section 7, and some of the non-book bibliographical sources noted in Section 4). From now on, most of the sources you examine will be drawn from the subject areas in Winchell, although they will be examined here as <u>basic</u> sources for <u>general</u> reference work.

15-24 A: It is obviously smaller, and not illustrated as heavily as the encyclopedia yearbooks.
　　　　In scope, it has broad coverage with a British and British Commonwealth slant. But like the encyclopedia yearbooks, it is limited to current information, not retrospective.
　　　　In arrangement, it is quite different. It is arranged by broad general topics, with specific access through the index. The topics themselves are actually quite similar to those in the encyclopedia yearbooks (names of countries, religion, science and technology, art, economics, etc.) but they are not arranged alphabetically. The arrangement can be seen easily through the Table of Contents.
　　　　Like the encyclopedia yearbooks, it has a list of deaths (obituaries) and a chronology of major events of the year.

15-25 A: Annual Register for 1969, see index under BBC radio and television for references to the general section on history of the United Kingdom.

15-26 A: None of the U.S. encyclopedia yearbooks examined date back that far (see Winchell annotations). The Annual Register began in 1758 so would cover that period; this of course would be a British point of view, which might be interesting in itself. However, Winchell lists under encyclopedia annuals another American annual source not currently published--Appleton's Annual Cyclopaedia and Register of Important Events (AD7)--which began in 1861 and should therefore give U.S. coverage of the event (see Winchell annotation).

15-27 A: New York Times Index (in Section 7) see questions #594 and #601. To get any viewpoints on the Civil War, and to get further detail on the Nobel Prize, you would have to refer to the newspaper itself, of course.

15-28 A: Yes, under the entry "Medicine." It might not seem as clear as it would in the encyclopedia yearbook articles, and it might require more references back and forth, and you might want to refer further to the newspaper articles themselves for details or clarification, but basically access to the information and much of the information

itself is there. The New York Times Index <u>annual cumulated volume</u> (A Book of Record) for 1964 has nearly nine pages of entries on medicine, many for specific countries other than the United States.

15-29 A: The encyclopedia yearbooks are <u>annual</u> publications only, and therefore they <u>will</u> be at least a year behind in their information all the time. If the Nobel Prize for medicine was awarded in October of 1970, it would not appear in the encyclopedia yearbook until <u>1971</u> (e. g. probably not be published until rather late in 1971. For very current information, you must go to a source which is issued more frequently. The New York Times Index is issued twice a month.

15-30 A: Facts on File, weekly world news digest with cumulative index. Published by Facts on File, New York. Appears weekly. See cover page in binder, or Winchell annotation.

15-31 A: Blue sheets in front of binder called "Guide to the Use of Facts on File," plus instructions for the index on the separator sheet for the index.

15-32 A: Facts on File appears weekly; New York Times Index appears twice a month. Facts on File is completely self-contained; it consists of a narrative digest of the news and a specific index to that digest. NY Times Index is itself an index, with references to another publication for fuller information, although it does give some digest of the news as well.

15-33 A: Index for 1971, under Nader, Ralph--item for Earth Action Group, which sounds like what you want. Reference is 1-12, 15A2; the announcement was made Jan. 12; the Facts on File story will be found on page 15 of the 1971 issues, top section of the page (A), column 2. (The reference in the Facts on File index is to the story in the same physical volume or binder as the index itself. It is not a reference to another publication, as it would be in the New York Times Index.)

15-34 A: Both are international in coverage with extensive coverage of United States' national affairs. New York Times Index is limited in scope, however, to that news which appears in the New York Times, while Facts on File draws on many publications which are listed in the blue sheets in the front of the binder ("Sources of information").

15-35 A: No. Facts on File does not quote or cite specifically from its sources.

15-36 A: Facts on File Index for 1970, under Heyerdahl or Ra 11. Two references given, one for setting out and one for completing the trip, and the dates therefore can be obtained directly from the index. It is necessary to turn to the first Facts on File article, to find the names of the crew members. Once the New York Times cumulated volume for 1970 is available, it is as easy to find references to the story (same entry word) and the dates are easily found in the Index itself, but it would probably be necessary to go to the newspaper itself for such details as the names of the crew members.

15-37 A: No, Facts on File is issued weekly but the index is continuously cumulated, so that it is rarely necessary to check in more than one or two places.

15-38 A: Yes, since the index eventually cumulates into an annual issue. The index is all that cumulates; the digests of news do not cumulate; it is still necessary to refer from the index to the individual weekly issues. But like the New York Times Index, the information is there, although not as concisely organized as in the Annual Register or the encyclopedia yearbooks. (Furthermore, the index also cumulates every five years.) However, Facts on File also publishes a yearbook-type of source called News Dictionary (not mentioned or listed in Winchell); it is very similar in size to the Annual Register, and has a dictionary arrangement of short topics, with cross-references and no index.

15-39 A: 1940 (see Winchell annotation).

15-40 A: Published in London since 1931, issued weekly.

15-41 A: Both Facts on File and Keesing's are international in scope, but Keesing's--a British (London) publication--is apt to have more stress on British and British Commonwealth activities.

15-42 A: Keesing's has no names in the index; the index is arranged by names of countries, with some names or topics sub-arranged under the countries. The Index for 1969 lists references for this topic under Israel --Jerusalem. There are references from Arab-Israel Conflict--Al Aksa Mosque Fire to Israel--Jerusalem. The trial is written up in the Nov. 22-29, 1969, issue of Keesing's. (It is not easy to see where each new week begins with Keesing's, but the pages are numbered continuously and the references in the index are to the page numbers, so this is not important.)

15-43 A: The 1969 Facts on File index has references under the name Rohan. It is probably easier to use the Facts on File index until one has mastered the arrangement of the Keesing's Index. However, the information given in Keesing's is far more detailed than that in Facts on File. The trial is reported in great detail in Keesing's, for example. Keesing's tends to cite its sources more specifically; Facts on File does not.

15-44 A: Yes, because the index cumulates. (The volume or binder contains two years rather than one, as in Facts on File, but this does not hinder you from obtaining an annual survey through the index.)

15-45 A: The news summaries, since they are prepared and issued weekly rather than annually, are closer to the facts and the situations and allow for very little perspective; all information pertinent at the moment is given. Basically, they do not attempt to offer judgment or interpretation of events.

The annual summaries of the encyclopedia yearbooks are prepared at somewhat greater distance from the events themselves, and are more selective; this offers the opportunity for fallible judgment in selection-- an event which seems very minor at the time may become of major importance later on, or vice versa.

The arrangement of these sources differs also. In the news summaries, events relating to one topic will be scattered throughout the weeks although brought together in the indexing. In the encyclopedia yearbooks, events related to one topic will be brought together.

The 1970 (e.g. 1969) Americana Annual has an article on consumer affairs; the facts and events upon which that article is based will probably be found indexed in the New York Times Index or Facts on File, plus more material, but all of it will require some time to search out in the newspapers or in the news digest of Facts on File.

15-46 A: The encyclopedia yearbook type of annual survey will show trends or developments more clearly.

The news summary type of annual survey will give facts, details, minor information more clearly, plus some primary source material for further research.

For example, it is probably easier to refer to the encyclopedia yearbooks for a general discussion of current trends in consumer affairs activities or current developments in ecology action. For specific facts such as the new student organization called Earth Action Group, the news summaries might be more useful; if it doesn't last, this group may never find its way into the 1972 (covering 1971) encyclopedia yearbook.

15-47 A: Anything current becomes retrospective. What is news today is history tomorrow. And for libraries especially, there is very little which is of current value only; all current material, however ephemeral, can be used for historical research on many levels. Not all libraries can afford to keep retrospective files of such sources, of course, but those which do have resources are of much value for research.

15-48 A: See ALA Glossary. This definition is essentially the same as that of a yearbook but does not stress the currency of information. Originally, almanacs were yearly publications containing calendar information such as planting dates, church festivals, weather forecasts, tide tables, etc. The almanacs to be examined here are of a somewhat broader scope, but the idea of being a miscellaneous compendium of information is certainly common to both types of almanacs.

15-49 A: 1868 (Winchell annotation).

15-50 A: It's not really easy to figure out what the arrangement of the World Almanac is, and unfortunately there is no Table of Contents page which lays out the arrangement for you. The almanac consists of a great many short articles, tables, charts, lists, etc., arranged in a vaguely subject-classed order. The arrangement of these items within the source itself is certainly not alphabetical, and to say it is subject-classed is even a bit far-fetched. You get, for example (in the 1971 edition) a section on Economics (beginning p. 81), followed by a section on Taxation (p. 98+), followed by a section on Trade and Transportation (p. 98+), followed by a section on Agriculture (p. 129+), which winds up with a page on zoos (p. 141) and a page on animals (p. 142), then a section on Education (p. 143+), etc. You also get a lot of smaller items and one page items set in at odd places, obviously where there is room rather than on any basis of classification of information: marriage information on p. 70, followed by "flower of the month," followed by Grounds for Divorce on p. 71. In any case, the arrangement is not similar to that in the encyclopedia yearbooks.

15-51 A: There is a specific subject index, located in the front. The index is in some ways astonishingly specific. Flowers of the month are indexed as "Flowers--Month, of the..."

15-52 A: a. p. 137, Agriculture--Nutritive value of foods (index under calories);
b. p. 189, Inventions--U.S. and foreign (index under inventions);
c. p. 411, U.S. Places of 2,500 or more population with zip codes (index under zip code);
d. p. 196, U.S.--Associations and societies (alphabetized under Hay rather than National)--(index under associations and societies);
e. p. 239, Noted personalities--entertainers (index under births--notable persons, dates);
f. p. 836, Sports--hockey (index under hockey) (could you have found this if you didn't know the Stanley Cup was for hockey?);
g. p. 94, Economics--Bureau of the Mint

(index under portrait);
h. p. 174, Education--magazine circulation (index under magazine-circulation);
i. p. 701, U.S. Superlatives (index under westernmost point; and superlatives);
j. p. 706, U.S. presidential election returns (index under election returns-- Presidents, by states; also under California--presidential vote).

15-53 A: a. p. 219 (index under passport);
b. p. 80 (index under first aid);
c. p. 222 (index under citizenship);
d. p. 948 (index under parcel post);
e. p. 176 (index under metric weights);
f. p. 98 (index under income tax, federal);
g. p. 218 (index under patents);
h. p. 217 (index under copyright law).

15-54 A: a. p. 926, located in the Chronology of Year's Events, beginning p. 910 (index under Heyerdahl);
b. p. 57, located under Late News, Addenda (the list of Nobel Prize Winners on p. 311 under Awards- Medals-Prizes goes only through 1969)--(index under Nobel Prize);
c. p. 54-55, Medical Developments during 1970 (index under medicine--developments, 1970);
d. p. 944-946, Deaths-Nov. 1, 1969 to Nov. 1, 1970 (index under obituaries; also under deaths--year (1970)).

15-55 A: The index--that is, either the specificity of the index, or your own ingenuity in figuring out the terminology used.

15-56 A: The almanacs and the encyclopedia yearbooks include, for the past year, chronologies, obituaries, summaries of developments in specific fields. Both include current up-to-date information such as prize winners. In addition, the almanacs include retrospective information (1950 winners of the Stanley Cup, birthday of Paul McCartney, inventor of the sliderule). In addition, the almanacs include standard information (nutritive values in food, first aid, copyright laws, income tax laws, citizenship laws, etc.).

15-57 A: Some of the so-called standard information does have a way of changing from time to time. This is just the sort of thing which is difficult to up-date in an encyclopedia. The westernmost point of the United States is presently in Alaska, but before Alaska became a state in 1958, the answer would have been different. The 1957 printing of an encyclopedia would have the out-of-date answer; the 1958 printing might have the new answer. The 1958 or 1959 almanac would be much more likely to have the new answer. In any case it is cheaper to buy a new almanac every year than a new encyclopedia printing every year. The almanacs are extremely useful for up-dating encyclopedia information in this way.

15-58 A: Basically it is the same in format and scope. The index is in the back. The table of contents page in the front is an alphabetical listing of major categories, similar to the Quick Reference Index on the verso of the title page of the World Almanac. Information Please includes a chronology and a list of deaths for the past year. It does not appear to have articles on developments in specific fields, but does include some articles on the environmental crisis, housing, population, education, etc., which are similar to the "special articles or features" appearing in the encyclopedia yearbooks. Much of the information is duplicated in both almanacs, but the Information Please Almanac has some features or sections (see Crossword Puzzle Guide, p. 533+, 1971 edition) not in the World Almanac, and vice versa.

15-59 A: 1947 (Winchell).

15-60 A: It is called an encyclopedic almanac and in many ways it is closer to the encyclopedia yearbooks than either the World Almanac or Information Please. To begin with, the arrangement is easier to grasp and the whole format is more attractive and readable.

There is a real Table of Contents which sets out the larger sub-divisions of information, so that you can, for example, turn directly to the entire section on astronomical information ("Stars/Planets/Space").

The index is in the back; in the 1970 edition it is similar to other almanac indexes, but in the 1971 index it is divided into three sections: lists and tables, articles, and names.

It has standard tables, lists, statistics of the other two almanacs, plus some not found in the others (and vice-versa).

It has the chronology of events, obituaries, and up-to-date information from the past year, as have the other almanacs and the encyclopedia yearbooks.

However, the New York Times almanac has many more signed and illustrated articles, on developments in general fields and on specifically current issues (violence, drugs, housing, women's liberation: 1971 edition), similar to those found in the encyclopedia yearbooks. There is more to read in the New York Times almanac.

Finally, it is more expensive.

15-61 A: Whitaker's is published in London, and as a British publication it can be expected to stress British and British Commonwealth material, even though the scope, like that of the three American publications, is world-wide.

15-62 A: It is probably most similar to the World Almanac in arrangement. The Table of Contents in the front does give a list of contents in order of appearance (rather than in alphabetical order), followed by an extensive alphabetical index.

15-63 A: Some sources are given, mostly for the tables, lists, statistics, population figures, etc. For example, the table of food values in the World Almanac, 1971, comes from the U.S. Department of Agriculture.

15-64 A: Obviously the 1971 almanacs will be more up to date than the 1970 encyclopedia yearbooks. However, it should also be remembered that the 1971 almanacs will be issued very early in 1971 and available for use throughout the year, while the 1971 encyclopedia yearbooks will probably not be issued till very late in 1971 if then. So that in actual use you are likely to have a more recent almanac than an encyclopedia yearbook.

15-65 A: World, 1971: Indexed under Tokyo--population.
p. 59: Population of World's Largest Urban Areas. Tokyo is listed as 14,770,727 according to the 1965 census.
p. 583: Population of Important World Cities. Tokyo is listed as 11,350,000. This is called "Greater" Tokyo; the date is not clear (the "latest available").
Information Please, 1971: Indexed under Tokyo.
p. 259: in article on Japan, lists as 8,960,000 estimated 1967; not clear whether urban center or city proper.
p. 761: (Cities, World) same information given.
New York Times, 1971: indexed in Articles under Tokyo, one reference is historical.
p. 340: World Population Facts. Tokyo City proper is listed as 9,102,000 in 1969. The short article does not indicate however the way in which the comparable position of New York City and Tokyo can be reserved depending on whether figures for the city proper or the urban area are used (in 1967).
All three sources used different figures, different years, different basis, and the differences are not always made clear.

15-66 A: World Almanac, 1971: p. 73 (indexed under births, illegitimate). 1968 is latest year listed, estimated number only since not all states report illegitimacy, methods of getting national estimates are explained, source of figures is Division of Vital Statistics, National Center for Health Statistics, U.S. Department of Health, Education and Welfare. Figure given is ratio only, you would have to figure the number by finding the number of live births in another table...
New York Times Encyclopedic Almanac, 1971: p. 393 (indexed in Lists, under Births, illegitimate). Number of births given but no indication of how the figures were obtained or any suggestion that not all states report illegitimacy. Source is U.S. Public Health Service.

15-67 A: New York Times Encyclopedic Almanac, 1971 edition, p. 330 (indexed in Lists index under Wildlife, Endangered; Animals --Endangered wildlife). Not in World, Information Please, or Whitaker's.

15-68 A: Information Please Almanac, 1971 edition, p. 459 (indexed under Libraries, Presidential; Presidential Libraries; and Presidents--Libraries). Not in World, NY Times, or Whitaker's. This information could also be found in the encyclopedias but it might not be up-to-date. The 1971 Information Please Almanac includes information about the Kennedy Library and the Johnson Library, and eventually there will probably be a Nixon Library.

15-69 A: Whitaker's, p. 1183 (1971), indexed under income tax.

15-70 A: World Almanac, 1971 edition, p. 308, Aviation Hall of Fame (indexed under Aviation Hall of Fame). Year of the first airplane flight by the Wright Brothers, p. 785 in Memorable Dates (indexed under Wright Brothers--first flight). For contemporary comments, you have to go to a source covering 1903, and there aren't too many from your list: Annual Register, and the Appleton's Annual Cyclopaedia noted in the answer to #15-26. The World Almanac and Whitaker's go back that far, and should lead you to newspaper articles on the event. The problem here is that the Wright Brothers flight probably did not seem nearly as significant in 1903 as it does in 1971.

15-71 A: You might expect this to be in Whitaker's as Canada is part of the British Commonwealth, but it isn't there, and it is unlikely to be in the American almanacs, so another possible source is a Canadian Almanac if one exists and you have access to it. Check Winchell, in the same section in which the American almanacs are listed, under the foreign country divisions, under Canada (item CG75).

15-72 A: World Almanac, Whitaker's Almanack, Britannica Book of the Year are all annuals; Ulrich's does not include annuals but Irregular Serials and Annuals (see section 5) does.
  Facts on File appears weekly, and should therefore be in Ulrich's as a periodical.
  Sources such as CBI, and BPR, BIP do not claim to include annual or yearbook publications but in fact they often do.

15-73 A: Current up-to-date information not yet in the encyclopedias or other older sources or that which is constantly changing (prize winners, population figures, etc.). Current developments, trends in certain fields or areas, which would possibly not yet be in the encyclopedias and in any case would not be as clearly set forth

(medicine, education, pollution, consumer affairs, etc.) In the older yearbooks, contemporary comments on events (Civil War, Wright Brothers, etc.) In the almanacs particularly, quick answers to factual questions.

15-74 A: The Statesman's Year-Book; statistical and historical annual of the states of the world for the year..published by MacMillan in London (also St. Martin's Press in New York). See title page, also Winchell.

15-75 A: It is an annual (see title, and see Winchell), published once a year. The double date is probably used because it comes out in the middle of the year (June) and the June 1970 publication would therefore be used through part of 1970 and part of 1971. The next issue would be dated 1971/72, so the date would always overlap.

15-76 A: See Contents pages (beginning p. vii, in 1970/71 edition). Basically, it is arranged by area: first, international organizations, beginning with the United Nations; then the Commonwealth, beginning with The United Kingdom; then The United States of America, with the states listed alphabetically; then "Other Countries" listed alphabetically. There is also an index.

15-77 A: That the stress is on the English-speaking world, since nearly the first half of the volume is devoted to The British Commonwealth and the United States.

15-78 A: History, constitution, government, present rulers, flag, national anthem, local governments, area, population, vital statistics, religion, education, number of newspapers, social welfare, justice, finance (currency, budget), defense, production, agriculture, fisheries, manufactures, power, tourism, commerce, shipping, roads, railways, aviation, post, banking, weights and measures; also information on the Faroe Islands and Greenland.

15-79 A: Statesman's Year-Book 1970/71, index under Nyasaland refers you to Malawi, and the main article on Malawi is located under the British Commonwealth. A short bibliography is at the end of the article, for further information, as is true for most of the articles.

15-80 A: Under Japan, then under Area and Population, then the list of leading cities: Tokyo is given as 8,893,000 for October 1965.

15-81 A: You would probably have to look up Sikkim in the index, unless you happened to know or guess that it would be listed in the Contents as part of The Commonwealth, under India, of which it is a Protectorate. Statesman's Year-Book 1970/71, p. 388-9, under "roads," states that there are no airfields.

15-82 A: This sounds like the kind of thing to turn
           up in the almanacs, but it isn't there.
           The Morse code itself is given in most of
           the dictionaries (Webster's Third unabridged,
           American Heritage, Funk and Wagnall's un-
           abridged). It is also given in the encyclo-
           pedias, no article but found in the indexes
           and in the article on Telegraph or Telegra-
           phy. The encyclopedia is the only likely
           source to give the difference between the
           Morse Code in the U.S. and the Interna-
           tional Code (see Americana).

15-83 A: Annual Register covering 1964; possibly
           Whitaker's Almanac covering 1964. Sources
           such as Facts on File, Keesing's, New
           York Times Index might give the informa-
           tion but you would not find it so easily.

15-84 A: World Almanac, 1971 edition, p. 338
           (indexed under Chinese Lunar Calendar, or
           Calendars--Chinese Lunar). Not in Infor-
           mation Please, NY Times, or Whitaker's
           (1971 editions).

15-85 A: To define I.Q., a dictionary would
           probably be sufficient. But to find out the
           tests used in determining I.Q., you would
           probably have to go to an encyclopedia for
           further information.

15-86 A: Encyclopedia year book covering 1969 (i.e.,
           Collier's, article on American Literature).

15-87 A: Any dictionary, or a pronunciation book
           such as the NBC Handbook of Pronunciation.

15-88 A: Statesman's Year-Book 1970/71, p. 1392
           (under Union of Soviet Socialist Republics,
           then under Justice). Possibly also an en-
           cyclopedia although information may not be
           up to date.

15-89 A: New York Times Index, Facts on File;
           almanacs covering 1970; possibly encyclo-
           pedia yearbooks covering 1970 when
           available.

15-90 A: Almanacs, indexed under Cambodia. States-
           man's Year Book, under Cambodia, then
           Finance. For up-to-the-minute informa-
           tion, you might try calling the foreign ex-
           change or international department of a
           local bank.

Section 16

Yearbook Supplements: Statistics

Questions #16/1-16/40

16-1   Under what heading are the almanacs classified in Winchell? Why?

16-2   What are statistics? Which of the questions that you previously answered through the yearbooks and almanacs are statistical in nature?

Statistical information is included extensively in most of the sources you have examined so far: especial-ly in the almanacs, to a great extent in the encyclopedias and encyclopedia yearbooks, to some extent in news surveys such as Facts on File (and of course in the New York Times itself), and even in the dic-tionaries (in population figures, for example).

The next set of sources to examine are examples of those which are specifically devoted to statistical in-formation. In a way they should be considered as supplementary to the unit on yearbooks, because much statistical information (population figures, for example) changes from year to year, and it is very impor-tant to have access to information which is as current and up-to-date as possible. Two of the sources to be examined for statistical information are, in fact, yearbooks. One is a retrospective source, and the last is a bibliographical source. The titles are:

            Statistical Abstract of the United States (CG49)
            Historical Statistics of the United States (CG51, 1CG6)

            Statistical Yearbook of the United Nations (CG32)
            Statistics Sources (CH108)

16-3   Who publishes the Statistical Abstract?

16-4   The almanacs in particular and to some extent the encyclopedia yearbooks are full of statistical informa-tion. Can you remember, or can you find by checking back in the almanacs, what types of statistical in-formation are given in these yearbook sources?

16-5   The U.S. Census Bureau is the source of a great number of statistics, as well as being responsible for the preparation of the Statistical Abstract. Where would you go to find out what the Census Bureau does, how often a census is taken, how the data from the census is published or made available?

16-6   How often is a major population census taken? When was the last one taken? Where would you look to find further general information on this last census?

16-7   Are figures and statistics from the 1970 census available in the 1971 almanacs?

16-8   What is the arrangement of the Statistical Abstract?

16-9   Statistical Abstract of the United States is not called a yearbook or almanac in its title. Is it a year-
         book?

16-10   Has anything new been added to the 1970 volume of Statistical Abstract? Where would you look to find
         out?

16-11   Can you find which state had the most elected Negro officials in 1970?

16-12   Does Statistical Abstract give only figures or data for the year preceding publication, or does it have
         retrospective data as well? Can you find, for example, the number of people killed in automobile acci-
         dents in 1968? Can you find comparable figures for 1960? What is the source of these figures?

16-13   What is the total estimated cost of the American Civil War? What is the total estimated cost of the
         Vietnam "conflict"? Is there anything special which should be noted about the Vietnam figure? Are those
         costs simply the expenses of waging the wars, or are other items included?

16-14   What are the latest figures you can find in Statistical Abstracts for the number of librarians currently
         employed?

16-15   Of the female librarians listed in table no. 337, 5.1% are "Negro and other." What is meant by "and
         other"?

16-16   Can you find, in the Statistical Abstract for 1970, the total number of new books including new editions
         published in the United States in 1969?

16-17   What is the source of these statistics? Knowing the source, what does this lead you to suspect about the
         types of material included in or excluded from these figures?

16-18   Does the table of new books published, as given in Statistical Abstract, state these omissions for you, or
         for others who might not even suspect such omissions?

16-19   Does Statistical Abstract 1970 have a figure for the number of books registered for copyright in 1969?

16-20   The number of books registered for copyright in 1969 is given as 83,000+, while the number of new books
         published is given as 29,000+. Are these figures really comparable? Are they really counting the same
         things?

16-21   Does the Statistical Abstract for 1970 list the number of daily newspapers in the United States in 1969?
         From what source are these figures taken?

16-22   Statistics are not always easy for the layman to understand, and there are many problems in using and
         interpreting statistics, even in reading statistical tables correctly. What are some of the problems
         which may seem evident from the questions you have answered so far? What are some of the things

you should look for in using and reading statistical information?

16-23   Is there any general difference between the statistical information given in Statistical Abstract and that given in the almanacs, for example?

16-24   Is all the statistical information given in the Statistical Abstract based on government figures or data?

16-25   Can you find in Statistical Abstract how many librarians there were in the United States in 1900? If not, where do you go for this information?

16-26   Historical Statistics of the United States exists as a retrospective supplement to the Statistical Abstract. Therefore its scope and arrangement are very similar to the Statistical Abstract itself, and it will be used in much the same way. What retrospective period is covered by this publication? Who is the publisher?

16-27   Will all the statistical tables in Historical Statistics then give figures from 1610 through 1962? For example, are there Consumer Price Indexes back to 1610?

16-28   Can you find out, through Historical Statistics, what the Consumer Price Index is, and how it works?

16-29   What historical statistics do exist for the colonial period? How can you locate them in Historical Abstracts? Can you find population figures for the American Colonies? Can you find figures for the amount of tea imported into the Colonies? What is the source of the figures on tea? Can you find the number of slaves brought into the United States? Were all of these actually slaves?

16-30   Do Historical Statistics and/or the Statistical Abstract give any international figures, or statistics from other countries? Can you find comparative figures for the food supply per person in the United States as compared to India?

16-31   Where would you look to find more detailed statistics on the food supply in India?

16-32   Where would you find general statistics for several countries or areas? Can you find the infant mortality rate in Guam? Can you find the number of infant deaths in Guam in any specific year?

16-33   Does the Statistical Yearbook of the United Nations indicate the sources of its data?

16-34   What is the point in knowing the source or sources for statistical data?

16-35   The next title on your list, Statistics Sources, provides further guidance in this area. What is the full title, the publisher, and the date of publication?

16-36   What is the arrangement of Statistics Sources?

16-37   Does Statistics Sources list only primary sources of data (i.e., Bowker Company)--that is, the organiza-
         tions, agencies, governments, businesses, etc., which collect the data--or also secondary sources (i.e,
         Statistical Abstract, World Almanac) in which statistical data is published?

16-38   Where could you write or call to get figures on the consumption and use of canned Irish potatoes?

16-39   Where could you find information on the profits made by drug companies?

16-40   If you wanted to know more about statistics, what they are, how to use them, etc., where would you
         look?

Section 16

Answers #16/1-16/40

16-1 A: CG, Statistics (part of Social Sciences). Probably because a large part of the information they contain is statistical in nature.

16-2 A: For a definition of statistics, see any dictionary. Examples of statistical information are the figures on illegitimate births (#15-66), the population of Tokyo (#15-65), the Presidential election returns (#15-52), etc.

16-3 A: It is a U.S. government publication, specifically the Bureau of the Census of the Department of Commerce. (See title page and Winchell citation).

16-4 A: Flipping through one of the almanacs to see what tables of figures are given is one way to see how much statistical information they contain. Somehow this seems more obvious in the World Almanac. For example, in the 1971 edition: U.S. Military Casualties in Southeast Asia (p. 35); Cost of Living in Various Cities of the World (p. 59); Employment Security (p. 65); the entire Vital Statistics section (p. 66-79); much of the information in the Economics section following; tables showing enrollment, teachers, attendance, expenditures in public schools (p. 170); Education Attainment by Age, Race and Sex (p. 172), and so on.

16-5 A: Try a general encyclopedia. There may not be an article on the Bureau itself but an article on the Census should give some information. Another more indirect source might be to see if there are any recent government publications which would be useful, by checking in the Monthly Catalog of Government Publications or in the GPO Price List which covers the census publications. For example: Census Bureau Programs and Publications; Area and Subject Guide (issued June 1968).

16-6 A: A population census is taken every 10 years (see article on Census in Collier's Encyclopedia, c.1966), and the last major census was in 1970. An encyclopedia yearbook (for 1971, covering 1970) would probably have an article on the 1970 census; the 1971 almanacs might also have information-- for example, in the 1971 New York Times Encyclopedic Almanac, p. 35, a short article on Census 1970 (indexed in Articles, under Census).

16-7 A: To some extent. Some of them give only preliminary figures. Many of the tables, charts, lists, etc., do not yet reflect changes from the 1970 census.

16-8 A: By broad subject grouping, such as population, vital statistics, immigration, education, etc. (see Contents pages) with a very specific index in the back.

16-9 A: Yes, because it is an annual publication, containing miscellaneous current and up-to-date information; in this case specifically statistical information. (See definition of yearbook, #15-3).

16-10 A: See Preface (Winchell annotation would not give it for anything as recent as the 1970 edition). More social awareness is found in this edition: coverage of minority groups, poverty, military affairs, pollution.

16-11 A: 1970 edition, p. 361, table no. 546, Negro Elected Officials, by Office--States: 1970. That is, as of February 1970 (see note following title of table). Indexed under Negro population--elected officials.

16-12 A: Yes. Some retrospective data for comparison is given. There is no set cut-off date; some tables go back further than others. Statistical Abstract 1970, p. 552, table no. 855, shows automobile accidents and goes back to 1960. Indexed under Motor Vehicles--Accidents (cross reference from Automobiles). The number for 1969 is 56,000. The source of the figures is given at the bottom of the table: The Travelers Insurance Companies, and a specific publication is cited for further reference.

16-13 A: Both figures are given in the 1970 edition, p. 248, table no. 371 (indexed under Wars, American, cost of). There is a reference note for the Vietnam figures which indicates that they are based on the assumption that the war would end by June 30, 1970.... Be sure to note that the cost of the Civil War, for example, is not 12 thousand dollars, but 12 million dollars; see note directly beneath the title of the table. The total estimated ultimate costs listed include all veterans' benefits and payments of interest on war loans as well as the military and national security costs.

16-14 A: Index under librarians has nothing; libraries, employment has three references, one of which turns out to be employment in federal libraries and one for employment in city and local government. Table no. 337 on p. 228 does apparently list "all" librarians but based on 1960 figures. Anyway, the table is broken down into "male" and "female"; presumably then you would have to add together the number of female librarians plus the number of male librarians to get a total. But there is no category for librarians under "male," and presumably they then fall under "Other prof., technical and kindred," so you can't really find an answer to your question.

16-15 A: See p. 2, in article on "Population" which gives some explanation of methodology. The paragraph on "Race" at the bottom of the page indicates that "and other" means anything other than white or Negro, except Mexicans who are counted as white, unless they are Indian in which case they are counted as "other"....

16-16 A: Table no. 869, p. 502, New Books and New Editions Published.... Indexed under Books, etc., in index, or you could find it through the Contents (Communications, then Books).

16-17 A: The source is in the Bowker Company and Publishers' Weekly. You already know that the listings in PW exclude certain types of publications--e.g., government publications, most subscription books, dissertations, pamphlets under 49 pages, and periodicals. You might then suspect that these types of publications are probably not included in the statistics from Bowker, and that therefore the figures as given are not strictly representative of all books published. For example, Statistical Abstract itself, although clearly a book, is not represented in the statistics from Bowker because it is a government publication.

16-18 A: Yes, following the title of the table.

16-19 A: Yes, following page 503, table no. 772.

16-20 A: The table on registration of copyright indicates that "books" includes pamphlets and leaflets, while the figure for new books clearly excludes pamphlets and, not so clearly perhaps, leaflets. The table on registration also indicates that it includes registrations from residents of foreign countries so that all registrations may not be for books published in the U.S. but only copyrighted here. In addition, you know yourself from the examination of the Catalog of Copyright Entries that many very odd kinds of publications appeared in that listing which did not appear in PW. Therefore the figures, even though for the same year, cannot really be considered as comparable.

16-21 A: Table no. 766 on p. 500, Newspapers and periodicals. 1969 and 1970 figures given, and some earlier figures. Source is the Ayer Directory. (Indexed under Newspapers--Frequency of publication, or found through Contents: Communications--Newspapers).

16-22 A: The date is important for timeliness and accuracy; for example, now that we have 1970 census figures, the various reference publications should begin to reflect these figures instead of earlier 1960 figures. Nomenclature (i.e., what comprises a "book," what comprises "and other," etc.) should be clarified, before you can determine exactly what the figures are telling you, or whether or not the figures are comparable. The source of the information is important, for further reference if necessary, or for general authority and accuracy. For example, you have some understanding about the statistics on books and newspapers because you are familiar with the sources --Ayer's, PW--from which they are taken; the figures on automobile accidents might not seem so deceptively simple if you were an insurance agent instead of a librarian. All footnotes or other descriptive or explanatory notes should always be read.

16-23 A: Statistical Abstract is careful to cite sources, dates, give sufficient explanatory and descriptive data. The almanacs are not always this careful; remember, for example, the wide range of answers found for population data on Tokyo.

16-24 A: No. The figures on books from Bowker Company, on newspapers from Ayer's, on automobile accidents from Travelers Insurance Company are not government data.

16-25 A: The next source on your list: Historical Statistics of the United States. This source is not a yearbook, as it is not published annually, and is strictly for retrospective rather than current information.

16-26 A: Historical Statistics goes back to "colonial times" (see title), actually to 1610 (see Winchell annotation). The basic volume itself covers up to 1957 (Winchell CG51), plus a supplement published in 1965 which brings it up to 1962 and makes some revisions (Winchell 1CG6). Both of these volumes are published by the United States Government Printing Office, as is Statistical Abstract. There is also a commercial publication by Fairfield Publishers (Horizon Press) which combines both the basic volume and the supplement into one volume, accomplished by interleaving the supplement continuations at the end of the chapters of the basic volume.

16-27 A: Statistics will be given retrospectively only for the years such statistics were kept, so most of the tables will not go back to colonial times. The Consumer Prices Indexes (beginning on p. 125 of the Fairfield volume), go back to 1851, although not all the breakdowns are available for all years. For example, there were no breakdowns of food into cereals, meats, dairy products, and fruits and vegetables until 1935. The Consumer Price Index on p. 125 of the Fairfield volume goes only to 1957. To get the continuation to 1962, you must turn to p. 130A-B.

16-28 A: Yes, see the notes at the beginning of the chapter on Prices and Price Indexes. Specific notes on the Consumer Price Indexes begin on p. 109 of the Fairfield volume. Historical Statistics contains much more explanatory material of this nature than does the Statistical Abstract.

16-29 A: Colonial statistics located in the last chapter (beginning p. 743, Fairfield). Population estimates, p. 756. Tea importation p. 767 (Series Z254-261). For the source, you have to go to the notes at the beginning of the chapter, looking under the series number. Slaves p. 769-70 for slave trade (Series Z281-303). See notes on these series (beginning of chapter); that for the slave trade in Virginia notes that until the middle of the 17th century, Negroes came here as servants, not as slaves.

16-30 A: Both are specifically for the United States. The Statistical Abstract does contain a section on comparative international statistics (p. 802+ of the 1970 volume). Table no. 1255 on p. 811 of the 1970 volume gives some figures on food supply per person by country. You can compare the number of calories available per person per day, or the number of pounds of meat available per person per year, for example. However, the figures for the U.S. are for 1967, and for India are for 1965/66 so they are comparable only in a general way. See also notes on p. 804 for further comments on comparability regarding the variations in which the data are collected, estimated, defined, etc.

16-31 A: Some statistical summary for India comparable to the Statistical Abstract of the United States. See Winchell, same section, under India. Item CG116, for example.

16-32 A: Some kind of international statistical source, which is likely to be published by an international organization such as the United Nations: see the next title on your list, Statistical Yearbook of the United Nations. This source has no specific index, so you must turn to the Table of Contents, checking under likely major subjects, where you find under Population, the Infant mortality rates (p. 78 of the 1969 yearbook--e.g., published in 1970, titled 1969, and giving statistics through 1968). Guam is on p. 79, under Oceania, latest rate available is for 1967. The rate is 22.7 per 1,000 live births. This is not the same thing as the number of deaths.

16-33 A: Yes, see information under "Sources" in Introduction.

16-34 A: See answer to question #16-23. Knowing the source gives you some idea of the accuracy, authority, impartiality, completeness, comparability, etc., of the data. Even more important, however, it gives you access to the complete raw data on which the statistics or statistical tables are based.

16-35 A: Statistics Sources; a subject guide to data on industrial, business, social, educational, financial, and other topics for the United States and Selected Foreign Countries. Published by Gale Research Company. (Title page). Copyright 1965 (verso of title page).

16-36 A: Subject (see title), alphabetically. No index so subject listing should be reasonably specific.

16-37 A: Both. See preface. See also "Selected Bibliography of Key Statistical Sources" following the preface.

16-38 A: Under Potatoes--Irish--Canned: gives National Canners Association, with address; notes also their "Canned Food Pack Statistics" as a (presumably) published source.

16-39 A: Drug or Drugs and Medicine in the alphabetical listing of Statistic Sources do not really give what you want, as most are related to the cost of drugs, to the number of employees in the industry, etc. Under Pharmaceuticals--Corporation assets and profits (no cross-reference from Drugs), you find that Fortune Magazine is a source of published information for this question.

16-40 A: Winchell lists some dictionaries of statistics (8th ed., p. 374) which might be helpful. Probably a better source would be an encyclopedia article on statistics, and if you are really mathematically ignorant or the whole area of statistics baffles you, then probably one of the children's encyclopedias such as World Book would be best.

Section 17

Handbooks and Manuals

Questions #17/1-17/85

17-1   What is meant by the term "ready reference" or quick reference? Which of the sources discussed so
        far, in the entire manual, can be considered as ready-reference sources? Do any seem to lend them-
        selves to this use more than others?

        The next set of sources to examine--the handbooks and manuals--are excellent sources for ready-
        reference use. The handbooks listed here, to be examined and discussed, are only examples from
        the many available, chosen to represent a certain type or a specific arrangement, etc.:

                Kane: Famous First Facts
                Guinness Book of World Records

                Benet: The Reader's Encyclopedia (BD18)
                Brewer's Dictionary of Phrase and Fable (BD48)

                Bartlett: Familiar Quotations (2BD16, BD75)
                Stevenson: Home Book of Quotations (BD83)
                Evans: Dictionary of Quotations (2BD18)

                Douglas: American Book of Days (CF22)
                Hazeltine: Anniversaries and Holidays (CF25)
                Steinberg: Historical Tables (DA47, IDA8)
                Langer: Encyclopedia of World History (DA42, 2AD5)
                Everyman's Dictionary of Dates (DA30)

                Emily Post's Etiquette (CF36, 1CF6)
                Menke: Encyclopedia of Sports (CB167)
                Roberts' Rules of Order (CI171)
                How-to-do-it Books: A Selected Guide (CB156)

17-2   What is a definition of a handbook? What is the definition of a manual?

17-3   The first two titles on the list--Kane's Famous First Facts, and the Guinness Book of World Records--
        are representative of a type often referred to as a "curiosity" handbook. What is the basic difference
        in scope between these two sources? Do they overlap?

17-4   How do they differ in arrangement?

17-5   Who was the first U.S. librarian to be paid for his services?

17-6   Where is the world's remotest inhabited island?

17-7   When was the first photograph taken?

17-8   What authority is there for the facts cited by Kane? Are any sources given? Are sources or authorities cited in Guinness?

17-9   For what is William Horlick famous?

17-10   Can you find out, through Kane or Guinness, what Olav Bjaaland is noted for?

17-11   Who was the first man to reach the South Pole?

17-12   Who is the youngest boxer ever to have won the world heavyweight championship?

17-13   How often are Kane and Guinness up-dated? Is currency important in such books?

17-14   What is the longest bridge in the world, according to Guinness? Do you think this information is still accurate? Where would you go to check on it? What additional or conflicting information can you find? Other than the need for current information, can you see any inherent problem in a question of this nature?

17-15   In the previous question dealing with the longest bridge in the world, would you have considered the encyclopedias as a reasonable source for an answer? In what way would the encyclopedias be useful to you in dealing with this question?

17-16   The next two sources on your list are Benet's Reader's Encyclopedia and Brewer's Dictionary of Phrase and Fable. How are these classified in Winchell?

        Both Benet and Brewer are examples of a type often referred to as "literary handbooks," but because of the broad scope of information included, they are very similar in some ways to the curiosity handbooks such as Kane and Guinness. In fact, many other titles listed in Winchell in the same section in which Brewer is found are also good examples of curiosity handbooks, such as Walsh's Handbook of Curious Information (BD55); Ackermann's Popular Fallacies (BD47).

17-17   What is the difference in scope between Benet and Brewer?

17-18   How are the Benet and Brewer books arranged?

17-19   Benet is considered here as a handbook. Why would it be listed in Winchell as an encyclopedia?

17-20   Oliver Optic is the pen name or pseudonym for the 19th-century author of many books for boys. He also edited a periodical for children. What is his real name and what is the name of the periodical?

17-21   Charles Dickens was an English novelist, 1812-1879. Could you find information on Dickens in Benet? in Brewer?

17-22   Uriah Heep is a character in a novel by Dickens. What is the name of the novel? What part does Heep play in the novel? Can you find this information in both Benet and Brewer?

17-23   If you came across a reference to Linnaeus' scientific classification system in your reading, could you find an explanation of it in Benet? In Brewer? If you wanted further information, where would you go?

17-24   What does it mean "to wear the willow?" How has this term come about?

17-25   How recently has Benet's Reader's Encyclopedia been revised? Does it seem to put much stress on recent names, allusions, etc.? Would you expect to find James Bond in Benet? in Brewer?

17-26   Nine is often thought of as a number of some mystical significance. Why is it considered mystical? What are some examples of the appearance of the number nine in literature and myth? What are some phrases using the word "nine"? What are the "nine points of the law" (as in, "possession is...")? Compare entries in Benet and Brewer.

17-27   What does "abracadabra" mean, how is it used, where did it come from?

17-28   Why are Benet and Brewer called "literary handbooks, and classified under "literature" in Winchell? Why is Benet called a reader's encyclopedia? Are Benet and Brewer limited to literary terms, characters in books, writers, etc.?

17-29   Another type of source related basically to the field of literature and classified under literature in Winchell are the books of quotations. These are considered here as handbooks, and are used extensively in libraries for ready-reference. Those discussed are only examples of many available. The first two-- Bartlett's Familiar Quotations and Stevenson's Home Book of Quotations--are examined here because they show two different approaches to the problem of quotations.
         How do Bartlett and Stevenson differ in arrangement?

17-30   Locate the quotation "The pen is mightier than the sword" in both Stevenson and Bartlett. How did you go about it? Who is the author of the quote? Is there any difference in the citation given in Stevenson and in Bartlett?

17-31   Would the quotation "The pen is mightier than the sword" be indexed only under pen in these quotation books? Why or why not?

17-32   Can you find a good quotation on foreign opinion of America such as you might use as inspiration for the text of a speech?

17-33   Does Stevenson have any limitations as a source for the preceding question (on quotes on foreign opinion of America)?

17-34   Edmund Burke is listed in the Table of Contents of the Stevenson book. Is this an indication that selections of quotations from his writings will be found in one place, as in Bartlett?

17-35   How would you go about finding the correct words and the title of a poem by John Masefield which you remember only vaguely as being about "the sea"?

17-36   The quotations in Bartlett are arranged by author. Where do quotations from the Bible appear? What, if anything, is done with those quotations which have no attributed author--for example, proverbs? According to the title of Bartlett, proverbs are included; where are they? Is "a stitch in time saves nine" listed in Bartlett?

17-37   Are there any sources which specifically list and index proverbs?

17-38   The latest revision of Bartlett is 1968. What recent, modern writers are included in Bartlett? Can you check Stevenson as easily as Bartlett?

17-39   Which of these two books of quotations--Bartlett and Stevenson--has the most useful arrangement?

17-40   The index in the Stevenson quotation book is referred to as an Index and Concordance, and some suggestions for its use are given immediately preceding the index (p. 2420 of the c.1967 edition). What is a concordance?

17-41   If you were searching for a quotation from Shakespeare, and you could not find it in any of the quotation books you had available, where else could you turn?

17-42   Both Bartlett and Stevenson, although recently revised, have long histories. When did they first appear?

17-43   A newer entry on the scene is Evans' Dictionary of Quotations, first published in 1968. How is it arranged?

17-44   Françoise Sagan (French novelist, born 1935) has been quoted as saying "Men have more problems than women." What is the rest of her comment, and is it a quotation from one of her novels?

17-45   Does the Evans quotation book appear to differ from Stevenson in any major way?

17-46   Do the quotation books include as sources only published material, or only literature, or only books?

17-47   What other sources have you examined which would be useful for identifying or verifying quotations?

17-48   When Neil Armstrong stepped from the lunar lander to the surface of the moon at the first moon landing, he uttered a statement which will, no doubt, be appearing in quotation books of the future. Did he say "That's one small step for man, one giant step for mankind"? Where can you look to check his exact words?

17-49   The next set of sources--those concerned with days and dates--are significant primarily for their arrangement: they approach knowledge from a chronological point of view. The first of these, Douglas' American Book of Days, is perhaps most similar in scope to the curiosity handbooks. What is its full title?

17-50   How is it arranged?

17-51   Is St. David's Day celebrated in the United States?

17-52   Is the information in Douglas limited only to information about celebrations of holidays and festivals?

17-53   Is the Fourth of July significant for any reason other than the American Declaration of Independence?

17-54   Is there any way in which you can tell from The American/Book of Days what local holidays and festivals are celebrated in the southwest of the United States?

17-55   Somewhat comparable to Douglas' American Book of Days is Hazeltine's Anniversaries and Holidays. How does Hazeltine compare to Douglas in arrangement and scope?

17-56   If you wanted further reading on St. David and St. David's Day than you found in The American Book of Days, where would you look?

17-57   Where would you find a list of the birthdays of several famous librarians?

17-58   What is one of the major limitations of the Hazeltine book? When was it published?

17-59   Where are the Hazeltine and Douglas books classified in Winchell?

17-60   Another chronological approach is represented by the next title on the list, Steinberg's Historical Tables. Under what subject is this title classified in Winchell?

17-61   What is the arrangement of Steinberg? What is the point of the arrangement?

17-62   The American Civil War began in the spring of 1861. What else happened in the world at that same time?

17-63   In Steinberg, under the list for "Western and Southern Europe" for the year 1861, a note is made that "Cavour" died. Can you tell through Steinberg who Cavour was?

17-64   Can you find out, through Steinberg, what was happening in Western Europe at the time of the collapse of the Byzantine Empire?

17-65   In contrast to the bare bones of history given in Steinberg is Langer's Encyclopedia of World History. How is this source arranged? Can you find out through Langer when the Byzantine empire collapsed?

17-66   Can you find out through Langer who Cavour was?

17-67   Where would you find a brief accounting of events of the Communist takeover of Czechoslovakia prior to the death of Jan Masaryk, Czechoslovakian foreign minister, in 1948?

17-68   The last of the date books is Everyman's Dictionary of Dates. What is the basic arrangement of this source? Is it similar to the other books on days and dates?

17-69   Can you find out the date of the collapse of the Byzantine Empire through the Everyman's Dictionary of Dates?

17-70   Can you find in Everyman's Dictionary of Dates comparative dates for the founding of the major national libraries? Can you also find this in Langer?

17-71   One of the confusing points which often arises in discussion of dates is that of the "old style" and "new style" calendar or dates. Where could you find a discussion of this problem?

The last sources on the list are chosen as examples of the vast number of specialized handbooks and manuals available for reference use. How-to-do-it Books is listed as a bibliographical source for further titles of that nature beyond what you can find in Winchell. The scope of these sources should be quite self-evident from the titles, and it is not really necessary at this stage to examine each of these individually, although checking the citations and annotations in Winchell might be helpful.

The following questions, then, are to be used as review for the entire section on handbooks and manuals, including the last few specialized sources which you have not yet specifically examined.

17-72   Where would you look to find a quotation on reading which would be suitable to use on the cover of a Great Books reading list you are compiling?

17-73   What is the meaning of the phrase "point of order" which many people seem compelled to shout out at intervals during business meetings?

17-74   What is Guy Fawkes Day? Who was Guy Fawkes?

17-75   What is the German title of Thomas Mann's novel The Magic Mountain?

17-76   Where is the wettest place in the world (other than something under water)?

17-77   Who wrote the nursery rhyme "Twinkle, twinkle, little star"?

17-78   What is the order of rank among government officials, both U.S. and foreign?

17-79   What are Movable Feasts and Fasts?

17-80   What does the phrase "the cat's pajamas" mean?

17-81   What are the rules of the game of rugby?

17-82   What was the first national holiday in the U.S.?

17-83   Where would you find a brief discussion of the major historical events in Hawaii prior to the annexation to the U.S.?

17-84   Who is Iphigenia, in Greek mythology? What is the plot of Euripides' play about Iphigenia? How do you pronounce Iphigenia?

17-85   How could you find out how to stuff and mount animals?

Section 17

Handbooks and Manuals

Answers #17/1-17/85

17-1 A: See ALA Glossary for definition of ready
reference. All of the sources studied so
far in the manual, including the bibliographical sources, are sources through
which factual questions can be answered
(i.e., who is the author of a specific book,
what is the meaning of a specific word,
etc.), and it depends therefore on how
easily the fact can be located in the source
as to whether it may truly be used as a
quick or ready-reference source. Some
of the sources--the college dictionaries, the
one-volume encyclopedias, the almanacs,
for example--because their scope is more
factual than in depth, because they are
more portable and therefore perhaps more
easily used, because their arrangement
tends towards the specific entry or because
they are so specifically indexed--seem to
lend themselves more to ready-reference
use.

17-2 A: See ALA Glossary on both. The ALA Glossary tends to define these terms similarly
--that is, a handbook as a manual, and a
manual as a handbook. The exact definition of a handbook is not really clear, and
it is somewhat arbitrary as to what sources are included within this type; some
sources seem to be called handbooks mainly because they do not fall into any other
category. In practice, the essential feature
of a handbook is that it is "handy," compact, concise, set up for reference use
rather than reading, usually with extensive
information within the limits of its scope,
usually concentrating more on basic,
known information than on that which is
constantly changing. A manual is generally
considered more in the how-to-do-it
realm, giving guidance, rules, instructions, etc. The terms are often used
interchangeably, especially in the titles
of publications.

17-3 A: Kane's is limited to "firsts"; while Guinness concerns itself with longest, shortest,
highest, lowest, biggest, smallest, etc.,
and in fact has comparatively few "firsts"
(more often referred to in Guinness as
"earliests"). Furthermore, Kane's is
limited to the United States; while Guinness
is worldwide. See title pages (neither
source is listed in Winchell).

17-4 A: Kane is arranged alphabetically by specific
item, with various indexes; years, days,
names, geographical. Guinness is
arranged on a classed basis--for example,

all items dealing with the natural world
brought together--with a specific subject
index.

17-5 A: Kane, main alphabetical arrangement under
Librarian (3rd ed., p. 342).

17-6 A: Guinness: indexed under "Island, remotest"
or in the section on "The Natural World,"
under Land--Islands.

17-7 A: Despite being a "first," you really have to
go to Guinness for this one. Kane lists
the first photograph taken in the United
States (3rd ed., p. 448, under Photograph,
taken...in the United States): 1839.
Guinness lists the first photograph taken
in the world, which was actually earlier,
1826 (6th ed., Bantam, p. 125, under
Photography, or indexed under Photograph,
earliest).

17-8 A: Kane: See the Preface for comments on
this. Some sources are occasionally listed, but as the preface states, these are
not necessarily the sources from which
the facts are obtained. Guinness: no
source cited, no comments made on sources or authority.

17-9 A: Kane, names index. Refers to Milk--malt-
ed milk, and when you look up Milk in the
main alphabetical list, you find that Horlick invented the first malted milk...

17-10 A: Not in Kane and no name index in
Guinness.

17-11 A: According to Guinness: Olav Bjaaland
(indexed under South Pole).

17-12 A: Guinness, indexed under boxing.

17-13 A: Kane is not up-dated very often: 2nd ed.,
1950; 3rd ed., 1964 (see verso of title
page). Guinness is up-dated more often
(again, see verso of title page), 5th
edition, 1966; 6th ed., 1968... Even so-
called "facts" do change as research
brings new information to light, and
"records," such as that of the youngest
boxer, change constantly. The kind of
facts included in Guinness are more subject to change than those in Kane.

17-14 A: Guinness (c1968), indexed under bridges,
indicates various possibilities, and here
you should immediately see the inherent
problem in this question and in others like

it: the longest bridge of what <u>type</u>. Possibilities are longest single span, longest suspension, steel arch, cantilever, etc. Guinness lists statistics for all these possibilities. It does not discuss the differences between the types.

Since new bridges are always being constructed, the possibility exists that this information is out-dated. More current sources likely to give this information would be the almanacs. World Almanac 1971 (indexed under bridges), for example, also lists by type, giving dates, lengths, etc. Like Guinness it does not discuss the difference between types. It would appear from both Guinness and World Almanac that probably what the average unsophisticated-about-bridges person means by "longest bridge" is longest single span, with the Verrazano-Narrows Bridge in New York holding the record as of 1970.

The New York Times Almanac 1971 gives similar information but adds a further element to the discussion by specifically listing "longest bridges" including the entire bridge span and the approach roads, with the honors going to the Lake Pontchartrain Causeway II in New Orleans, completed in 1969.

17-15 A: Since this is the type of information so commonly found in almanacs, and since there is always an element of datedness involved, it hardly seems worthwhile to even bother with the encyclopedias. However, there still remains the unresolved problem of the difference between the various types (single span, suspension, steel arch, cantilever, etc.) of bridges; finding the answer to this problem may be the real key to determining the correct answer to the question for some people, and the differences in types of bridge construction is one which is probably best answered from an encyclopedia.

17-16 A: Both are listed under BD: Literature (in Humanities). Brewer is listed as a handbook and Benet as a dictionary encyclopedia.

17-17 A: Brewer stresses phrases and terms (see "to put on the lugs," "as light as St. Luke's bird," p. 568, Cassell 1963 edition). But since phrases can be interpreted quite broadly, this includes many names of people (Lucy, St.; Lucy Stoner), places (Lud's Town, Ludgate, Lutetia), things (lunar month, lutestring), etc. It has many similarities to the information found in the slang and etymological dictionaries, and some similarities also to usage sources such as Fowler, Evans. Benet includes more names of writers, titles of books, etc. Brewer includes pronunciation.

17-18 A: Both are dictionary arrangements, very short entries on specific topics listed alphabetically with all cross-references

within the work itself and no separate index.

17-19 A: Possibly because of its title, or its dictionary arrangement, or the fact that the information given in its entries is sometimes rather lengthy. This is a good example of the difficulties in "classifying" or defining handbooks.

17-20 A: Benet. Under Optic, Oliver: gives real name (William Taylor Adams) and some information. Does not say see also, but the real name is given in small capital letters indicating an article also on Adams, and the article on Adams gives the name of the periodical he edited. It is therefore necessary to look under <u>all</u> possible entries for the fullest information. (Not in Brewer).

17-21 A: In Benet, which includes author, writers, etc. Not in Brewer.

17-22 A: Both Benet and Brewer indicate the name of the novel (<u>David Copperfield</u>) in which Uriah Heep appears, and both indicate the kind of generally unpleasant character he represents. Benet tends to relate this more specifically to the plot of the novel.

17-23 A: Both Benet and Brewer have entries; Benet under the name of the man (Linnaeus, Carolus) and Brewer only for his system (Linnaean system). The information given is sketchy, although it might be sufficient for your needs at the moment. For further discussion, you could go to a regular encyclopedia.

17-24 A: Brewer (dictionary of <u>phrase</u> and fable). Not in Benet; which does <u>not</u> attempt to include phrases in the same way as Brewer. This is an example of the somewhat confusing arrangement of Brewer; this phrase, to wear the willow, is not listed in strictly alphabetical order, under "to," or even under "wear," but rather "willow" (considered by Brewer as the key word in the phrase) along with some other phrases also dealing with willow. Brewer tends to group phrases under related key words. The typography does not make this too clear.

17-25 A: Benet had a major revision in 1965. This is not exactly up-to-the-minute revision, of course. There is not a lot of stress on recent material, although it is included (there <u>is</u> a reference for James Bond, and for Ian Fleming, in Benet), probably on the theory that the modern reader will not need an explanation of James Bond as much as he will need one of Oliver Optic. Brewer, although also revised from time to time (most recent, 1963), seems to stress modern items even less than Benet. Brewer ignores James Bond.

17-26 A: Both have entries directly under "Nine." Brewer is much more extensive, explains the reason for the mystical significance of nine, includes phrases using the number, explains what the nine points of the law are. Both list many examples of the appearance of the number nine in literature and myth. The Benet account appears to have been taken almost verbatim from Brewer, with some of Brewer left out. See preface to Benet on its relation to Brewer and other such handbooks.

17-27 A: See Benet and/or Brewer (entries are almost word for word the same).

17-28 A: Neither are limited only to literary information (see #17-23 on Linnaeus), although Benet in particular does heavily stress the literary. They aim to provide a handy source of information on names, words, phrases, allusions of all kinds which the general reader may come across. The information is extensive in coverage, but limited in depth.

17-29 A: Bartlett is arranged by author, chronologically. Stevenson is arranged by subject, alphabetically. Both have an index by authors alphabetically, and an index of key words alphabetically.

17-30 A: For Bartlett, it is necessary to check in the key word index and then follow up the reference to the page on which the quote appears. For Stevenson, you could either check the key word index as in Bartlett, or you could look in the alphabetical table of contents for the broad topic of Pen, then Pen and Sword and turn to the page to which that refers you. Both cite Bulwer-Lytton as the author and give the title, act, and scene of the play in which it appears. Bartlett further gives the date of the play, and the author's full name and dates are also given on the same page as the quote. In Stevenson it is necessary to refer to the alphabetical author list.

17-31 A: No, it should be indexed under all important key words (pen, sword, probably mightier). The point is to have as many accesses as possible in case you have the sense but not the correct words, also to provide, in Bartlett's, a subject access under both pen and sword.

17-32 A: To use Bartlett for this, you have to look in the index under "America," perhaps also "American," then check out each reference (or those that seem suitable); a tedious and time-consuming process, and besides this only gives you access to those quotations or phrases which specifically refer to America. In Stevenson, you can refer directly to the subject of America-- foreign opinion (see Table of Contents) where many quotes on this subject are grouped together.

17-33 A: It is limited in terms of current material (latest quote is dated 1931) and international scope (mostly Englishmen and Americans are quoted).

17-34 A: No. Edmund Burke is listed in the Table of Contents of Stevenson (as are other writers) as a subject entry. The list of quotations referred to are about Burke, not by him.

17-35 A: To use Stevenson for this, you would turn to the sections on "Sea" and on "Ships," and then look through several pages of quotes in each to see if something by Masefield is listed which strikes the right chord in your memory. To use Bartlett, you could turn directly to the section of quotes from Masefield (probably turning first to the author index to find out where Masefield is located in the chronological list.

17-36 A: This is not too clear from either the Table of Contents or the introductory material, and the Winchell annotation is not much help either. If you just root around in the book itself, you find that quotations from the Bible (and from a few other religious sources) are listed at the beginning, following a few items from Ancient Egypt. Anonymous listings, including some nursery rhymes, are put at the end of the author section. For the problem of proverbs, it is not at all clear. Many proverbs of course can be attributed somehow to some author, and thus in Bartlett' they would appear under that author rather than anonymously. If you check out "a stitch in time saves nine," through the index, you find that it is listed, unattributed, in a footnote under quotes from Persius, along with the quotation about necessity being the mother of invention. (If you look under the quotes from Petronius you discover that "one good turn deserves another," which would seem to be a good candidate for an anonymous proverb, is in fact attributable to Petronius.) There is almost as much information in the footnotes of Bartlett as there is in the main body of the source; the footnotes are indexed, however.

17-37 A: See Winchell, 8th ed., p. 244-5. (Indexed under "Proverbs, collections.")

17-38 A: Since the authors in Bartlett are arranged chronologically (by birth), you can check toward the end of the list to see what younger people are included. (It should not be assumed that all the additions to the 14th, 1968, edition will be added onto the end of the chronological list, however.) Yevtushenko, Martin Luther King, Jack Kerouac, James Baldwin, Allen Ginsberg, J.D. Salinger, etc., are included. Starting with the year 1900 (p. 1046 of the 14th edition) as an arbitrary indication of what twentieth century people are included, you start right out with Louis Armstrong and Humphrey Bogart.

Since Stevenson has no chronological list of authors, you cannot check it in the same way, but of course you can check individual authors' names (Ginsberg, Salinger, Kerouac, etc.) in the alphabetical author list.

17-39 A: The usefulness of the arrangement depends on the question. The problem is similar to that of the dictionary of synonyms vs. the thesaurus of synonyms (or of slang words). Stevenson brings together in one place all the quotes on one subject, and if you have a problem with essentially a subject approach (foreign opinion of America) then Stevenson, or other quotation books arranged on a similar pattern, are probably most helpful. For an author approach (Masefield), Bartlett is most helpful. For checking on the source of a specific quotation (the pen is mightier than the sword), either one will do; the only problem is to find a quotation book which includes the quotation you are looking for.

17-40 A: See ALA Glossary and/or any dictionary. The comments in Stevenson are also helpful. A concordance is essentially a word index, and it is usually done for the works of one author (or for the Bible). It lists all words or all significant words in that author's work, giving references to their specific appearance. It can be used as a source for locating specific citations for quotations if the author is known.

17-41 A: Check a concordance of Shakespeare's works if one is available, since a concordance would presumably give you access to all appearances of any key word and would therefore be much broader. See Winchell (index under Shakespeare, concordances), 8th ed., p. 272; two concordances of Shakespeare are listed, one by Bartlett, one by Stevenson...

17-42 A: Bartlett in 1855 and Stevenson in 1934 (see Winchell annotations).

17-43 A: Like Stevenson.

17-44 A: Evans: see under subject of Men and Women. (Indexed under "women," or under author's name). Taken from New York Times.

17-45 A: It seems to be somewhat more selective in choice of quotations, and is probably generally more modern. The topics under which quotes are arranged are often quite different than the Stevenson choice, and often more specific (stiff upper lip, Pickwickian, ozymandias, no soap, etc.). Evans also has comments on many of the quotations included (see under Ammunition, Muffet, etc.). In general, the Evans book

has a certain charm of its own, not unlike that of his Dictionary of Contemporary American Usage.

17-46 A: No. The quotation from Humphrey Bogart (#17-38) in Bartlett was from a movie. The quotation from Françoise Sagan (#17-44) in Evans was from the New York Times.

17-47 A: Any of the dictionary sources which used quotes as examples, especially the Oxford English Dictionary.

17-48 A: A source giving reasonably full coverage of news events of that year (1969): for example, the 1969 New York Times Index, or an encyclopedia yearbook (i.e., frontispiece of the Collier's yearbook for 1970 covering 1969 is a footprint on the moon with the quotation given but no author noted.)

17-49 A: The American Book of Days; a compendium of information about holidays, festivals, notable anniversaries and Christian and Jewish holy days with notes on other American anniversaries worthy of remembrance.

17-50 A: By day of the month (e.g., January 26, January 27, January 28, etc.) with a subject index.

17-51 A: Douglas: look first in index under St. David's Day for reference to page number, where you find that it falls on the first of March. The article discusses various celebrations and gives historical and legendary information about St. David.

17-52 A: No, it includes much historical and biographical material as well as folklore and custom. See the preface, but better yet see the Contents: first flag of Washington's Army, Millard Fillmore's birthday, first balloon ascension, etc.

17-53 A: Philippine Independence. American Book of Days, under July 4.

17-54 A: Only by going through the Contents or the index and choosing those which seem to be appropriate, which would be a very inadequate approach.

17-55 A: The first part of Hazeltine is arranged as is Douglas, by day of the month. The second part is a bibliographical source, a list of books about holidays divided into several broad categories. There is a classified index and a general index. The entries in Hazeltine are not as full as in Douglas, but Hazeltine cites sources and further readings, and is generally more international in scope.

17-56 A: Check Hazeltine, under March 1st; several numbers are listed which are reference numbers to the bibliography in the second half of the book.

17-57 A: Hazeltine, classified index, under Librarians, etc.

17-58 A: It is quite out of date by now, as it was published in 1944. The holidays and most of the information about them are not likely to change, but the bibliographic sources are now very old.

17-59 A: CF: Folklore and popular customs, specifically Holidays.

17-60 A: DA: History and Area Studies--General.

17-61 A: Strictly by year, chronologically, with items divided into 6 major classifications per double page. The object is to show the general reader what was going on in a given age in various parts of the world in different fields of activity (see Foreword and Preface).

17-62 A: Emancipation of the serfs in Russia, Wagner's opera Tannhäuser was produced in Paris, and Hans Christian Andersen's Fairy Tales was published.

17-63 A: No. Steinberg gives only the bare facts, no descriptions, discussions, explanations.

17-64 A: No, only if you already happen to know the date of the fall of the Byzantine Empire. The only access in Steinberg is by date. There is no index.

17-65 A: Chronologically also--by general period (i.e., Prehistoric, ancient, etc.), but within that overall period, broken down geographically (i.e., Paleolithic period--Europe, Africa, Asia, etc.). There is a specific index, and you can find Byzantine Empire, collapse of, with references to page numbers (not dates) on which you can find the fall of Constantinople in 1204 and, eventually, the end of the Byzantine Empire in 1453. (And you can then refer back to Steinberg under 1453 and find out that in 1453, Gutenberg and Fust were printing the Mazarin Bible.)

17-66 A: Yes, index under Cavour (Italian statesman), references to several pages which discuss (although briefly) his activity in the unification of Italy.

17-67 A: Langer: The World Since 1939--Europe--Czechoslovakia (or index under Masaryk).

17-68 A: This is an example of a date book with an alphabetical arrangement, similar to a dictionary or encyclopedia. This is a handbook of miscellaneous information with the stress on events, on dates.

17-69 A: Yes, perhaps more easily than in Langer, since you only have to read one short article in Everyman's, instead of skipping through several references and cross-references as in Langer.

17-70 A: In Everyman's under Libraries, modern. Libraries as such not indexed in Langer, although a few specific ones are, but the information is very scattered and therefore more difficult to find.

17-71 A: Hazeltine has a discussion of the problem in the bibliographic section, under "Time and the Calendar" plus many other references. Douglas' American Book of Days has a brief discussion under "Calendar" in the Appendices. Any general encyclopedia also should have information. Brief mention in Everyman's in introductory matter under Calendars.

17-72 A: Quotation book with subject arrangement--i.e., Stevenson's or Evans'.

17-73 A: Robert's Rules of Order, indexed under Point of Order.

17-74 A: Douglas' American Book of Days, or Hazeltine. Also a mention in Brewer in entry for "Guy."

17-75 A: Benet's Reader's Encyclopedia, under Magic Mountain, The.

17-76 A: Guinness, under Weather (indexed under weather and rain).

17-77 A: Bartlett's Familiar Quotations, key word index under twinkle.

17-78 A: Emily Post for unofficial guidelines; there is no official government policy. (Part II: Protocol in official circles).

17-79 A: Hazeltine has a whole section on Movable Feasts (between March and April in the calendar section), also indexed under Movable Feasts. Nothing in Douglas. Brewer under Feast.

17-80 A: Brewer, listed under cat.

17-81 A: Encyclopedia of Sports. (Contents or index under rugby).

17-82 A: Kane's Famous First Facts (under Holiday).

17-83 A: Langer's Encyclopedia of World History, check index under Hawaii and follow up references. Section on Hawaii, 1778-1919 would give you what you want. You need some discussion of events, so a simple date book would not be sufficient.

17-84 A: Brewer's Dictionary of Phrase and Fable. Also in Benet. Pronunciation in Brewer only.

17-85 A: Check How-to-Do-It Books for a manual on the subject (under taxidermy).

Section 18

Directories

Questions #18/1-18/55

18-1   Where would you look, in the sources you have already examined, to find out what the Royal Society (of Great Britain) is or does? Where would you look to find out what its current address is?

        The next set of sources deal with information about organizations of all kinds including those not so well known as to be included in the encyclopedias.   These titles also represent a specific type of source: directories.

                    Encyclopedia of Associations (2AC1, AC28)
                    Foundations Directory (2AC2)
                    Research Centers Directory (2AC3, 1AC5, 1AC6)
                    Yearbook of International Organizations (CJ143)
                    Klein: Guide to American Directories (CH98)

18-2   What is the definition of a directory?

18-3   In other words, a directory is simply a list of names and addresses, such as a telephone directory. It may in addition give other, fuller information.   A directory can be a list of either people or organizations (or both); directories of people will be dealt with specifically in the next section, on biographical sources. The directories examined here are concerned with organizations.
        What is an organization? What other words are often used to express the same idea? Where are most of the directories on your list classified in Winchell?

18-4   In which of the sources you have previously examined would you expect to find directory information about organizations or associations?

18-5   The first title to examine is the Encyclopedia of Associations published by the Gale Research Company. This source starts right out to confuse the issue by calling itself an encyclopedia instead of a directory, but in size alone it does appear to be quite encyclopedic.   How many volumes are there for this source, and how is it arranged?

18-6   Does the Encyclopedia of Associations attempt to define the term organization or association, as used in its titles and included in its scope?

18-7   Which of the following organizations would you expect to find in the Encyclopedia of Associations: Alcoholics Anonymous, Republican Party, Civil Air Patrol, Peace Corps, Television Information Office, American Library Association, R.R. Bowker Company, American Booksellers Association, American Legion, Elks Club, American Council of Learned Societies, Weathermen?

18-8   Is there an organization for people who own or are interested in Model T Fords?

18-9   Who is the president of the Amalgamated Flying Saucer Clubs of America?

18-10   Where are most of the associations and organizations listed in the Gale publication located?

18-11   Does a source such as the Encyclopedia of Associations need to be revised and brought up-to-date frequently? How is this accomplished with this particular source?

18-12   Does the title of vol. 3--New Associations and Projects--reflect any change in the scope of the source?

18-13   How is the up-dating service arranged? To check for an organization is it necessary to check each issue?

18-14   When was Zero Population Growth founded?

18-15   How would you go about getting names and information for all of the various ecology action groups now working to save us from ourselves?

18-16   What are the names and addresses of some organizations from which you can get information on mental telepathy, clairvoyance, ESP, and other psychic phenomena?

18-17   Organizations and associations are excellent sources for current and highly specialized information. Why is it important for a reference librarian to realize this?

18-18   Another useful thing for librarians to remember about organizations and associations is that they publish material--lots of useful, cheap, frequently free materials which will not necessarily appear in the bibliographic sources. Can the Encyclopedia of Associations be any help in a bibliographic way? Can you find through this source what publications, if any, are put out by the Wilderness Society?

18-19   What is the headquarters' address of the National Association for Gifted Children? What does the organization do?

18-20   How would you find out if there is a chapter or branch of the National Association for Gifted Children in your city?

18-21   Where are the headquarters of the AAAS located?

18-22   The Encyclopedia of Associations does appear to index some acronyms although not abbreviations. What is the object of the group which calls itself NOSE?

18-23   The next directory is an example of one which is somewhat more specialized: The Foundation Directory. What is the scope of this publication? How is a foundation defined, for inclusion in this source? Does this differ much from a dictionary definition?

18-24   The introduction to the third edition of the Foundation Directory states that at least 18,000 foundations are presently active in the United States; yet less than half of these are listed in the directory. What is another limiting factor?

18-25   How is the Foundation Directory arranged? What is the purpose and what are the general assets of the Joseph P. Kennedy, Jr., Foundation?

18-26   Can you find through this source what foundations exist to aid conservation activities?

18-27   Where can you find some comparative figures showing major fields in which foundation grants were given in the 1960's--for example, how much foundation money went to welfare aid as compared to international activities?

18-28   Another directory published by the Gale Research Company is the next one on your list, titled Research Centers Directory. How does this differ in scope from the Encyclopedia of Associations?

18-29   How is the Research Centers Directory arranged?

18-30   What areas of research are presently being carried on at the Biomedical Information Service Center of Wayne State University? Are the results published anywhere?

18-31   What further sources of information on psychical research (ESP, etc.) can you find through the Research Centers Directory?

18-32   Encyclopedia of Associations includes basically only organizations of the United States. The next source is titled Yearbook of International Organizations. Would this source list political organizations in France, for example?

18-33   What kinds of organizations are included?

18-34   What international organizations are there in the field of bibliography?

18-35   What publications are put out by the International Federation for Documentation?

18-36   Does an organization exist to study and determine standards on a world-wide basis for various kinds of instruments used for measuring?

18-37   The last title on the list is essentially a bibliographical source for directories. What is the full title of Klein's Guide to American Directories? Does it have any limitations in scope?

18-38   Besides providing a list of directories for librarians, does Klein's Guide to American Directories have any other purpose?

18-39   Can you find a list of manufacturers in the state of Nebraska?

18-40   Is there an international directory of libraries?

18-41   What does Klein list under the heading "bibliography"?

The following questions are REVIEW questions for directories, and all the sources previously covered in Part II of the manual.

18-42   Is sousaphone a word of American origin?

18-43   Which language has the shortest alphabet?

18-44   Antonio Palau y Dulcet is a Spanish bibliographer whose famous Manual del Librero Hispano-Americano (Winchell AA688) is one of the most comprehensive lists of material published in Spain and Spanish America.   When and where was he born?

18-45   Where does the phrase "mad as a hatter" come from?

18-46   Where could you find a map of New York City?

18-47   Where can you find the pronunciation of the word "pusillanimous" given in the International Phonetic Alphabet?

18-48   How many different kinds of dog clubs are there in the United States?

18-49   Where would you find information about the ceremony, participants, etc., perhaps with illustrations, of the Investiture of the Prince of Wales, in Great Britain, in 1969?

18-50   Who won the Cy Young Award in 1965? What is the award for?

18-51   What is the address of the Keep Britain Tidy Group?

18-52   What is the density of the population in Pakistan?

18-53   Where would you find some general but current information about the New Hebrides--how big it is, how many people live there, what kind of educational system it has, what kind of commerce it has, if any, etc. ?

18-54   Who is the chairman of the Presidential task force on low-income housing, and what will it do?

18-55   Where would you look to find out where you could take your air conditioner to get it repaired?

Section 18

Directories

Answers #18/1-18/55

18-1 A: An organization as venerable as the Royal Society should be included in an encyclopedia (see Britannica, for example). For the current address, check an almanac (Whitaker's, for example).

18-2 A: See ALA Glossary. Also see any dictionary, but the ALA Glossary comes closest to a clear explanation of a directory as a specific type of reference source.

18-3 A: Any dictionary to define organization. A dictionary or synonym book would give other possible words, such as association, society, group. Winchell lists most general directories under AC: Societies.

18-4 A: All of the sources may have some information on organizations or associations. The dictionary and supplementary language sources may have information in the sense that they may define or identify a particular group, and the abbreviations dictionaries are particularly useful in this way. But information would not be extensive. Encyclopedias may give background, purpose, scope, history, etc., for some of the major associations and groups, but would not be likely go give specific directory-type information such as addresses, officers, etc. In the yearbook sources for current information you can often find a lot of directory information on organizations; the almanacs all have special lists of names and addresses; the Statesman's Year-Book is a further source of current information for groups in specific countries. News summaries will of course give information on groups which are active, in the news, or so new they do not yet appear in the more standard sources.

18-5 A: 6th edition, 1970 has 3 volumes. 1st volume called National Organizations of the United States, organizations are arranged under broad subject headings, with an alphabetical index of names of organizations and more specific subject headings; 2nd volume is a geographical and executive (persons) index; 3rd volume is a loose-leaf binder for the up-dating service, called New Associations and Projects.

18-6 A: The introduction says it includes nonprofit American membership organizations of national scope. Also some foreign organizations and some non-membership organizations if significant. The terms organization or association are not really defined. Many groups are included in the Encyclopedia of Associations which one might not expect to

find there. See the quotation from Alexis De Tocqueville at the head of the Contents page.

18-7 A: All are there except R.R. Bowker Company, which is a commercial firm (e.g., not non-profit). The Republican Party is represented by the Republican National Committee, the Peace Corps by the Peace Corps National Advisory Committee.

18-8 A: Yes. Model T Ford Club International, listed in Section 13 (Hobby and Avocational Organizations), alphabetically under automobile. Also indexed under Model T, and under Ford.

18-9 A: Encyclopedia of Associations vol. 1, (indexed under Amalgamated, etc.).

18-10 A: Volume 2, see statistical summary of geographical index, preceding the geographic index itself.

18-11 A: Organizations die and proliferate like people, and even those which continue on change officers, addresses, etc. Any directory of organizations is soon out-dated. The Encyclopedia of Associations is kept up to date by a quarterly supplement (see vol. 3, binder) called New Associations and Projects.

18-12 A: Yes, see introduction to March 1970 issue.

18-13 A: Alphabetically by name of organization, rather than broad subject groupings, but with an index of names of organizations and keywords. The index cumulates in each issue, so you only need to check the latest for specific organization names.

18-14 A: Vol. 3 (March 1970 issue).

18-15 A: Check the keyword subject index. Vol. 1 has only a few under ecology but lots under conservation (such as Save the Redwoods) which have similar purposes. Vol. 3 has, also mostly under conservation, a lot more, which is to be expected as many such groups have evolved in the past year or so.

18-16 A: Key is to find the proper keyword. These organizations are classified under Section 4, Science and Technology, and indexed under "psychical." Once you get to the right group of organizations, there are some marvelous sources: see especially the Association for Research and Enlightenment, which has a library, loans material, does indexing, publishes information, etc. Also see Haunt Hunters, which is a clearing house for such information.

18-17 A: Reference librarians need not stop the search for information or knowledge only with the materials in their own library. Librarians, library users or researchers can be referred to other more complete sources of information.

18-18 A: Yes, main entries for each organization list publications (often briefly) if applicable.

18-19 A: Indexed under National Association for Gifted Children, and under gifted children. Refers to main entry which gives address, and tells purpose of organization.

18-20 A: Check your local telephone directory. (Encyclopedia of Associations does not necessarily list local chapters.)

18-21 A: Problem is to find what AAAS stands for, as Encyclopedia of Associations does not index abbreviations. Go to Acronym and Initialisms Dictionary (also published by Gale) or De Sola Dictionary of Abbreviations from Section 13. Each lists three possibilities, two of which are also found in the Encyclopedia of Association.

18-22 A: Vol. 3, December 1970 issue. Reference is made to a larger group, the Student Legal Action Organizations, for full information. The various groups listed under this Organization are excellent examples of acronyms.

18-23 A: See preface of Foundation Directory for scope of the source. Specifies non-governmental and non-profit. Dictionary definitions are not necessarily this limiting.

18-24 A: Money; they must have assets of $200,000 or more to be included.

18-25 A: Arranged geographically, by state, with specific name index. Index under Kennedy (Joseph P.), Jr. Foundation, gives page reference.

18-26 A: Yes, see fields of interest index.

18-27 A: See Introduction to Foundation Directory (p. 36-44 of 3rd edition).

18-28 A: See Introduction, under "Types of Research Units Listed."

18-29 A: Similarly to Encyclopedia of Associations, under broad subject groupings, with alphabetical indexes for keyword subjects, names of the centers, names of people, and in addition names of the parent institutions.

18-30 A: Research Centers Directory, Research Centers index under Biomedical.

18-31 A: Keyword subject index under Parapsychology (cross-reference from psychical). Four centers listed, three of which are also listed in the Encyclopedia of Associations.

18-32 A: It is international in scope in the sense that it lists organizations whose aims or activities are international in character, not international in the sense that it includes all organizations from all countries.

18-33 A: See introductory matter, p. 11 of 1968/69 editions: "What kind of organizations are included."

18-34 A: See entry for bibliography in main dictionary alphabetical list. (Subject cross-references are interfiled with names of the organizations.) Some organizations listed, also a reference to numbers in the classified list.

18-35 A: Yearbook of International Organizations, main alphabetical list under name of organization (International Federation for Documentation).

18-36 A: Here you really have to know the word for measuring instruments: metrology, which is the subject keyword used in the main alphabetical list to refer you to the International Organization of Legal Metrology.

18-37 A: Guide to American Directories; a guide to the major business directories of the United States, covering all industrial, professional, and mercantile categories. Limitations: American or U.S.; business.

18-38 A: See Preface, "designed to aid each type of business and industry in locating new markets..."

18-39 A: Klein's Guide to American Directories will give you the name of a source which contains such a list: see sections on Manufacturers, geographical arrangement, under Nebraska.

18-40 A: See Winchell. See also Klein: Guide to American Directories, under Libraries, look for one which fits this description. The International Library Directory as listed is published in London, therefore one which you would not expect to find in Klein according to its stated scope.

18-41 A: A really strange collection of things, most of which hardly seem to fall under the definition of "directory," which shows that one should take all definitions and all sources with a grain of salt.

18-42 A: Mathews' Dictionary of Americanisms.

18-43 A: Guinness World Records (Under The Arts --Language--Alphabet).

18-44 A: Born 1867 in Montblanch according to Espasa (Spanish encyclopedia--AD68), under Palau y Dulcet, Antonio.

18-45 A: Not from Alice in Wonderland. See Brewer, 1965, p. 573, under "mad." This may sound like a quotation book problem, and actually it is in Evans although not in Bartlett.

18-46 A: Encyclopedias are a good source for this type of thing--see Americana.

18-47 A: NBC Handbook of Pronunciation (see #13-65).

18-48 A: Encyclopedia of Associations, Section 13 (Hobby and Avocational Organizations) under Dogs. Or index under "dogs" as keyword.

18-49 A: Encyclopedia yearbooks, news surveys, possibly almanacs. See the Annual Register, for example.

18-50 A: Almanacs. See World Almanac, indexed under Cy Young award.

18-51 A: Encyclopedia of Associations is U.S. only. Whitaker's Almanack, under Societies and Institutions, lists it.

18-52 A: Statistical Yearbook of the United Nations.

18-53 A: Statesman's Year-Book.

18-54 A: Encyclopedia of Associations, vol. 3 (New Associations and Projects).

18-55 A: Yellow pages of your local telephone directory.

Section 19

Biographical Sources: Universal

Questions #19/1-19/68

19-1   What is a "biography?"

19-2   Biographical reference sources do not necessarily present entire "lives" of individuals but may be limited only to some very essential facts. What kinds of questions or problems may be considered as "biographical" in nature?

19-3   What sources have you examined so far which give you biographical information?

In other words, all reference/information sources are potentially useful for biographical information. The next set of sources to examine deal specifically with biographical material:

    Webster's Biographical Dictionary (AJ25)
    Chambers's Biographical Dictionary (AJ14)
    Lippincott's Biographical Dictionary (AJ23)
    New Century Cyclopedia of Names (AJ19)

    International Who's Who (AJ29)
    Current Biography (AJ28)

    Biography Index (AJ2)

19-4   The first title on the list is Webster's Biographical Dictionary. Who is the publisher and what else have they published that you are familiar with?

19-5   What was one of the chief differences between Webster's Third unabridged dictionary and Webster's second, regarding biographical information?

19-6   Is there anything in the title which might tell you how the source is arranged? Is this in fact the arrangement?

19-7   Can you find out, through Webster's Biographical Dictionary, what Marie Antoinette's full name was and how she died?

19-8   One of the complaints made about Webster's Third was that it doesn't even tell who Jesus Christ was. Does the Webster's Biographical Dictionary? What about Buddha?

19-9   Can you find out, through Webster's Biographical Dictionary, who was nicknamed or known as the "Old Pretender"?

19-10   Can you find out, through Webster's Biographical Dictionary, who invented the chronometer?

19-11   Can you find out anything about Guy Fawkes Day through Webster's Biographical Dictionary?

19-12   Does Webster's Biographical Dictionary include George Washington? Lyndon Johnson? Richard Nixon? John F. Kennedy? Robert Kennedy? Ted (Edward) Kennedy?

19-13   Do the entries in Webster's Biographical Dictionary give bibliographical references, or cite further sources? Are the entries signed by the authors? What authority is given for the information?

19-14   What factors should be considered in determining the scope of a biographical source?

19-15   One of the major problems both in using and in compiling biographical sources is that of deciding who is or who should be included. In determining a "selection policy" (or exclusion policy, as the case may be), what possible factors may be considered?

19-16   What is the scope of Webster's Biographical Dictionary? Are the people included in it limited geographically? By chronological period? Does it include living people as well as those who have died?

19-17   Since Webster's includes only some 40,000 entries (see Preface), it must have some limitations, however. How did the editors decide who to include and who to leave out? What is their "selection policy"?

19-18   In selecting names from such a broad scope for such a comparatively limited list, it is usually considered most difficult to choose from the modern or contemporary names. Why is this?

19-19   Another biographical source similar in scope and arrangement to Webster is Chambers's Biographical Dictionary. The Preface to Chambers is particularly readable and to the point on the problem of selection, making clear that the real choice lies not so much with any objective criteria as with "who is most likely to be looked up."
         Compare the entries in Webster and Chambers on D. H. Lawrence. What are the differences, if any? Does the entry in Chambers appear to be entirely factual or does it offer any value judgements?

19-20   One of the differences in the entries on D. H. Lawrence is that Webster states that his wife Frieda was the sister of World War I flying ace Baron von Richthofen (repeated in the entry under Richthofen), and Chambers says she was his cousin. Where could you look to clear up this difficulty?

19-21   Does Chambers list Washington, Nixon, Johnson, John F. Kennedy, Robert Kennedy, Ted Kennedy?

19-22   What is Robert Dodsley known for? Is there a full-length biography about him?

19-23   Can you find out, through Chambers, who was known as the Old Pretender? Can you find out who invented the chronometer?

19-24   What would seem to be the major differences between Chambers and Webster, if any?

19-25   Do both Webster and Chambers note pronunciation?

19-26   In which of these sources would you find a list of the rulers of Great Britain?

19-27   How are Webster and Chambers kept up to date?

19-28   The third title on the list, Lippincott's Biographical Dictionary, is an old one, most recently revised in 1930 (5th edition), but it supplements the first two titles in a special way. What is the full title of this source, what does the title tell you about its scope and arrangement?

19-29   In which of the three sources so far examined--Webster, Chambers, and Lippincott--would you find: who Oceanus was? a portrait of Robert Louis Stevenson? some information about Martin Luther King?

19-30   Another source somewhat similar to Lippincott's Biographical Dictionary but rather more recently revised (1954) is the New Century Cyclopedia of Names. Using the Winchell annotation only, how does the scope of this work compare with that of Webster's and Chambers's? How does it compare with Lippincott's Biographical Dictionary?

19-31   Is the New Century Cyclopedia of Names connected with any source you have previously examined?

19-32   James McDougal Hart was a nineteenth-century landscape painter. What particular aspect of landscape painting was he noted for?

19-33   What is the origin of the use of the name "Gotham" in reference to New York City?

19-34   Sir Oliver Martext is a character in one of Shakespeare's plays, As you Like It. Would you expect to find information about him in any of the biographical sources you have examined so far? Would you expect to find information about him in any of the sources you have examined previous to this section?

19-35   Obviously, all four of the sources so far examined can be considered "retrospective" in scope. Do they also include "current" personalities? Do they attempt to exclude people who are still living?

19-36   The next source is the International Who's Who. Obviously, from the title, its scope is international, people from all countries. Equally obviously, there must be some limitations on this. Does the book give any indication of the limitations, or of the selection policy?

19-37   Does the International Who's Who include John F. Kennedy? Lyndon B. Johnson? Richard M. Nixon? Wouldn't John F. Kennedy be considered as known outside of his own country? What further limitation is set on inclusion of names. Is there anything in the title which might lead you to think this?

19-38   The International Who's Who then must be considered as a <u>current</u> biographical source, as compared to retrospective.   What information is given for those included in <u>International Who's Who</u>?   Where does the information come from?

19-39   What can you find about the educational background of General Nguyen Cao Ky?

19-40   What can you find about the educational background of John Lennon (Beatle)?   What are his leisure interests?

19-41   How often is International Who's Who issued, and how long has it been appearing?

19-42   Are older editions of International Who's Who of any reference value?

19-43   Adam Malik is the Foreign Minister of Indonesia.   Would you expect to find an entry for him in International Who's Who?   Would you expect the entry to give you any information on Malik's attitudes toward Sukarno, towards Communism, towards American policies in Indochina?

19-44   The next source on the list, Current Biography, is one which attempts to provide the kind of detailed and discursive biographical information not found in the brief factual entries of the sources you have examined so far.   Is there anything in the title of this source which further defines its scope?   What is the publication pattern of Current Biography (that is, how often does it appear)?   Who is the publisher?

19-45   What is the criteria for inclusion in Current Biography?   Are the people who are written up primarily in the entertainment field, or in government?   Are they limited to Americans?

19-46   What is the arrangement of Current Biography?   Can you find an article on Malik?

19-47   Who wrote the article on Malik?   What are the sources of information used?   Is there any way you can determine its authority?

19-48   The prefatory material in each monthly issue, "About this publication," states that these biographies are "objective rather than authorized biographies."   What does this mean?

19-49   Paul Ehrlich is the author of the best-selling <u>The Population Bomb</u> and advocate of close population controls.   How many children does he have?

19-50   Sir John Wolfenden was appointed Director and Principal Librarian of the British Museum early in 1969. What were his activities prior to this appointment?   What background if any does he have in librarianship or in education?   Where would you expect to find biographical material on Wolfenden?

19-51   Are the articles in Current Biography ever revised or up-dated?

19-52   Information on currently newsworthy people is not always easy to find, especially for those suddenly thrust into the public eye. Question #19-18 noted the problem of choosing from contemporary names for the universal but limited sources such as Webster's Biographical Dictionary, or even the encyclopedias. A source which gives only current coverage, such as International Who's Who, is of some help here, but the information is limited and the choice of names is perhaps even more limited, to those who have already proved themselves. Current Biography is an attempt to help fill in this gap, but even this extremely useful source is limited to some 300-400 names per year, and there is some delay in getting the material into print. What other sources can you turn to, then, for information on currently newsworthy names?

19-53   The last source is one which specifically guides you to these further sources of information: The Biography Index. Who is the publisher of this source? What is its publication pattern?

19-54   What is the scope of Biography Index? How does it differ from the Readers' Guide? Could you find biographical material through the Readers' Guide?

19-55   Biography Index indexes currently published magazines and books. Does this mean that only living persons, or persons of current interest will appear in this source? Would Biography Index list Martin Luther? Martin Luther King? Coretta King? John Lennon? Plato?

19-56   Can you find out, generally, through Biography Index, who Plato was?

19-57   The Current Biography article on Joe Namath was published in 1966, but he has been much in the news since then. What recent biographical material or magazine articles have appeared about him?

19-58   Is there any point in checking the Readers' Guide as well as Biography Index for material on Joe Namath?

19-59   What is the title of a recently published full-length biography of Senator Everett Dirksen?

19-60   Would Biography Index give you access to current studies of the work of Galileo?

19-61   If you were searching for a biography of Queen Victoria suitable for an elementary school student to read, would Biography Index be of any use to you?

19-62   Does Biography Index have any subject access at all? If you were doing research on the problem of modern museums, would Biography Index be of any use to you?

19-63   Biography Index includes a "Checklist of Composite Books Analyzed." What does this mean? Why is this list included?

19-64   The children's television program "Sesame Street" was first broadcast in the 1969/70 season. Where can you find information about its genesis, its staff, some of the studies done on it, etc.? Can you find this information through the biographical sources?

19-65   Where would you look to find out who is the U.S. ambassador to Indonesia?

19-66   Who invented the ice cream cone?

19-67   Of the biographical sources which you have examined so far, can you make any generalizations about the <u>arrangement</u> of the material, and about the access to the material? What information do you need before you can make use of them?

19-68   Of the biographical sources which you have examined so far, can you make any generalizations about the <u>scope</u>? Do you see any patterns forming in the way the scope of such sources can be limited? Do you see any relationships between the geographical and chronological coverage, and the selection policies for those names included? between the geographical and chronological coverage, and the amount of information given?

Section 19

Biographical Sources: Universal

Answers #19/1-19/68

19-1 A: See any dictionary.

19-2 A: Who is A? When was B born? Where was
          C born? What is D noted for? Where
          was E educated? Where does F live? and
          so on... Also, why did G do such-and-
          such? When did H do such-and-such? Also,
          who did such-and-such?

19-3 A: Dictionaries if they include names, either
          separately or interfiled (Webster's Third
          doesn't, Webster's Second does, etc.) En-
          cyclopedias, especially through the indexes;
          information may be in some depth for well-
          known people. Encyclopedia yearbooks, and
          news surveys, especially for people of very
          current interest. Almanacs to some extent;
          they include much information about specific
          people but which is not indexed under the
          specific name of the person--such as winners
          of the Nobel Prize. Handbooks, especially
          the curiosity and literary types. Quotation
          books and bibliographies can also be very
          useful sources of bibliographical information;
          it is possible that you might find people
          listed in these sources who do not appear
          elsewhere. Directories of organizations,
          especially if they have "names" indexes.

19-4 A: G. and C. Merriam Co.; publishers of
          Webster's Third International Dictionary,
          Webster's Dictionary of Synonyms.

19-5 A: Biographical information in Webster's Second
          was given in a special list called a Pronounc-
          ing Biographical Dictionary. No biographical
          information was given in Webster's Third at
          all unless it was indirectly through a name
          used as an adjective.

19-6 A: Dictionary, therefore possibly the arrange-
          ment would be a so-called dictionary type,
          all entries in one single alphabet.
          Yes, the source is arranged this way--all
          entries, including cross-references, in a
          single alphabet.

19-7 A: Yes, entry under Marie Antoinette.

19-8 A: Entries for both Jesus Christ (under Jesus
          with cross-reference from Christ) and
          Buddha. These are two of the longer
          entries in this source.

19-9 A: Yes, cross-reference from Old Pretender.

19-10 A: No; no subject entries or subject index.

19-11 A: Yes, it is mentioned in the entry for
          Fawkes, Guy.

19-12 A: Johnson, Nixon (entry had not been corrected
          to include him as President, however, in
          the c.1969 edition), Kennedy all listed, al-
          though information given is sparse. Robert
          Kennedy is listed within the entry for John
          F. Kennedy. Ted Kennedy is not included
          at all (c.1969). Washington is listed. How-
          ever, note the length of the entry for Wash-
          ington as compared to those for current
          presidents.

19-13 A: No bibliographical references are given; for
          authors, some of their works are cited, of
          course, but no bibliographic references or
          further sources for the subject of the entry
          are given. The entries are not signed. In-
          dication of authority, writers of the entries,
          sources consulted, etc., are given in the
          preface.

19-14 A: Two main factors: who is listed in it, and
          how much information is given.

19-15 A: Geographical (national, regional, etc.);
          Period (retrospective, current; another way
          of putting it, with biographical sources, is
          living or dead); "Subject"--i.e., occupation,
          profession; also perhaps race, sex, religion.

19-16 A: Universal or general scope. No limiting
          factors such as nationality, period, subject,
          etc. See Preface, first sentence. As is
          usually the case, however, American and
          British names are stressed.

19-17 A: See sub-title on title page: "noteworthy
          persons." The editors admit (see Preface)
          that the limited size of the source makes
          necessary a restriction in the names included,
          and they do not specifically state their cri-
          teria for inclusion other than experience
          (e.g., theirs), objectivity, and a list of
          sources referred to.

19-18 A: See Preface to Webster on this. The
          problem is similar to that of the encyclo-
          pedia yearbooks or news surveys--knowing
          at the moment what is likely to prove most
          noteworthy.

19-19 A: Both give dates, birth information, informa-
          tion on birth and marriage, and titles of
          some of his books. Chambers gives fuller
          biographical information on his life, plus

further references to biographies, studies, letters, etc. Chambers also gives some evaluative comments on his writing.

19-20 A: By checking in other sources. D.H. Lawrence and Baron Von Richthofen are both well enough known to be included in encyclopedias, and that might be sufficient, but probably a better source, if available, would be a full length biography of any of these three people: Chambers cites biographies for D.H. Lawrence, and for Richthofen in the entry for him. You could also check bibliographical sources with subject access.

19-21 A: Nixon and Johnson are both listed in the main list. The Addenda (following the Preface) of the revised 1968 edition brings their entries up-to-date to the presidential nominations in the summer of 1968, and adds an entry on Hubert Humphrey, who up to that time had apparently not been considered most likely to be looked up. John F. Kennedy is listed, and both Robert and Edward are noted in the entry for John. Information on all of these is fuller in Chambers than in Webster. Washington is listed.

19-22 A: Chambers, entry is Dodsley. Among other things, started the Annual Register. A biography (by Strauss) is cited--with the very briefest of biographical information-- in the Chambers entry.

19-23 A: Yes, both through index. Old Pretender listed under Nicknames and Personalities. Chronometer under Science and Industry.

19-24 A: Both are universal or general in scope, not limited geographically or by period. Webster has more entries (40,000) compared to Chambers (15,000). Chambers is published in Great Britain and might be considered therefore to stress British names. Chambers, with somewhat less entries, has also fuller entries, gives bibliographical notes; as the preface says, it attempts to be something more than a catalogue of facts. Chambers has a subject index, of sorts.

19-25 A: Webster makes a major point of doing this. Chambers does when it seems necessary.

19-26 A: Webster: see special tables at the back.

19-27 A: Webster in particular seems to practice a kind of continuous revision (see copyright dates on verso of title page); Chambers has periodically revised editions (1961, 1968, etc., also on verso of title page).

19-28 A: Universal Pronouncing Dictionary of Biography and Mythology. (Title page and Winchell). Arrangement is dictionary, all in one alphabet, like Webster and Chambers. Scope is universal, like Webster and Chambers. Scope also includes mythology,

unlike Webster and Chambers. Also puts great stress on pronunciation; Preface and Introduction is almost entirely devoted to this problem.

19-29 A: Oceanus is a god in classical mythology; therefore only in Lippincott. Neither Webster nor Chambers include any illustrations, but Lippincott does, therefore the portrait of Robert Louis Stevenson can only be found there.
     Only Webster or Chambers are recent enough to be likely to include Martin Luther King.

19-30 A: New Century Cyclopedia of Names expands the idea of "names" to its broadest scope--including names of places, of events, of works of art or literature or music. It includes biographical information, but it is not limited to biographical information, although it is limited in entries to names. Lippincott's is more limited, to biographical information but extending this idea to include names of people in mythology, that is people who never lived. Webster and Chambers are more limited yet, to actual people.

19-31 A: The Century Dictionary and Cyclopedia from Section 12 on dictionaries. See Winchell annotation.

19-32 A: Webster's Biographical Dictionary has an entry, lists landscape painting only. New Century Dictionary goes further and notes especially sheep and cattle.

19-33 A: New Century Dictionary of Names, entry under Gotham. Look also at following entry under Gotham, England, for significance of the reference.

19-34 A: New Century Dictionary of Names. Also in Readers' Encyclopedia.

19-35 A: All include current personalities and they do not attempt to exclude those who are still living. This is seen easily in Webster and Chambers, who include for example Washington (retrospective), Kennedy (current, but not living), Nixon (current and living). Lippincott and Century are less likely to include very current personalities simply because they are not so recently revised but they do not exclude current or living persons; this can be seen by glancing through the pages and finding many entries with only birth dates given.

19-36 A: Prefatory material indicates "attempts to include everyone whose name is known outside his own country."

19-37 A: Johnson and Nixon are included; Kennedy isn't. (Mrs. Kennedy, now Mrs. Onassis, is.) Further limitation is that persons included must be living. This is not stated in the source. The only clue you get is the title: who's who (who is who).

19-38 A: Full date and place of birth, parentage, mar-
           riage, children, education, publications,
           leisure interests, posts held, etc., and ad-
           dress, sometimes telephone number. All
           information not always given for each entry.
           See preface for methods of obtaining informa-
           tion; from subject himself through ques-
           tionnaires, otherwise from government of-
           fices and institutions, etc.

19-39 A: See entry for Ky in International Who's Who.

19-40 A: See his entry in International Who's Who.

19-41 A: Annually since 1935, according to the
           Winchell annotation.

19-42 A: Yes, for those persons who have died and
           have therefore been dropped from succeeding
           editions. See obituary list in each volume.

19-43 A: Yes, you would expect to find Malik, listed
           in International Who's Who, since he fits
           the criteria of being known outside of his
           own country. However, the entry will give
           you only the barest facts of his career and
           will not tell you anything about his attitudes,
           beliefs, policies, etc.

19-44 A: Current Biography--apparently some stress
           on current interest. In line with this, it
           appears in monthly issues, cumulating an-
           nually into the Current Biography Yearbook.
           Published by Wilson Company.

19-45 A: See "About this publication" in monthly
           issues: people who are prominent in the
           news, in all areas, internationally.
           Preface to annual volumes: living leaders
           in all fields of human accomplishment the
           world over.

19-46 A: Entries arranged alphabetically by name of
           the person discussed. Monthly and annual
           issues and annual volumes include a list of
           the names classified loosely by profession,
           also a necrology or list of obituary notices
           of those who have died since the last issue.
           There are cumulative name indexes in each
           monthly issue and each annual volume.
           The article on Malik is found in the 1970
           Yearbook volume. Check the index of the
           last issue and the index of the last bound
           volume.

19-47 A: Articles are not signed, and no writers' or
           compilers' names are given anywhere. The
           prefatory matter indicates that sources of
           information are newspapers, magazines,
           books, sometimes the biographee, and that
           careful researching is done. A list of
           further references is given at the end of
           each article.

19-48 A: That the articles have been written by
           someone other than the biographee, and
           that they have been written to be objective
           rather than to please the biographee.

19-49 A: Current Biography 1970 volume.

19-50 A: Possibly he would be in International Who's
           Who, but information would be sketchy. Be-
           cause of his sudden rise to prominence in
           the library world, you might expect an
           article on him in Current Biography, which
           there is, in the 1970 volume.

19-51 A: Minor changes, revisions, etc., are not
           necessarily made. Some older articles are
           superseded by new articles reflecting a
           major change in the biographee's situation.
           See the 1970 article on Shirley Temple
           Black, reflecting her current activities in
           politics and as a U.N. delegate, supersed-
           ing the 1945 article.

19-52 A: New York Times Index, for some informa-
           tion and further references on anyone in
           the news. Facts on File and Keesing's may
           be of some help. Readers' Guide and other
           periodical indexes may list useful references.
           Many of the references cited in the Current
           Biography articles are from periodicals and
           news magazines indexed in Readers' Guide.

19-53 A: Wilson Company. It appears quarterly and
           cumulates each year, then every three years.

19-54 A: See Prefatory Note in quarterly issues, or
           Winchell annotation. Biography Index lists
           or indexes biographical material appearing
           in periodicals, books, etc. The Readers'
           Guide indexes only periodicals; Biography
           Index indexes books as well, plus some
           periodicals not indexed in Readers' Guide.
           Biographical material could be located
           through the Readers' Guide, indexed under
           the name of the person as subject.

19-55 A: All persons, all times.

19-56 A: Yes, if you find an entry for him. See
           Sept. 1968-August 1969 volume. Entries
           given dates and brief identifying label (i.e.,
           Greek philosopher).

19-57 A: See Biography Index cumulations and issues
           since 1966.

19-58 A: Biography Index duplicates, for biographical
           material, what is in Readers' Guide. But
           Biography Index appears only quarterly, and
           Readers' Guide appears twice a month,
           thus Readers' Guide might give you more
           current access for periodicals, in addition
           to the broader scope of materials you would
           find indexed in Biography Index.

19-59 A: See Biography Index under Dirksen (February
           1971 issue, or cumulation which includes
           this). Separately-published biographies are
           listed, or indexed, in Biography Index.

19-60 A: Yes, see February 1971 issue.

19-61 A: Yes, juvenile literature is included and so

noted. See February 1971 issue, for example.

19-62 A: Biography Index has a kind of subject access in
its "index to profession and occupations." You
could, for example, check under "Museum
directors and curators" in each issue for
names of specific people, then check the
main index itself under these names for
articles or other biographical material about
them. The biographical material, if at all
extensive, would undoubtedly contribute something to your research.

19-63 A: These are books containing "composite" biographical material--that is, not limited only
to one person--which are analyzed or specifically indexed in Biography Index. For
example, Harold Schonberg's Lives of the
Great Composers (published by Norton in
1970) is indexed or analyzed in the February 1971 issue; that is, the book will be
cited, giving the pertinent pages, under the
names of each of the composers (Beethoven,
Bach, Mozart, Schumann, etc.) whose lives
it covers. These books are listed in the
Checklist so that libraries may use it as a
purchasing guide; it is pointless to have the
index if you do not have the books or periodicals in which the information is located.

19-64 A: The encyclopedia yearbooks for 1969 might
seem to be a good source for this information, but in fact they are not. Another
source might be through periodical indexes,
such as Readers' Guide, which would lead
you to periodical articles about the show.
Another approach, not so obvious, is the
biographical; the article on Joan Ganz
Cooney, executive director of the Children's
Television workshop, in Current Biography
(1970 volume) gives extensive background and
information on the show itself.

19-65 A: You have the title, but not the name. You
need the name to find it through the biographical sources. Statesman's Year-Book
under Indonesia, gives this information,
reasonably up-to-date.

19-66 A: Try Kane's Famous First Facts. Again,
you do not have the name; you have the
event, or the fact, so you have to work
from that approach.

19-67 A: Those sources which are specifically biographical in nature are, in general, always
arranged alphabetically by the name of the
person. They are nearly always in dictionary or directory form (Webster being
an example of a dictionary form; International Who's Who being an example of a
directory form). Current Biography, because
its entries go beyond brief dictionary length
into encyclopedic length articles, is perhaps
an exception here, but even this source is
arranged strictly alphabetically by name of
the person. Subject access is non-existent
in most of the sources and that which does
exist is very limited.

In general, then, the biographical sources
are best approached by specific name. It is
possible to find subject information in the
biographical sources, but sometimes this
is best done by using other approaches to
get the name, then using the biographical
sources for further information.

19-68 A: All of the biographical sources which you
have examined so far have been very broad
in scope; universal or general. The only
pattern which is forming so far is that of
specifically current material (International
Who's Who, living persons only; Current
Biography, people "prominent in the news")
as opposed to retrospective-and-current
(Webster's Biographical Dictionary, etc.).
The broader the scope is geographically and
chronologically, the more the choice of
persons included must be limited to the
well-known and very noteworthy. The
broader the scope is geographically and
chronologically, the less information you get
about each person included. These patterns
and relationships may not seem clear yet,
as you have examined only the more general
sources. Keep them in mind as you work
through the next section.

Section 20

Biographical Sources: National and Subject

Questions #20/1-20/83

The biographical sources which you examined in the previous section were all very broad in scope: general or universal. That is, they included persons from all places, all times. With such a broad basic scope, the principle limiting factor in these sources became a matter of the space available; therefore, limits are put on the number of and which names are chosen, the amount of information given about each name.

20-1   In this section, you will examine sources which are more limited in scope and therefore less limited in information. On what basis would you expect these more limited sources to be organized? Think in terms of the patterns of organization of other information/reference sources you have examined. Look in Winchell and see how the biographical sources are arranged, under what headings they are grouped.

The next set of sources to be examined are:

          Who's Who in America (AJ45)
          Who Was Who in America (AJ40)
          Who's Who (AJ155)
          Who was Who (AJ152)

          Dictionary of National Biography (AJ144)
          Concise Dictionary of National Biography (see AJ144)
          Dictionary of American Biography (AJ32)
          Concise Dictionary of American Biography (AJ33)
          National Cyclopaedia of American Biography (AJ34)

          American Men of Science (1EA34, 35, 2EA35, 2CA10)
          Who's Who in American Art (BE78)

          Slocum: Biographical Dictionaries and Related Works (2AJ1)

20-2   The major pattern which appeared in the biographical sources examined in the previous section was that some of the sources were limited specifically to current names: e.g., either people who are living (International Who's Who) or people prominent in the news (Current Biography). The first of the national sources to examine, Who's Who in America, fits into this pattern. What can you tell from the full title about its scope and arrangement?

20-3   Who publishes Who's Who in America? How often does it appear? How long has it been published?

20-4   Approximately how many names are there in the most recent edition of Who's Who in America? What percentage is this of the total population?

20-5   What are the criteria for inclusion in Who's Who in America? In other words, who or what do you have to be to get in?

20-6   What information is given in the entries? How is the information obtained?

20-7   Is the information given in Who's Who in America evaluative, or is it purely descriptive?

20-8   In theory, Who's Who in America lists only living persons. Is Robert Kennedy included? Martin Luther King? John F. Kennedy? Adlai Stevenson?

20-9   In Section 7, you found through the New York Times Index that Dr. N.E. Borloug won the 1970 Nobel Peace Prize. Is Dr. Borloug listed in Who's Who in America?

20-10   If by some remote chance you did not know that Mrs. Jacqueline Kennedy is now Mrs. Aristotle Onassis, could you still find her entry in Who's Who in America? What does the star following her entry mean?

20-11   Who's Who in America lists only a small percentage of the total population of the United States. Are there any similar sources which, by narrowing the scope, can provide access to a larger number of people?

20-12   Is there any usefulness in back volumes or outdated volumes of Who's Who in America?

20-13   Is there any way to get access to those names dropped because of death, other than through the earlier or outdated volumes?

20-14   How is the series of Who Was Who in America arranged?

20-15   If you were trying to locate the entry for Albert Schweitzer in Who Was Who in America, would you have to know the year in which he died in order to find it?

20-16   Who's Who in America goes back only to 1899. Is there coverage of this type prior to this date?

20-17   Do the Who Was Who volumes include only entries from the original Who's Who in America series?

20-18   The next title on the list is simply known as Who's Who, and properly it should have been considered prior to Who's Who in America, since it existed prior to the American source. Who's Who is the British counterpart to Who's Who in America. Who publishes Who's Who, and how long has it been appearing?

20-19   How does Who's Who compare to Who's Who in America in format and arrangement?

20-20   How do the two sources compare in scope? Does Who's Who include only Britishers? Are Lyndon Johnson and Richard Nixon listed in Who's Who? What is the criteria for inclusion in Who's Who? Is it similar to Who's Who in America?

20-21   What information is given in Who's Who?   Is it similar to that in Who's Who in America?

20-22   What does Who's Who tell you about John Lennon (Beatle)?   Is he listed in Who's Who in America?

20-23   Does Who's Who have retrospective volumes for the deceased, as does Who's Who in America?   What period is covered?   Is there an index to the volume?

20-24   Who is the present Chancellor of the Federal Republic of Germany (West)?   Where would you look to find a brief biographical sketch about him?

20-25   Where would you look to find a similar sketch or information about a minor public official of the Federal Republic of Germany?

20-26   So far you have examined current (who is who type) and retrospective (who was who type) sources for the United States and Great Britain.   Are there other retrospective biographical sources organized by country?   What other retrospective biographical sources exist for Great Britain?

20-27   The major retrospective biographical source for Great Britain is the Dictionary of National Biography. Although called a "dictionary" in the title, this source is really more of an encyclopedia.   What is its scope?

20-28   The Dictionary of National Biography was published in parts over a period of time, much like some of the bibliographical sources.   It was later reprinted.   The Winchell annotation may seem somewhat confusing, and the arrangement of the source itself is not always clear.   Mainly, it is important to remember that the scope excludes living persons (in other words, includes only those deceased) and that there are a number of supplementary volumes.   How many volumes are there to the set, and how is it arranged?

20-29   On what basis are names added to each of the chronological supplementary volumes to the DNB?

20-30   If you wanted to find the biographical article in the DNB on Sir Edward Charles Blount and you did not know in what year he died, would you have to go through all of the volumes?

20-31   Where was Sir Walter Scott born?

20-32   Who wrote the article on Sir Walter Scott (author of the Waverley Novels)?   Where would you look to find the qualifications of the author of the article?

20-33   Does the article on Sir Walter Scott give further sources or references?

20-34   What is the Concise Dictionary of National Biography?   How is related to the DNB itself?

20-35   Is there any subject access to the DNB? If you wanted information on the establishment of the Irish
         Free State, could you find it through the DNB?

20-36   The DNB is a British retrospective source. Would you expect to find a biographical article on John
         Hancock, signer of the American Declaration of Independence? George Washington? Benjamin Franklin?
         John Adams? Paul Revere? Daniel Boone? Thomas Paine? Anne Bradstreet (first New England poet)?
         John Eliot (translated Bible into an Indian language)?

20-37   When was the DNB first published? When were many of its articles written? What advantages and/or
         disadvantages does this give it as a biographical source?

20-38   An example of the way a contemporary account can be somewhat misleading is in the DNB article for
         Sir Leslie Stephen himself. The biographical article on Stephen in the DNB and the introductory article
         on Stephen as editor, in the first volume, both mention his two marriages and the fact that he had two
         sons, and that one of his sons was a scholar of Trinity College, Cambridge. Both articles were written
         in the very early 1900's. Neither mentions who his daughters were. One of his daughters is now in fact
         probably more well-known than her father. Where would you look to find who their daughter is?

20-39   A source similar in purpose to the Dictionary of National Biography is its American version, the Dic-
         tionary of American Biography. What is the basic arrangement of this set? How does the arrangement
         compare to the DNB?

20-40   Is there an abridged version of the Dictionary of American Biography as there is with the DNB?

20-41   How does the scope of the Dictionary of American Biography differ from or compare to that of the Dic-
         tionary of National Biography?

20-42   Former President Franklin D. Roosevelt is certainly a notable American, no longer living. Is he includ-
         ed in the Dictionary of American Biography?

20-43   Why not?

20-44   Would you expect to find articles in the Dictionary of American Biography for John Hancock? George
         Washington? Benjamin Franklin? John Adams? Paul Revere? Daniel Boone? Thomas Paine? Anne
         Bradstreet? John Eliot?

20-45   John Burgoyne, William Howe, and Henry Clinton were all generals of the British Army during the Amer-
         ican Revolution. Presumably therefore they would not be included in the Dictionary of American Biogra-
         phy (and they are not). Where would you look for biographical information on these men?

20-46   Thomas Hutchinson (born in Boston) was governor of the Massachusetts Bay Colony at the time of the
         Boston Tea Party and was loyal to the Crown during events preceding the Declaration of Independence.
         He was succeeded as governor by General Thomas Gage (born in England) who later became commander-
         in-chief, for a brief time, of the British forces in North America. Would you expect these men to be
         included in the Dictionary of American Biography? in the Dictionary of National Biography?

20-47   Who wrote the article on Hutchinson in the DAB?   Are bibliographical references given?

20-48   Is the biographical information given in the Dictionary of National Biography and the Dictionary of American Biography limited to factual, objective information, or is it evaluative as well?   Does this have any relationship to your ability to find out who wrote the articles?

20-49   How does the biographical information given in the DNB and the DAB compare with that given in the other retrospective sources you have examined, Who Was Who in America and Who Was Who?

20-50   In general, articles in the Dictionary of American Biography are thorough, scholarly, reliable, signed, with bibliographical references.   One limitation to the source, however, is that it covers really only the major names in American retrospective biography (nearly 15,000, according to the Preface of the Concise DAB).   What other retrospective sources for American biography are available?

20-51   How does the scope of the National Cyclopaedia of American Biography compare to the DAB, according to Winchell?

20-52   What is the arrangement of the National Cyclopaedia?   Look at the source itself, not at the Winchell annotation, and see if you can figure it out.

20-53   Anna P. Dinnies was an American poet, quite minor.   What can you find out about her through the National Cyclopaedia?

20-54   Does the index (indexes) to the National Cyclopaedia give you any access to the material other than by personal name?   If you were doing research on the history of printing in the United States, would the National Cyclopaedia be helpful to you?

20-55   Actually, the National Cyclopaedia is not so impossible to use as it may appear at first glance, but it is somewhat more complicated than the other biographical sources.   What is its primary use?

20-56   Is there a retrospective biographical source for Australians, which is scholarly, definitive, gives information in depth, and is reasonably recently published?

20-57   So far, you have seen that the biographical sources are organized, like bibliographical sources, on a national basis, current vs. retrospective.   For example, if you needed information on a contemporary Belgian scientist, where would you look?

20-58   In what further way can biographical sources be limited in scope, thus expanded in coverage?   If you didn't find the contemporary Belgian scientist in the who's who for Belgium type of source, how else could you approach the problem?

20-59   The next two sources on the list are examples of subject-limited biographical sources.   There are some subject lists which have a general or universal scope, but these two are examples which further fit into the pattern of division along national lines.
         The first of these, American Men of Science, is another multi-volumed source.   What is the basic

arrangement? Does this biographical source appear on an annual basis? How is it updated?

20-60   What information is given for each entry, and how is the information obtained?

20-61   What are the criteria for inclusion in American Men of Science? Is it limited to living persons only?

20-62   The next title is Who's Who in American Art. What does this title tell you about the source, without even looking at it? What can you guess about the arrangement and scope of the source, without looking at it? Would you expect to find and can you find information about Andrew Wyeth in this source, without bothering to read through the preface, introduction, check the Winchell annotation, etc.?

20-63   The data given on Wyeth in Who's Who in American Art is limited to bare facts. Where might you find an article discussing his life and activities?

20-64   Where are American Men of Science and Who's Who in American Art classified in Winchell?

20-65   What is the name of the professional biographical dictionary or directory for librarians?

20-66   Winchell has a section, AK, titled Genealogy, following the section on Biography. What is genealogy?

20-67   What bibliographic sources do you have thus far which will give you access to further biographic publications?

20-68   The last title on the list is another bibliographical source: Slocum's Biographical Dictionaries and Related Works. How is this source arranged? Does it give you access to biographical material about a specific person, such as you get through the Biography Index?

20-69   Can you find through Slocum a list of biographical sources which would be useful to you if you were doing research in the history of printing?

20-70   If you were searching for information on a person whom you knew to be a native of the New Hebrides Islands, could you find, through Slocum, a source which might help you?

20-71   Could you answer both of the previous questions through Winchell?

20-72   How would you deal with the following question: where was Robert Boyle born?

20-73   If you don't know anything and can't get a clue about Robert Boyle, what would your procedure be? Where would you start? Is there any relationship between the scope of the source and your likelihood of finding a particular name in it?

The following questions can be used as REVIEW for the biographical sources; keep all of the other previously examined sources in mind, however.

20-74   What is Marshall McLuhan's telephone number?

20-75   Where would you find a fairly lengthy and authoritative article on John Baskerville, an English printer and typefounder, which includes the comments of some of his contemporaries about him?

20-76   Who is the present governor of New Caledonia?

20-77   Becky Sharp appears in the novel Vanity Fair by Thackeray. Where would you look to find information about her?

20-78   How much does Dustin Hoffman pay per month for his New York apartment?

20-79   What factor led Henry Clay Folger to develop his book collecting interests? How did he make his money?

20-80   Who was the first governor of Illinois?

20-81   Where would you find information on the life of Captain Bligh of the H.M.S. Bounty?

20-82   What are the names of some people who are currently interested in the study of flying saucers or other unexplained aerial phenomenon?

20-83   Rootabaga Stories is the name of a book of tales for children. Who wrote it?

Section 20

Biographical Sources: National and Subject

Answers #20/1-20/83

20-1 A: Biographical sources tend to be organized on a <u>national</u> basis. Winchell lists first general and international works, then works for the United States, then works for other countries, arranged alphabetically by name of country.

This is very similar to the way <u>bibliographical</u> sources are organized. Just as complete universal bibliographical sources are difficult if not impossible to achieve, universal biographical sources tend to be very limited in information. Fuller coverage can be obtained on a national basis.

In a way, we can say that all reference sources are organized, broadly, on a national or geographical basis. Dictionaries, for example, are organized by language, which is similar to a national or geographical division. Most encyclopedias are general or universal in coverage, but they tend to stress material of the country or language in which they are published, therefore, we think of them as American, British, German, etc. It is really more correct to say that most reference sources are <u>published</u> on a national basis and therefore tend to have a geographical or language bias which makes them most useful from a national or geographical approach. However, the national biographical sources are more clearly <u>limited</u> in scope to national coverage.

20-2 A: Full title (see title page): Who's Who in America; with World Notables; a Biographical Dictionary of Notable Living Men and Women. Who is Who, therefore people who are still living--also noted in subtitle. In America but also includes "world notables," so scope is not limited to America but stresses America. Dictionary, therefore alphabetical arrangement, one list.

20-3 A: Publisher: Marquis-Who's Who, Inc, Chicago. Appears: biennially (every two years). Published since: 1899. (All information from title page, as well as Winchell annotation).

20-4 A: 1970/71 edition states in preface that approximately 64,000 names are listed. The table given on the verso of the title page states that an estimated 62,825 "full sketches" are included and that this represents 3.09 names per each 10,000 persons of the U.S. population (which isn't the same thing as percentage of the total population,

but does give you an idea of the relationship between the total population and the number of names in the source).

20-5 A: See "Standards for Admission" on page opposite title page. Many people are included automatically by virtue of their position; others are decided by a "judicious process" which is not entirely spelled out.

20-6 A: Information given is similar to that in International Who's Who: name, birth, parents, marriage, family, education, positions held, membership in organizations, publications, address. In general, information is obtained from the biographees themselves. Some data is gathered by the publisher if the biographee fails to furnish it. (See Preface.)

20-7 A: Purely descriptive, objective. To some people, of course, the inclusion of the listing itself is an evaluative comment.

20-8 A: John F. Kennedy and Adlai Stevenson are not listed; Robert Kennedy and Martin Luther King are listed in 1970/71, with date of death (1968) given. This is an indication that all deceased persons are not <u>immediately</u> dropped from the next revision.

20-9 A: 1970/71; yes. Nobel Peace Prize is not yet listed among his accomplishments, however.

20-10 A: Some cross-references are given in the main alphabetical list, including that from Kennedy, Jacqueline to Onassis. For the explanation of the star, see list of abbreviations, etc., in the prefatory matter.

20-11 A: Yes, with the organizational pattern still on a geographical basis. Winchell lists several regional who's who sources, published by Marquis and following the same format of the main source (see items AJ46, 47, 48, 49); Winchell also notes that state publications are available although not listed there.

20-12 A: Some names are dropped because of deaths and some names are dropped for reasons other than death (these reasons not being clearly stated); information on those persons would of course be available only in earlier editions. Some entries in current editions have had to be shortened for space considerations, and reference is made to earlier editions (see explanation of symbols in the Table of Abbreviations).

20-13 A: Names dropped because of death are found in Marquis' series called Who Was Who in America. See Winchell annotation under Who's Who in America, and next title on list.

20-14 A: There are (as of 1971) four volumes divided chronologically (i.e., 1897-1942, 1943-1950, etc.), which are compilations of the original sketches from Who's Who in America, 1899+. Each volume is arranged alphabetically by name of person, just as the current or contemporary volumes are.

20-15 A: No; there is a cumulative index for all volumes in the most recent volume.

20-16 A: Marquis has also published a "Historical Volume," covering 1607-1896, on the same plan but using original research since there were no volumes of Who's Who in America to draw on for that time. All of the volumes together--the Historical Volume, the four (as of 1971) Who Was Who Volumes, the current Who's Who volumes--make up the Marquis series known as "Who's Who in American History."

20-17 A: See Preface to vol. 4. Some entries, in the addendum, represent names overlooked in the original Who's Who in America series, as well as corrections and deaths received too late to be added to the main alphabetical list.

20-18 A: Published in London by Black (U.S. edition by St. Martin's Press), since 1849. (See Winchell annotation).

20-19 A: In arrangement they are similar; in format they are similar although Who's Who is smaller. Who's Who is published annually, while Who's Who in America appears biennially.

20-20 A: In scope the sources are similar. Who's Who includes names of important people other than Britishers--Johnson and Nixon, for example. The criteria for inclusion in Who's Who is not stated, as it is in Who's Who in America, except to say that one does not have to pay for the privilege.

20-21 A: Information given in both is similar, limited to objectively stated facts. Who's Who tends to include recreations, and the various parts of the entry (education, publications, etc.) are clearly set out by the use of italic type.

20-22 A: John Lennon is not listed in Who's Who, despite having received the Order of the British Empire. He is listed in Who's Who in America.

20-23 A: Yes, see Who Was Who. Who Was Who goes back only to 1897, although Who's Who itself goes back to 1849. No index; you must check each volume or know the year of death.

20-24 A: You would have to go to some source such as Statesman's Yearbook to find the name of the present Chancellor. Statesman's Yearbook 1970/71 lists Willy Brandt as the Chancellor. You would expect to find him listed in Who's Who in America since he is one of those foreign heads of government automatically listed, and he is.

20-25 A: Look for a who's-who-in-Germany type of source. Winchell, under Germany-- Contemporary, lists one (item AJ142).

20-26 A: See Winchell, biography section under Great Britain, where several sources are listed. The first is the next title on your list to examine.

20-27 A: All noteworthy inhabitants of the British Isles and the Colonies, exclusive of living persons (see Winchell annotation). "From earliest times to 1900" (title page of vol. 1), with supplements to 1950. The DNB itself has no real preface explaining its scope.

20-28 A: The basic arrangement is under name of person with entries all in one alphabetical list (dictionary). There are 22 basic volumes covering "earliest times to 1900"; the first 21 are one alphabetical list, the 22nd volume includes additions of persons who died too late for inclusion in vols. 1-21. Thus vol. 22 forms a kind of supplement to the "beginning to 1900" set. Then there are several supplementary volumes for the twentieth century, divided chronologically, each arranged alphabetically as is the basic set.

20-29 A: On the death of the biographee, as with the Who Was Who volumes.

20-30 A: There is a cumulative index in the last of the supplementary volumes (1940-51) which gives all names in the supplementary volumes plus birth and dates. This tells you that Blount died in 1905 so you can check the 1901-11 volume.

20-31 A: The problem here is which Sir Walter Scott; there are four Walter Scotts listed in the main set of the DNB, two of them "Sirs." The last listed, author of the Waverley novels, is probably the best known.

20-32 A: The article is signed L.S. and you must refer back to the list of contributors in vol. 1 (or in the same volume in some older editions) to find that the author is Leslie Stephen. Stephen is actually one of the editors of the DNB, and you could find out more about him by reading the article on him in the DNB itself; he died in 1904 and is therefore in the first of the 20th century supplementary volumes.

20-33 A: Yes, many further sources are listed. The DNB is particularly helpful for bibliographic references.

20-34 A: The concise DNB is an abridged version of the DNB, with the articles themselves shortened or abstracted. All names from the DNB are included. Some errors are corrected. (See Preface to vol. 1 of the Concise DNB.) It serves then as an index to the larger DNB as well as a smaller and less expensive version.

20-35 A: There is a subject index of sorts (similar to that in Chambers's Biographical Dictionary) in the back of the first volume of the Concise DNB. You could use it to check under Ireland, then Irish Free State, then find names of persons presumably active in that field, and look at the articles under their names.

20-36 A: The DNB claims to include "noteworthy" Americans of the Colonial period. Of the names listed, only Paine, Bradstreet, and Eliot are included in the DNB. These three were born in England, and the others were not, which may explain their inclusion.

20-37 A: Originally published from 1885 on and therefore written at that time or earlier (see Winchell annotation). It has the disadvantage of being by now out-of-date in some respects, not reflecting current scholarship and discoveries. (Some revision and corrections are found in the Concise DNB). However, it has the great advantage of giving what are nearly contemporary accounts of the people included, or accounts based on contemporary views.

20-38 A: Webster's Biographical Dictionary, under Stephen, Leslie, refers to his two daughters by their first names and refers you to the entries for their husbands, through which circuitous means you can find that one daughter was writer Virginia Woolf. Chambers's Biographical Dictionary is somewhat clearer, in the entry for Stephen, Leslie, that Virginia Woolf is one of his daughters. At the time the DNB articles were written, of course, she was still a very young woman. There is a DNB article for Virginia Woolf herself (she died in 1941).

20-39 A: Like the DNB, it is arranged alphabetically by the name of the person. It was first published in 20 volumes plus two supplements which brought it up to date to 1935, then 1940. There is one alphabetical list in the basic set, then two more alphabetical lists in each of the two supplements. (There is an 11 volume reprint edition which includes both supplements, as two separate lists, in the 11th volume. According to the Winchell annotation, there is an index

volume published at the time of the original edition; this index volume is not part of the 11 volume reprint.)

20-40 A: Yes, Concise Dictionary of American Biography; follows essentially the same pattern as the Concise DNB.

20-41 A: The DNB is essentially a biographical source for Britishers, and the DAB is essentially a source for Americans. See Preface of source for statement of scope. The DAB (like the DNB) excludes living persons. It is restricted to those persons who have actually lived in the United States (or in the territory now known as the United States) although not restricted to those born in the United States. It specifically excludes British officers who served in the colonies after independence was declared (e.g., those not on our side). Included, within these restrictions, are those who have made some significant contribution to American life.

20-42 A: No.

20-43 A: He died after 1940, and the DAB only goes up to 1940.

20-44 A: Yes, all are included.

20-45 A: All three are included in the Dictionary of National Biography.

20-46 A: Both Hutchinson and Gage are in the DAB and in the DNB. (Both left the colonies for England prior to the Declaration of Independence.)

20-47 A: As in the DNB, articles are signed with initials (contributors identified in the front of each volume of the DAB). Also as in the DNB, extensive bibliographical references are given for the articles.

20-48 A: In general, DNB and DAB entries are evaluative as well as factual. As examples, see the articles in both sources on Hutchinson, particularly the final paragraphs. See also the entry on Melvil Dewey in the Concise DAB. In any source where value judgments are given, it is important to know who wrote the material, who is giving the judgment, what are his qualifications for doing so.

20-49 A: The Who Was Who volumes, like the current who's who type, give strictly objective statements of fact (see #20-7). The information is quite limited compared to that found in the encyclopedic type entries of the DNB and DAB.

20-50 A: See Winchell, same section as the DAB. Also the Winchell annotation for the DAB itself compares the scope of the DAB to two other major retrospective sources, Appleton's Cyclopedia (AJ31) and the National Cyclopaedia of American Biography, the next title on your list.

20-51 A: National Cyclopaedia is much more com-prehensive, less limited and selective. (See Winchell annotation).

20-52 A: The National Cyclopaedia is a good example of a thoroughly confusing source. All of the biographic sources examined so far have been arranged alphabetically by the name of the person. Looking at the single volumes of the National Cyclopaedia shows no obvious rationale behind the arrangement of the material. It is not alphabetically, and not obviously chronologically. Since it is a biographical source, and since there are clearly separate entries each headed with the name of a person, the need is for some sort of access by personal name, preferably alphabetically, and the obvious thing to look for, then, is an index of some sort. Each volume has a separate index, but there are more than 50 volumes, so checking each volume would be a tedious task. Again, the obvious thing to look for is some sort of cumulative index.

A separately published Index to vols. 1-51 only was published in 1969. This helps con-siderably. An earlier index also includes current loose-leaf-type indexes to the cur-rently published volumes (from 52 on). Both indexes can be checked; or the 1969 index plus each separate volume from v. 52 on.

20-53 A: Look in the Index to Vols. 1-51 (1969) under Dinnies, Anna P., which refers you to vol. 13, p. 149, where you find the entry for her with biographical information.

20-54 A: There is subject access as well as name ac-cess through the indexes. For example, there are extensive references under the heading of "Printing," plus some see also references to other related subject headings.

20-55 A: It is useful primarily for its comprehensive-ness; see Winchell annotation. The entries are more extensive than in Who's Who, for example. It includes living persons so pro-vides more current coverage. It has some subject access.

20-56 A: See Winchell, biography section, under Australia, item AJ67, a 1949 publication patterned on the DNB. But better yet, see the first supplement to Winchell, item 1AJ5, the Australian Dictionary of Biography. Note that this source, unlike most of those you have examined, has a basic chronological arrangement.

20-57 A: In a current (who's who type) source for Belgium.

20-58 A: Subject limitations; i.e., lists of scientists, artists, musicians, etc.

20-59 A: The basic arrangement is alphabetical by name. The last edition was in 1965, and since then there have been periodic supplements with new names to up-date it.

20-60 A: Same type of factual achievements as is listed in who's-who-type sources: educa-tion, degrees, positions, membership, spe-cific scientific fields of interest (see entries themselves). The information is obtained from the biographees themselves, through questionnaires; again, similar to the who's-who-type sources (see Editor's Preface of vol. 1, 1965 edition).

20-61 A: Criteria listed in Editor's Preface. The source does not clearly state it is limited to living persons only, but its nature (the fact that the information is based on questionnaires filled in by the biographees, for example) dictates that it is probably limited in this way.

20-62 A: This is a who's who type source, therefore probably limited to living persons and giv-ing the basic factual data obtained from the biographee himself; no evaluative comments or discursive treatment of his work. It is limited to Americans and limited (not to artists) to people working in the field of art, artists, craftsmen, teachers, writers, critics, etc. You can assume it will be arranged alphabetically by name of person. You can expect to find Andrew Wyeth listed there, and you will find him in the W's as you would expect. The one thing you can't assume is that the source will be revised or issued every year, and you should there-fore check the date of publication to see how recent it is.

20-63 A: Try Current Biography. Also try Biography Index for magazine articles, parts of books, etc.

20-64 A: Under the subject (i.e., E: Pure and Ap-plied Sciences; BE: Fine Arts), then under biography; not in the Biography (AJ) section.

20-65 A: Check Winchell under the subject area of librarianship (AB), then under Biography, where you find two significant titles of the who's who type: one British, and one for the United States (Who's Who in Library Service, item AB75). Checking the supple-ments to see if anything more current has been published, you similarly find a 4th edition, 1965 (item 1AB8). (A 5th edition, not yet in Winchell, was published in 1970, titled A Biographical Directory of Librarians in the U.S. and Canada.)

20-66 A: See Winchell, 8th ed., p. 190.

20-67 A: Winchell, Biography Index, any of the na-tional biographical sources with subject access (under name of biographee as subject, or checking under Biography itself as the subject), any of the periodical indexes.

20-68 A: Slocum is a list of biographical sources ar-ranged by scope--that is, universal, then national or area, then vocational (or subject). There are author and title indexes for the biographies, but there is no index for names of persons listed in the biographies, as that would be an impossible undertaking.

20-69 A: Yes, under "Biography by Vocation," then "Library Science and Book Arts."

20-70 A: Yes, under "National or Area Biography," then under "New Hebrides."

20-71 A: Yes. See index of basic volume: New Hebrides, biography; Printing, biography. Slocum tends to list many more biographic sources than are included in Winchell, however.

20-72 A: You need to know more than just the name of the person. In the first place, there are no doubt many many Robert Boyles. Which do you want? In the second place, you need to know what source to turn to first, so you should have some idea of the time period of the person, and some idea of his nationality. In library reference work, you would ordinarily expect to get some sort of clue from the inquirer about the particular person he is searching for. Hopefully, your own reading and general knowledge background might be helpful. You can also make some assumptions or guesses; for example, from the name it would seem reasonable that Robert Boyle is English or American.

20-73 A: Start with the universal sources, work through national, regional, special, subject, etc. Work from broadest scope to narrow scope. The broader the coverage of the source, the less insignificant names it will include.

20-74 A: Curiously enough, this information is given in the entry for McLuhan in the International Who's Who.

20-75 A: Dictionary of National Biography.

20-76 A: Statesman's Yearbook will give fairly recent information.

20-77 A: New Century Cyclopedia of Names; Reader's Encyclopedia.

20-78 A: This is the kind of information which frequently appears in Current Biography articles.

20-79 A: Dictionary of American Biography.

20-80 A: Try an encyclopedia, under Illinois.

20-81 A: Captain Bligh was actually a real person; the novel Mutiny on the Bounty was based on a real incident. There is an article on Captain (William) Bligh in the Dictionary of National Biography.

20-82 A: Try directories of organizations, such as Encyclopedia of Associations, under flying saucers as subject entry, to get names of officers.

20-83 A: Title of literary work, see New Century Dictionary of Names. See also Readers' Encyclopedia. See also BIP, title volume, where you will of course find it only if it is still in print.

Section 21

Geographical Sources: Gazetteers and Guidebooks

Questions #21/1-21/91

21-1   What is the arrangement of Winchell's Guide to Reference Books?

21-2   If you were looking in Winchell for material on a specific subject (for example, education), where would you look?

21-3   In which of these major divisions have most of the bibliographical and reference sources which you have examined so far been classified?

21-4   In what ways have the bibliographical and reference sources you have previously examined been general rather than subject sources?

21-5   The final sections of this manual cover geographical sources. How are geographical sources classified in Winchell?

The geographical sources, then, can be examined as an example of <u>sources within a subject field,</u> as well as of basic reference sources. The first set of titles to examine is:

      Wright and Platt: Aids to Geographical Research (CK1)

      Columbia Lippincott Gazetteer of the World (CK30)
      Webster's Geographical Dictionary (CK34)

      Neal: Reference Guide for Travellers
      California (American Guide Series) (see CK265)
      Hotel and Motel Red Book (CK267)

21-6   Geography is treated as a subject area in Winchell, but is included in most reference textbooks and library school reference courses as part of the basic or general or non-subject areas. In what ways is geography a part of general, as opposed to subject, reference work?

21-7   What is the study of the field of geography? Where would you look for a simple definition? Where would you look for a fuller description, with some discussion of the major divisions or branches of the field and some information on its historical development?

21-8   Geography is classified in Winchell as part of the social sciences. How would you find out how geography is classified in a library collection? Why is it important to know how a subject field is classified in a library collection?

21-9   Which sources that you have previously examined have included geographical information, including maps?

21-10   Does Winchell give any general background on the subject of geography--what it covers, how it is related
to other fields, etc.?

21-11   Winchell lists bibliographies and other reference sources for geography in Section CK. Does Winchell
attempt to list all such sources? Does Winchell attempt to be comprehensive for subject areas?   What
is the scope of Winchell's Guide to Reference Books, especially in relation to the subject fields?

21-12   Where do you look, then, for more comprehensive and specialized coverage of the subject field?

21-13   Wright and Platt is listed in Winchell as a "guide." Since there are many kinds of guides used in
reference work, perhaps a better designation for this particular type of source is "guide to the literature." What is a guide to the literature?

21-14   Probably the best way to see what a guide to the literature is, is to examine one. The first title on the
list, Aids to Geographical Research by Wright and Platt, is a good example of a guide to the literature
of a subject field.   What is the purpose of the Wright and Platt book?   What is its scope?

21-15   What are some of the main topics or divisions into which the study of geography is divided?

21-16   Does Wright and Platt give any information about how geographers work?   what kind of facts, data, information they deal with?   what geographical research attempts to do or to discover or to explain?

21-17   Does Wright and Platt make any suggestions how the student of or researcher in (or librarian in) the
field of geography might go about exploring the literature of his subject?

21-18   Does Wright and Platt give any general guidance on the ways in which geographical materials are most
likely to be arranged?

21-19   Does Wright and Platt discuss ways in which libraries may be used in the search for geographical information?   (Remember that the book was written for geographers, not librarians).   Are other collections
of material, besides libraries, suggested for use?

21-20   Does Wright and Platt discuss or suggest ways in which people and organizations may be used in the
search for geographical information?   (Note the name of the organization responsible for the publication
of Wright and Platt itself; see title page).

21-21   What is one major drawback to the Wright and Platt book?

21-22   What parts of the Wright and Platt work are most affected by the fact that the book is 25 years old?

21-23   Does Wright and Platt list any bibliographies of bibliographies in the field of geography? Does Winchell?

21-24   What access do you have, through the national bibliographic sources studied in Part I of this manual, to information on current U.S. or English geographical publications?

21-25   Are there any bibliographies currently published (i.e., on an on-going basis as are CBI, BPR, etc.) which are specifically limited to geographical publications?

21-26   Neither Winchell nor Wright and Platt indicate whether these current sources are in fact still currently appearing. Where would you check to find out?

21-27   What access do you have, through the national bibliographic sources, to retrospective geographical publications?

21-28   Are there any bibliographies specifically limited to geographic materials which do give better retrospective coverage?

21-29   Is there a selective bibliography available in the field of geography, for retrospective and current materials?

21-30   Does Winchell list bibliographies specifically on the subject of phytogeography (plant geography)?   on agricultural geography? Does Wright and Platt? Which appears to be more useful for the specialized aspects of the subject: Winchell or a guide to the subject literature?

21-31   Where would you look, in the sources you have previously examined, to find the titles of some periodicals in the field of geography?

21-32   Is there a list of periodicals limited specifically to those in the field of geography?

21-33   Is there a union list of serials or periodicals in the field of geography?

21-34   Is there a periodical indexing and/or abstracting service (similar to Readers' Guide) limited to geographical materials?

21-35   What access do you have to government publications in the field of geography?

21-36   Other than bibliographies, what types of reference sources have you examined so far?

21-37   The examples you examined of these types of reference sources have been of a general nature, not subject-limited. The same types of sources exist in the subject fields, and their scope (within the limits set by the subject) and arrangement tend to be similar to the general sources you have already examined, so that once you know or assume the existence of such sources, you already know how they can be used and for what kinds of information they will be most useful.

How would you find out what dictionaries, for example, exist in the subject field of geography?

21-38   Can you tell, from checking in Winchell, and Wright and Platt, what is the title of the most basic, most useful dictionary of technical terms in the field of geography?

21-39   You could find in the general encyclopedia an article on geography itself, what it consists of, some history of its development, etc. Where would you look to find out what is currently being done in this field?

21-40   What kind of handbooks are there in the field of geography?

21-41   Is there a directory of organizations for geography?

21-42   The directories for geography seem to list both people and organizations. Are there any biographical/ sources for the field other than these? Where would you look for current biographical information on geographers living and working in the field today?

21-43   The types of reference sources which you have examined throughout this course are found also in the subject field of geography, as they are in most subjects. In addition, subject fields tend to have types of sources peculiar to that particular field, related to the kinds of information and the need for approaches to information peculiar to that particular field. To understand these specialized types of sources, it is often helpful to have some knowledge about the subject area itself and what kind of work is done in it.
         Winchell lists four specialized types of sources for geography. What are they?

21-44   Atlases will be taken up in a separate section, but the other specialized sources for geography will be examined in this section of the manual. The first special type is the gazetteer. What is a gazetteer?

21-45   Is there anything in the title of the Columbia Lippincott Gazetteer which indicates its scope? its arrangement?

21-46   How up-to-date is the Columbia Lippincott Gazetteer? How important is it for such sources to be up-to-date?

21-47   Would you expect to find all of the following in the Columbia Lippincott Gazetteer: Iran, Moscow, Hainan Island, Thames River, Stonehenge, Mount Kilimanjaro, Niagara Falls, Botswana?

21-48   What does the Columbia Lippincott Gazetteer give as the population for Aiea, Hawaii? What does the entry itself have to say about the location of Aiea? What does T.H. stand for? What is the date for the population figure given?

21-49   Is this information brought up to date in any way in the Columbia Lippincott Gazetteer?

21-50   Are there later census figures than 1960? Where would you find information on the latest census figures for Aeia?

21-51   The scope of the Columbia Lippincott Gazetteer is world-wide, but it must have some limitations in what it can include. As the universal biographical sources attempted to limit their scope by including only the most "important" names, does Columbia Lippincott attempt to limit its scope by, for example, the relative size of the places it lists?

21-52   What is the full title of Webster's Geographical Dictionary? Is it a gazetteer?

21-53   Who is the publisher of Webster's Geographical Dictionary?

21-54   What is one of the chief differences between Webster's Third unabridged dictionary and Webster's second, regarding geographical information?

21-55   How current is Webster's Geographical Dictionary? How is it kept up to date?

21-56   Webster's Geographical Dictionary is obviously, by size alone, more limited in scope than Columbia Lippincott. What kind of limitations has it set on the places it includes?

21-57   Does Webster's Geographical Dictionary include Botswana? recent population figures for Aiea, Hawaii?

21-58   What is the county seat of Sequatchie county, Tennessee, according to Webster's Geographical Dictionary?

21-59   How old is the city of Katmandu, and what of interest can be seen there? Compare Webster's and Columbia Lippincott.

21-60   Where would you find a more recent population figure for Katmandu?

21-61   What kind of industry, if any, is there in the town of Poggio Rusco in Italy? What is the population?

21-62   Where is Yezo or Yeso?

21-63   What is the difference between the name Yezo and Hokkaido?

21-64   Webster's Geographical Dictionary includes only U.S. towns with population of 1,500+; Columbia Lippincott includes only incorporated towns listed in 1950 census. Neither includes New Tazewell, Tennessee. Where else could you look, of the sources previously examined, to find the location, population, and general information on manufacturing and industry, if any, for New Tazewell, Tennessee?

21-65   How many islands are there in the Philippine Island group? Can you find information showing the relative size and placement of the major islands? Can you find the location of Calayan Island, in the Philippines? Compare Columbia Lippincott and Webster's.

21-66   In general, does the Columbia Lippincott Gazetteer have maps? Can you, however, locate Calayan Island on any map through the information given in the entry in Columbia Lippincott?

21-67   Where was the ancient country or territory of Phoenicia located? Is there now a geographical area called Phoenicia?

21-68   What are the major differences between the Columbia Lippincott Gazetteer and Webster's Geographical Dictionary?

21-69   The ALA Glossary defines a gazetteer simply as a geographical dictionary. Is this strictly accurate? For example, can you find in either the Columbia Lippincott or Webster's definitions of such terms as mountain, ocean, pond, sea-level, estuary, desert, topographic?

21-70   Where would you look to find definitions of such terms? For example, what is the difference in the use of the word "river" and "stream" to geographers?

21-71   Where is the Mohave Desert located in California, according to the gazetteers? Is that the correct spelling for the name?

21-72   The spelling of geographical names often varies, and problems arise in knowing which is the correct or approved spelling, and in knowing what variants exist under which the place may be listed in a gazetteer or called on a map. Is there any official way in which such problems are resolved?

21-73   What are the two agencies which are concerned with the problems of variance of spelling of American and English place names? What publications are available which set out their decisions?

21-74   What is the meaning or origin of the word mojave (or mohave) in the name Mojave Desert?

21-75   The next type of specialized source for geography taken up in Winchell are the atlases. These will be examined in the next section. The fourth of the specialized sources in Winchell are "guidebooks." What is the definition of "guidebook" as it is used in this context?

21-76   There are several series of guidebooks available (i.e., Baedeker's, Muirhead's, Nagel's, Fodor's, etc.) noted in Winchell, but Winchell does not attempt to give specific listings for the individual titles in these series or for guidebooks not published in such series. The next title on your list to examine is a specialized bibliographical source for guidebooks: Neal's Reference Guide for Travellers. How recently was this bibliography published? Who is the publisher?

21-77   If you became intrigued by the Columbia Lippincott Gazetteer's description of Katmandu in Nepal, and you decided you wanted to visit there, where could you find further information on the city, the interesting spots to visit, hotels to stay in, etc.?

21-78   If you were traveling to Africa, and wanted to read up on the country before you left on your trip, would Neal's Reference Guide for Travellers be useful to you?

21-79   If you were trying to decide whether you should get a Fodor or Nagel or Baedeker guidebook for Great Britain, where would you find some comparative discussion of the information given in each, recency, etc.?

21-80   One of the best known, although very old, series of guidebooks is the American Guide. This series includes guides to each of the states, as well as some cities and some regions. The next title to examine--California; a Guide to the Golden State--is from this series. When was this guide originally published, and when was the latest revision?

21-81   In what way does this guidebook give information useful to tourists? Can you find out through it whether or not you can visit San Simeon, William Randolph Hearst's former estate? how you get into the movie studios and how you can see the TV programs in Los Angeles? what motels and hotels you can stay at near Disneyland? how old the Golden Gate Bridge is?

21-82   Does this guidebook give any historical background on the state, as well as information of purely current interest?

21-83   Where is the town of Petaluma located, in California? Is there any special industry there? What does the name mean?

21-84   If you were planning to visit California, and wanted to do some reading about the state before your trip, would this guidebook be useful to you?

21-85   What is the difference between the information given in a guidebook and that given in a gazetteer? How are guidebooks of use to a library?

21-86   Does the American Guide series' book on California give you room rates for the Ahwanee Hotel in Yosemite National Park?

21-87   Is the Hotel and Motel Red Book a comprehensive listing of all hotels and motels in the world?

21-88   What is the approximate price of a double room in the Sheraton Hotel in Tel Aviv?

21-89   Is there a Holiday Inn in Tulsa, Oklahoma?

21-90   If you were planning a meeting of approximately 1,000 people in Los Angeles, what hotels could provide you with a banquet room which would seat all your guests, plus an auditorium or meeting room which would seat all your members, plus availability of movie and slide projectors and a P.A. system?

21-91   Where would you look to find out what cruises to the South Pacific make stopovers in Fiji?

Section 21

Geographical Sources: Gazetteers and Guidebooks

Answers #21/1-21/91

21-1 A: See Contents page. Five major divisions:
A, General Reference Works; B, Humanities;
C, Social Sciences; D, History and Area
Studies; E, Pure and Applied Sciences.
(See also Preface, "Arrangement.")

21-2 A: Under the section for that specific subject;
for education, in the major division C for
Social Sciences, then in section CB for
Education.

21-3 A: Nearly all have been in the major division
A, General Reference Works. A few
(especially in the sections on yearbooks
and almanacs, handbooks and manuals)
have been classified in subject areas; for
example, the statistics sources in section
16 under Social Sciences--Statistics.

21-4 A: In scope, they have covered all (or at least
most) of the subject areas. They have
not been limited to or primarily limited
to one subject area, or even one broad
subject area such as science. In some of
the sections of this manual, you have
examined a few examples of specifically
subject limited sources, such as American
Men of Science and Who's Who in American
Art in the biographical sources.

21-5 A: As a subject area, Section CK, major
division of Social Sciences.

21-6 A: Geographical questions and problems like
biographical questions are frequently en-
countered in general library reference
work: questions like where is X, how big
is Y, how many people are there in Z,
what is the climate of A, what is the capital
of B, what are the principle cities of C,
etc.
   Geography is an extremely broad subject field, overlapping, contributing to, and
being dependent upon many other subject
disciplines, especially in the sciences and
social sciences (anthropology, history,
geology, mathematics, etc.).

21-7 A: A general dictionary for a simple basic
definition; an encyclopedia for a general
basis discussion. All three major adult
encyclopedias have articles on geography.

21-8 A: You need to know how, or where, a subject is classified in a library collection so
that you can know generally where in the
building the material itself is located and
can be found. The same knowledge will
tell you generally where the reference
material on a subject field can be found

in the library's reference collection.
   To find out how the subject is classified
in the library, you can check the two
basic subject classifications schemes used
in libraries: Dewey (Dewey Decimal
Classification and Relative Index, see
Winchell item AB121) and Library of
Congress (Outline of the Library of Congress Classification, plus detailed schedules
for each class, see Winchell item AB119).
   In LC, for example, geography is
classified, with anthropology and recreation,
in G--following history (C, D, E and F)
and preceding Social Sciences (H) which
puts it generally in the area of Social
Sciences. The geography categories go
from G through GF, including divisions
for voyages and travels, polar regions,
atlases, maps, mathematical geography,
cartography, physical geography, geo-
morphology, oceanography, anthropogeogra-
phy, and human ecology.
   In Dewey, geography and history are in
the last of the 10 major classes (900),
general geography being specifically in
910, with divisions for historical geography (911), then atlases and maps, etc.
(912), then divisions by area (ancient
world, modern Europe, modern Asia, etc.)
This classification separates geography
from the other social sciences but shows
its relationship to history.

21-9 A: Some of the dictionaries (Webster's 2nd
unabridged, for example, but not Webster's 3rd unabridged; Random House, etc.).
   All of the encyclopedias--articles on
major countries and cities, etc., references in the indexes to specific place
names. Good pictorial representations of
all kinds, including maps. Foreign encyclopedias especially good for information on
foreign countries or place names.
   Encyclopedia yearbooks to some extent
and news summaries to some extent,
especially for up-to-date geographical
changes, new place names, population
figures, etc.
   Almanacs have some maps, some specific geographical information, population
figures, etc.
   Handbooks do include some geographical
information and place names (the curiosity
and literary handbooks in particular).
   As with biography, every source is a
potential source of geographical information
if only indirectly. For example, a bibliography
about Thailand will include sources of geographical information on Thailand.

21-10 A: No, only a few paragraphs at the beginning of Section CK specifically on the library needs in the field.

21-11 A: For Winchell's scope, see Preface, under "Scope." Winchell is selective, not all-inclusive.

21-12 A: See Preface to Winchell again, which suggests consulting the manuals, guides and bibliographies in the subject fields. In the opening paragraphs on CK: Geography, Winchell also suggests Wright and Platt's Aids to Geographical Research as a very valuable guide for geographical reference material. This is the first title listed in Winchell for geography, and the first title on your list to examine.

21-13 A: ALA Glossary has no such entry, and the term is too specialized for general dictionaries. Winchell, in introductory section titled "Reference Materials for Special Subjects," notes such sources under "I. Guides and Manuals" (8th ed., p. xvii), but does not really define what they are. Guides to the literature are basically bibliographic sources, but the most useful guides are more than simply lists of sources; they are also bibliographic guidebooks, handbooks, manuals, giving some information about the subject field and guidance in use of the material.

21-14 A: See first paragraph, Introduction. Purpose: to serve advanced students and professional workers in geography. Scope: observations on the nature of geographical studies, general discussion of published aids to geographical research, selected list of bibliographies, etc.; not references to primary works but information guiding to other works which will open up the literature.

21-15 A: See Wright and Platt, Contents, II: Topical Aids (historico-geographical, physical geography, mathematical geography, phytogeography, urban geography, etc.). See also the general encyclopedia articles on geography, and to a limited extent, see the Dewey and/or LC classification schemes under geography.

21-16 A: Introduction, sections titled "Field work and indoor work," "Geographical description and interpretation," also "Aids to geographical field research," "Aids to geographical study indoors."

21-17 A: Through the use of bibliographic aids; see Introduction, section so titled.

21-18 A: See Introduction: "Classification and arrangement of the material in bibliographic aids."

21-19 A: See Introduction, "Guides to collections." Wright and Platt does not give any dis-cussion of use of the card catalog, library classification schemes, reference and circulation policies, etc., which are found in some other literature guides. Also suggested are museums, botanical and zoological gardens.

21-20 A: See Introduction, section titled "Guides to Individuals and Institutions"; see also list of people, institutions, organizations in the Appendix (badly out of date now, of course, but still useful as an example of what kind of information can be found in a guide to the literature). Wright and Platt published "for the American Geographical Society."

21-21 A: Out of date; published (2nd ed.) in 1947.

21-22 A: Lists of titles of specific sources. The sources listed still exist, of course, but more recently published and therefore more current sources are now available. The introductory material is generally un-dated.

21-23 A: Under General Aids, Geographical Bibliographies: Bibliographies of geographical bibliographies. Notes two, one of which is only partly on geography and the other was published in 1881. Winchell has none listed.
           Wright and Platt itself, of course, forms a bibliography of bibliographies in the field of geography, although it makes no claim to be comprehensive.

21-24 A: Any bibliographic record with subject access: Subject Guide to Books in Print, American Book Publishing Record, and BPR Cumulative, Subject Guide to Forthcoming Books, Cumulative Book Index, LC Subject Catalog.

21-25 A: Winchell--under Geography, Bibliography, Current Surveys, lists three (items CK17, CK18, CK19), none published in the U.S. or Great Britain. Another (CK12a), published in London, is listed under Bibliography. Another (2CK1) is listed in the second supplement, under Bibliography. See also Wright and Platt--General Aids, Geographical Bibliographies, Current, p. 51+ (includes same titles as Winchell, with extensive annotation on two of them).

21-26 A: Ulrich's Periodical Directory; Irregular Serials and Annuals.

21-27 A: Those with subject access: American Catalogue and U.S. Catalog (preceding CBI); Evans. (Nothing really very satisfactory prior to the 20th century.)

21-28 A: See Winchell--Geography, Bibliography, titles listed CK2-CK14. See Wright and Platt, General Aids, Geographical bibliographies, retrospective... (p. 58+).

21-29 A: Winchell, 1CK1, Church and Zelinsky: A
Basic Geographical Library; a selected
and annotated book list...published 1966,
so includes relatively recent publications
as well as retrospective. In Wright and
Platt, not too clear. However, see Bibliographies of Works for Teachers of
Geography (p. 61+). Church and Zelinsky
is much too recent to be included in Wright
and Platt, of course.

21-30 A: Wright and Platt, in the section on "Topical
Aids," lists bibliographic sources under
various subjects such as plant geography,
agricultural geography, etc. Most of the
bibliographies listed are parts of other books.
Winchell does not include those bibliographies which are published as parts of other
books, but some of the major bibliographies
listed in Wright and Platt are also found in
Winchell. Winchell lists under bibliographies, for Geography, only those dealing
with the overall subject. Other bibliographies are found under related subjects, such
as agriculture, botany, etc. For example,
Wright and Platt lists under phytogeography a
book titled Geographical Guide to Floras of
the World which includes "Floristic works";
this is cited in Winchell, under Biological
Sciences-Botany-General Works-Bibliography.

21-31 A: Ulrich's Periodical Directory.

21-32 A: Winchell, Geography-Bibliography-Periodicals
(8th ed., p. 443), cited two such lists
(items CK15 and CK16), one of serials in
England and one international.

 Wright and Platt itself gives a short list
with discussion (p. 66+); out of date, of
course, but the major periodicals listed
are probably still appearing and in any case
are still available for retrospective searching.

21-33 A: Winchell: same place, item CK16 annotation
shows that there was one; the revision
(Harris and Fellman's International List of
Geographical Serials) does not indicate locations but does give references to other union
lists.

21-34 A: Winchell 1st supplement, item 1CK2, lists
Geographical Abstracts, 1966+. It is not clear
from the annotation whether this includes
books, and/or periodical articles or what.
All of the items noted in question #21-25
include periodical articles as well as books.
Check also in Kujoth: Subject Guide to
Periodical Indexes (Section 7 of this manual).
Most of the subject-limited indexing/abstract-
ing services tend to include books and other
publications as well as periodical articles
(see question #552).

21-35 A: Try Leidy and Jackson subject guides; neither
have entries for geography as such but have
related entries (maps, travel, surveying,
climatology, agriculture, etc.).

 No U.S. GPO price list for geography as
such, but for related topics: maps, states of

the U.S. and their resources, national
parks, Census publications, etc.

 Wright and Platt lists (p. 26+) under
bibliographies for teachers, a very dated
list (1938) titled Government Publications
of Use to Teachers of Geography and
Science (by Grace S. Wright).

 A publication similar to that listed in
Wright but more up to date, and not listed
in Winchell is: U.S. Government Publications for Research and Teaching in Geography and Related Social and Natural Sciences,
by C.L. and A.G. Vinge (Totowa, New
Jersey, Littlefield, Adams and Co., 1967).

21-36 A: Dictionaries, encyclopedias, yearbooks or
annuals, handbooks and manuals, directories (organizational and biographical).

21-37 A: Check Winchell, then further check a guide
to the literature, such as Wright and Platt.
Winchell is sometimes easier to work with,
since it is organized according to these
general types of sources and follows the
same pattern you have used for learning the
general sources. However, the sources in
Winchell are selective and therefore it may
be necessary to use other guides as well.
It is also useful to realize that the distinction between the types of sources is not always completely clear, and one guide may
classify a title as a handbook while another
guide may classify it as a dictionary, etc.

21-38 A: Winchell, under Geography, lists dictionaries and encyclopedias together, making no
clear distinction between the two types. In
the basic set and two supplements, there
are three titles in English which appear to
be limited to technical geographical terms:
Moore (2CK5 and CK23), Monkhouse (1CK6),
and Stamp: Glossary of geographical terms
(CK20). Annotations for all of them indicate that either the Stamp or the Monkhouse
are the fullest.

 Wright and Platt is perhaps less clear.
They seem to lump dictionaries and encyclopedias and anything else with an alphabetical
order arrangement under the heading "Gazetteers and Related Works" (p. 74+); that section discusses mainly the gazetteers, and
refers to Winchell (Mudge=Winchell) for
general dictionaries and encyclopedias. For
technical dictionaries and glossaries, one is
referred to a listing in another source.

21-39 A: A yearbook or annual of some sort. Winchell
lists only one, in the second supplement
(2CK9, New Geography, 1966/67+). A
regular encyclopedia yearbook might be helpful; see for example a short article on
geography in the Americana Annual 1970
(i.e., 1969). Nothing in Collier's Yearbook
for 1969.

21-40 A: Winchell: one on deserts of the world (2CK7),
one on identifying old maps and globes (1CK7),
one on the world's mountains (CK24) and on
the world's oceans and islands (CK25). As

an example of the difficulties of classifying into types, especially in the subject
fields: Winchell's basic volume lists the
Standard Encyclopedia of the World's Mountains (CK24) and a similar source on oceans
and islands (CK25) as handbooks. In the
first supplement, a similar source on the
world's rivers and lakes is listed under
"Dictionaries and encyclopedias." Wright
and Platt lists some titles which might
seem to fall into this designation under
"General Geographical Manuals" (p. 71+).

21-41 A: Winchell, under Geography--Directories,
            lists Orbis Geographicus (CK28), which
            appears to be a comprehensive directory
            of organizations, institutions, and people
            in the field, and is up-dated periodically.
            Another title, Geographisches Taschenbuch
            (CK27), is listed under Directories, called
            a handbook in the annotation, and appears
            every two years with reports of expeditions,
            etc., so could serve as a yearbook type of
            source for current development. It also
            lists organizations and people.

21-42 A: See Winchell, 1st supplement, item 1CK8, a
            list of mapmakers, universal (all countries,
            all periods). Other than the two German
            (but apparently universal) sources listed in
            Winchell, there appear to be no current
            directories for people in this field, so you
            would have to turn to a broader scope--
            e.g., probably social sciences. See
            section CA in Winchell, Social Sciences--
            General--Biography, which refers you to
            American Men of Science which includes
            persons in the social sciences as well as
            the physical and biological sciences, and as
            such specifically includes geographers. (It
            will not however give you access to those
            persons working in geography unless you
            know their names.)

21-43 A: Following the section headed "General Works,"
            listing guides, bibliographies, dictionaries
            and encyclopedias, handbooks, and direc-
            tories, Winchell lists:
            Gazetteers (General, then U.S., then by
            country). Geographical names and terms
            (the same); Atlases (the same); Guidebooks
            (basically only general and U.S.).

21-44 A: See ALA Glossary, or a regular dictionary,
            or the paragraph in Winchell under "Gazet-
            teers," or the first paragraph of the
            Preface to the next source to examine, the
            Columbia Lippincott Gazetteer.

21-45 A: Scope is "of the world." The word Gazetteer
            in the title, meaning dictionary of geo-
            graphical place names, indicates that its ar-
            rangement will probably be (dictionary-type)
            in one alphabetical list.

21-46 A: Columbia Lippincott published in 1952, with a
            1961 supplement added to the back of the
            volume in the 1962 printing. See Winchell;
            see title page, verso of title page, and page

facing title page of the source. Some geographical information will remain the same
but much will change.

21-47 A: All are included except Botswana, an inde-
            pendent African nation established in 1966
            and therefore too recent for even the 1961
            supplement of Columbia Lippincott. Mount
            Kilimanjaro is entered as Kilimanjaro. The
            gazetteer lists not only names of countries
            and cities and towns, but all geographical
            features such as rivers, oceans, deserts,
            waterfalls, etc., also historical features
            such as Stonehenge.

21-48 A: The entry, under Aiea, lists it as popula-
            tion 3,714, located in Oahu, T.H. T.H.
            stands for Territory of Hawaii (see abbrevi-
            ations list in front matter), which im-
            mediately shows it is out ot date. The
            front matter also lists a "key to population
            figures" which shows, under Hawaii, that
            1950 figures have been used.

21-49 A: Yes, in the 1961 supplement. There is no
            entry for Aiea as such. The entry for
            Hawaii in the supplement brings it to state-
            hood (1959). A list of 1960 Census popu-
            lation figures for U.S. cities, arranged by
            state, is also given in the supplement; here
            you can find Aiea with 11,826 population in
            1960.

21-50 A: 1970 Census; try 1971 almanacs for latest
            census figures. (See #16-5, 16-6, 16-7 in
            Section 16 on Statistics.)

21-51 A: See Preface. Columbia Lippincott claims
            to list all U.S. cities and incorporated towns
            listed in the 1950 census; the 1960 census
            list in the supplement is limited to places
            of 1,000 or more population.

21-52 A: Webster's Geographical Dictionary; a dic-
            tionary of names of places with geographical
            and historical information and pronuncia-
            tions. Yes, it is a gazetteer.

21-53 A: G. and C. Merriam Co., publishers of
            Webster's New Third International Dictionary,
            Webster's New Dictionary of Synonyms, Web-
            ster's Biographical Dictionary.

21-54 A: Geographical information in Webster's
            Second is given in a special list called a
            Pronouncing Gazetteer. No geographical
            information is given in Webster's Third at
            all unless it is indirectly through a name
            used as an adjective.

21-55 A: Webster's Geographical Dictionary practices
            a form of continuous revision, like the other
            Merriam publications you have looked at. See
            Winchell annotation and verso of title page
            of source.

21-56 A: See Preface. Stresses United States and
            Canada. Has specific minimum population
            figures (varies with the country) for

inclusion; U.S. cities must have 1,500+ population (as of 1950 census? not clear).

21-57 A: C.1969 edition: Botswana is listed, giving a see reference to its former name before independence (Bechunaland Protectorate). Aiea is listed with population of 11,826 (1960 census figures according to Preface).

21-58 A: Webster's Geographical Dictionary (1969) under Sequatchie, refers to "table" at Tennessee; under Tennessee, table lists all counties of the state and gives their county seat. (Columbia Lippincott gives name of county seat in entry for Sequatchie County.)

21-59 A: Columbia Lippincott gives a much more extensive description than Webster's of its background, the temples, palaces, and pilgrimage sites there. Webster's merely locates it. Columbia Lippincott gives its population according to 1920 figures; Webster's (1969) lists same population figures with no indication that it is out-dated.

21-60 A: World Almanac 1971 gives figure for Nepal only. Statesman's Yearbook 1970/71 gives figure for Katmandu as 195,260; doesn't give year but figure given for Nepal indicates 1964 estimate.

21-61 A: Not in Webster's (too small). In Columbia Lippincott. Macaroni manufacturing. Population given is 2,705, but since this is for the 1936 census (see "Key to Population Figures" in front) this is hardly significant at this point.

21-62 A: Northernmost island of Japan, Hokkaido. Webster's has cross-references to Hokkaido from both Yezo and Yeso. Columbia has cross-reference from Yezo only.

21-63 A: Columbia Lippincott entry explains that the island was called Yezo (and variations on that), then renamed Hokkaido following restoration of imperial power (1868). Webster's doesn't give the information.

21-64 A: Try the Ayer Directory of Newspapers, which includes descriptions of all the places in which the newspapers listed are published. (See question #462 in section 5).

21-65 A: Both Columbia Lippincott and Webster's have an entry for the Philippine Islands and give the number of islands. Columbia Lippincott has discussion about the relative size and placement of the islands, but only Webster's has a map which gives that information easily and visually. Calayan Island (north of Luzon) can be located on the Webster's map. Both Columbia Lippincott and Webster's have also a separate entry for Calayan Island telling where it is located, but only through the map in Webster's can you see its location.

21-66 A: Columbia Lippincott has no maps; Webster's has some. The entry in Columbia Lippincott for Calayan Island gives geographical coordinates (latitude and longitude) which would allow you to locate it on other maps in other sources.

21-67 A: Phoenicia is not a meaningful geographical name for the modern world, but both Columbia Lippincott and Webster's have entries for it giving its meaning in historical terms.

21-68 A: Columbia is larger, has more entries and tends to give more information for entries. Webster's is more selective in entries, primarily directed to American users. Webster's is more up-to-date; Columbia is out-of-date in many respects. Columbia is more expensive. Webster's has maps.

21-69 A: No. These gazetteers are more accurately called dictionaries of places. They list only place names and define only actual place names. They do not define technical terms in the field.

21-70 A: Use a technical dictionary (see answer to #21-38). For example, A Glossary of Geographical Terms, edited by Sir Dudley Stamp (Winchell item CK20), under "river," gives the definition according to the OED and Webster's, then comments on these definitions according to geographical usage.

21-71 A: Both Columbia Lippincott and Webster's gives cross references from Mohave to Mojave. Webster's indicates that both spellings are permissable, but Mojave preferred. Columbia Lippincott lists other place names, similar in location, for which the spelling Mohave is apparently preferred.

21-72 A: See Preface to Columbia Lippincott Gazetteer, which discusses this problem. The second group of specialized geographical sources in Winchell--Geographical Names and Terms--deal with this area. It is also discussed in Wright and Platt in the section titled "Spelling of Geographical Names" (see table of contents).

21-73 A: United States Board on Geographic Names (under U.S. Dept. of the Interior), for publications see Winchell item CK87. Permanent Committee on Geographical Names for British Official Use, for publications see Winchell items CK85, 86, 86a. (Also in Wright and Platt, p. 78+, with more information and some references to periodical articles explaining the work of these agencies.)

21-74 A: Sometimes the origins or meanings of words used in place names will be given in dictionaries, especially if the name is a commonly used one or if the word is used in other ways than just as a place name. Origins may be given in gazetteers. Some meanings or origins are given in the place name "decisions" lists put out by the U. S. Board on Geographic Names. In addition, there are specialized sources which exist just to describe place names in terms of their meaning or origin. These are listed in Winchell, specifically by country, following the general sources which gave official decisions on place names. For the U.S., there is no source specifically listed for California but instead a bibliography (item CK88, 2CK12) of "place-name literature" through which you could find if a source existed for California, in which you could then find the information on Mojave.

21-75 A: See ALA Glossary. See also a general dictionary, since guidebook in this sense is a very common word. Winchell does not specifically define the term, nor does Wright and Platt in its section covering these sources (p. 80+). All definitions seem to indicate that guidebooks are prepared specifically for travelers or tourists.

21-76 A: Published by Bowker, in 1969.

21-77 A: Neal (arranged by country) under Nepal, gives guidebooks for Nepal which would include Katmandu, also one specifically on Katmandu which is comparatively recent and gives tourist information. (Katmandu is also in the index.)

21-78 A: Yes, suggested reading (such as Dinesen, Hemingway--other than the listed guidebooks) given for each country.

21-79 A: Winchell is a little help (see general paragraphs preceding list of guidebooks, 8th ed., p. 460). Wright and Platt not much help. Neal probably of most help here, see information under Great Britain. An even better way would be to examine these guidebook series yourself, to see which gave the general information you wanted, and which most appealed to you in format, style, etc. If possible, locate and examine one or two examples from these series. A bookstore or a public library is probably one of the easier places in which to do this.

21-80 A: Originally published 1939, complete revision 1967 (see verso of title page).

21-81 A: The guidebook does give this type of information, which you can find most easily through checking the index (for San Simeon, Disneyland, Golden Gate Bridge). The information on the movie and TV studios is not indexed, and can be found in the chapter on the city of Hollywood, rather than in the chapter on Los Angeles. This guidebook does not attempt to offer detailed information on motels, accommodations, prices, opening times, etc., thus it does not become dated as quickly as those guide-

books which rely heavily on this type of tourist information.

21-82 A: Yes, much historical background is given, one of the especially useful features of the American Guide series; see Part I: California, from past to present.

21-83 A: See index for reference to specific information.

21-84 A: Yes, extensive lists of further reading; see Appendices.

21-85 A: See Winchell, paragraphs preceding the list of guidebooks (8th ed., p. 460).

21-86 A: The Ahwanee Hotel is mentioned (see index) but no room rates, times, etc., given. For this information, the next title on your list, the Hotel and Motel Red Book, would be useful.

21-87 A: No, only those "accepted" as members of the American Hotel and Motel Association (required to meet high standards, etc.). See "An important message from the President of the American Hotel and Motel Association," following title page.

21-88 A: Hotel and Motel Red Book: Asia, then Israel, then Tel Aviv, then Sheraton-Tel Aviv Hotel, prices given; advertisement on opposite page offers Israel's only American style coffee shop, open 24 hours... (1970 edition).

21-89 A: Yes, see Hotel and Motel Red Book under Oklahoma, then Tulsa.

21-90 A: See Hotel and Motel Red Book, blue pages section for Facilities for Business Meetings, under California, then Los Angeles.

21-91 A: Official steamship guide (Winchell CK270). Winchell also lists similar sources for airlines, railways, and buses (see "Timetables," 8th ed., p. 461).

Section 22

Geographical Sources: Atlases

Questions #22/1-22/100

22-1   How would you go about determining who wrote the following: "As soon as men begin to talk about any-
        thing that really matters, someone has to go and get the atlas"?

        Atlases are a very specialized type of reference source which can provide a wealth of information, both
        general and geographical, if carefully used. The atlases listed here for examination in this section are
        only a selection of many available:

                    Rand McNally New Cosmopolitan World Atlas (1CK28)
                    Hammond Ambassador World Atlas (1CK21-23)
                        or
                    Hammond Medallion World Atlas (1CK21-23)
                    Odyssey World Atlas (1CK27)
                    Goode's World Atlas (CK212)
                    Rand McNally Commercial Atlas (CK220)
                    Times Atlas of the World, Comprehensive ed. (2CK24)
                    Times Index-Gazetteer of the World (1CK9)

22-2   What is an atlas?

22-3   What are the criteria on which you should judge an atlas? What things should you look for in examining
        an atlas?

22-4   Since an atlas is basically a collection of maps, it is also helpful to have some understanding of maps
        in general. What is a map? Is there any difference between "map" and "chart"? Where would you look
        to find the origin of the word "map"?

22-5   What is cartography?

22-6   If you wanted to get some background information on maps and map-making--for example, if you were a
        librarian suddenly put in charge of a collection of maps and/or geographical material--where would you
        go for help?

22-7   What kinds of maps are there? What can be shown by means of a map?

22-8   The first atlas to be examined is the Rand McNally New Cosmopolitan World Atlas, published by Rand
        McNally and Company in Chicago. One of the items you have checked for in nearly every source
        examined is the date of the source, to know how current the information is and how frequently it is re-
        vised. What is the date of the atlas you are examining? What is the revision policy for the New
        Cosmopolitan?

22-9   The New Cosmopolitan was first published, then, in 1965. What is one way in which you can check to see if the edition you are looking at has been brought up to date further than that?

22-10   What is the scope of this atlas, according to its title and according to the table of contents? It is published in the United States; is it an atlas only for the United States?

22-11   How much of this atlas is devoted to the United States, however? How does this compare with the space given to the rest of the world?

22-12   Although world-wide in scope, half of this atlas is devoted to coverage of the United States. Is this surprising?

22-13   What is the general arrangement in this atlas? Is it alphabetical? Is the map for Alaska between that for Africa and that for Australia?

22-14   What kind of maps are found in the New Cosmopolitan World Atlas? Can you find a map which shows the political boundaries of Laos? Can you find a relief map showing elevation and mountainous areas of Laos? Can you find a map which shows population density of Laos? How are these maps grouped? Are all the various kinds of maps dealing with Laos or Asia grouped together?

22-15   What are map projections? Are these explained in this atlas?

22-16   On the political map of Cambodia, Laos, etc., is the type of map projection used indicated? Could you find out through the atlas how this particular projection is formed?

22-17   Why is it important to realize the type of projection used in a map and to know how the projection is formed?

22-18   On this same map, is the scale indicated? What is meant by "scale" in maps? In what ways can the scale of a map be represented or indicated?

22-19   The scale of the map of Cambodia and Laos, etc., is 1:8,000,000. The scale of the map following, of India and Pakistan, etc., is 1:16,000,000. Is the scale of the map for Cambodia larger or smaller than that of the map of India? Is the map of Cambodia therefore more detailed or less detailed than the map of India?

22-20   Locate the map for Rhode Island in the New Cosmopolitan. Is the scale of that map larger (and therefore capable of being more detailed) than the map of Laos?

22-21   Is there anything in the New Cosmopolitan by which you can compare Laos to Rhode Island in size, in area?

22-22   Can you also compare the population? Are dates given for the population figures? Is anything shown to indicate the source of all this information?

22-23   Are the maps themselves, in the New Cosmopolitan World Atlas, dated? How can you tell if they have been revised or brought up to date?

22-24   On the physical or relief map of Eurasia, which includes Laos, what is the significance of the broken black lines in the general area of Laos, Thailand, Vietnam? of the solid red line? of the white area around the coast of Thailand?

22-25   How would you go about locating New Tazewell, Tennessee on a map in this atlas?

22-26   What does 768 in the index reference for New Tazewell stand for? Is this the page number of the map?

22-27   Having found the map of Tennessee on p. 117, how do you locate New Tazewell? What is the closest town to New Tazewell? Is this town larger or smaller than New Tazewell? What is the name of the railroad line which runs through New Tazewell? What is the name of the river which runs north of New Tazewell?

22-28   Does the index of the New Cosmopolitan World Atlas include all the names which appear on all of the maps within the atlas? Does it include any names not appearing on the maps within the atlas?

22-29   Does the Rand McNally New Cosmopolitan World Atlas consist only of maps and an index to those maps?

22-30   Is this additional information available only in the atlas or is it available also in other sources?

22-31   Another atlas similar in scope, size, etc., to the Rand McNally New Cosmopolitan, and published by another well-known mapping company, is the Hammond Ambassador World Atlas. Hammond published three other atlases at the same time that the Ambassador was published (including the Medallion World Atlas). How do these four atlases differ?

22-32   What is the scope of the Hammond Ambassador or the Medallion atlas? How much of it, comparatively, is devoted to the United States?

22-33   How recent is this atlas? Can you tell anything about its revision policies? Are the maps dated? Is Botswana included?

22-34   Does the Hammond Ambassador/Medallion atlas include political, physical, and topical maps? How are the maps arranged? Is it similar in arrangement to the Rand McNally Cosmopolitan? Look at the maps for Alaska and for Brazil, for example.

22-35   Is there a map in the Hammond Ambassador/Medallion showing population distribution for the world?

22-36   What is the scale of the political map which shows Laos?   How does it compare to that in the New Cosmopolitan?

22-37   Is the projection of the map indicated?   Is that type of projection explained in the atlas itself?

22-38   There are indexes for each separate political map in Hammond's Ambassador/Medallion atlas. Is there a cumulated or general index?   Does this include names not on any of the maps?   Does it include all of the names on the maps?

22-39   Can you locate New Tazewell, Tennessee, in this atlas?   Is the population given?

22-40   Once you have located New Tazewell, on the Tennessee map (method similar to that used in New Cosmopolitan), do you see any differences between the maps in the Hammond Ambassador/Medallion and those in the New Cosmopolitan?

22-41   Does the atlas give any sources for the information it includes, such as population figures and other statistics?

22-42   Does Hammond's Ambassador/Medallion atlas have supplementary gazetteer or encyclopedia information as the New Cosmopolitan does?

22-43   The third atlas, the Odyssey World Atlas, is also similar in size and scope to the Rand McNally New Cosmopolitan World Atlas and the Hammond Ambassador/Medallion World Atlas, and can be examined by comparison.   What is the name of the publisher of this atlas?   What is the name of the company or organization which prepared the maps for this atlas?

22-44   How recent is this atlas?   Can you tell what the revision policy is?   Are the maps dated?   Is Botswana included?

22-45   What is the scope of the Odyssey atlas?   How much of it is devoted to the United States?   How does this compare to the New Cosmopolitan and the Ambassador/Medallion?

22-46   What is the arrangement of the maps?   How does this compare to the other atlases?

22-47   Does the Odyssey atlas have very many thematic maps, in comparison to the other atlases you have examined?

22-48   Are the projection and scale noted on each of the maps?   Are they further explained in the text?

22-49   Is there a map of Laos similar to those in the New Cosmopolitan and Hammond Ambassador/Medallion? How does the scale compare?

22-50   Can you locate New Tazewell, Tennessee, in this atlas?

22-51   Stalingrad, in Russia, is no longer known by that name. Can you locate it in the Odyssey atlas?
         Where would you look to find out when the name was changed? It is unlikely it was called Stalingrad
         before 1879 (year of Stalin's birth); what was it called before it was called Stalingrad?

22-52   Are sources for information given in the Odyssey atlas?

22-53   What supplementary information is given in the Odyssey atlas?

22-54   The next atlas to examine, Goode's World Atlas, is an example of a school atlas useful also because of
         its handier size. Who is the publisher of Goode's?

22-55   Presumably then Rand McNally maps are used, probably some of those included in the New Cosmopolitan.
         What would have to be done to the New Cosmopolitan maps if they were to be used in Goode's (or vice
         versa)?

22-56   What is the revision policy for Goode's?

22-57   To be useful as a school atlas, what would you expect this particular atlas to stress?

22-58   Does Goode's provide these things? How does it compare with the New Cosmopolitan in this respect?

22-59   Does Goode's have the same kind of political maps as the larger atlases?

22-60   Does Goode's have a general index? Are population figures included? Is any special information in-
         cluded? How are the places located on the maps?

22-61   Does Goode's contain a lot of supplementary or encyclopedic type information?

22-62   Does Goode's stress the United States as much as the New Cosmopolitan?

22-63   The next atlas is an example of a rather specialized atlas, and one which is extremely useful for its
         very detailed coverage of the United States--the Rand McNally Commercial Atlas and Marketing Guide.
         What is the scope of the Commercial Atlas? How much of it is U.S.? Is there any world coverage?

22-64   What is the purpose of the Commercial Atlas?

22-65   How up to date is the Commercial Atlas?   How is it kept up to date?

22-66   What information does the Commercial Atlas give you about cities and towns in the U.S.?   (See sample entry in introductory material.)

22-
67/68   What else can you find out about New Tazewell, Tennessee, through the Commercial Atlas?   How does this compare to what you found in Ayer (see #22-64)?

22-69   What is the date of the population figures given in the Commercial Atlas?

22-70   The last atlas to examine, but by no means the least, is the Times Atlas of the World, Comprehensive Edition.   Where was this atlas published, originally?   Who made the maps?

22-71   When was this atlas published and what is its previous history?

22-72   What is the scope of this atlas?   What is the coverage given to the United States?   Is there a full map for California?   Where was this atlas originally published?

22-73   How is the atlas arranged?

22-74   Does the Contents list in this atlas give you any information which is helpful in making comparisons of the map themselves, without even seeing the maps?

22-75   Can you find a map for Perth, Australia which shows Guildford Road and locates the Parliament House?

22-76   How does the map for London compare with that for Paris?   for New York City?

22-77   Can you locate the British Museum on the map of London?

22-78   Locate the map for Laos.   Are both political and physical maps given?   How does the scale compare with that of the other atlases?   Is the projection given?

22-79   Are the projections and scales explained in the atlas?

22-80   Is New Tazewell, Tennessee, found in the Times Atlas?

22-81   Could you find New Tazewell, Tennessee, on a map in the New Cosmopolitan Atlas from the information given in the index of the Times Atlas?

22-82   One of the problems with the five-volume Midcentury Edition of the Times Atlas is that each of the five-volumes has its own index and there was no cumulative or general index for the entire atlas. This was remedied in 1965 when the Times Publishing Company put out the Times Index Gazetteer of the World, which is the last title on your list. Although this is a gazetteer, and so listed in Winchell, it is being examined here in conjunction with the atlases because it differs considerably in scope and use from the other gazetteers. In what way does it differ?

22-83   What is the purpose of giving latitude and longitude?

22-84   The Times Index-Gazetteer thus serves as an index to any atlas or any map. Where is Guy Fawkes located?

22-85   Does the Times Index Gazetteer list Botswana? Timbuktu? Brussels, Belgium? Stonehenge? Stalingrad? Phoenicia?

22-86   How many places' names are given in the Times Index Gazetteer? How does this compare with other sources, such as the Columbia Lippincott Gazetteer? the Odyssey World Atlas? the Times Atlas?

22-87   Honey Creek, Wisconsin is listed in the Times Index Gazetteer but not shown on the Times Atlas maps. Can you locate it on a map in any of the other atlases? Would you expect that it would not be indexed in the other atlases?

22-88   Is there an atlas devoted specifically to the Philippines?

22-89   Are there any bibliographical sources for atlases? for maps? Where would you look to find them?

22-90   What is a globe? What is the particular usefulness of a globe as compared to maps?

The following questions can be used as REVIEW for the geographical sources.

22-91   Where is Clayton, Missouri and how big is it?

22-92   Pitcairn Island is in the Pacific Ocean, and is about two miles long. Where can you find a map of it which shows the location of Bounty Bay and Pt. Christian?

22-93   Where can you find a pictorial representation of the world's volcanic and earthquake zones?

22-94   What is a Mercator projection?

22-95   Sing Sing is an American prison.   Where is it located?

22-96   Where would you look to find the names and addresses and price ranges of some places to stay overnight in Kennebunkport, Maine?

22-97   Where can you find a map showing major military installations in the entire United States--that is, a map which will show you clearly where such installations are concentrated?

22-98   What does the world "holm" mean in the name of the city Stockholm (Sweden)?

22-99   Is Niagara Falls the biggest waterfall in the world?

22-100   Where could you find a map showing the location of the Bibliothèque Nationale in Paris and some information on what hours it is open during the summer?

Section 22

Geographical Sources: Atlases

Answers #20/1-20/100

22-1 A: Quotation books. Rudyard Kipling wrote it.

22-2 A: See ALA Glossary, or any dictionary, or
           technical dictionary in geography (question
           #21-38).

22-3 A: See Winchell, outline guide for examining
           atlases, in paragraphs preceding list of
           atlases (8th ed., p. 435-4).

22-4 A: See ALA Glossary on map and chart for
           library-related definition. See any dic-
           tionary. See technical dictionary for
           geography (as in #21-38). For origin,
           see Oxford English Dictionary. (A Glos-
           sary of Geographical Terms, edited by
           Stamp, quoted OED on origin as well as
           giving definition.)

22-5 A: See any dictionary.

22-6 A: Start with one or more articles from the
           general encyclopedias. Wright and Platt
           has some rather specialized information
           (p. 83+). Follow up bibliographic
           references in encyclopedias for further
           reading. Find some periodicals (through
           Ulrich's?) which deal with the subject
           and make a habit of perusing them from
           time to time.

22-7 A: Wright and Platt divides them into loca-
           tional (those with which most people are
           familiar) and topical (those which show
           specialized aspects such as population,
           railways, resources, vegetation, climate,
           etc.).
               Locational maps are also called political
           (showing boundaries and places) or physical
           or topographic (showing landforms, physical
           features, relief, etc.).
               Topical maps are also called thematic
           maps. Atlases which are devoted to spe-
           cific and specialized themes (such as a
           climatological atlas) are found in the sub-
           ject areas.

22-8 A: Date given on title page as "edition" and on
           verso of title page in copyright statement.
           Some form of continuous revision seems
           likely from the number of dates given in
           the copyright statement but this is not
           clearly stated. Winchell annotation for
           this atlas says that the 1965 edition was a
           "new" edition with "New" added to the title of
           the old Rand McNally Cosmopolitan World
           Atlas, published in various editions since
           1949.

22-9 A: Check the maps or the information given to

see if changes have been made. For example, look at the map of Africa to see if
Botswana (new name as of 1966), see question #21-47) is shown. (Yes, it is, in
1968 edition.)

22-10 A: World Atlas, Contents lists the world,
           Europe, Asia, Africa, etc., as well as the
           United States. (In fact, it includes the
           Solar System and the Moon).

22-11 A: You can tell this most easily from the
           table of contents. The atlas contains ap-
           proximately 125 pages of "World Reference
           Maps," of which half (p. 61-125) are de-
           voted to North America and all but 15
           pages of that to the United States. The
           same general proportion of U.S. to world
           information is true for the other sections
           of the atlas.

22-12 A: It shouldn't be by now, since nearly all the
           reference sources you have examined here--
           even though world-wide or universal in
           scope--tended to emphasize information for
           the country in which they were published.
           This "bias" is probably most easily seen
           in the atlases.

22-13 A: See Contents. Not alphabetical. Maps
           are grouped by geographical regions. World
           first, then Europe (including individual
           maps for British Isles, France, Germany,
           etc.), Asia (including individual maps for
           China, Japan, etc.), etc. Maps for indi-
           vidual states are grouped under the United
           States which is under North America.

22-14 A: New Cosmopolitan has political, physical,
           and topical maps. The major map section
           is political maps, which includes under
           Asia a map showing Cambodia, Laos,
           Vietnam, Thailand, and Malaysia together,
           giving political boundaries and location of
           cities and towns, etc. Following all the
           political maps is a much shorter set of
           physical maps emphasizing landforms
           (mountains, etc.), which includes a map of
           Eurasia, (a much larger area than the
           political map of Laos). Following the
           physical maps are a few topical maps
           (climate, vegetation, population, races,
           languages, religions) on a world basis only
           (but which does show you the general popu-
           lation density of Laos if you know where
           Laos is), plus an extensive section of his-
           torical maps. The various kinds of maps
           are grouped separately--political, then
           physical, then topical.

22-15 A: Map projections are ways by which the earth's curved surface is portrayed on a flat (map) surface. See Contents for reference to the two pages in the New Cosmopolitan introductory section in which projections are explained and illustrated.

22-16 A: Projection indicated at the bottom of the page of the map; types of projections discussed and illustrated in the introductory material of the atlas. This specific projection is included.

22-17 A: To understand the extent to which distortion may occur in the map.

22-18 A: Scale is the relationship of the size of an area on the map to the area it represents. It also is discussed in the introductory material to the New Cosmopolitan World Atlas. It can be represented or stated in three ways: fractional or numerical, or sometimes called natural:
> 1:8,000,000;
> written or word: 1 inch = 126 statute miles;
> graphic or linear or bar: divisions of the bar showing the stated distance.
The scale on the map in the New Cosmopolitan is shown in all three ways.

22-19 A: As the lower number of the fraction decreases, the scale becomes larger. As the scale becomes larger, the amount of detail which can be given increases. The scale of the map for Cambodia is larger than that for India, therefore more detail can be given in the map for Cambodia. This can be seen visually also, since part of Laos and most of Thailand appear in the far right side of the map of India and Pakistan, etc., and they are obviously smaller than they appear in the map which features them.

22-20 A: The map for Rhode Island is on the same page as the map for Connecticut, and therefore not in alphabetical order and is most easily located by using the Table of Contents. The scale for the Rhode Island map is larger (1:731,000 or 1 inch=11.5 statute miles) than that for Laos (1:8,000,000).

22-21 A: See World Political Information Table, following the maps. Laos is listed as 91,429 square miles; Rhode Island as 1,214 square miles.

22-22 A: Total population and population density (per square mile) are also given. Population figures are "estimated" as of January 1965; nothing is said about what this estimate is based on. No source is indicated for any of the information.

22-23 A: No, they are not dated. You can tell about revisions only if you know something significant you can check for (such as Botswana, as in question #22-9).

22-24 A: Broken black line is political boundary, solid red line is railroad (see physical map symbols preceding the maps themselves, p. 127 of the 1968 edition). The white area is 500 feet below sea level, see relief scale in lower left of the map itself.

22-25 A: Turn to general index of place names in back, alphabetical, find New Tazewell, Tennessee, which gives you 768, C10, 117.

22-26 A: 768 is the population figure ("latest available"); see "Explanation of the Index and Abbreivations." The page number of the map is 117.

22-27 A: The reference given in the index is C10; the letters are given on the right side (the C somewhat obliterated by the map in this instance) and the numbers along the top of the middle section (Tennessee being split in half in order to get it on the page). Follow C across and 10 down and then poke about a bit for New Tazewell, somewhat to the southwest of the C10 intersection. The closest town is Tazewell. Both Tazewell and New Tazewell are represented by dots of approximately the same size, but Tazewell is an open circle. To discover the significance of this, it is necessary to turn back to the introduction to the political map section (p. xix of the 1968 edition) which explains "Map Symbols" and the index reference system. This tells you that dots of the same size represent the same sized cities or towns and that an open dot is a county seat. The railroad is SOU and it is not made clear what this stands for (although the Railroad map on p. 226 does give the abbreviations), and the river is the Powell River. The features noted in light blue letters are not easily read.

22-28 A: See "Explanation of the Index and Abbreviations." Only "important" names from the maps are given. Some names are included that were not on the maps, signified by an *.

22-29 A: No, there is a section of over 50 pages of "Geographical Facts, Figures and Information about the World and the United States."

22-30 A: It is also available in other sources--encyclopedias, almanacs, statistical sources, for example; also in gazetteers and guidebooks.

22-31 A: See Winchell annotation for them. The same maps and information are used in all. By reducing the information, the indexing, and the size of the maps, the company has issued the same material in four different publications at a range in price from approximately $5 to $20. (This is relatively common practice with atlases, and therefore, before purchasing atlases, it is well to check reviews or other independent sources to make sure that you are not simply repurchasing something you already have in another form). For the questions on this atlas, either the Medallion or Ambassador versions may be used, since the maps themselves are similar and the primary difference is in the extent of the indexing.

22-32 A: Scope is <u>world</u> wide. Of about 320 pages (excluding the index), over 130 pages, or at least one-third, is devoted to the United States.

22-33 A: Winchell citation lists it as new and up-to-date when first published in 1966. Revision policy is not clear. Maps are not dated. Botswana is sometimes included--it is not on the world page map (p. 2-3); it is noted on most of the African maps, but more as an afterthought.

22-34 A: The types of maps included is not clear from the Contents, although the arrangement is. It is strictly geographical, the world first, then Europe, then Asia, etc. This is similar to the New Cosmopolitan.

Looking at the map(s) for Brazil (South America), you find 4 pages, including a political map, a topographic (physical) map, a topical map showing agriculture, industry and resources, plus a detailed map for the capital city, a detailed map for the southeastern area, a highway map for that area, an index for states, cities, towns; general area, population, etc., information for the country, a picture of the flag, and an indication of where Brazil is in relation to the rest of South America. The same general plan is followed for Alaska. Thus, the Hammond Ambassador/Medallion atlas does include political, physical, topical (some) maps, and they are grouped together by area. This differs from the arrangement of the New Cosmopolitan where political maps were together, followed by physical, followed by topical, etc.

22-35 A: Not on a world-wide basis as in New Cosmopolitan. It is shown for general regions, such as Europe, Asia, etc.

22-36 A: Map for Burma, Thailand, Indochina, and Malaya, p. 72-4. The scale of the political map is shown in the linear bar only and is somewhat difficult to compare then with the new Cosmopolitan without actually measuring the two bars. (The scale is approximately the same.)

22-37 A: Type of projection noted on the map. Projection mentioned but not explained in "Introduction to the Maps and Indexes." Projection discussed with illustrations at the end of the volume (following the index).

22-38 A: General index, called "Index of the World" at the end. Lists "major" and "principal" places. Does not say that it includes items not on the maps.

22-39 A: New Tazewell, Tennessee, is listed in the general index in the Medallion version, but is not listed in the general index in the Ambassador version. In both it is listed in the individual index for Tennessee. Population given only in the individual indexes, not in the general index.

The Medallion index has approximately 100,000 place names; this was cut down to 25,000 in the Ambassador version by listing only the more "important" names. (See Winchell annotation.)

22-40 A: Hammond Ambassador/Medallion seems less cluttered, easier to distinguish county boundaries, easier to read name of river; but at the same time less information is given--railroad line not indicated, for example. Hammond Ambassador shows major highways on another map for Tennessee on the preceding page.

22-41 A: See Gazetteer-Index of the World in the front, which is an attempt to give sources but not specific enough to be much help. It does, however, indicate whether figures are from official censuses or otherwise, and the date, which is more than the New Cosmopolitan did.

22-42 A: Yes, but perhaps not as much. Some terms, distance table, statistics at the end of the atlas. Some of this type of information given with each set of maps for each country or state. In addition, the Medallion version includes a color section titled "The Universe, earth, and man."

22-43 A: Publisher is Odyssey Books, New York (see title page). Maps by General Drafting Co., see name on each of the maps themselves, also indicated on the verso of the title page, also indicated in Winchell annotation. This is an entirely different organization from Rand McNally and Company, which did the maps for the New Cosmopolitan, and from Hammond, Inc., which did the maps for the Ambassador/Medallion.

22-44 A: According to Winchell, published in 1966 as a new work; maps are not dated, but if they are new for this publication, they should not be much older than 1966. Revision policy not indicated. Botswana is included.

22-45 A: Scope is <u>world-wide</u>. P. 50-91 of about 188 p. devoted to U.S.; about one-fourth. Much better balance than either New Cosmopolitan or Ambassador/Medallion.

22-46 A: Arrangement by geographical region (e.g., world, then North America, including United States, then South America, etc.), with physical, political, and topical or thematic maps for the region or country all together. This is similar to Ambassador/Medallion; different from new Cosmopolitan.

22-47 A: Odyssey has a lot. New Cosmopolitan has only a few. Ambassador /Medallion had at least one for each country or state, but not so many world or regional thematic maps.

22-48 A: Noted on the maps and explained in the text (preceding the Introduction).

22-49 A: See Quick Reference Index in front for Laos, map on p. 146. Similar to the others in that it includes Thailand, Cambodia, Viet-Nam. Scale is larger in the Odyssey (1:6, 900, 000 compared to 1:8, 000, 000).

22-50 A: Listed in general index in the back. Gives population (768), page of map (71), locator reference (H5).

22-51 A: Index under Stalingrad has cross-reference to Volgograd, which can be located. Map does not identify Volgograd as formerly Stalingrad. For information such as when the name was changed, you would have to go to a gazetteer (or an encyclopedia, or even a dictionary; American College Dictionary c.1964 gives all of this information).

22-52 A: In general, no. Some of the thematic maps do give sources (see Canada: agriculture, forestry maps. World: metals, minerals). Consultants listed on page preceding title page, acknowledgments given on verso of title page.

22-53 A: Some is given in the back--the usual list of countries and regions of the world with population and area, lists of largest cities in the world and urbanized areas of the U.S., world facts and figures, short glossary of geographical terms, foreign geographical terms, abbreviations.

22-54 A: Rand McNally and Company, publishers of New Cosmopolitan.

22-55 A: Reduced in size to fit pages (or vice versa).

22-56 A: More or less continuous revision. See title page and verso of title page: 13th edition, c.1970. Winchell annotation says "frequently revised."

22-57 A: General information on how to use an atlas and maps. Topical or thematic maps showing rainfall, population, resources, vegetation, trade, transportation, etc.

22-58 A: Yes. Introduction is good and covers a lot of needed general information on projections and scale, etc. Extensive topical or thematic maps for the entire world. New Cosmopolitan had very little in the way of thematic maps.

22-59 A: No. Political boundaries and names of places superimposed on physical or topographic maps in Goode's. Less detail given for names of places.

22-60 A: Yes, there is a general index in the back. Population figures not given. Some pronunciation given. Places are located by giving page of map, and geographical coordinates (latitude and longitude).

22-61 A: Very little in comparison to the New Cosmopolitan, for example. Some comparisons (islands, mountains, etc.), principal countries with area and population, glossary of foreign geographical terms.

22-62 A: No, more on rest of the world.

22-63 A: Most of it is U.S. There is some world coverage but not at all on the same scale. Maps for other parts of the world appear to be mostly for simple reference.

22-64 A: This is not specifically noted in the introductory material or in Winchell. Purpose is perhaps best given in the title--commercial and marketing guide. Primarily for business firms who need information on where best market areas are for particular types of goods, what kind of supply routes (post offices, railroads, etc.) are available, where the shopping is done, what the population is, what type of people live there (college age, military families, etc.).

22-65 A: Annual revision (see cover and title page, also see Winchell annotation). Libraries "subscribe" to this atlas; this is actually a rental system--the atlas belongs to Rand McNally and is returned to them each year and a new revised issue received (see front cover and front end papers). List of "late changes" on first page.

22-66 A: Sample entry is for Atlanta, Georgia, and tells you the extensive information given in this atlas. In this way, it is similar to a gazetteer and in fact goes beyond the information given in most gazetteers for small places.

22-67/68 A: The index entry tells you that it has a railway express agency office, a post office, that it is incorporated, that the 1960 population was 768, and the population now is 1, 861 including areas annexed since the last census. Also gives zip code. Ayer gives manufacturing and agriculture information.

22-69 A: Estimates as of 1970 (in 1970 edition); see Introduction and Explanation.

22-70 A: Originally published by the Times of London. Published in the U.S. by Houghton Mifflin, Boston (title page.) Maps by John Bartholomew and Son Ltd., Edinburgh (verso of title page).

22-71 A: Published 1967 (see verso of title page). For history, see Foreword or Winchell annotation. Previous publication was a five-volume edition called the Midcentury Edition, published 1955-59. 1967 Comprehensive Edition is in one volume and contains some revised material.

22-72 A: Scope is world-wide. The United States gets about 13 pages out of 123, much less in proportion than in other atlases you have examined. There is no state map for California. California is shown in a two-page map of "Pacific Coast South" including Arizona, Utah and Nevada. (Texas and Alaska do each have double-page spreads, however.) This is not an American-made atlas. It was originally published in Great Britain.

22-73 A: Similarly to most of the other atlases: by geographical area (world, followed by Orient, etc.). All maps including thematic or topical maps for an area are together.

22-74 A: The Contents lists give the scale of the map as well as the plate number, so that you can make an instant comparison of the general coverage you can expect to get. For example, the map of the U.S. is 1/12,500,000; those for the northwest, southeast, etc., regions are all at 1/2,500,000, showing much more detail.

22-75 A: Inset map for Perth (scale 1/250,000) on plate for Australia West.

22-76 A: London and environs, scale of 1/100,000. Paris the same. New York City smaller (1/250,000). See Contents.

22-77 A: Only if you know where to look for it. It is shown on the map. It is not indexed, however.

22-78 A: See list of States and Territories in the front; lists Laos, map at plate 25. Scale is 1/5,000,000--larger than New Cosmopolitan, Hammond, Odyssey. Projection (Mercator) is given.
Maps in Times are physical or topographic with political (boundaries, cities, etc.) overlaid.

22-79 A: No, not as in the other atlases you have examined. Brief mention given in the definitions of geographical terms in the back.

22-80 A: See index, on map plate 105, locator reference D1.

22-81 A: Yes. Times Index gives geographical coordinates (latitude and longitude) which can be used on any map which shows latitude and longitude.

22-82 A: See Foreword. Intentionally not a descriptive gazetteer-index. Purpose is comprehensive, quick, handy locational guide. Place names only give larger area (i.e.,

country, state, etc.) plus latitude and longitude, plus reference to maps in the Times Midcentury Edition for those names which appear on the maps in that atlas.

22-83 A: So that a place can be located on any map which gives parallels and meridians. See Foreword. See also question #21-66.

22-84 A: Three Guy Fawkes listed in Times Index Gazetteer. One is a river in Tasmania, with reference to a map in the Times Midcentury Edition (no geographical coordinates given). One is an island in the Galapagos Islands, not located on a map in the Times atlas but geographical coordinates given. The third is a city or town in Australia, also not located on a map in the Times atlas but geographical coordinates given.

22-85 A: Timbuktu and Brussels cross-referenced from English version to vernacular version. Stalingrad is not listed, no reference to Volgograd, although Volgograd is listed and indicates formerly Stalingrad. Botswana is not listed (too early, 1965). Stonehenge listed (still exists as a place). Phoenicia not listed (except as a town or city in New York state); historical place which no longer exists. The Foreword of the Times Index-Gazetteer is particularly good to read on the problems of name changes, spelling variations, etc.

22-86 A: Times Index-Gazetteer lists 345,000 place names (see Foreword and Winchell).
Columbia Lippincott: 130,000.
Odyssey World Atlas: 105,000.
Times Atlas, Comprehensive edition: 200,000.

22-87 A: You can locate it on other maps through the geographical coordinates. It may be indexed in other atlases, especially those with strong coverage for the U.S. Using the Odyssey atlas map for Wisconsin (p.66), you can locate the point for the geographical coordinates, which would actually put Honey Creek in Illinois, rather than in Wisconsin. Honey Creek is located in the Odyssey atlas (see index) in the inset map for the Milwaukee area in the lower left of the Wisconsin map--just above Burlington. (This is more like a latitude 42.45 than 42.15).

22-88 A: See Winchell, section on Atlases--National and Regional--Philippines.

22-89 A: See Winchell: Geography--Atlases--Bibliography (on both maps and atlases). See also Wright and Platt.

22-90 A: See any dictionary. A globe is an accurate visual representation of the world's surface, as opposed to the distortion of the various map projections. Globes cannot give any information which cannot also be found through maps, but they have a special visual impact and effectiveness which enhances the information found through maps and atlases.

22-91 A: Gazetteers, atlases, perhaps encyclopedias or dictionaries. May need to check something continuously brought up to date such as Ayer or Rand McNally Commercial Atlas for recent population figure.

22-92 A: Times Atlas a likely choice since it gives very detailed maps. Odyssey Atlas also has a detailed map for Pitcairn.

22-93 A: Odyssey World Atlas, world map section, thematic map shown under the main physical map of the world.

22-94 A: See almost any atlas which gives illustrated discussion of projections.

22-95 A: Gazetteers (or encyclopedias or dictionaries). Atlases very unlikely to give this type of information. Rand McNally Commercial Atlas lists prisons.

22-96 A: Hotel and Motel Red Book, possibly a guidebook for that region.

22-97 A: Rand McNally Commercial Atlas has such a map.

22-98 A: See lists of geographical equivalents or foreign geographical terms in supplementary material in most of the atlases.

22-99 A: Problem is what do you mean by biggest? longest? highest? widest? most water? Some atlases have lists of waterfalls in "world facts" sections in the back, but usually list only highest. Gazetteers have entries for Niagara Falls but are not comparative. Almanacs, as usual, are most helpful here since they tend to give lots of comparisons. Try also Guinness Book of Records.

22-100 A: Guidebook for Paris, or guidebook for France which includes Paris.

Section 23

Review of Part II

Questions # 23/1-23/60

This section is a review of Part II: Basic Reference Sources, Sections 12-22.

In this review, you should follow the same procedure used in Section 11 (Review of Part I): you can either search out the specific answers in the sources, or simplify the process by deciding which source(s) you would use to answer the question, or use a combination of both methods. What you do should depend on how much time you have and how much practice and review you think you need.

In either case, you should begin by deciding which source or sources to use. Think in terms of the type of information required by the questions and the type of sources available. In deciding which source(s) to use, think first of the type of source (generic name) and then a specific title (brand name) which is an example of that source and which would--because of its scope and arrangement--be likely to give you the answer to that question.

For many of the questions, there may be several possible sources in which you could find the answer. This is even more true of the sources in Part II than for the bibliographical sources in Part I. You should try to think of as many possibilities as you can, because you may find yourself working in a library which will not have all of the sources studied in this manual. Also, you cannot rely on the specificity of the general reference sources in the same way that you can with the bibliographical sources. For example, if you are searching for the price of a book, you can be reasonably sure that a source which claims to include price, such as BPR or CPI, will in fact include that information for all the items listed. If you are searching for a fact such as a man's birthplace, you cannot be at all sure that the biographical sources will include that information for all persons listed; you may have to check further in other sources also giving biographical information.

However, in this review section, you should again assume that you have available all of the sources studied in the manual, and you should then think in terms of which would be the best or the most likely source to use and why. Think in terms of the existing pattern or structure of the available reference sources. For example, the general encyclopedias will in fact frequently provide factual answers for a large proportion of reference questions. But in using the encyclopedias for such factual material, you always have to consider the problems of how accurate, how up-to-date, how detailed, etc., the information is. There may be other more direct, more current, more easily used sources.

As before, if you find that you are not really sure which source(s) you should choose, and why, then it may be that you need more practice in and use of the sources to clarify your understanding of them. Try searching out the answer to the question in various likely sources, and see if this procedure helps you to compare the usefulness and scope of the sources.

Throughout Part II of the manual, no specific suggestions were given for making the kind of review charts which you made for the bibliographical sources. If you have not made any such charts or brief comparative notes, you might find it useful now to review the material by going over the sections, noting down the various types (generic names: i.e., unabridged English language dictionary, usage book, synonym dictionary or synonym thesaurus, general adult American encyclopedia, encyclopedia yearbooks, directory of organizations, etc.) of sources, then noting down the kinds of information for which those sources are most useful (i.e., definition of words in English language, etc.), then trying to remember, or coordinate from the list in the Table of Contents of the Self-Study Manual, various specific titles which are examples of types of sources.

Then turn to the review questions, trying to answer them, without the aid of your notes. There are plenty of review questions for practice.

23-1   Where would you find a discussion of recent developments in organ transplants (i.e., heart, kidneys, etc.) in the past few years?

23-2   How does a computer work?

23-3   What is the origin of the word Hoosier, and is it used to mean Indiana or someone from Indiana?

23-4   When and where was movie actor James Garner born? Is that his real name?

23-5   Where would you look to find the titles of some biographies about nurses for a student interested in nursing as a career?

23-6   What are the major retail sales areas of the United States? How are these distributed geographically throughout the country?

23-7   Where would you find statistics on coffee production in the Philippines in the early 1960's?

23-8   John Jones (not a made-up name) was the personal physician of Benjamin Franklin and wrote an article about Franklin's last illness. Where would you find further information about Jones' education and career with further bibliographical references, and which would probably also include a reference to the article on Franklin?

23-9   Swaziland is an African nation which became independent in 1968. What was its previous history? What kind of government does it currently have? Does it have an ambassador to the United States and if so, who is currently in that post?

23-10   What are some well-known statements or comments which have been made about patriotism?

23-11   A word currently much used is "parameters." What exactly does it mean?

23-12   What is the difference between whom and whomever?

23-13   How large is the Oritani Motor Hotel in Hackensack, New Jersey?

23-14   Where would you find information on the exact date, number of people killed, area covered, etc. for the recent earthquake in Southern California?

23-15   Where can you find information about Zoroaster?

23-16   What is a word which is similar in meaning to "negotiate" but is not quite so formal?

23-17   Where would you find information on Women's Lib writer Kate Millett? Is she married? Does she believe in marriage? What kind of family life did she have as a child?

23-18   What were the names of the original states of Germany before its division at the end of World War II? What are the present states of the (West) German Federal Republic?

23-19   What is the present form of government in the West German Federal Republic, and who is its head?

23-20   What is the meaning of the word "saucefleem," used in the 15th century (Middle English)?

23-21   Who said "It is not observed that...librarians are wiser men than others"?

23-22   What is the OAS, an organization active in Algeria?

23-23   Where would you find a list of books on fortune telling?

23-24   Where would you find a short bibliography on folk music?

23-25   If you were asked to conduct a meeting, where would you find information on what order of business to follow?

23-26   How many and what railroads serve Peoria, Illinois?

23-27   What is the name of the long suffering female in Chaucer's A Clerk's Tale?

23-28   Where would you find comparative figures showing the number of telephones in the United States in the late 1800's, early 1900's, mid-1900's?

23-29   What was Ikhnaton, an Egyptian king of the 14th century, noted for?

23-30   If your small boy was interested in the weather and wanted to set up a weather observation station in your yard, where could you look to help him? What if he wanted to know specifically how an anemometer works?

23-31   What does "cockamamie" mean (as in, what is this cockamamie school all about anyway)?

23-32   A well-known German bookseller is the firm of Otto Harrassowitz, presently located in Wiesbaden. Can you find out anything of the earlier history of this firm?

23-33   Henry Green is the pseudonym of an English novelist. What is his real name?

23-34   Where would you find some statistics on the consumption of tobacco products in the U.S., and on the changes if any in cigarette smoking habits in the U.S. in recent years?

23-35   What are the names and addresses of some places to stay overnight in New Orleans?

23-36   What is the meaning of the word "cubomancy"?

23-37   Truman Capote is the author of the non-fiction novel <u>In Cold Blood</u>. What is his address?

23-38   Where would you look to find a pictorial representation of the major food-producing areas of the world?

23-39   What is the origin of April Fools' Day?

23-40   Where can you find an explanation of "new math" for a confused "old math" parent?

23-41   Where can you find a reproduction of Masolino's painting called "Banchetto di Erode"?

23-42   Where is Madison, Wisconsin located? What is it known for? Is there any major industry or manufacturing there? What is its approximate population?

23-43   Where would you look for clarification of the usage of "Junior," "II," "III," etc. for a man given the same name as his father or blood relatives?

23-44   What does the Center for Research on Conflict Resolution at the University of Michigan concern itself with?

23-45   Who invented the ice cream cone?

23-46   What is the origin of the phrase "First catch your hare"?

23-47   Where would you look to get some ideas for decorating a school bulletin board for the month of June?

23-48   Who or what or where is Chandra?

23-49   In what year did Albert Schweitzer win the Nobel Peace Prize?

23-50   What is the purpose of the group which calls itself Fly Without Fear? Who are its current officers, and where can you write to them?

23-51   Where would you find useful information for someone who wanted advice on purchasing an encyclopedia for his home?

23-52   Specifically where are the Mexican volcanoes of Ixtacihautl and Popocatepetl, and how do you pronounce them?

23-53   Where would you find a list of various natural disasters (floods, fire, earthquakes, etc.) for the past year or so?

23-54   Where would you look to find the date of the first climbing of Mount Kilimanjaro?

23-55   Where would you find a detailed map of New Guinea?

23-56   Where would you find some historical and descriptive information about Nevada, giving details about the interesting things to see and do there?

23-57   To whom could you write to get really up-to-date information on research in the development and testing of pesticides?

23-58   What is the author and title of a recently-published fictionalized biography of Mao Tse-Tung?

23-59   What are some slang terms having to do with being exhausted, tired out (i.e., "beat to the socks")?

23-60   What is the source of: Better is the end of a thing than the beginning thereof?

Section 23

Review of Part II

Answers #23/1-23/60

23-1 A: Encyclopedia yearbook (Americana Annual, Collier's Year Book, Britannica Book of the Year), probably under "medicine." This source would probably not be available yet for the past year, but would be available for the few years preceding last year. Other sources, such as New York Times Index or Facts on File, which would give news of such developments could also be used and would be available for the past year, but they do not really give a "discussion" and since you must search in them under various headings (i.e., kidney transplants) in various issues (weekly or semi-monthly) they are not really as convenient for a general view as the encyclopedia yearbooks.

23-2 A: General information, fuller than a dictionary would give: general encyclopedia, Britannica, Americana, Collier's--depending on level of comprehension of person who wants to know. Perhaps even a children's encyclopedia would be useful (World Book, Compton's).

23-3 A: Historical or etymological dictionary: Mathews' Dictionary of Americanisms. General dictionary might also give it.

23-4 A: Biographical information; this can be easily found in almanacs. World Almanac gives birth date and place for "Noted Personalities." Information Please in addition gives real name.

23-5 A: Bibliographical source for biographies: Biography Index, which has an "occupations" index and indicates juvenile books.

23-6 A: Atlas, specifically in this case the Rand McNally Commercial Atlas--the only source you've had so far which is really likely to answer this question.

23-7 A: Statistical source with international scope: Statistical Yearbook of the United Nations.

23-8 A: Biographical source with encyclopedic-type information and bibliographic references, for American no longer living: Dictionary of American Biography. General encyclopedia might be used but probably would not be so extensive on such a minor figure.

23-9 A: Current information needed--Statesman's Year-Book is best as it should answer all these questions and more, and should be comparatively current. Almanac may also be useful but unlikely to give name of

ambassador.

23-10 A: Quotation book; in this case, probably one with a subject approach such as Stevenson's Home Book of Quotations would be easiest to use.

23-11 A: General dictionary.

23-12 A: This is a usage problem. The dictionaries, especially the unabridged, may give some help, but a fuller discussion would be found in the supplementary sources specifically covering usage, such as Fowler's Dictionary of Modern English Usage or Evans' Dictionary of Contemporary American Usage.

23-13 A: Travel/tourist information; guidebook or accommodations directory: Hotel and Motel Red Book will do it.

23-14 A: News summary service (Facts on File or New York Times Index).

23-15 A: Name given only, perhaps not clear if this is a real person, myth or literature, whether living or not, or what area. Start with universal sources, such as Webster's Biographical Dictionary, New Century Cyclopedia of Names, or a general encyclopedia.

23-16 A: Synonym. Dictionary may be helpful, but a better source would be those which specifically cover synonyms, and in this case, one which tries to "discriminate" between meanings of words (Webster's Dictionary of Synonyms) rather than one which simply lists synonymous words.

23-17 A: Current biographical information on currently popular figure. More than just basic biographical data. Current Biography is a likely source. If not there, try Biographical Index for references to magazine articles, etc.

23-18 A: See Webster's Geographical Dictionary or Columbia Lippincott Gazetteer under Germany. Encyclopedia probably would also be helpful.

23-19 A: See most recent Statesman's Year-Book or almanac.

23-20 A: Dictionary which includes words not in current usage. Oxford English Dictionary under saucefleme; Century Dictionary under sausefleme.

23-21 A: Quotation book, can be answered through keyword-type index; Bartlett's Familiar Quotations or Stevenson's Home Book of Quotations.

23-22 A: Abbreviations or acronym source (Acronyms and Initialisms, for example). Might be in dictionaries, might also be in encyclopedias. (Sounds from the way the question is phrased as if it is a geographical problem; however, since it deals with an organization, it cannot be answered through the geographical sources).

23-23 A: Bibliographical source: encyclopedias might be useful but perhaps an even better source would be How-To-Do-It Books.

23-24 A: General encyclopedias usually include short bibliographies or list of references for major articles. Americana, Collier's, Britannica, perhaps World Book or Compton's depending on reading level you wanted.

23-25 A: Manual covering this specific topic: Roberts' Rules of Order.

23-26 A: Official Guide to Railways, if you had it. Another useful and current source for this information is the Rand McNally Commercial Atlas. Some other atlases might show railway routes but would not necessarily be as current or detailed enough to show Peoria.

23-27 A: Literary handbook: Benet's The Reader's Encyclopedia. You have the name of the literary work and need a source which will give you some general information on plot and characters. Biographical sources not helpful as you need the name, but do not know it.

23-28 A: Statistical source: Historical Statistics of the United States.

23-29 A: Biographical source with universal scope, limited information: Webster's Biographical Dictionary or Chambers's Biographical Dictionary.

23-30 A: Children's encyclopedia: World Book or Compton's.

23-31 A: Slang term not in general dictionaries-- see special dictionaries of slang. Probably easier to use one with dictionary arrangement such as Wentworth and Flexner's Dictionary of American Slang.

23-32 A: Foreign (German) encyclopedia for details on minor item. Try Brockhaus Enzyklopaedia.

23-33 A: Literary handbook; Benet's The Reader's Encyclopedia.

23-34 A: Statistical source: probably Statistical Abstract of the U.S., perhaps used in conjunction with Historical Statistics of the U.S. This sort of thing can often be found in the almanacs also.

23-35 A: Tourist /travel information; guidebooks and accommodations directories. Hotel and Motel Red Book.

23-36 A: General dictionary.

23-37 A: General very current biographical information on comparatively "noted" American, living: Who's Who in America.

23-38 A: An atlas for pictorial representation, in map form. Goode's World Atlas and Odyssey World Atlas both have a lot of thematic maps.

23-39 A: Source which deals with holidays: Hazeltine's Anniversaries and Holidays, or Douglas' American Book of Days. Literary handbooks might also be useful.

23-40 A: Encyclopedia. Children's encyclopedias perhaps even better on this than adults, not because material is "written down" but because the children's encyclopedias do try to include general information helpful to parents as well as to children.

23-41 A: Foreign encyclopedia for minor things which might not be in general American encyclopedias. Enciclopedia Italiana is both Italian and noted for art reproductions.

23-42 A: Probably a gazetteer for this one. An atlas would locate it (through the index, then looking at a map) and would probably give the population, but would not give information on industries, etc. Columbia Lippincott Gazetteer of the World would give population figures for 1960 (in supplement) which would probably be sufficient for "approximate." (Webster's Geographical Dictionary would be more current; a recent almanac would probably be even more current.)

23-43 A: General dictionary or usage book might be helpful; but probably a better source would be a manual on etiquette, such as Emily Post.

23-44 A: Directory of organizations, specifically the Research Center Directory.

23-45 A: Sounds like a biographical approach but since it is subject-access rather than name-access, the biographical sources may not be much help. This is actually one of those "curious" facts to be found in Kane's Famous First Facts. "Who invented" is often synonymous with "first." An encyclopedia might also be helpful.

23-46 A: Sounds like a quotation book, but in this

case the phrase is not really a correct quotation but somewhat of a corruption, so the quotation books don't help. Brewer's Dictionary of <u>Phrase</u> and Fable.

23-47 A: Hazeltine's Anniversaries and Holidays or Douglas' American Book of Days, both under June.

23-48 A: Try New Century Cyclopedia of Names, since it may not be clear whether this is biographical, geographical, or literary.

23-49 A: You can approach this from two ways: biographical under Schweitzer or subject under Nobel Peace Prize. Almanacs list such prizes with past winners and this is probably the quickest route. Universal sources such as Webster's Biographical Dictionary or encyclopedias would be best for biographical approach; Schweitzer is dead (therefore not in International Who's Who) and not an American or Englishman (therefore not in Who Was Who or Who Was Who in America, or Dictionary of National Biography or Dictionary of American Biography).

23-50 A: Directory of organizations; Encyclopedia of Associations.

23-51 A: General Encyclopedias in Print and/or Subscription Books Bulletin Reviews.

23-52 A: Source which locates geographically and gives pronunciation: Webster's Geographical Dictionary. Columbia Lippincott Gazetteer would probably give pronunciation also. NBC Handbook of Pronunciation would probably give pronunciation but would not locate. Dictionary giving geographical information might also be useful.

23-53 A: Almanacs are useful. New York Times Encyclopedic Almanac has a list of disasters and catastrophes by year; World Almanac and Information Please list by subject (e.g., type of disaster).

23-54 A: Several possible approaches; gazetteers might do it (Webster's doesn't; Columbia Lippincott does); encyclopedias might do it; date books (Everyman's Dictionary of Dates includes it).

23-55 A: Atlas. Probably Times Atlas of the World, since it is excellent for relatively large-scale maps of world coverage.

23-56 A: Encyclopedia might be useful, but better would be a guidebook for the state of Nevada, such as one of the American Guide series.

23-57 A: See Encyclopedia of Associations, Research Center Directory--subject approach.

23-58 A: Bibliographical source for biography: Biography Index, under Mao as subject.

23-59 A: Dictionary specializing in slang terms-- either a dictionary-arrangement (Wentworth and Flexner: Dictionary of American Slang) or thesaurus arrangement (Berrey and Van den Bark: American Thesaurus of Slang) would be helpful, but in this case, since you are not after the meaning of a specific word, but rather a general list or group of words, the thesaurus approach would be better.

23-60 A: Quotation book, using keyword index. (Ecclesiastes 7:8.)